'What happens in the Indian Ocean will define India's strategic future, and that in turn will do a great deal to set Asia's course in the Asian Century. David Brewster gives us a perfect guide to the forces shaping India's role in the Ocean that bears its name. It is a lucid, lively, comprehensive and judicious account of one of the central strategic questions of our times.'

Professor Hugh White, *Australian National University*

'A knowledgeable India hand, David Brewster explores India's maritime ambitions and provides an incisive assessment of its potential to wield influence across the Indian Ocean region. Amidst current speculation about turbulent regional geopolitics, this Antipodean study illuminates a zone of uncertainty and holds a mirror to Indians, laypersons and strategic thinkers alike.'

Admiral Arun Prakash (Retd), Chief of Naval Staff, *Indian Navy 2004–06*

'It is fashionable for strategic analysts to claim to understand India's growing role and the increasing centrality of the Indian Ocean as a zone of geopolitical competition. It is also easy to assert that India's domestic problems and troubled neighbourhood will forever hobble its maritime ambitions. In this book, David Brewster offers a convincing and carefully-researched alternative—outlining a realistic trajectory for India as an Indian Ocean power. In so doing he explains the power relationships and the subregional dynamics that will determine how smooth or otherwise this course will be. This book fills an important gap for scholars and policymakers striving to understand how India will affect the Indo-Pacific strategic order in the 21st century.'

Rory Medcalf, Director, *International Security Program,*
Lowy Institute, Australia

'This is an excellent contribution to understanding the power dynamics in the Indian Ocean, the bridge between Europe and Asia. It brings out the centrality of this ocean region—the new global centre of trade and energy flows—and the key role India will play in influencing the regional order.'

Brahma Chellaney, Professor of Strategic Studies,
Centre for Policy Research, India

GW00691596

LD 4787961 0

India's Ocean

This book assesses India's role as a major power in the Indian Ocean. Many see the Indian Ocean as naturally falling within India's sphere of influence but, as this book demonstrates, India has a long way to go before it could achieve regional dominance. The book outlines the development of Indian thinking on its role in the Indian Ocean and examines India's strategic relationships in the region, including with maritime South Asia, the Indian Ocean islands, East Africa, the Middle East, Southeast Asia and Australia. The book then discusses India's ambivalent relationship with the United States and explores its attitude towards China's growing power in the Indian Ocean. It concludes by discussing the region's evolving strategic order—does India have what it takes to become the leading power in the region?

David Brewster, a former mergers and acquisitions lawyer, is a Visiting Fellow at the Australian National University and has written extensively on India's strategic relations. He is also the author of *India as an Asia Pacific Power*.

Routledge Security in Asia Pacific Series

Series Editors
Leszek Buszynski, Strategic and Defence Studies Centre, the Australian National University, and William Tow, Australian National University

Security issues have become more prominent in the Asia Pacific region because of the presence of global players, rising great powers, and confident middle powers, which intersect in complicated ways. This series puts forward important new work on key security issues in the region. It embraces the roles of the major actors, their defense policies and postures and their security interaction over the key issues of the region. It includes coverage of the United States, China, Japan, Russia, the Koreas, as well as the middle powers of ASEAN and South Asia. It also covers issues relating to environmental and economic security as well as transnational actors and regional groupings.

1 **Bush and Asia**
   America's evolving relations
   with East Asia
   Edited by Mark Beeson

2 **Japan, Australia and
   Asia-Pacific Security**
   *Edited by Brad Williams
   and Andrew Newman*

3 **Regional Cooperation and Its
   Enemies in Northeast Asia**
   The impact of domestic forces
   *Edited by Edward Friedman
   and Sung Chull Kim*

4 **Energy Security in Asia**
   Edited by Michael Wesley

5 **Australia as an Asia Pacific
   Regional Power**
   Friendships in flux?
   Edited by Brendan Taylor

6 **Securing Southeast Asia**
   The politics of security
   sector reform
   *Mark Beeson and
   Alex J. Bellamy*

7 **Pakistan's Nuclear Weapons**
   Bhumitra Chakma

8 **Human Security in East Asia**
   Challenges for
   collaborative action
   Edited by Sorpong Peou

9 **Security and International
   Politics in the South China Sea**
   Towards a co-operative
   management regime
   *Edited by Sam Bateman
   and Ralf Emmers*

10 **Japan's Peace Building
   Diplomacy in Asia**
   Seeking a more active
   political role
   Lam Peng Er

11 **Geopolitics and Maritime
   Territorial Disputes in East Asia**
   Ralf Emmers

12 **North Korea's
   Military-Diplomatic
   Campaigns, 1966–2008**
   Narushige Michishita

13 **Political Change, Democratic Transitions and Security in Southeast Asia**
Mely Caballero-Anthony

14 **American Sanctions in the Asia-Pacific**
Brendan Taylor

15 **Southeast Asia and the Rise of Chinese and Indian Naval Power**
Between rising naval powers
Edited by Sam Bateman and Joshua Ho

16 **Human Security in Southeast Asia**
Yukiko Nishikawa

17 **ASEAN and the Institutionalization of East Asia**
Ralf Emmers

18 **India as an Asia Pacific Power**
David Brewster

19 **ASEAN Regionalism**
Cooperation, values and institutionalisation
Christopher B. Roberts

20 **Nuclear Power and Energy Security in Asia**
Edited by Rajesh Basrur and Koh Swee Lean Collin

21 **Maritime Challenges and Priorities in Asia**
Implications for regional security
Edited by Joshua Ho and Sam Bateman

22 **Human Security and Climate Change in Southeast Asia**
Managing risk and resilience
Edited by Lorraine Elliott and Mely Caballero-Anthony

23 **Ten Years After 9/11— Rethinking the Jihadist Threat**
Arabinda Acharya

24 **Bilateralism, Multilateralism and Asia-Pacific Security**
Contending cooperation
Edited by William T. Tow and Brendan Taylor

25 **Negotiating with North Korea**
The Six Party Talks and the Nuclear Issue
Leszek Buszynski

26 **India's Ocean**
The story of India's bid for regional leadership
David Brewster

27 **Defence Planning and Uncertainty**
Preparing for the next Asia-Pacific war
Stephan Frühling

India's Ocean

The story of India's bid for
regional leadership

David Brewster

Routledge
Taylor & Francis Group

LONDON AND NEW YORK

First published 2014
by Routledge
2 Park Square, Milton Park, Abingdon, Oxfordshire OX14 4RN

and by Routledge
711 Third Avenue, New York, NY 10017

Routledge is an imprint of the Taylor and Francis Group, an informa business

First issued in paperback 2015

British Library Cataloguing in Publication Data
A catalogue record for this book is available from the British Library

Library of Congress Cataloging in Publication Data
Brewster, David.
    India's ocean : the story of India's bid for regional leadership / David Brewster.
        pages cm. -- (Routledge security in Asia Pacific series ; 26)
    Summary: "This book assesses India's role as a major power in the Indian
Ocean. Many see the Indian Ocean as naturally falling within India's sphere of
influence but, as this book demonstrates, India has a long way to go before it
could achieve regional dominance. The book outlines the development of Indian
thinking on its role in the Indian Ocean and examines India's strategic
relationships in the region. The book then discusses India's ambivalent
relationship with the United States and explores its attitude towards China's
growing power in the Indian Ocean. It concludes by discussing the region's
evolving strategic order - does India have what it takes to become the leading
power in the region?"-- Provided by publisher.
    Includes bibliographical references and index.
    1. Regionalism--India. 2. India--Politics and government. 3. India--Foreign
relations. 4. Indian Ocean--Strategic aspects. 5. Indian Ocean--International
status. 6. India--Politics and government. 7. India--Foreign relations. I. Title.
    JQ220.R43B74 2014
    327.54--dc23
        2013033787

ISBN 978-0-415-52059-1 (hbk)
ISBN 978-1-138-18307-0 (pbk)
ISBN 978-1-315-81524-4 (ebk)

Typeset in Times New Roman
by Taylor & Francis Books

Thanks to Christine, Jack, Juliette, Bronte, Essie and Artie for their continuing love, patience, support and understanding in this crazy project. Many thanks also to my dedicated editorial team. May 2013

Contents

List of maps   xii
List of abbreviations   xiii

1 The shifting balance of power in the Indian Ocean   1

2 Indian strategic thinking about the Indian Ocean   18

3 Maritime South Asia   43

4 The Southwest Indian Ocean   69

5 East and Southern Africa   85

6 The Northwest Indian Ocean   103

7 The Northeast Indian Ocean   123

8 Australia   147

9 The United States   163

10 China   182

11 India as an Indian Ocean power   199

   References   208
   Index   225

List of maps

1.1 The Indian Ocean region   xvi
3.1 Maritime South Asia   42
4.1 The Southwest   68
5.1 East and Southern Africa   84
6.1 The Northwest   102
7.1 The Northeast   122
8.1 The view from Australia   146

Abbreviations

ANZUS	Security Treaty among Australia, New Zealand and the United States
APEC	Asia Pacific Economic Cooperation
ASEAN	Association of South East Asian Nations
BIMSTEC	Bay of Bengal Initiative for Multi-Sectoral Technical and Economic Cooperation
BRICS	Brazil, Russia, India, China and South Africa
CENTO	Central Treaty Organization
CTF 150	Combined Task Force 150—multinational coalition naval task force undertaking maritime security operations in the Horn of Africa region
CTF 151	Combined Task Force 151—multinational coalition naval task force undertaking anti-piracy operations in the Gulf of Aden area
EEZ	Exclusive Economic Zone
FDI	Foreign Direct Investment
IBSA	India, Brazil and South Africa
IBSAMAR	joint military exercises conducted by the Indian, Brazilian and South African Navies
IMF	International Monetary Fund
IONS	Indian Ocean Naval Symposium
IOR-ARC	Indian Ocean Rim Association for Regional Cooperation
IOZOP	Indian Ocean Zone of Peace
LeT	Lashkar-e-Taiba (literally *Army of the Good*), one of the most active terrorist Islamist organizations in South Asia,
LTTE	Liberation Tigers of Tamil Eelam (also known the Tamil Tigers)
MILAN	a multilateral naval exercise hosted by the Indian Navy in the Andaman Islands
NALT	Naval Arms Limitation Treaty
NAM	Non-Aligned Movement
NPT	Nuclear Non-Proliferation Treaty

RAW	Research and Analysis Wing, India's main external intelligence agency
SAARC	South Asian Association for Regional Cooperation
SEATO	South East Asian Treaty Organization
SLOC	Sea Lines of Communication
USCENTCOM	United States Central Command, the US military command with responsibility for the Middle East
USPACOM	United States Pacific Command, the US military command with responsibility for the Asia Pacific and much of the Indian Ocean.

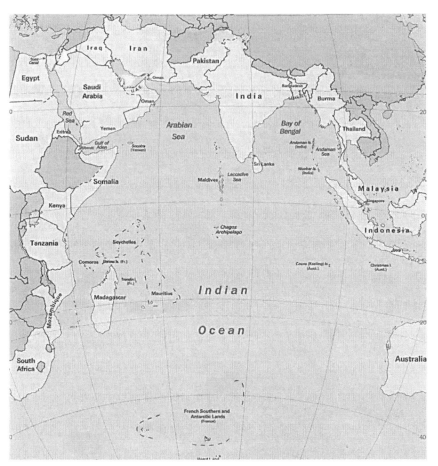

Map 1.1 The Indian Ocean region
   Adapted from the University of Texas Libraries collection.

1 The shifting balance of power in the Indian Ocean

India aspires to be the dominant power in the Indian Ocean, and this goal may come within its reach in coming decades. This book looks at India's strategic ambitions in the Indian Ocean as part of the shifting balance of power in Asia. It will ask whether India has the wherewithal to become the leading power in the Indian Ocean.

India has long seen itself as the natural leader in the Indian Ocean—and wants to ensure that it remains 'India's Ocean'. During the colonial era, India was the hub of Britain's Indian Ocean empire and, after a gap of some 60 years, India is slowly re-emerging as the natural centre of gravity for the region. Its rise as a global economic and military power is leading it to it look towards an expanded strategic role in the region and on the world stage. Some in New Delhi see control over the Indian Ocean as essential to prevent the possible 'encirclement' of India by hostile powers. Others regard an Indian sphere of influence in the Indian Ocean region as an essential building block in the fulfillment of India's destiny to become a global power. But most Indians would strongly reject the idea that India has any hegemonic ambitions in the Indian Ocean, instead seeing it as a friendly policeman that can provide security in a troubled region and help keep unwanted outsiders away. Over the last decade or so, India has successfully presented itself as a benign and cooperative security provider throughout much of the Indian Ocean. But India also tends to have a hierarchical view of the international order which may have consequences for the region.

Over the last decade, India has experienced an unprecedented period of economic growth that is giving it many of the material and military capabilities to become a major regional power—perhaps one day even a world power. But India also has many weaknesses that could prevent it from achieving its regional leadership ambitions. In addition to the many internal constraints it faces, India will need to deal with other major powers, the United States and China, as well as important middle powers in the region. These constraints and competition, combined with a lack of clear strategic direction in New Delhi, create many uncertainties about its future role.

This chapter will make a strategic survey of the Indian Ocean as a basis for understanding India's future strategic role. It will consider in what ways the

Indian Ocean is important to the world and how it currently functions (or not) as a region. It will also look at the history of domination of the Indian Ocean by extra-regional powers and examine India's historical role as the region's natural centre of gravity. Lastly, it will discuss India's ambitions to become an Indian Ocean power.

Is the Indian Ocean important?

One strategic analyst has famously argued that the Indian Ocean will become 'centre stage' in the twenty-first century, the place where many global struggles will be played out—including conflicts over energy, clashes between Islam and the West, and rivalry between a rising China and India.[1] Certainly, the Indian Ocean region is an important part of the global economic power shifts that are taking place in Asia. The rise of both China and India as major economic powers means that the Indian Ocean region will only become ever more important as a highway for trade and a centre of economic power. But the region is also home to many poor countries, including a large proportion of the world's fragile or failed states.

For centuries the Indian Ocean has been the main thoroughfare for trade between Asia and Europe, and over the last century or so the region has acted as the world's principal source of energy and the highway over which that energy is transported to the rest of the world. In 2011, some 48 per cent of the world's proven oil reserves and 32 per cent of total oil production was in the Middle East. Many countries, particularly in South and East Asia, rely heavily on oil produced in the Middle East or shipped across the Indian Ocean. The vulnerability of trade through the Indian Ocean is heightened by its unusual geography. The ocean is largely enclosed on three sides, with a handful of narrow entry and exit points (often called 'chokepoints') to and from adjacent waters. These include the Strait of Hormuz, which joins the Indian Ocean with the Persian Gulf, and the Strait of Malacca, which is the primary exit/entrance between the Indian and Pacific oceans. Other chokepoints include the Bab el-Mandab, the narrow strait that links the Indian Ocean with the Red Sea and the Mediterranean, and the Mozambique Channel/Cape of Good Hope, which is the gateway between the Indian and South Atlantic oceans.

The Strait of Hormuz, located at the head of the Persian Gulf between Iran and Oman, is the world's most important oil chokepoint. In 2011, around 35 per cent of the world's seaborne trade in oil was moved by tanker through the Strait, largely destined for Asia, Western Europe and the United States.[2] This included some 63 per cent of India's total oil imports, 42 per cent of China's, 82 per cent of Japan's imports and 74 per cent of South Korea's. The other major chokepoint is the Strait of Malacca, between Indonesia and Malaysia, which is the major trading route between the Indian and Pacific oceans. It is transited by around one-third of global trade, including the bulk of energy supplies carried from the Middle East to East Asia. China relies heavily on the Malacca Strait, through which around 82 per cent of its oil imports pass (including imports from the Sudan and West Africa).[3] A blockage of the strait would mean that almost half of the world's shipping fleet would need to reroute through the Sunda or Lombok straits, two other narrow straits through the Indonesian archipelago which are themselves vulnerable to blockade.

The importance of the energy supplies that transit the Indian Ocean to Asia will likely rise in coming years. Between 2011 and 2035, global consumption of oil is expected to rise by around 28 per cent and natural gas by around 47 per cent. Much of this growth will come from Indian and Chinese imports from the Middle East.[4] But at the same time, the direct importance to the United States of the Middle East as a source of energy is likely to fall. Technological developments in extraction of gas and oil have led to major increases in production in North America over the last several years, and although the United States still depends on the Persian Gulf for much of its oil its dependence is falling. In 2011, only 16 per cent of the oil imported by the United States came from the Persian Gulf (down from 24.5 per cent in 1990)[5] and this is likely to fall further. The International Energy Agency has predicted that the US will become a net exporter of natural gas by 2020 and a net exporter of oil in the years after.[6] While the Middle East is likely to remain very important for the United States and its allies, reduced oil dependence may give the United States increasing strategic room to manouevre in the region.

Since the late 1970s, the growth of radical Islamist ideologies has also been a major security issue in the Indian Ocean region. Over the last decade or so this has been an important factor in several major external military interventions, including large-scale wars and insurgencies in Iraq and Afghanistan. The winding down of US military involvement in Iraq and Afghanistan is allowing it to withdraw forces from the region and it is possible that Islamic radicalism may be less of a source of international conflict in coming years. But the fundamentalist Islamic regime in Iran also remains a major source of regional instability; this includes its potential to provoke a regional nuclear weapons race and its capacity to block the Strait of Hormuz in times of crisis.

There is also a significant possibility that the Indian Ocean will become a key theatre for rivalry between India and China, the two great rising powers of Asia. India's aspirations to become the dominant power in the Indian Ocean may not be consistent with China's strategic imperatives, especially its need to secure its sea lines of communication to the Middle East. Some believe that the Indian Ocean is currently witnessing a 'security dilemma' in which moves by India and China to enhance their own security only create greater insecurity for the other. The United States, which has been the predominant power in the Indian Ocean and will likely remain so for many years to come, will increasingly need to manage the balance between the two rising powers. The tussle between these three powers, both inside and outside the Indian Ocean, forms an important backdrop to India's rise as an Indian Ocean power.

Despite these various sources of instability and its importance as a source of energy, in many ways the Indian Ocean has historically been a secondary region of international relations. For more than 500 years the world's major economic and military powers have been situated in the Northern Hemisphere—in Europe, North America and Northeast Asia—and major strategic developments in the Indian Ocean has often been merely a byproduct of rivalries elsewhere. Ever since the Portuguese explorer, Vasco da Gama, sailed from Europe to India, the Indian Ocean has been subject to external domination: first by Portugal, later Britain and more recently by the United States. This history of external domination, the vast distances across the Indian Ocean and the diversity of states in and around it has meant that there is relatively little strategic interaction across the 'region'. While there may be considerable strategic interaction within areas of the Indian Ocean littoral, say *within* South Asia, or *within* Southeast Asia, there is little sustained interaction *between,* say, Southeast Asia and Africa, or *between* Australia and South Asia. For hundreds of years the Indian Ocean has not provided a central focus for its surrounding states, binding them together. Instead it has largely acted as a crossroads for those headed elsewhere.

The relatively low level of strategic interaction among the states fringing the Indian Ocean has led many strategists to question whether it is meaningful to analyse the Indian Ocean as a 'region'.[7] Does an examination of the Indian Ocean as a whole help us understand the strategic behaviour of the states bordering it? For strategic analysts, the states surrounding the Indian Ocean would not, for example, qualify as a *regional security complex,* i.e. a group of states whose primary security concerns are linked together sufficiently closely that their national securities cannot realistically be considered apart from one another.[8] Barry Buzan, a leading regional theorist, concluded that 'the attempt to conjure up an Indian Ocean region tends to detract more from an understanding than it adds'.[9] According to Buzan, the Indian Ocean is actually a collection of regions, including Southern Africa, the Middle East, South Asia and Southeast Asia. This lack of interdependence underlies why attempts to create pan-Indian Ocean organisations have not been successful—its members have had relatively few common interests to bind them together.

But does a relative lack of strategic interaction within the Indian Ocean mean that it should not be considered as a single strategic 'space'? On a map, the Indian Ocean and its surrounds looks like it should be a region, perhaps even more so than other political constructs such as the 'Asia Pacific' which many now regard as a region in strategic terms. The northern powers that have controlled the Indian Ocean for several hundred years have often treated it as a defined strategic space, even though there was little interaction between its constituent parts. Portugal and Britain both gained control over the Indian Ocean through taking control of the main chokepoints to and from the Atlantic and Pacific oceans and the Mediterranean Sea and developing intermediate bases to facilitate the movement of military forces over the huge distances across the ocean. In fact, the domination of the Indian Ocean by external powers is a key reason for the relative lack of political and economic interaction between its constituent parts. Since Portugal gained control of the Indian Ocean in the early sixteenth century, the most important political, economic and security relationships of local rulers have often been with a far-off power in the northern hemisphere. The history of the Indian Ocean 'region' has not been a story of local powers jostling for position (which was the case in Europe) or of weaker states constantly calibrating their relationships with a dominant regional power (as has been the case in the Americas).

The rise of India as a major economic and military power now has the potential to change the entire character of the Indian Ocean. If India is successful in its ambitions, for the first time in its history a littoral state will be the predominant power. This could have the effect of binding its disparate parts together through their respective strategic and economic relationships with India. No longer would the majority of Indian Ocean states look elsewhere for their security—or their enemies. In the future, India may create a region out of the Indian Ocean, where relationships with India may be more important than relationships with outside powers.

The domination of the Indian Ocean by extra-regional powers

As noted before, over the last 500 years the Indian Ocean has been dominated by a succession of European or Western powers: first, Portugal, later Britain and now the United States. To a significant extent they have formed the current strategic landscape of the Indian Ocean.

The Indian Ocean was first opened to European naval power in 1498 by Vasco da Gama, and within two decades Portugal had taken control of the main trading routes across it. The Portuguese regarded the Indian Ocean as a strategic whole, referring to the entire region from the Cape of Good Hope to Timor as the 'State of India'. Their strategy, which is most closely associated with the adventurer and imperialist, Afonso de Albuquerque, involved transforming the Indian Ocean into a *mare clausum* (or 'closed sea') over which Portugal had exclusive jurisdiction. Their main objective was to monopolise the trade in precious spices and other luxuries from East Asia and India to Europe. The Portuguese tried to keep out Arab traders and European competitors by interdicting and confiscating any ship that was found without a Portuguese *cartaz* or permit.

Portugal implemented its strategy by taking control of all major entry points into the Indian Ocean and major points in between. During the early years of the sixteenth century, Portuguese forces took the ports of Malacca (on the Strait of Malacca), which controlled the key entry point from the Pacific Ocean; Mozambique Island (in the Mozambique Channel), the chief trading route to and from the Atlantic Ocean; and Hormuz (on the Strait of Hormuz), which controlled trade to and from the Persian Gulf. They developed several intermediate bases, for instance at Mombasa in East Africa, Goa in India and Colombo in Sri Lanka. Portugal's small population meant that it did not have the capacity to colonise or control large swathes of territories, although it established a small colony at Goa which was used as Portugal's administrative capital in the Indian Ocean. This system formed the basis for Portuguese military and economic domination of the Indian Ocean for more than a century.

The Dutch ended Portuguese predominance in the mid-seventeenth century when they captured Malacca and Ceylon (now Sri Lanka) and established a settlement at the Cape of Good Hope. Nevertheless, Albuquerque's ideas live on to this day and continue to be highly influential in strategic thinking about the Indian Ocean. The Indian Navy's 2007 *Maritime Military Strategy* expressly invokes Albuquerque's name to justify India's strategy of controlling the same Indian Ocean chokepoints, just like the Portuguese.[10] As the Indian Navy's 2004 *Indian Naval Doctrine* comments: 'Control of the chokepoints could be useful as a bargaining chip in the international power game, where the currency of military power remains a stark reality.'[11]

Britain gained control of the Indian Ocean when it became the dominant global naval power at the beginning of the nineteenth century. Britain's primary objectives in the Indian Ocean region over the next 150 years were to maintain its rule of India, protect India from maritime threats, and contain the southward drive of Russia towards the Indian Ocean. From the beginning of the twentieth century another key objective was added: to protect and monopolise the sources of oil in the Middle East. Like the Portuguese before them, they seized control of key oceanic chokepoints, building naval bases at Singapore on the Malacca Strait; at Cape Town in South Africa; and Aden on the Red Sea. The British also built numerous intermediate bases to provide strategic depth and facilitate the movement of forces throughout the region, including major naval bases at Bombay, Trincomalee, Mombasa and Mauritius. Britain's strategy allowed it to dominate the Indian Ocean for some 150 years with relatively small naval forces. Even at the height of Britain's imperial power in 1914, the Royal Navy deployed only 12 major warships in the Indian Ocean compared with 43 in the Pacific, where Britain had far fewer interests.[12] By facilitating the movement of expeditionary forces throughout the Indian Ocean, Britain also avoided the need to maintain large standing armies in the region.

In many ways the Indian Ocean represented the central point of the entire British Empire. The Indian Ocean was a 'British Lake' around which lay almost half the total area of its empire and some 80 per cent of its population.[13] At the geographic and strategic centre of the British Lake lay India. Britain formally claimed or was the suzerain power over most of the territory surrounding the Indian Ocean, including most of Southern and East Africa, much of the Middle East and the Persian Gulf, all of South Asia, Burma, Malaya and the entire continent of Australia. Maritime security in the Indian Ocean was almost entirely the preserve of the Royal Navy, but the British Indian Army was often responsible for territorial security. According to one historian, 'the Royal Navy was the key instrument of British power in the Indian Ocean along with the Indian Army, the "hammer and anvil" upon which Britain's paramount power depended'.[14]

Britain's colonial territories were often controlled by small local army detachments backed by expeditionary forces that could be quickly deployed from India or intermediate bases to respond to local threats and insurgencies. Britain relied heavily on an Indian mercenary army for imperial commitments. In 1890 the British Army had some 70,000 troops in India, which were largely required to maintain domestic security on the subcontinent, while the Indian Army consisted of some 150,000 troops, many of whom were available for imperial duties.[15] Indian troops were cheaper, could be deployed without parliamentary approval and were considered better suited for tropical climates than British forces.[16] British Indian forces formed the backbone of major military campaigns throughout the Indian Ocean region, in locations as diverse as Afghanistan (1839–42; and 1878–80), Persia/Iran (1856–7; 1914–18; and 1941–7), Mesopotamia/Iraq (1914–18; and 1941–3), Egypt (1882; and 1940–3), Sudan (1885–6; and 1896–8), Abyssinia/Ethiopia (1868; and 1940–41), Somaliland (1901–10), Kenya (1896–1900), Uganda (1897–90); Tanganyika (1914–15); Burma (1885–87; 1942–5), Malaya (1874–6; and 1941–2), Java (1811; and 1945–6) and China (1856–60; and 1900), and many other brushfire and constabulary actions too numerous to list. Only in a few parts of the Indian Ocean littoral, such as Australia, did the Indian Army not have a key security role.

To the territories they controlled throughout the Indian Ocean the British also brought with them millions of Indian indentured workers, administrators and traders. Between 1834 and 1937 an estimated 30 million Indians worked overseas.[17] These migrant workers formed the basis of large Indian communities throughout the Indian Ocean littoral, particularly in South Africa, East Africa, Mauritius, Burma and Malaya. This changed the demographics of the region, including in Mauritius, where some 70 per cent of the population is now of Indian descent; in Sri Lanka some 18 per cent; and in Malaysia some 8 per cent. As will be seen, this has had a lasting impact on India's strategic relationships in the region.

While British imperial territories elsewhere in the world were usually administered by colonial governors reporting directly to London, much of Britain's Indian Ocean Empire was administered through India.[18] The British Indian government administered virtually the whole of the Indian subcontinent and Burma either directly or through protectorate relationships with the so-called princely states. In the northwest Indian Ocean, the British Raj administered Aden directly, as well as much of the Arabian peninsula and the Horn of Africa through protectorate arrangements, including Kuwait, Bahrain, the Trucial States (now United Arab Emirates), Muscat and Oman, British Somaliland and Zanzibar. These gave the British Indian government suzerain rights equivalent to the rights it exercised with respect to the princely states on the Indian subcontinent, including a veto over relationships with 'external' powers and special protections for British (including British Indian) subjects.[19] In the northeast, the British rulers of Calcutta founded and administered the Straits Settlements (Penang, Malacca and Singapore), until local traders obtained autonomy.

While British India's strategy was conceived within the context of the overall interests of the British Empire, the British Indian government had its own style and often reflected India's particular strategic, economic and political perspectives. The British Indian government was not permitted to conduct a foreign policy that was detrimental to British interests, but through necessity it was given latitude to develop an approach driven by its particular regional perspectives.[20] As Thomas Metcalf put it, the continuous deployment of Indian forces in the Indian Ocean region created:

> An arc of power emanating from the [British Indian] government's mountaintop aerie at Simla and extending throughout this Indian Ocean arena. India remained always, to be sure, a subordinate partner in the larger British Empire, but from Africa to eastern Asia, its army made possible the empire's very existence.[21]

Delhi's strategic perspectives were often very different from London's and there was frequent friction with London over both substantive issues and political style, although in major disputes London generally won. Of course, at least until the last years of the Raj, no Indians were asked for their opinions about India's strategic needs. Nevertheless, the British Indian government often applied a particularly Indo-centric view of the world, if also an imperialistic one. In the years following World War I, the British Indian government lobbied London to take over Tanganyika and Mesopotamia as colonies for returned Indian soldiers as a gesture of goodwill towards them and a way of consolidating Indian control of the western Indian Ocean. In the 1930s, as political independence for India came closer, the British Indian government strongly resisted the transfer of Aden from India to Britain due to its particular strategic importance to India.

The centrality of India in Britain's Indian Ocean system meant that the independence of India in 1947 inevitably placed Britain's predominance in the Indian Ocean in eclipse, even if it hung on to many colonial possessions for decades afterwards. But while the United States became the dominant global military and economic power after World War II, its primary strategic concerns lay in Europe and Northeast Asia. Washington was content for the Indian Ocean to remain a 'British Lake' under the responsibility of the Royal Navy for as long as possible. Nehru and other leaders of a newly independent India also took a generally indulgent view of the Royal Navy, seeing it as a stabilising presence during the final years of the colonial period while India built its own capabilities. But Britain forced the issue in the late 1960s with its announcement of the withdrawal of the Royal Navy from 'East of Suez'. In the following years, Britain actively cooperated with the United States in handing over security responsibilities in the Indian Ocean, including transitioning many of its colonial relationships in the Persian Gulf, East Africa and Southeast Asia. In 1965 Britain created the British Indian Ocean Territory as a new, unpopulated territory in the central Indian Ocean by excising the Chagos islands from colonial administration by Mauritius and Seychelles and then deporting its plantation workers. The island of Diego Garcia was then leased to the United States to enable it to construct a naval and air base there, now a key element in the US regional security system.

As the predominant power in the Indian Ocean since the early 1970s, the United States has followed a somewhat different strategic approach to its predecessor. Its primary objectives in the Indian Ocean region have been to secure Middle Eastern oil and the energy transportation routes to the Northern Hemisphere and, during the Cold War, to contain the Soviet Union and prevent it from expanding its influence southwards into the Middle East and southern Asia. In pursuing these objectives, the United States sought to rely as much as possible on alliances with local states, including the multilateral Central Treaty Organization (or CENTO pact) with Turkey, Iraq, Iran and Pakistan; and the South East Asian Treaty Organization (or SEATO pact) whose members included Pakistan, Thailand and Australia. The United States also had a separate ANZUS treaty relationship with Australia and New Zealand. All these multilateral alliances fell apart in the 1970s and 1980s, to be replaced by numerous formal or informal bilateral security relationships in which the United States acts as a 'hub'. This has been called a system of 'multi-bilateralism', in which US security partners interact with each other *through* the United States.

The US backed its alliance relationships in the Indian Ocean with substantial naval and air forces, mostly concentrated in and around the Persian Gulf. The United States established USCENTCOM as a separate unified military command with responsibility for the Middle East, with operating headquarters in Qatar. USCENTCOM commands considerable US military forces throughout the western Indian Ocean, including the US Navy's Fifth Fleet, based at Bahrain. The United States operates numerous military bases or has access to local infrastructure throughout the Persian Gulf (including Iraq, Kuwait, Saudi Arabia, Bahrain, UAE, Qatar, Oman, Djibouti), South Asia (Pakistan and Afghanistan), Indian Ocean islands (including Diego Garcia and Seychelles), Southeast Asia (including Thailand and Singapore) and Australia.

The US military base on Diego Garcia has a crucial role in US military strategy in the Indian Ocean and the world. The United States identified Diego Garcia in the 1960s as a future hub for its base network in the Indian Ocean. Its many advantages as a military base included its geographical centrality, its position on the territory of a close ally, its isolated location and its lack of a local population. The United States built up Diego Garcia through the 1970s and 1980s in response to the growth of a Soviet presence in the Indian Ocean. Diego Garcia was a launch point for B-52 bombers in the event of nuclear war with the Soviet Union, and after the Cold War it was used as a major staging point for US attacks on Iraq in 1990 and 2003 and Afghanistan from 2001. Today the base has four main functions. It is: a semi-permanent anchorage for a fleet of ships that can deliver prepositioned equipment sufficient for US Army and Marine Corps brigades to be deployed anywhere in the Indian Ocean region within one week; a hub for fast attack submarines and surface ships operating in the Indian Ocean; an airbase that supports the 'Global Strike' concept under which the US Strategic Command can make conventional strikes anywhere on the earth's surface; and the regional hub for communications, SIGINT and satellite-tracking capabilities.[22] The base is currently being upgraded to host a nuclear-powered cruise missile submarine which, with the cruise missile firepower of an entire carrier strike group, will be a key part of America's 'over the horizon' strategy in the Indian Ocean in coming years. Along with Guam in the Pacific Ocean, Diego Garcia is now a crucial element in a system that allows the United States to pivot military power throughout the world. According to one analyst, Diego Garcia is the single most important military facility the United States has, allowing it to control half of Africa and the southern sides of Asia and Eurasia.[23]

Like America's predecessors, the Indian subcontinent plays a crucial role in the US strategic system in the Indian Ocean, but until recently, America's primary alignment has been with Pakistan. From its establishment following the Partition of India in 1947, Pakistan made itself a willing ally of the United States against the Soviet Union; it is now a somewhat less willing ally in the US struggle against Islamic radicalism. This arrangement has provided Pakistan with considerable material and political benefits in opposing what it saw as its real enemy, India. Throughout the Cold War, Pakistan acted as a regional anchor for the United States, bolstering US relationships with Muslim states throughout the northeast Indian Ocean, helping to destabilise the Soviet Union's southern periphery and keeping India, a potential regional competitor, strategically preoccupied with South Asia. In 1971 the United States saved West Pakistan from invasion and possible dismemberment by India, an act which soured US–Indian relations for decades. In the last decade or so, the United States has tried to reduce its reliance on Pakistan and has moved to make India its key strategic partner in the Indian Ocean.

The Soviet Union briefly challenged US predominance when it attempted to use the opportunity created by the British withdrawal from the Indian Ocean to expand its influence in the region. Through the 1970s and 1980s, the Soviet Union and the United States jostled for influence among the weak states in the region, often vying for access to port or air facilities. This competition was heightened by the Soviet intervention in Afghanistan in 1979, which Washington believed was part of a Soviet push to breach its containment barrier and gain access to the Indian Ocean. But Washington's assessment of the Soviet Union's strategic aims in Afghanistan was wrong and, in any event, the Soviet Union never developed more than a modest military presence in the Indian Ocean.

Although formal and informal alliance relationships between the United States and Pakistan and other Muslim states in the northeast Indian Ocean have sometimes been problematic, these alliances have generally helped the United States minimise the need to deploy land forces in the region. Over the last four decades, the United States has only been required to conduct significant land-based military interventions in the Indian Ocean region on a few occasions; these included the campaigns against Iraq (in 1991 and 2003–11) to protect US oil interests in the Persian Gulf, and a punitive campaign against Islamic fundamentalists in Afghanistan (2001–present), part of the so-called 'War on Terror'. The US 'Rebalancing' strategy, announced in late 2011, signals a greater US strategic focus on balancing China's power in East Asia and relatively less focus on the Indian Ocean. The end of major land wars in Iraq and Afghanistan will permit a significant reduction in US forces committed in West Asia. As a result, the United States will seek to maintain its power in the region through greater reliance on local allies and greater use of what it has called the 'offshore' option—the relatively low-cost projection of power from offshore naval forces and use of unmanned vehicles. The United States will also leverage its military force by swinging resources between the Pacific and Indian oceans to a much greater extent than previously.

India's ambitions to become an Indian Ocean power

India has long seen itself as destined to become not only a major regional power but also a global power. Jawaharlal Nehru spoke of India's 'manifest destiny' to become the third or fourth greatest power in the world, and in recent years it has become commonplace for Indian leaders to talk of India's destiny as a great power.[24] George Tanham, an American observer of Indian strategic culture, claimed that the Indian elite see 'a hierarchical layering of nations according to world power', essentially an extension of Brahmin hierarchical social concepts to the international system, and naturally they wish to see India at or near the top of that hierachy.[25]

But the nature of India's destined 'greatness' remains the subject of some debate within India. There has long been a strong element of exceptionalism among the Indian elite, who see India as a spiritual or moral leader of the world. This was a key ideological foundation of India's nonaligned posture during the Cold War, when India's supposedly 'moral' approach to international relations was often contrasted with what was disparagingly referred to as the 'power politics' practised by the United States and others. Although beliefs in Indian moral exceptionalism have been muted since the end of the Cold War, they still remain an important factor in Indian strategic behaviour. As Indian Foreign Minister Yashwant Sinha commented in 2004:

> It is important therefore that India distances itself from the conventional idea of power, as the ability of a nation to bend other nations to its will through coercive use of force. It is also essential to make clear at the very outset that India approaches the notion of power with an alternate vision and a deep consciousness of responsibilities. There can be no other way for India.[26]

But while India officially rejects territorial ambitions or any aspirations towards regional hegemony, it has long had ambitions to be the dominant power in the Indian Ocean, and this creates somewhat of a paradox for India's future role.

Though few might publicly admit it, many in New Delhi believe that the Indian Ocean must be, and must be seen to be, 'India's Ocean'. This involves several ideas—first, domination of the Indian Ocean is not merely a strategic choice but part of India's 'manifest destiny'; second, India must establish a defence perimeter as deep into the Indian Ocean as possible to preclude the possibility of extra-regional intervention in the subcontinent; and third, that the development of a sphere of influence in the Indian Ocean is a necessary step towards India's status as a global power.

Although India formed the centre of gravity of Britain's Indian Ocean empire, independence and Partition in 1947 left it with a legacy of strategic ambitions that were not remotely matched by economic or military capabilities. At independence, India was one of the poorest nations in the world. This poverty was compounded in the following decades by government policies promoting economic autonomy and a high level of state control of the economy, which in practice led to economic isolation and stagnation. Up until the 1990s, India's so-called 'Hindu rate of growth', averaging around 3 per cent per annum, made it a by-word for failed economic policies.[27] For many decades, India was preoccupied with immediate security threats in South Asia from Pakistan and China and had few resources to spare for the Indian Ocean region.

India first began asserting its destiny to be the leading power in the Indian Ocean in the early 1970s, when the Royal Navy was withdrawing from east of Suez. India tried, without success, to stop the handover of power in the Indian Ocean to the United States. It sponsored a treaty that would exclude the US and other extra-regional powers from the Indian Ocean, and the Indian Navy announced ambitious (but unfunded) expansion plans to build a fleet of 250–300 vessels. Although these plans were largely unimplemented, they signified a major change in India's naval ambitions in the region: from an emphasis on coastal defence towards an attempt to alter the naval balance in the Indian Ocean. India also became more assertive in projecting power throughout the region, including planning or implementing military interventions in several Indian Ocean states, such as Mauritius (1983); Sri Lanka (1983–90); Seychelles (1986) and Maldives (1988). But the failure of India's peacekeeping force in Sri Lanka and the assassination of Rajiv Gandhi by Sri Lankan terrorists in 1991 severely undermined the political will of India's leadership to embark on regional military adventures.

In coming decades India may be in a position to achieve many of its strategic ambitions. In 1991, India began a process of transforming its economy comparable to the transformation of the Chinese economy from the late 1970s under Deng Xiaoping. The removal of many of the barriers to trade and economic activity that had been in place under the Nehruvian system led to a dramatic acceleration in India's economic growth, from 0.8 per cent per annum in 1991/92 to around 7.2 per cent per annum in 2011. India's GDP has grown from US$267 billion in 1991 to an estimated US$1,676 billion in 2011.[28] In 2007 Goldman Sachs predicted that India's GDP (in US dollar terms) will exceed the United States by 2050.[29]

Despite many predictions that India is on the threshold of becoming a global economic power, the current reality is somewhat less impressive. India is now the eleventh largest economy in the world in exchange rate terms and third largest in purchasing power parity terms.[30] However, India remains a poor country, with annual per capita GDP of US$3,700 in purchasing power parity terms, placing it far below major Indian Ocean powers. By comparison, in 2011 annual per capita GDP for the United States was US$49,000; Australia, US$40,800; South Africa, US$11,100; China, US$8,500; and Indonesia, US$4,700.[31] Although the total size of India's economy is large due to its huge population, the low per capita GDP and its limited ability to raise taxation constrains India's ability to mobilise its economic surplus for military purposes.

Nevertheless, India's rapid economic growth is being translated into expanded military capabilities, particularly its ability to project power. Defence expenditure has increased from Rs 196 billion (US$13.8 billion) in 1991 to Rs 2,330 billion (US$44.2 billion) in 2011, making it the eighth largest defence spender in the world (less than Saudi Arabia but more than Germany).[32] India's defence budget for 2012–13 showed an increase of 18 per cent over the previous year and is likely to increase significantly in coming years. Much of the increase in India's defence expenditure has been devoted to modernising the army and air force and transforming the navy into a blue water navy that can project power throughout the Indian Ocean. The navy's share of total defence expenditure (particularly capital expenditure) has increased very significantly in recent years, from 11 per cent in 1992/93 to around 18 per cent in 2008/9.

India has a very large military establishment. It has the world's second largest army (around 1.1 million active regular personnel), the world's fourth largest air force (around 850 combat aircraft), and one of the world's largest navies. But India has only a limited ability to project power beyond South Asia. Much of its huge army deals with domestic insurgencies or is deployed in defensive roles along its western and northern borders. The Indian Navy has major expansion plans for the next decade or so, involving a fleet of over 160 ships by 2022, including three aircraft carriers and 60 major combatant ships, as well as almost 400 naval aircraft. But the navy remains deficient in many areas. The air force remains largely focused on Pakistan and China and has only token capabilities to project power beyond the subcontinent. Although India is a declared nuclear weapons state with approximately 50–60 nuclear devices as at 2007,[33] there are significant limitations to its long-range nuclear weapon delivery capabilities, meaning that while India can deploy nuclear devices against all of Pakistan, it is unable to deploy nuclear devices against eastern China.

India's defence modernisation over the last decade or so has placed considerable emphasis on improving power projection capabilities across the Indian Ocean region. This includes air power, expeditionary capabilities, intelligence, surveillance and reconnaissance, and nuclear capabilities. India is enhancing its ability to project air power beyond the subcontinent, with the Air Force reportedly revising its war doctrine to include taking pre-emptive and retaliatory action across a region stretching from the Persian Gulf to the Straits of Malacca'.[34] However, its long-range strike capabilities are restricted by limited in-flight refuelling capacity and little access to forward airfields. India has focused on aircraft carriers as a means of projecting air power throughout the Indian Ocean area and also, not coincidentally, as symbols of great power status. Since the early 1980s, when Australia retired its last carrier, India has been the only Asian or Indian Ocean state to have an operational aircraft carrier.[35] The Indian Navy currently operates one obsolete aircraft carrier laid down in 1944 and is in the process of commissioning a large Soviet-built carrier. Two other locally built aircraft carriers are under construction. According to former Indian chief of naval staff, Admiral Arun Prakash, India aims to exercise selective sea control through task forces built around three aircraft carriers that will form the core of separate fleets in the Bay of Bengal, the Indian Ocean and the Arabian Sea. While three operational carrier task forces are likely to remain in the realm of imagination for many years to come, there is little doubt that new aircraft carriers will allow India to project air power far beyond its current capabilities.

India is also focusing on improving its expeditionary capabilities. At the end of World War II, the Indian Army was one of the most experienced expeditionary forces in the world. It has retained limited expeditionary experience through its participation in UN peacekeeping operations but most of its amphibious capabilities have been lost. In 2011, the Army announced the redesignation of an infantry division for amphibious operations, with one brigade based in south India for deployment on the Indian Ocean, another in west India for deployment around the Arabian Sea, and a third in the Andaman and Nicobar Islands. Over the last decade the Navy has developed its amphibious capabilities through the acquisition of the amphibious dock ship, INS *Jalashwa* from the United States, and is procuring up to four large multi-role support vessels and increasing the size of its Marine Commando force. The Air Force will also significantly increase its strategic airlift capacity to support expeditionary forces through the acquisition of up to 16 C-17 Globemaster transports from the United States.

India is also developing surveillance and reconnaissance (ISR) capabilities in order to enhance its maritime domain awareness (MDA) throughout the Indian Ocean.[36] According to India's 2007 *Maritime Military Strategy,* 'this singular factor—MDA—has the potential and capability to widen the gap between the capabilities of the Indian Navy and other regional maritime forces in the IOR [Indian Ocean Region]'.[37] The Indian Navy has expanded its fleet of medium-range maritime surveillance aircraft, and is taking delivery of up to 24 Boeing P-8i long-range multi-mission maritime aircraft, which are capable of broad-area, maritime and littoral operations. They are likely to be complemented by the Global Hawk broad-area maritime surveillance drones, which will massively enhance India's maritime ISR capabilities. India is also launching a dedicated naval communications satellite to provide coverage from the east coast of Africa to the Malacca Strait as part of an effort to create a 'network-enabled navy'.

The Indian Navy is also developing its nuclear weapon delivery capabilities as the third leg of a nuclear triad. The desire for submarine-launched ballistic missile capabilities is driven by the limited range of India's land-based missiles, as well as by a desire for international status—to match the capabilities of the 'Permanent 5' members of the UN Security Council. In 2012, the Navy leased a nuclear-powered submarine from Russia. A locally constructed nuclear submarine is scheduled for induction and work has commenced on two other nuclear submarines, which will be based at a dedicated new base on India's east coast. It remains to be seen whether India will deploy its nuclear submarine capabilities into the Pacific against China.

But while India has ambitious military expansion plans, their significance should not be overstated. India has a long tradition of allowing its strategic ambitions to outstrip its capabilities and plans to go unfulfilled. The Indian Navy, the main service by which India projects military power in the Indian Ocean, remains a junior partner in the Indian Armed Forces, and its spending is a tiny fraction of US naval spending. Over the last several decades, the Indian Navy has received a share of around 11–14 per cent of the total defence budget and in 2012–2013 its budget allocation of US$7.6 billion represented around 19 per cent of total defence spending (which proportion is likely to decline somewhat in coming years).[38] By contrast, in 2012 US spending on its navy (including the Marine Corps) was US$161 billion, or approximately 29 per cent of the aggregate US defence budget.[39] At the height of the British Empire, in the period 1900–1914, spending on the Royal Navy represented around 60 per cent of Britain's total defence spending.[40] India will need to enhance its capabilities considerably if it is to meet its strategic ambitions in the Indian Ocean.

Notes

1 Robert D. Kaplan (2009) 'Center stage for the twenty-first century', *Foreign Affairs*, Vol. 88, No. 2, pp. 16–29.
2 US Energy Information Administration (2012) *World Oil Transit Chokepoints*, 22 August.
3 United States, Department of Defense, *Annual Report to Congress: Military and Security Developments Involving the People's Republic of China 2012*, p. 42.
4 US Energy Information Administration (2011) *International Energy Outlook 2011*, 19 September.
5 Standard Life (2012) *The Weekly Focus: a market and economic update*, 8 October.
6 International Energy Agency (2012) *World Energy Outlook, 2012*, Paris: OECD.
7 See, for example, William L. Dowdy (1985) 'The Indian Ocean region as a concept and reality', in William L. Dowdy and Russell B. Trood (eds), *The Indian Ocean: Perspectives on a Strategic Arena*, Durham, NC: Duke University Press, pp. 3–26.
8 Barry Buzan and Ole Wæver (2003) *Regions and Powers: The Structure of International Security*, Cambridge: Cambridge University Press.
9 Barry Buzan (1982) 'The Indian Ocean in global politics', *Survival*, Vol. 24, p. 44.
10 Indian Navy (2007) *Freedom to Use the Seas: India's Maritime Military Strategy*, p. 59.
11 India Navy (2004) *Indian Maritime Doctrine*, p. 64.
12 Michael Naylor Pearson (2003) *The Indian Ocean*, London: Routledge, p. 191.

13 D.H. Cole (1931) *Imperial Military Geography, 6th edition*, London: Sifton Praed, p. 81.
14 Ashley Jackson (2011) 'Britain in the Indian Ocean', *Journal of the Indian Ocean Region*, Vol. 7, No. 2, December, pp. 145–60.
15 Karen A. Rasler, William R. Thompson (1994) *The Great Powers and Global Struggle, 1490–1990*, Lexington, KY: University Press of Kentucky, p. 149.
16 The use of Indian troops instead of British troops for expeditionary commitments also helped to ensure that the ratio of British to Indian forces stationed in India did not fall below 1:2, which was considered important to deter an Indian army mutiny. T.A. Heathcote (1995) *The Military in British India: the development of British land forces in South Asia, 1600–1947*, Manchester: Manchester University Press, p. 152.
17 Pearson, *The Indian Ocean*, p. 223.
18 See generally, Robert J. Blyth (2003) *The Empire of the Raj: India, Eastern Africa and the Middle East 1858–1947*, London: Palgrave Macmillan.
19 See James Onley (2009) 'The Raj reconsidered: British India's informal empire and spheres of influence in Asia and Africa', *Asian Affairs*, Vol. 40, No. 1, pp. 44–62.
20 Blyth, *The Empire of the Raj*, p. 3.
21 Thomas R. Cole (2007) *Imperial Connections: India in the Indian Ocean Arena 1860–1920,* Berkeley, CA: University of California Press, p. 69.
22 See generally, Andrew S. Erickson, Walter C. Ladwig and Justin D. Mikolay (2010) 'Diego Garcia and the United States' emerging Indian Ocean strategy', *Asian Security*, Vol. 6, No. 3, pp. 214–37.
23 David Vine and Laura Jeffrey (2009) '"Give us back Diego Garcia': unity and division among activists in the Indian Ocean', in Catherine Lutz (ed.), *The Bases of Empire: the Global Struggle against US Military Posts*, New York: New York University Press, p. 211.
24 Vernon Marston Hewitt (1992) *The International Politics of South Asia*, Manchester: Manchester University Press, p. 195.
25 George Tanham (1992) *Indian Strategic Thought: an interpretive essay*, Santa Monica, CA: Rand, p. 131
26 Yashwant Sinha (2004) 'Geopolitics: What it takes to be a world power', speech in New Delhi, 12 March.
27 From which must be deducted population growth of around 2 per cent per annum for real GDP growth per capita.
28 In exchange-rate terms. CIA World Factbook. Online: www.cia.gov/library/publications/the-world-factbook/ (accessed 10 October 2013).
29 Dominic Wilson and Anna Stupnytska (2007) 'The N11: More than an Acronym', Goldman Sachs Global Economics Paper No. 153, 28 March.
30 International Monetary Fund (2012) World Economic Outlook Database, April.
31 2011 estimates, each at purchasing power parity. CIA World Factbook. Online: www.cia.gov/library/publications/the-world-factbook/ (accessed 10 October 2013).
32 Excluding expenditure on nuclear weapons. US dollar figures are at constant 2010 exchange rates. Stockholm International Peace Research Institute. Online: www.sipri.org/research/armaments/milex (accessed 10 October 2013).
33 'India's Nuclear Forces, 2007' (2007) *Bulletin of Atomic Scientists*, Vol. 63, No. 4, July/August, pp. 74–8.
34 'India: Air Force' (2009) *Jane's World Air Forces*, 1 June, p. 11.
35 The Royal Thai Navy acquired a small aircraft carrier in 1997 that has never been operational. In 2011, China commissioned the ex-Soviet aircraft carrier *Varyag* as a training vessel.
36 See generally, W. Lawrence S. Prabhakar (2009) 'India's maritime surveillance and reconnaissance Initiatives and the quest to secure its maritime-aerospace', *Strategic Affairs*, September.

37 Indian Navy, *Freedom to Use the Seas*, p. 117.
38 Laxman K. Behera (2012) 'India's defence budget 2012–13', *IDSA Comment*, 20 March.
39 US Department of Defense (2011) *National Defense Budge Estimates for FY 2012*, March, p. 92.
40 Peter Padfield (1974) *The Great Naval Race: Anglo-German Naval Rivalry 1900–1914*, London: Hart-Davis, MacGibbon, p. 210.

2 Indian strategic thinking about the Indian Ocean

While India's growing military and economic capacity may provide a material basis for it to become a major regional power, how it will exercise that power will be a function of its strategic objectives and intentions. Indian strategic thinking about the Indian Ocean derives from several traditions and themes. These include a legacy of geostrategic thinking from its British imperial past; India's strong Nehruvian tradition of nonalignment and strategic autonomy; and claims to an Indian Monroe Doctrine. These streams of thinking are not always either consistent or clear to outsiders (or even insiders for that matter). This partly reflects the fact that India has traditionally been strategically focused on its land borders and, as a result, thinking about its oceanic environment is still evolving in many respects. As one analyst described it, India's approach to maritime affairs as 'amorphous, syncretic and incremental'.[1]

Some of these streams of thought represent a resurrection of perspectives from previous times and others reflect the application of ideas previously applied to South Asia to the broader Indian Ocean region. This chapter will examine these streams of Indian strategic thought about the Indian Ocean and their likely impact on Indian strategic behaviour.

The imperial legacy in strategic thinking about the Indian Ocean

British imperial perspectives provide an important foundation for Indian strategic thinking. These traditions were passed on to an independent India in a variety of ways which are still evident today, including through a tendency towards geostrategic thinking among strategic analysts, the habits and practices of the bureaucrats in South Block and the Indian Navy's cultural inheritance from the Royal Navy. In ruling India the British often built upon existing traditions of the Indian subcontinent. In other ways, British strategies, particularly those relating to India's role in the Indian Ocean, represented a significant departure from Indian traditions, in which there was little history of military or political adventures beyond the limits of the subcontinent. Although pre-colonial India exerted considerable cultural and religious influence in the Indian Ocean region, particularly in Southeast Asia, this was never converted into political or territorial control.

Britain's control of the subcontinent was characterised by an idiosyncratic mixture of direct and indirect rule which was partly inherited from their Mughal predecessors. The British ruled only parts of South Asia directly and relied on a patchwork of suzerain relationships to control the rest. Protectorates or 'princely states', covering around half the Indian subcontinent, were allowed a high degree of political autonomy on local matters but were not permitted to develop relationships with foreign powers. Lord Curzon, the British Viceroy of India at the beginning of the twentieth century and a key strategic thinker of the British Raj, is closely associated with the pursuit of an active strategic role for imperial India throughout the Indian Ocean region. Curzon was comfortable with the imprecise nature of India's control over the region, calling India's borders a 'Threefold Frontier'—*first*, an administrative boundary within which the government of India exercised full authority, *second*, a zone claimed as Indian territory but autonomously governed, and *third*, independent kingdoms or protectorates that were tied by special treaties of friendship and obligation to the government of India.[2] This included neighbouring independent or semi-independent kingdoms in southern Asia such as Afghanistan, Tibet, Nepal, Sikkim, Bhutan and Siam.

Consistent with these indistinct spheres of control, Lord Curzon advocated a so-called Forward Policy to secure India. The so-called 'Forward School' of Curzon's followers argued that India's security demanded control of the maritime routes and key ports *en route* to India, the use of buffer states to insulate direct contact with other empires, and for British India to take an active role in managing the affairs of the buffer zones. Britain took a great deal of trouble to ensure that these buffer states were politically subordinated to British interests or the influence of potentially competing powers such as Russia, China or France was otherwise neutralised. As previously discussed, British strategy in the broader Indian Ocean involved reliance on the Royal Navy to deter extra-regional powers and facilitate the free movement of British and Indian army forces to maintain security throughout the region. British India, in effect, formed the centre point of a security system that encompassed the entire Indian Ocean region. The supremacy of the Royal Navy meant that there were few credible maritime threats to India and instead British Indian defence planners focused on land-based threats to India's north.

Importantly, the British saw close links between India's external and internal security. The threat represented by an expansion of Russian influence into southern Asia during the nineteenth century (the so-called 'Great Game') was not principally seen in terms of the threat of external invasion. Rather, the British were worried that unrest on the frontier created by foreign influences would trigger internal uprisings in India. These close links between internal and external security continue to be a significant factor in modern India.

In 1942, as Independence became increasingly inevitable, the British Indian Foreign Secretary, Sir Olaf Caroe, established a group to study the strategic needs and role of an independent India as part of a British-led Commonwealth. Caroe envisaged a natural Indian pre-eminence in the Indian Ocean, a 'central constellation from which others in the Indian Ocean in the long run are likely to radiate', and hoped to position a post-independence India as a part of a global Anglo-Saxon security system.[3] Caroe's study group strongly influenced the thinking of early Indian strategists, including India's most famous Indian Ocean strategist, K. M. Panikkar, who remains one of the most influential exponents of Indian geostrategic thinking. His 1945 book which arose out of these discussions, *India and the Indian Ocean: An Essay on the Influence of Sea Power on Indian History*,[4] is still required reading for Indian naval officers and remains foundational to Indian strategic thinking about the Indian Ocean. Panikkar deliberately named his book after a well-known work by the nineteenth century US naval strategist, Alfred Thayer Mahan, who advocated the use of sea power by major powers to extend their international influence.

In advocating India's post-independence strategy, Panikkar emphasised the amphibious character of European colonisation of India. He claimed that India's security could only be guaranteed through control of the Indian Ocean, arguing that 'to India it is the vital sea. ... The Indian Ocean must therefore remain truly Indian ... '.[5] According to Panikkar, this goal could only be achieved through the establishment of a system of forward bases at or near the Indian Ocean chokepoints, including in the Bay of Bengal and at Singapore, Ceylon, Mauritius and Socotra (near Aden). The Indian Navy would have primary responsibility for guarding this 'steel ring'.[6] Panikkar recognised the limitations on an independent India's capabilities and proposed that India and Britain, as equal partners, should make the Indian Ocean a 'reserved sphere of Anglo-Indian influence'.[7] This would be administered by a council of regional powers chaired by India and including Britain, Australia and South Africa. This system would allow Britain to maintain a measure of its global role in a post-colonial world while providing an essential bolster to India's security.

Pannikar's proposal never came to pass. In the decades after independence this geostrategic tradition used by thinkers such as Panikkar was largely discarded in Indian strategic rhetoric (if not always in practice). But in the last decade or so geostrategy and the imperial legacy have again become prominent features in Indian strategic discourse, particularly among those interested in maritime affairs.[8]

The Nehruvian strategic tradition and India's quest for strategic autonomy

Independence brought a major change in Indian strategic thinking. Rhetorically at least, India turned its back on imperial traditions. In its place India adopted a distinctive strategic approach that was nationalist and inward-looking and at the same time internationalist, promoting international cooperation while rejecting alliances with friendly states. What is now called 'Nehruvian' strategic doctrine was employed by Jawaharlal Nehru and followed, at least rhetorically, by his daughter, Indira Gandhi, and grandson, Rajiv Gandhi. At its core was the concept of nonalignment, whose key principles, as espoused by India, were nonviolence, international cooperation, Afro-Asian solidarity, and the preservation of India's freedom of action through refusing to align India with any Cold War bloc.

Nonalignment was seen as quite different from mere 'neutrality' and represented an insistence that even relatively weak powers could choose to stay aloof from great power rivalries. In this respect, nonalignment resembled America's nineteenth century strategy of avoiding 'entangling alliances'. Through its advocacy of nonalignment India sought to overcome its material weaknesses, claim a measure of strategic space and pursue its perceived destiny of international leadership. Although Indian strategic practice was progressively modified towards a more realist stance following India's defeat at the hands of China in 1962, a consensus around Nehruvian ideas largely remained in place. Nehruvian strategic principles were an intellectual anchor to Indian strategic thinking and dominated Indian strategic rhetoric up to the end of the Cold War. It continues to be influential today.

Through much of the Cold War, India used its position as a leader of the nonaligned movement to exert considerable ideological influence over newly independent Indian Ocean states in an effort to persuade them against entering into alliances with extra-regional powers. In short, India hoped that the entire Indian Ocean littoral could become nonaligned, with itself sitting at the centre. But while India was relatively successful in promoting nonalignment as a rhetorical objective among many states in the region, it was less successful in building an Indian Ocean security system around the idea. The Indian Ocean Zone of Peace (IOZOP) was a proposed international agreement that would effectively exclude the superpowers from the India Ocean. The proposal was prompted by the withdrawal of the Royal Navy from the Indian Ocean in the early 1970s, when India tried to head off the United States and Soviet Union from filling the so-called 'power vacuum'. Nonaligned ideology held that the 'intrusion' of great powers (particularly Western powers) into any part of the developing world was inherently illegitimate and the primary (if not only) source of insecurity among developing states. According to this logic, the withdrawal of the military presence of great powers from any region would *ipso facto* lead to greater security. India insisted that the IOZOP should exclude extra-regional powers from the Indian Ocean but not involve the general demilitarisation of the region.[9]

The IOZOP proposal, which was formalised in a UN General Assembly resolution in December 1971, called for consultations between great powers and littoral states to halt the military expansion of the great powers in the Indian Ocean and to eliminate military bases, nuclear weapons and other manifestations of great power rivalry. However, no consensus on the proposal could be reached in the face of overt or covert opposition of the key extra-regional powers—the United States, Britain, France and the Soviet Union. Many littoral states, particularly among India's South Asian neighbours, also had misgivings about the proposal. Although the exclusion of the great powers from the Indian Ocean was consistent with nonaligned principles to which many of them subscribed, in the long term it would also have left India as the most powerful state in the region. Many littoral states advocated a more general demilitarisation of the Indian Ocean and the declaration of South Asia as a nuclear-free zone, proposals that India strongly opposed. While many in New Delhi firmly believed their own rhetoric that moral arguments would lead the United States and the Soviet Union to exclude themselves from the region, wiser heads saw the IOZOP proposal as a diplomatic stick to use against the superpowers and a way of demonstrating India's regional leadership role. However, India found itself largely powerless to alter the military balance in the Indian Ocean and by the end of the 1970s it had become clear that India would not be able to achieve its objectives. New Delhi nevertheless kept the proposal alive as a means of leverage against the great powers.[10]

The end of the Cold War forced India to re-examine the viability of non-alignment in guiding India's strategic stance. The idea seemed to lose its *raison d'être* with the collapse of the Soviet Union and India's leaders were instead forced to fashion a new set of strategic goals based on a more pragmatic view of the world. While many ideas were debated within the Indian strategic community, by the end of the 1990s the dominant emphasis in Indian strategic thinking had settled on building a new partnership with the United States as part of a multidirectional engagement with other major powers. India's self-declaration as a nuclear power, made through the 'Pokhran II' nuclear tests in 1998, also provided India with a new international status and led to a transformation of its relationship with the United States. According to C. Raja Mohan, a leading 'modernist' in Indian strategic thinking, after Pokhran II, India's self-perception as an emerging great power armed with nuclear weapons allowed it to negotiate with other powers without the sense of defensiveness that permeated earlier relationships. India's successful transition to a nuclear power also helped to move India's intellectual balance in favour of realists and pragmatists and effectively ended the long-standing dominance of Nehruvians and left-of-centre internationalists in the foreign policy discourse.[11]

Despite these developments, the term 'nonalignment' retains a considerable degree of emotional currency in India, although its modern-day use often bears little resemblance to Nehruvian doctrine.[12] Other features of Indian strategic culture that were associated with the policy of nonalignment also continue to have a significant influence on strategic thought and behaviour. One important factor is India's hesitancy to use military force beyond South Asia. George Tanham's study of India's strategic culture in the early 1990s characterised Indian strategic thinking as being 'defensive' and having a 'lack of an expansionist military tradition'.[13] A common view among the Indian elite is that India does not project military power. A related factor is what US analyst, Stephen Cohen, calls a culture of 'strategic restraint'. According to Cohen, this is deeply rooted in the Indian strategic psyche and is derived from a political culture that stresses disengagement, avoidance of confrontation and a defensive mindset. This culture of restraint is likely to continue to be an important limiting factor in India's strategic behaviour even as India gains the material resources to play a more active strategic role beyond South Asia.[14]

India's quest for strategic autonomy

One of the most important ideas in India's strategic lexicon, which is often connected with nonalignment, is the concept of 'strategic autonomy'. Strategic autonomy has been the 'Holy Grail' of Indian security policy since Independence.[15] Although in the post-Cold War years India's elite largely discarded India's failed policies of economic autonomy, the idea of strategic autonomy remains a patriotic touchstone. While its meaning is rarely defined, the idea is closely connected to a belief in India's destiny to become a great power, beholden to no one. The Indian concept of strategic autonomy shares many of the underlying elements of nonalignment and has been described as 'a realist mutation of the traditional non-aligned posture'.[16]

For many Indian strategists, strategic autonomy is the *sine qua non* of great power status. According to Sumit Ganguly the phrase has acquired 'almost talismanic status' in Indian foreign policy discussions.[17] For some, particularly those influenced by Nehruvian traditions, it is an absolute imperative: any compromise of India's strategic autonomy will also compromise India's destiny to become a great power. To Nehruvian traditionalists, the imperative of maintaining strategic autonomy not only forbids any strategic alignment with the United States and its regional allies but also casts considerable doubt on any security cooperation with states outside the US alliance system. Others would concede that India's interests may be served by entering into security relationships with other states, provided that India retains significant freedom of action. More cynical observers see India's insistence on strategic autonomy as often just a convenient justification for what is actually a state of policy paralysis—for decision-makers in New Delhi, doing nothing, and particularly doing nothing with the United States, is almost always safer than taking any action.[18]

Raja Mohan argues that India should rethink its attachment to strategic autonomy, claiming that autonomy is for weak powers who are trying to insulate themselves from great powers, and that Delhi's task in coming years will be to contribute to the management of the international order, not to seek autonomy from it.[19] But India's preoccupation with strategic autonomy may be less quixotic than it might initially seem: it should be remembered that the United States followed an analogous policy of avoiding 'foreign entanglements' for more than a century and only abandoned it in the twentieth century when the prospect of German domination of Europe forced it to take an active role in managing the international order. Indeed, strong domestic opposition to entering into foreign alliances only fell away after the Japanese attack on Pearl Harbour in 1941.

In the case of India, the prospect of Chinese domination of East Asia might force it to take a more active management role in the international order, but that seems a long way off. The idea of strategic autonomy is strongly ingrained in the Indian strategic psyche and is likely to be a guiding principle (if a relatively undefined one) for many years to come. However, it is likely that the concept will evolve in coming years, just as Indian ideas about nonalignment evolved through the Cold War.

The impact of ideas about strategic autonomy on India's behaviour in the Indian Ocean region will be discussed in detail in later chapters. As will be seen there are considerable unresolved tensions between this goal and a pragmatic recognition of the need to cooperate with the United States in the Indian Ocean. In recent years India has tried to benefit from cooperation with the United States while also trying to avoid the appearance of cooperation. The goal of strategic autonomy is also a major factor in India's considerable reluctance in participating in multilateral security arrangements. In the Indian Ocean, it has only shown enthusiasm for developing close security relationships with very small or weak states (e.g. Singapore, Maldives, Mauritius, Oman). India has been much more cautious of 'entanglements' with larger states.

India's Monroe Doctrine

Another key strand of Indian strategic thinking has come to be called 'India's Monroe Doctrine'. This is an expression of South Asia as a single strategic unit, with India having a special role as the custodian of regional security. This concept is quite different from nonalignment and in practice is often inconsistent with its underlying principles. Despite considerable inconsistencies and vagaries in its application, the doctrine continues to represent a basic goal in Indian strategic thinking about South Asia, as well as potentially having broader application in the Indian Ocean region. Some Indian analysts deny that a Monroe Doctrine has ever functioned in southern Asia and, since the 1960s, Indian leaders have avoided mentioning it in public. However, its spirit—at least a 'soft' version of it—is alive and well in much of Indian strategic thinking about its neighbourhood. As Raja Mohan comments, the Indian variation of the Monroe Doctrine 'has not been entirely successful in the past, but it has been an article of faith for many in the Indian strategic community'.[20]

What is India's Monroe Doctrine?

The Monroe Doctrine had an early place in strategic thinking in modern India. It was used both as an expression of the newly independent India's determination to rid the subcontinent of residual colonial influence and a desire to exclude other powers from the entire South Asian region. In the days leading up to India's independence in 1947, Jawaharlal Nehru argued that 'The doctrine expounded by President Monroe had saved America from foreign aggression for nearly a 100 years, and now the time has come when a similar doctrine must be expounded with respect to Asian countries'.[21]

In 1961, Nehru expanded on this to justify India's use of military force to take over the Portuguese colony of Goa, when he commented:

Even some time after the United States established itself as a strong power, there was fear of interference by European powers in the American continents, and this led to the famous declaration by President Monroe of the United States [that] any interference by a European country would be interference with the American political system. I submit that ... the Portuguese retention of Goa is a continuing interference with the political system established in India today. I shall go a step further and say that any interference by any other power would also be an interference with the political system of India today. ... any attempt by a foreign power to interfere in any way with India is a thing which India cannot tolerate, and which, subject to her strength, she will oppose. That is the broad doctrine I lay down.[22]

Nehru's version of a Monroe Doctrine for India was given a muscular revision by his daughter, Indira Gandhi. In 1983, as India began its ill-fated intervention in the Sri Lanka civil war—discussed in Chapter 3—the influential foreign policy analyst, Bhabani Sen Gupta, provided the clearest articulation of what some called the 'Indira Doctrine'.[23] This version of India's Monroe Doctrine included the following propositions:

- India has no intention of intervening in the internal conflicts of a South Asian country and it strongly opposes intervention by any other.
- India will not tolerate external intervention in a conflict situation in any South Asian country if the intervention has any implicit or explicit anti-Indian implication.
- No South Asian government should therefore ask for external assistance with an anti-Indian bias from any country.
- If a South Asian country genuinely needs external help to deal with a serious internal conflict situation or an intolerable threat to a government legitimately established, it should ask help from a number of neighbouring countries, including India.
- The exclusion of India from such a contingency will be considered to be an anti-Indian move on the part of the government concerned.

Such ideas have an obvious foundation in British Imperial perspectives. As discussed earlier, the British Raj viewed the relationship between Delhi and peripheral or minor states in South Asia as essentially one of suzerainty. During the colonial era, nearly all of India's current neighbours were governed directly by New Delhi (Pakistan; Bangladesh; and Burma until 1937), were in a protectorate relationship with New Delhi (the Himalayan states), or were separately administered by Britain consistent with New Delhi's interests (Ceylon/Sri Lanka; the Maldives; and Burma from 1937). An independent India was merely continuing to expect that neighbouring territories would not act inconsistently with New Delhi's interests or form strategic attachments with potentially hostile states. Post-colonial South Asia may no longer have *political* unity, but an independent India proceeded as if it had the right to enforce the *strategic* unity that existed under British rule.

But Nehru did not invoke British imperial precedent to justify India's prerogatives over its neighbours—he instead consciously fashioned India's policies after the 'Monroe Doctrine' of the United States. Perhaps he saw this as being more ideologically justifiable in a post-colonial world and more palatable to the United States itself. The doctrine was positioned as a natural corollary to nonalignment—even if it was a type of nonalignment unilaterally imposed by India.

The US Monroe Doctrine was a set of principles originally articulated by President Monroe in 1823 as a way of rejecting all new colonial claims of European powers in the Americas. It was modified many times in later years, often involving ever-greater American prerogatives over the affairs of neighbouring states. At the turn of the twentieth century, Alfred Mahan, who was a close advisor to President Theodore Roosevelt, saw the Monroe Doctrine primarily in terms of an imperative to control the sea lines of communication between the Pacific and Atlantic oceans. Washington was increasingly concerned that Germany might obtain naval bases in the Caribbean basin near the Panama Canal from corrupt or bankrupt states, thereby threatening the primary means of communication between America's east and west coasts. In 1904, President Roosevelt proclaimed that the United States might reluctantly be forced to act preemptively as an 'international police power' to prevent European powers from developing a maritime security presence in the Americas.[24] These unilateral pronouncements were initially rejected by European powers, particularly while the United States had no power to enforce them, but, as discussed below, Britain later found it convenient to support the US policy so as to limit the influence of its European rivals in the Americas.

India's Monroe Doctrine did not sit easily with India's highly vocal advocacy of state sovereignty and nonalignment in the international system. Certainly, nonalignment provides an ideological basis for opposing alignments between nearby states and extra-regional powers. The principle of non-interference also justifies India's opposition to perceived instances of interference by extra-regional powers in the affairs of its neighbours. However, New Delhi has never been able to explain how India's self-proclaimed prerogative to restrict its neighbour's freedom to form security relationships with other states and a purported right to intervene in the affairs of its neighbours to enforce that prerogative can be squared with the principles of state sovereignty and non-intervention. Indian strategic thinkers consider India's Monroe Doctrine in terms of a defensive avoidance of external 'intrusions' into India's strategic space and usually bridle at suggestions that India has ever acted as a regional hegemon.

India's attempts to assert regional hegemony within the paradigm of the Monroe Doctrine (either explicit or implicit) has long encountered resistance from its neighbours. As one Bangladeshi military officer commented, 'While India considers the security of the smaller nations to be integral to her own, they perceive India as their principal source of insecurity'.[25] Pakistan, in particular, vehemently rejects any notion that India has any 'special rights' as a keeper of regional security. As Pakistani foreign minister, Agha Shahi, commented in 1988, India's Monroe Doctrine:

> Cannot be acceptable to India's neighbours as it violates basic principles of the Charter of the United Nations, the Nonalignment Movement and Peaceful Co-existence. The concern of exclusion of non-regional powers from the region … is a thin disguise for the assertion of a hegemonic status and a claim to establish one's own sphere of influence over other South Asian countries.[26]

While India's other neighbours are similarly resentful of Indian hegemony, they tend to be more or less discreet in dealing with India's presumptions and generally prudent in the extent of their extra-regional security relationships.

India's policy has also encountered resistance from extra-regional powers, particularly China and the United States.[27] China argues that the international relationships of India's neighbours are exclusively for them to decide and that it is not acceptable for India to place limits on those relationships.[28] But while China frequently acts in contradiction to India's Monroe Doctrine, it also does pay some heed to India's sensitivities. Although the United States has not accepted the application of the Monroe Doctrine to Pakistan, since at least the early 1980s it has implicitly accepted India's special role elsewhere in South Asia. Indeed, Chester Bowles, the US ambassador to India during the 1950s and 1960s, tried on several occasions to persuade Nehru that India should, with the informal backing of the United States, institute an 'Asian Monroe Doctrine' covering the whole of southern Asia (including Iran, Afghanistan, Pakistan, Burma and Thailand). Nehru declined the suggestion.[29]

The application of India's Monroe Doctrine to South Asia

India has applied its Monroe Doctrine in South Asia in several different phases. In the immediate post-independence period it focused on ridding the subcontinent of any residual colonial legacy. In 1947–48, the newly independent India used its energies to incorporate into the Indian Union some 570 princely states and protectorates that had not been under direct British rule, including using force to discourage local rulers from joining Pakistan or claiming independence. New Delhi negotiated an end to France's small colonies on the subcontinent by 1954, but in 1961 used military force to evict Portugal from Goa and related territories. In the early years after independence, India also imposed suzerainty over its Himalayan neighbours with the aim of excluding any non-Indian influence. While Communist China moved to consolidate its position in Tibet in 1950, India confirmed or renegotiated colonial-era protectorate relationships with Bhutan (in 1949), Sikkim (in 1950) and Nepal (in 1950 and 1951). Although India allowed these states a significant degree of internal political autonomy, they were required to accept severe limitations on their ability to form relationships with other powers.

In the decades following independence, India also conducted several military interventions in neighbouring South Asian states to maintain internal security or enforce its prerogatives. This included interventions in Nepal (1951–3; and 1960–2); Bangladesh (1971); Sikkim (1973; annexed in 1975); Sri Lanka (1971; and 1983–90) and Maldives (1988–9). Many of these interventions were justified by India as being in response to real or imagined fears about the influence of what it regarded as 'outside' forces. Several interventions also involved a claim by India of an extraterritorial interest in protecting Indian ethnic minorities and the right to pre-empt any potential transborder ethnic conflict.

India has also resisted what it saw as the 'intrusion' of other naval powers into the waters around South Asia. India initially took an indulgent view of the continued presence of the Royal Navy in the Indian Ocean, including the maintenance of British naval bases at Trincomalee in Sri Lanka until 1958 and at Gan in the Maldives until 1976.[30] This may have reflected thinking about an Anglo-Indian sphere of influence in the Indian Ocean (consistent with Panikkar's earlier proposals), or merely a view that the British naval presence was temporarily convenient and should be allowed to wither peacefully. However, New Delhi took a very dim view of attempts by various other powers to develop a naval presence in South Asia (at Trincomalee, Gan or Diego Garcia) or conduct manoeuvres in nearby waters.

India's belief in its special regional role was strongly reinforced by its successful military intervention in East Pakistan (now Bangladesh). This was seen as proof that India could use force to order the strategic affairs of South Asia even in the face of opposition from the United States. But Indian thinking about its regional role was further modified by India's disastrous intervention in Sri Lanka in the 1980s. As will be discussed in Chapter 3, India's attempt to impose a *Pax Indica* on the warring Sri Lankan ethnic groups led to the humiliating defeat of the Indian Army and the assassination of Rajiv Gandhi. Burnt by the experience, India adopted a hands-off policy towards Sri Lanka for more than a decade. The Sri Lankan debacle and an image of India as a regional bully led New Delhi to try to demonstrate greater awareness of local political sensitivities and greater self-restraint in its dealings with its neighbours. The end of the Cold War also reduced motivations behind what New Delhi saw as foreign meddling in South Asia and the Indian Ocean.

From 1996, I.K. Gujral (first as Indian foreign minister and then as prime minister) sought to soften the 'Indira Doctrine' by proclaiming the so-called 'Gujral Doctrine'. This aimed to reassure India's smaller neighbours by claiming that India would not always ask for reciprocity in its dealings with its neighbours but would give what it could in good faith and trust. It also emphasised non-interference in internal affairs, mutual respect for territorial integrity and sovereignty, and the settlement of disputes through peaceful bilateral negotiations.[31]

Gujral hoped that these principles would achieve a fundamental recasting of South Asia's regional relationships and generate a climate of mutually benign cooperation in the region. Whether or not India's neighbours were wholly reassured by these pronouncements, the Gujral Doctrine signalled a more restrained and mature approach by India to its regional relationships. As Foreign Minister Pranab Mukherjee commented in 2007: 'India does not seek an exclusive sphere of influence, but a shared sphere of mutual development and cooperation'.[32]

Since the end of the Cold War, New Delhi has also to some extent come to terms with the fact of a US security presence in and around South Asia (including in Pakistan, Afghanistan, the Maldives and Diego Garcia). Many Indian strategists now quietly see the benefit of a limited US presence as a regional stabiliser. India has taken a cooperative approach to the United States in attempting to stabilise several South Asian states, including Afghanistan and Nepal. In Sri Lanka, India and the US coordinated security assistance to the government during the last years of the civil war and since the end of the war they have coordinated their diplomatic positions on Sri Lanka to a considerable extent—indeed, in some cases New Delhi has found it politically convenient to allow Washington to take a leading role. The focus of concerns about extra-regional 'intrusion' into its neighbourhood has mostly shifted to China. Indian strategists have long been affronted by China's *de facto* alliance with Pakistan, including its role in proliferating nuclear weapons to its neighbour. Links between China and India's other South Asian neighbours such as Nepal, Bangladesh and Sri Lanka, whether they be economic, political or defence-related, are often seen in New Delhi as illegitimate and ultimately aimed at India.

The Gujral Doctrine signalled a move away from the 'hard' version of the Monroe Doctrine as expounded under Indira and Rajiv Gandhi towards a greater emphasis on regional cooperation and respect for sovereignty. But it did not signal the abandonment of New Delhi's opposition to a military presence in the region by powers that it saw as contrary to India's interests. Importantly, India's Monroe Doctrine, however formulated, should not be seen as a legalistic bright line pronouncement but more as a guiding principle. On the one hand, an overly explicit enunciation of the Monroe Doctrine could well be counter-productive and in some cases cause India's smaller neighbours to develop links with China as a defensive measure.[33] There is also debate about the extent to which India is practically able to impose hegemony over South Asia. Bhanani Sen Gupta himself concluded that 'India has neither the power nor the culture, nor the wherewithal to be a truly hegemonic power'.[34] These limitations are only heightened in a globalised world. Raja Mohan asserts that India is no longer able to claim South Asia as an exclusive geopolitical space and that it must now pursue a strategy of regional leadership.[35] According to Mohan, India should recast its regional stance through rewriting India's 'protectorate' treaty relationships with Nepal and Bhutan, transcending its preoccupation with Pakistan, economically integrating with its neighbours, working with its neighbours to resolve regional conflicts and working with friendly great powers to promote reasonable solutions to regional conflicts. While India has in practice moved towards such an approach, the ideas behind the Monroe Doctrine still have a powerful emotional hold on Indian strategic thinking.

The Monroe Doctrine and the Indian Ocean

Although India's Monroe Doctrine nominally applies only to South Asia and its immediate maritime surrounds, it has also had considerable influence on Indian strategic thinking about the entire Indian Ocean region. Holmes, Winner and Yoshihara, senior strategists at the US Naval War College, argue that Nehru's 1961 declaration of an Indian Monroe Doctrine laid the groundwork for a policy of primacy in the Indian Ocean and continues to form an important part of India's strategic lexicon.[36] If it is not actually a policy, then it is at least a preferred objective.

From the early 1970s, India strenuously, if selectively, opposed any military presence of extra-regional powers in the Indian Ocean region. Indian leaders emphatically rejected claims that the British withdrawal from east of Suez would leave a 'power vacuum' that should be filled by the United States and the Indian chief of naval staff, Admiral A. K. Chatterji, ambitiously claimed that the Indian Navy would thenceforth assume 'total charge of the Indian Ocean'.[37] But, like many such pronouncements from Indian strategists and military leaders, India did not have the capabilities to fulfil these aspirations.

Over the following two decades, India's principal focus in the Indian Ocean was to oppose the US military presence in the region. India's concerns about the US naval presence in the Indian Ocean were initially triggered by the deployment of a US naval task force headed by the nuclear-armed aircraft carrier USS *Enterprise* in the northeast Indian Ocean in the closing days of the Bangladesh War in December 1971. Although the secession of Bangladesh was by then a foregone conclusion, the deployment was ordered by US President Nixon as one of several measures to pressure New Delhi to end the war before India invaded and possibly dismembered West Pakistan. The US administration, based on an intelligence source in or near the Indian cabinet, believed that Indira Gandhi was planning a military strike westward as soon as it was able. As US secretary of state, Henry Kissinger, commented to Nixon, 'If we do nothing, there is a certainty of disaster [in West Pakistan]'.[38] Apart from the political consequences of allowing the destruction of a US ally, Nixon and Kissinger were deeply concerned that a large-scale Indian invasion of West Pakistan would set off a chain of events: China might intervene on behalf of Pakistan, leading Russia to intervene on behalf of India—potentially the conflict could slide into a broader Sino–Soviet war.[39]

The United States made the deployment of its naval task force as public as possible, giving Moscow prior notice and ensuring that the task force sailed through the Malacca Strait in daylight hours.[40] Washington also took other measures to prevent an invasion of West Pakistan, including persuading Moscow to place pressure on Gandhi to halt the conflict. It is difficult to say to what extent, if at all, the deployment of the USS *Enterprise* contributed to the Indian announcement of a ceasefire in West Pakistan. But Nixon certainly miscalculated the long-term consequences of the action. The 'intrusion' of the USS *Enterprise* into the Bay of Bengal was deeply humiliating for India at its moment of great military triumph in a way that few can now fully appreciate. For many it echoed the earlier arrival of European imperialists on India's shores. Although essentially symbolic, it was remembered with bitterness for many decades. The incident was seen as justifying the suspicions of many in New Delhi about US intentions in South Asia and the need for India to rely on the Soviet Union as a counterbalance to the United States.[41] To New Delhi, the development of the US base at Diego Garcia in the following years represented an ever-present threat to intervene in South Asia.

For the remainder of the Cold War most Indian analysts believed that rivalry between the United States and the Soviet Union in the Indian Ocean represented an immediate threat to India, potentially bringing nuclear war between the superpowers to the Indian Ocean. The Soviet presence in the Indian Ocean was often considered as less threatening than the United States' and more of an unfortunate consequence of the US presence. According to one report, some New Delhi officials believed that as the Soviet Union was 'nearly a littoral state' of the Indian Ocean it was entitled to deploy naval power of whatever level it considered necessary.[42] As noted earlier, India responded to the growing US and Soviet naval presence in the Indian Ocean by promoting the Indian Ocean Zone of Peace, which would ban extra-regional military presences from the region. India also responded with plans for a significant expansion of its naval capabilities. In 1978, the Indian Navy announced an ambitious 20-year programme to build a 'Blue Water' fleet of 250–300 vessels with a focus on sea denial capabilities. According to Admiral A. K. Chatterji, India's objective was to create a 'force equal in size and competence to the naval forces of any one of the superpowers now formally operating in the area'.[43] Other senior Indian naval officers reportedly argued that if India was not able to match the naval capabilities of the superpowers, it could at least raise the 'threshold of intervention' in the region of the Indian peninsula.[44] But once again these plans went unfulfilled, largely because India was unable to pay for them. In 1980, India's total defence budget was around US$4 billion, compared with a US defence budget of US$303 billion.[45]

Attitudes of the Indian security community towards the US presence in the Indian Ocean have evolved considerably since the 1980s. India has grudgingly accepted that the United States, with its base at Diego Garcia and its naval facilities in the Gulf, will likely remain the predominant naval power in the Indian Ocean region for some time. As will be discussed in Chapter 9, the United States seems willing to cede—and indeed encourage—a major regional naval role for India across the Indian Ocean. Cooperation between the United States and India to achieve India's own ambitions in the Indian Ocean is not as paradoxical as it may seem. As former US secretary of state, Dean

Acheson, once admitted, during the nineteenth century the United States relied on the then superpower, Britain (then in relative decline), to enforce its Monroe Doctrine in the Western Hemisphere until the United States was sufficiently strong to do so itself.[46] Britain found the US stance a convenient way of helping to exclude its European competitors from the region, even if the United States was not capable of fully implementing the policy by itself.

But with the exception of the United States, India will likely resist the presence of other extra-regional navies in the Indian Ocean unless they recognise India's leadership status. Japan, for example, has made it clear that it considers India to have a leading role in the Indian Ocean and will rely upon it as a provider of maritime security. As the chairman of joint staff of the Japanese Defence Agency, Admiral Natsukawa, commented in 2006, 'Only India has the capability and intention for security cooperation in [the Indian Ocean] this huge sea area, the west side of the Malacca Strait.'[47] In contrast, China has made clear that it will not allow the Indian Ocean to become 'India's Ocean'. China's relationships in the Indian Ocean region are viewed with considerable suspicion in New Delhi, and China is perceived by the Indian Navy to be its primary long-term threat. Many Indian strategists see China's political and security relationships in the Indian Ocean region as part of a policy of 'encirclement' of India that justifies the development of a 'defensive' sphere of influence by India. As Admiral Prakash, the former Indian chief of naval staff, put it: 'The appropriate counter to China's encirclement of India is to build our own relations, particularly in our neighbourhood, on the basis of our national interests and magnanimity towards smaller neighbours'.[48]

What does the Monroe Doctrine tell us about India's likely strategic behaviour in the Indian Ocean? Holmes, Winner and Yoshihara, from the US Naval War College, have examined how the Monroe Doctrine was implemented by the United States as a guide to roles that India could play in the Indian Ocean, calling them 'Free Rider', 'Strongman' and 'Constable' strategies.[49] A 'Free Rider' model would involve India relying on the United States as the region's dominant naval power while India built its national power. India would undertake limited efforts in maritime policing (e.g. against piracy and terrorism) to develop goodwill and lay the framework for a more assertive role. A 'Constable' model would involve more forceful but limited management of security in the Indian Ocean basin. The principles of the Monroe Doctrine would be applied where vital national interests were at stake, but India would generally act with restraint while it expands its power. A 'Strongman' model would involve a more muscular exercise of hegemony, potentially over the whole Indian Ocean region, and a willingness to use force where there are perceived threats to national interests. Holmes, Winner and Yoshihara conclude that, based on India's power projection capabilities, India intends to follow something between a Free Rider and a Constable strategy.

These categorisations provide a useful menu of some of the roles that India might play as a security provider in the Indian Ocean. But they do not provide a guide to India's intentions. It is important to remember that India's

'Monroe Doctrine' should be seen only as an imperfect reflection, using borrowed American terminology, of Indian instincts towards an area of influence in which inimical powers are excluded.

The development of a maritime strategic perspective

The evolution of Indian strategic thinking about the Indian Ocean also reflects a gradual change in India's strategic orientation from a purely continental outlook towards a more balanced perspective that gives more weight to maritime concerns. This has helped fuel India's ambitions to become the predominant naval power in the Indian Ocean region. As its economic and military power grows, India may be in the process of developing what the German naval strategist, Admiral Wolfgang Wegener, called a 'Strategic Will to the Sea'.[50]

Indian strategic thinking has historically had a strong continental outlook. Military threats to India have long been perceived as coming over land, primarily from India's northwest, and the domination of the Indian Ocean by the Royal Navy during the colonial era only served to reinforce this continental focus. During the twentieth century, military threats to India were land-based: from the northeast (Japan, 1941–5), the northwest (Pakistan, 1947 and after) and the north (China, 1962 and after). The continuing threats on India's western and northern borders and from domestic insurgencies has led to the Indian Army holding an indisputably dominant position within the Indian military establishment, in comparison to which the Indian Navy and its supporters have had relatively little influence.

But Indian maritime strategists, led by the Indian Navy, are now seeking to expand the Indian 'mental map' in strategic affairs to include the seafaring dimension. If this change occurs, it might be compared to the fundamental shifts in strategic culture experienced by other rising powers, including Japan in the nineteenth century (as a result of the intrusion of a US fleet under Admiral Perry) and the United States in the twentieth century (following its acquisition of Spanish colonial territories and the attack on Pearl Harbour).[51] Other great power aspirants such as the former Soviet Union and, now, China, have also come to see maritime power as a *sine qua non* of great power status. Some Indian political leaders see a close connection between India's maritime ambitions and its destiny as a great power. According to Indian Foreign Minister, Pranab Mukherjee:

> After nearly a millennia of inward and landward focus, we are once again turning our gaze outwards and seawards, which is the natural direction of view for a nation seeking to re-establish itself, not simply as a continental power, but even more so as a maritime power, *and consequently as one that is of significance on the world stage* (emphasis added).[52]

An important factor in an increased focus on the Indian Ocean is that any significant geographic expansion of Indian influence can arguably *only* take place in the maritime domain. As Rajiv Sikri, a former Indian diplomat, commented: 'If India aspires to be a great power, then the only direction in which India's strategic influence can spread is across the seas. In every other direction there are formidable constraints'.[53] Some also see the conventional and nuclear balance of power between India and China and Pakistan as effectively holding India 'hostage' as a land power and argue that India could 'liberate' itself from this constraint through developing its capabilities in the maritime realm.[54]

There is also a common view among Indian maritime strategists that control of the Indian Ocean could give India the ability to dominate the whole of maritime Asia. Many Indian analysts enthusiastically repeat a statement attributed to Mahan that: 'Whoever controls the Indian Ocean dominates Asia. … In the twenty-first century, the destiny of the world will be decided on its waters'. Although the attribution of the statement has been shown to be fictitious, this has not inhibited the enthusiasm for the ideas that it carries. But while control of the SLOCs across the Indian Ocean could provide India with a degree of bargaining power over other states, there are only very limited circumstances in which that power could be used, particularly against nuclear-armed adversaries.

A key factor in the expansion of India's role in the Indian Ocean has been the Indian Navy, which remains strongly influenced by a strategic culture and global outlook inherited from the Royal Navy. This includes an openness to developing relationships with others that is not matched elsewhere in India's defence and security establishment. Although the Indian Navy may have been at the receiving end of US gunboat diplomacy in 1971, since the early 1990s it has been the leading advocate of increased military cooperation with the United States. Over the last decades the Indian Navy has actively developed security relationships throughout the Indian Ocean that are intended to enhance India's ability to project power and restrict China's ability to develop relationships in the region. The Indian Navy has promoted itself as a benign provider of public goods, emphasising its capabilities in such things as humanitarian and disaster relief, anti-piracy and hydrographic research. The Indian Navy has also sought to institutionalise itself as the leading Indian Ocean navy through such initiatives as sponsoring the biennial Indian Ocean Naval Symposium, to which the navies of all Indian Ocean littoral states have been invited.[55]

Although the USS *Enterprise* incident in 1971 prompted a temporary shift in the Indian Navy's strategic focus towards one of sea denial, its cultural bias towards sea control and power projection quickly reasserted itself after the Cold War. Like the Royal Navy before it, the Indian Navy now pays particular attention to controlling the chokepoints at entrances to the Indian Ocean around southern Africa, the Arabian peninsula and the straits connecting the Indian and Pacific Oceans.[56] According to the Indian Navy's 2004 *Maritime Doctrine,* control of the chokepoints is a 'useful bargaining chip'.[57] India's security relationships with small states such as Mauritius and Seychelles in the southwest, Oman in the northwest and Singapore in the northeast are undoubtedly driven by this strategy. To these chokepoints at the entrances of the Indian Ocean, India has added a further 'chokepoint' in the central Indian Ocean, where the key east-west trading routes run between the Maldives and the southern tip of India.

India's naval aspirations have not been without sceptics who question India's ability to transform itself from a continental to a maritime power. Varun Sahni, for example, warns that the Soviet Union's failed attempts to become a naval power in the 1970s and 1980s should act as 'a cautionary tale for India's Mahanian navalists … [and] a grim warning of what happens to a continental state that harbours overly grandiose maritime ambitions'.[58] Given the long-standing lack of coordination in strategic planning between the military services and within government itself, the Indian Navy's activist role in the Indian Ocean has often been ahead of the views within the other armed services and the government. According to Harsh Pant,'the Indian navy's attempt to come up with its own strategy and doctrine, though welcome in many respects, has little meaning in the absence of a national security strategy from the Indian government'.[59]

An Indian sphere of influence in the Indian Ocean?

One of the questions that this book will examine is whether, as India's economic and military capabilities grow, it will seek to create an extended sphere of influence in the Indian Ocean. Some might consider this to be a natural consequence of the rise of India as a major power and a normal part of the international system. According to Saul Bernard Cohen, a noted geopolitical theorist, spheres of influence are essential to the preservation of national and regional expression, '. … the alternative is either a monolithic world system or utter chaos'.[60] A key feature distinguishing a sphere of influence from the mere ability to project military power is an acknowledgement from other states of a hierarchical relationship where the larger power plays a leadership role and provides security to lesser powers. This book considers whether India has the ideological and material resources to build a hierarchical system in the Indian Ocean, and will consider what such a system might look like.

According to some there is now a 'well-established tradition' within the Indian strategic community that the Indian Ocean is, or should be, 'India's Ocean'.[61] As one US analyst commented:

> New Delhi regards the Indian Ocean as its backyard and deems it both natural and desirable that India function as, eventually, the leader and the predominant influence in this region—the world's only region and ocean named after a single state.[62]

This viewpoint is often justified by India's geographic domination of the northern Indian Ocean, but it also seems to involve a large slice of nominative determinism. As Indian ambassador to the United States, Ronan Sen, told

President George Bush in 2005, 'There are good reasons why it is called the Indian Ocean ... it has always been in the Indian sphere of influence'.[63] But it nevertheless remains an open question as to how this general aspiration can be translated into reality.

Over the last decade India has claimed a much expanded area of strategic interest in the Indian Ocean region. The Indian Navy now sees itself as destined to be the predominant maritime security provider from the Red Sea to Singapore and having a significant security role in areas beyond, including the South China Sea.[64] This appears to have broad support among India's political leaders. The Ministry of Defence describes India's *security environment* as extending from the Persian Gulf in the west to the Straits of Malacca in the east,[65] an area which the former BJP foreign minister Jaswant Singh called India's *sphere of influence*[66] and the current prime minister Manmohan Singh has perhaps more diplomatically called India's *strategic footprint*.[67] In 2007, Indian foreign minister, Pranab Mukherjee, described what he called the *primary area of Indian maritime interest* in even broader terms as extending 'from the Persian Gulf in the north, to Antarctica in the South, and from the Cape of Good Hope and the East Coast of Africa in the west, to the Straits of Malacca ... and Indonesia in the east'.[68]

Many Indian leaders and strategic thinkers see India as the future dominant power in this extended area. According to Prime Minister Singh, there is 'no doubt that the Indian Navy must be the most important maritime power in this region'.[69] Similarly, Foreign Secretary Nirupama Rao argued that 'as the main resident power in the Indian Ocean region ... India is well poised to play a leadership role' in the region.[70] These views appear to have strong support among the Indian public. According to a 2013 opinion poll, some 94 per cent of Indians agreed that India should have the most powerful navy in the Indian Ocean.[71]

Indian leaders and strategic thinkers have used the American concept of 'manifest destiny' in describing India's future role. This phrase was used in the United States in the nineteenth century to justify its claims over the entire North American continent, and was also closely associated with the idea that the United States is an exceptional or divinely inspired nation with a mission to spread its form of civilisation. When Nehru spoke of India's 'manifest destiny' to become the third or fourth greatest power in the world it is not clear whether he intended to refer not only to India's fate but also to India's supposed moral exceptionalism. Similarly, K. Subrahmanyam, the doyen of Indian strategists, argued that it is India's 'manifest destiny to control Southern Asia and the Indian Ocean sea-lanes around us'.[72] Talk of India's manifest destiny in the Indian Ocean was echoed by Indian chief of naval staff, Admiral Sureesh Mehta in the Indian Navy's 2007 *Maritime Military Doctrine*.[73] These claims to 'destiny', while perhaps having some emotive value to an Indian audience, may be seen by others as claims to hegemony.

But India's elite overwhelmingly sees India as an international leader and not as a hegemon. In the early 1990s, George Tanham described India's self-perceived regional role as 'a friendly policeman that seeks peace and stability for the entire Indian Ocean region'. According to Tanham, it denies any hegemonistic designs or territorial ambitions and 'wants not only to play the role of regional peace-keeper but also to be acknowledged and endorsed in that role by others, especially the great powers'.[74] According to the former Indian chief of naval staff, Admiral Nirmal Verma, India does not aspire to play the role of a 'headmaster' in the region.[75] Certainly India's sensitivities over being seen as a hegemon often cause it to move very slowly and cautiously and in practice underplay its strategic strengths.

But India does have a particular preoccupation with ensuring that other states recognise its special status in the Indian Ocean. Tanham argues that 'gaining recognition of India's status in the region ... plays a pivotal role in Indian strategic thinking. Indeed external recognition and validation of India's place is almost as important as having that status'. According to Tanham, Indians are greatly frustrated by the failure of external powers to acknowledge the fact that India dominates the Indian Ocean.[76] The refusal of China in recent years to acknowledge India's leadership role is particularly infuriating. In contrast, the United States is happy to give rhetorical encouragement to India's rise as a great power even though it clearly dominates the region. The middle powers in the Indian Ocean, such as Australia, Indonesia and South Africa, may be more or less prepared to acknowledge an undefined 'leading role' for India in the Indian Ocean, although there will be definite limits on what they might accept this to mean in practice.

While there are many uncertainties about how India will seek to exercise its growing power in the Indian Ocean, one can nevertheless identify several themes in Indian strategic thinking, including:

- an instinct to exclude any extra-regional military presence in the Indian Ocean region, which is now almost entirely focused on China. As the relative balance of power changes in coming decades, India may also have less patience with the continuing US military presence;
- a perceived connection between India's ability to exercise an extended sphere of influence in the Indian Ocean and its claim to great power status;
- the perceived importance of external recognition of its leadership status;
- a desire to avoid multilateral security cooperation and a preference for cooperating only with small or weak states;
- a growing interest in the protection of Indian ethnic minorities outside India; and
- an inclination to expand its influence outside of South Asia in a cooperative and non-confrontational manner.

The following chapters will consider India's strategic relationships in different parts of the Indian Ocean in light of these themes.

Notes

1 Iskander Rehman (2011) 'An ocean at the intersection of two emerging maritime narratives',*ISDA Issue Brief*, 11 July.
2 See Ainslie T. Embree (1989) 'Frontiers into boundaries: the evolution of the modern state' in Ainslie T. Embree, *Imagining India: essays on Indian history*, New York: Oxford University Press, pp. 67–84.
3 Peter John Brobst (2005) *The Future of the Great Game: Sir Olaf Caroe, India's Independence and the Defence of Asia*, Akron, OH: University of Akron Press, p. 13.
4 K.M. Panikkar (1945) *India and the Indian Ocean: An Essay on the Influence of Sea Power on Indian History*, London: George Allen & Unwin.
5 Ibid., p. 20.
6 Ibid., p. 95.
7 Ibid., p. 15.
8 See, for example, C. Raja Mohan (2013) 'India's regional security cooperation: the Nehru Raj legacy', ISAS Working Paper No. 168, 7 March.
9 Although the UN resolution was formally proposed by Sri Lanka, India had considerable influence over its form, particularly in narrowing the resolution to apply only to the military activities of extra-regional powers.
10 By 2009, the so-called UN Ad Hoc Committee established to implement the IOZOP proposal had met 453 times without result.
11 C. Raja Mohan (2003) *Crossing the Rubicon: the Shaping of India's New Foreign Policy*, London: Palgrave Macmillan, p. 27.
12 See, for example, Sunil Khilnani, Rajiv Kumar, Pratap Bhanu Mehta, Prakash Menon, Nandan Nilekani, Srinath Raghavan, Shyam Saran, Siddharth Varadarajan, *Nonalignment 2.0: A Foreign and Strategic Policy for India in the Twenty-first Century*. Online: www.cprindia.org/sites/default/files/NonAlignment%202.0_1.pdf (accessed 10 October 2013).
13 George Tanham (1996) 'Indian Strategic Thought: An Interpretive Essay', in George Tanham, Kanti P. Bajpai and Amitabh Mattoo (eds), *Securing India: Strategic Thought and Practice in an Emerging Power*, New Delhi: Manhora, p. 73.
14 See generally, Stephen P. Cohen and Sunil Dasgupta (2010) *Arming without Aiming: India's Military Modernisation*, Washington, DC: Brookings Institution Press.
15 Varun Sahni (2006) 'India and the Asian Security Architecture', *Current History*, Vol.105, 690, April, pp. 163–7.
16 Guillem Monsonis (2010) 'India's Strategic Autonomy and Rapprochement with the US', *Strategic Analysis*, Vol. 34, No. 4, July, pp. 611–24 at p. 624.
17 Sumit Ganguly (2012) 'India's Misguided Autonomy', *The Diplomat*, 25 June.
18 Thomas E. Ricks (2012) 'Why India is so half-hearted about the US rebalance towards Asia' *Foreign Policy*, 14 August.
19 C. Raja Mohan (2010) 'India and the Changing Geopolitics of the Indian Ocean', speech at the National Maritime Foundation, New Delhi, 19 July.
20 C. Raja Mohan (2004–5) 'What if Pakistan fails? India isn't worried. … yet', *Washington Quarterly*, Vol. 28, No. 1, p. 127.
21 Jawaharlal Nehru (1985) *Selected Works of Jawaharlal Nehru, Volume 3 Series 2*, New Delhi: Jawaharlal Nehru Memorial Fund, p. 133.
22 Jawaharlal Nehru (1961) *India's Foreign Policy: Selected Speeches, September 1946–April 1961*, Delhi: Government of India, pp. 113–15.
23 Bhabani Sen Gupta (1983) 'The Indian Doctrine', *India Today*, 31 August. There is little doubt that Sen Gupta was used as a conduit to reflect the views of Indian leadership. As he commented later, 'The officials denied it officially'. Mani Shankar Aiyar (ed.) (1993) *Rajiv Ghandi's India: a golden jubilee retrospective, Vol. 3*, New Delhi: UBSPD, p. 68.

24 See generally, James R. Holmes, Andrew C. Winner and Toshi Yoshihara (2009) *Indian Naval Strategy in the Twenty-first Century*, Abingdon: Routledge, pp. 46–50.

25 Brig (Retd) Hafiz (1995) 'An insecure security', *The Morning Sun* (Dhaka), 17 June.

26 Agha Shahi (1988) *Pakistan's Security and Foreign Policy*, Lahore: Progressive Publishers, p. 192.

27 J. Mohan Malik (2004) 'India and China: Bound to Collide' in P. R. Kumaraswamy (ed.), *Security beyond survival: essays for K. Subrahmanyam*, New Delhi: Sage, pp. 127–65.

28 John. W. Garver (1992) 'China and South Asia', *Annals of the American Academy of Political and Social Science*, Vol. 519, January, p. 72.

29 Howard B. Schaffer (1993) *Chester Bowles: New Dealer in the Cold War*, Cambridge, MA: Harvard University Press, Ch. 5.

30 The Indian Navy even took part in combined exercises with the Royal Navy, the Pakistan Navy and the Royal Ceylon Navy out of the Royal Naval base at Trincomalee as late as 1958.

31 Padmaja Murthy (1999) 'The Gujral Doctrine and beyond', *Strategic Analysis*, Vol. 23, No. 4, pp. 639–52. Some believe that this doctrine was actually authored by Gujral's close friend and 'Saturday Group' member Bhabani Sen Gupta, who originally articulated the 'Indira Doctrine' in 1983. V.N. Khanna (1997) *Foreign Policy of India*, New Delhi: Vikas, p. 41.

32 Amit Baruah (2007) 'Not seeking exclusive sphere of influence', *The Hindu*, 11 February.

33 John W. Garver (2001) *Protracted Contest: Sino–Indian Rivalry in the Twentieth Century*, Washington, DC: University of Washington Press, p. 17.

34 Maharajakrishna Rasgotra (ed.) (1998) *Rajiv Gandhi's India: A Golden Jubilee Retrospective Vol.3: Ending the Quest for Dominance*, New Delhi: UPSPD, p. 67.

35 C. Raja Mohan (2003) 'Beyond India's Monroe Doctrine', *The Hindu*, 2 January.

36 Holmes, Winner and Yoshihara, *Indian Naval Strategy in the Twenty-first Century*, p. 45.

37 *The Times* (London), 4 March 1968, p. 5.

38 United States, Department of State (2005) *Foreign relations of the United States, 1969–1976: Vol XI, South Asia crisis, 1971*, Washington, DC: US GPO, p. 779.

39 Henry Kissinger (1979) *The White House Years*, Boston, MA: Little, Brown, pp. 903–13.

40 Elmo R. Zumwalt (1976) *On Watch: A Memoir*, New York: Quadrangle, p. 367.

41 New Delhi's anger at the USS *Enterprise* contrasts sharply with its attitude towards the dispatch of the British assault carrier, HMS *Albion*, towards the Bay of Bengal in December 1971, ostensibly to evacuate refugees from Dhaka. This attracted little or no comment.

42 *The Guardian*, 4 March 1974.

43 Walter K. Andersen (1979) 'India in Asia: walking on a tightrope', *Asian Survey*, Vol. 19, No. 12, pp. 1241–53, at p. 1251.

44 Raju G.C. Thomas (1989) 'The Sources of Indian Naval Expansion', in Robert H. Bruce, *The Modern Indian Navy in the Indian Ocean*, Perth: Centre for Indian Ocean Regional Studies, pp. 95–107, at p. 98.

45 At 1980 exchange rates. George J. Gilboy, Eric Heginbotham (2012) *Chinese and Indian Strategic Behaviour: Growing Power and Alarm*, New York: Cambridge University Press, p. 103.

46 Dean G. Acheson (1955) *A Democrat Looks at his Party*, New York: Harper, p. 64.

47 Kazuya Natsukawa (2006) Opening Address, Indo–Japan Dialogue on Ocean Security, Tokyo, 12 October.

48 Admiral Arun Prakash (2006) 'China and the Indian Ocean region', *Indian Defence Review*, Vol. 21, No. 4, p. 11.

49 Holmes, Winner and Yoshihara, *Indian Naval Strategy in the Twenty-first Century*.

50 See James R. Holmes and Toshi Yoshihara (2009) 'History Rhymes: The German Precedent for Chinese Seapower', *Orbis*, pp. 14–34.
51 Holmes, Winner and Yoshihara, *Indian Naval Strategy in the Twenty-first Century*, p. 33.
52 Pranab Mukherjee (2007) Speech for the Admiral A.K. Chatterjee Memorial Lecture, Kolkata, 30 June.
53 Rajiv Sikri (2009) *Challenge and Strategy: Rethinking India's Foreign Policy*, New Delhi: Sage, p. 250.
54 Cohen and Dasgupta, *Arming without Aiming*, p. 71.
55 Including France (which India recognises as a littoral state by virtue of its colonial territories), but not Britain, the United States or China.
56 Although the relationship with the Soviet Union seems to have had little lasting impact on Indian naval thinking, there are interesting parallels between India's chokepoint strategy and Soviet naval doctrine, which emphasised the use of chokepoints as part of a strategically defensive concept of 'area defence' under which superior forces would be locked out from the USSR's 'inner defence perimeter'. Iskander Rehman, 'India's aspirational naval doctrine', in Harsh V. Pant (ed.) (2012) *The Rise of the Indian Navy: Internal Vulnerabilities, External Challenges*, Farnham: Ashgate, pp. 55–79.
57 Ministry of Defence, *Indian Maritime Doctrine*, p. 64.
58 Varun Sahni (2005) 'India's Security Challenges out to 2000', paper presented at the Australia–India Security Roundtable, Canberra, 11–12 April.
59 Harsh V. Pant (2009) 'India in the Indian Ocean: Growing mismatch between ambitions and capabilities', *Pacific Affairs*, Vol. 82, No. 2, Summer, pp. 279–97, at p. 297.
60 Saul B. Cohen (1973) *Geography and Politics in a World Divided*, 2nd edn, New York: Oxford University Press, p. viii.
61 David Scott (2006) 'India's 'Grand Strategy' for the Indian Ocean: Mahanian Visions', *Asia Pacific Review*, Vol. 13, No. 2, pp. 97–129.
62 Donald L. Berlin (2006) 'India in the Indian Ocean', *Naval War College Review*, Vol. 59, No. 2, Spring, p. 60.
63 Chidanand Rajghatta (2005) 'India Shows its Sphere of Influence to the World', *Times of India*, 5 January.
64 Scott, 'India's 'Grand Strategy' for the Indian Ocean'.
65 India, Ministry of Defence, *Annual Report 2000–2001*.
66 Chidanand Rajghatta (2001) 'Singhing Bush's Praise', *Times of India*, 13 April.
67 Singh, 'PM's Address at the Combined Commander's Conference'.
68 Pranab Mukherjee (2007) 'International Relations and Maritime Affairs—Strategic Imperatives', speech for the Admiral A.K. Chatterjee Memorial Lecture, Kolkota, 30 June.
69 Singh (2009) 'PM Inaugurates Naval Academy at Ezhimala', 8 January.
70 Nirupama Rao (2010) 'India as a Consensual Stakeholder in the Indian Ocean: Policy Contours', speech to the National Maritime Foundation, 19 November.
71 Rory Medcalf (2013) 'India Poll 2013: Facing the future—Indian views of the world ahead', Lowy Institute for International Policy.
72 Holmes, Winner and Yoshihara, *Indian Naval Strategy in the Twenty-first Century*, p. 38.
73 Indian Navy, *Freedom to Use the Seas*.
74 Tanham, 'Indian Strategic Thought: An Interpretive Essay', p. 69.
75 Sridhar Kumaraswami (2010) 'India not taking role of headmaster', *Asian Age*, 5 February.
76 Tanham, *Indian Strategic Thought*, pp. 82–3.

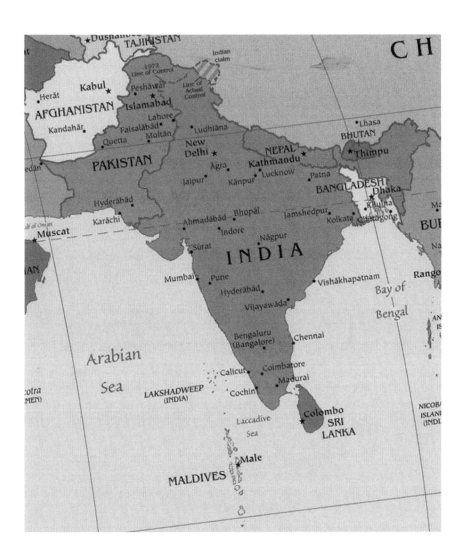

Map 3.1 Maritime South Asia
Adapted from the University of Texas Libraries collection.

3 Maritime South Asia

India is the predominant power in South Asia, where it claims special rights and responsibilities in managing regional security. This chapter will focus on India's strategic role in maritime South Asia, especially its security relationships with the island states of Sri Lanka and the Maldives. India's experiences in maritime South Asia illuminate the strategic approaches and policies that may be used elsewhere in the Indian Ocean.

India's strategic predominance in South Asia

South Asia comprises India, Pakistan, Nepal, Bhutan, Bangladesh, Sri Lanka, the Maldives and, perhaps, Afghanistan. India is without doubt the predominant power in South Asia and its predominance has many dimensions. It is by far the most populous state in South Asia (its population comprises approximately 75 per cent of the region),[1] has the biggest economy (Indian GDP comprises approximately 79 per cent of the region)[2] and is the largest in physical size (India's land area represents 75 per cent of South Asia). It has by far the largest and most capable military establishment in the region. India's central position on the subcontinent means that it borders every other state in South Asia, while none of its South Asian neighbours border another—a geographical factor which has considerable strategic consequences. India sees itself as a civilisational state that essentially defines South Asia and its neighbours as more or less subsidiary entities in that civilisation.

South Asia is regarded by most international relations practitioners as a clearly defined strategic region. From a geopolitical standpoint the subcontinent is a virtual island, cut off from the rest of Eurasia: it is surrounded by the Indian Ocean in the south, the Himalayas in the north, desert in the west and almost impassable jungle ranges in the east. According to Barry Buzan, a leading exponent of regional security analysis, South Asia is a clear example of a 'regional security complex', that is, a set of states whose major security perceptions and concerns are so interlinked that their national security problems cannot reasonably be analysed or resolved apart from one another.[3] Regional security complexes are generally defined by a pattern of rivalry and balance of power among the main powers within the region. Balance of power logic encourages local rivals to call in outside help, and by this mechanism the local patterns of rivalry become linked to the global ones. Despite these external linkages, the security dynamics of South Asia have historically operated somewhat separately to the dynamics of neighbouring security regions. India's predominance in South Asia is increasingly allowing it to transcend South Asia and project power and influence into the Indian Ocean and beyond. However, much of India's strategic behaviour, aspirations and constraints remains rooted in the Indian subcontinent.

Although South Asia may be a well-defined region, regional institutions are weak. The South Asian Association for Regional Cooperation (SAARC) acts as a regional grouping, comprising India and all its South Asian neighbours. But since its establishment in 1985 it has been hobbled by the India–Pakistan dispute and India's insistence that it not be used to deal with the numerous security issues that afflict the region. There is little indication that SAARC will become a real engine for regional cooperation any time soon. As a result, regional security dynamics are primarily defined by each country's relationship with India. India has long perceived itself as being the regional security manager with special prerogatives and responsibilities to ensure the stability of its smaller neighbours, manage transborder ethnic conflicts and exclude any 'external' security presence. Although many would contest India's special rights, there is also an implicit acceptance by many of India's smaller neighbours of restrictions on their ability to form security relationships with outside powers.

Another feature of South Asia is its very low degree of economic integration—a cumulative result of the India–Pakistan dispute, fears of Indian economic domination, and India's protectionist policies. According to one study, South Asia is the least economically integrated region in the world. In 2008, intraregional trade among the South Asian states constituted a mere 4 per cent of all their international trade. Trade between India and its neighbours constituted less than 3 per cent of its total foreign trade.[4] In comparison, in the Asia Pacific, intra-regional trade constitutes around 50 per cent of total trade. In recent years India has paid greater attention to economic integration as a tool to promote political stability and regional cooperation and this is now seen as a key part of India's regional strategy.[5]

India's relations in maritime South Asia

The maritime states of South Asia include India, Pakistan, Bangladesh, Sri Lanka and the Maldives. India's long peninsular forms a triangle jutting deep into the northern Indian Ocean. On either side of India sit Pakistan in the northwest Indian Ocean and Bangladesh in the northeast; to the south are the island states of Sri Lanka and the Maldives. All these neighbouring states are unstable and are seen by India as potential sources of security threat of one type or another.

Pakistan is the most militarily powerful state in maritime South Asia after India and has been India's principal adversary since Partition in 1947. For decades Pakistan has kept India strategically preoccupied in South Asia, and since the early 1990s it has also been a nuclear-armed adversary. India's defeat of Pakistan in the 1971 war and the secession of Bangladesh crystallised India's role as the clearly dominant naval power in South Asia, and since that time Pakistan has represented a gradually decreasing maritime threat to India. Over the last two decades India has demonstrated a determination to transcend its security preoccupations in South Asia and has had some success in 'de-hyphenating' itself from Pakistan in international perceptions. But Pakistan continues to be a significant source of terrorist violence against India and it continues to challenge India's regional predominance even as its own credibility wanes. The impact of Pakistan on India's strategic role in the northwest Indian Ocean will be discussed in more detail in Chapter 6.

To the east of India is Bangladesh. India played a pivotal role in the birth of Bangladesh in 1971 when it provided military support to Bangladeshi nationalists and then invaded and occupied East Pakistan in the space of two weeks. The subsequent division of East and West Pakistan into separate states changed the whole balance of power in South Asia and allowed India to focus on what it saw as the greater military threat from Islamabad. Despite India's role in the 'liberation' of Bangladesh, the relationship is not an easy one and is frequently strained by Islamic politics. But while Bangladesh has a large population (some 150 million in 2011) and a long coastline in the Bay of Bengal, it remains very poor and internally preoccupied and is not currently a significant factor in India's ambitions in the Indian Ocean. Bangladesh possesses only two viable ports (Cox's Bazaar and Chittagong) and the Bangladesh Navy is essentially a coastal constabulary force. Bangladesh's poverty, its dependence on foreign aid for survival and a weak political system largely precludes it from playing a significant strategic role in the wider Indian Ocean region.

For many years Bangladesh has engaged in some limited balancing against its huge neighbour, which includes using China as the principal provider of defence equipment and training to the Bangladesh armed forces. But while Bangladesh tries to keep some options open, it is careful not to threaten India's regional interests. The security relationship between India and Bangladesh is largely focused on their 4,000 km-land border. The delineation of the border in the days before the 1947 partition produced a mish-mash of enclaves and enclaves-within-enclaves.[6] There are numerous security-related issues along this border, including illegal immigration, smuggling, disputes over water usage, border demarcation, transit rights and the activities of transborder insurgent groups. Over the last decade or so, consistent with the Gujral Doctrine, India has more or less followed a 'good neighbour policy' with its neighbour. But while Bangladesh is not currently a major factor in India's *ambitions* in the Indian Ocean, it has the potential to become a significant security *problem* for India. Internal political instability or non-political events such as rising sea levels and the resultant inundation of large portions of Bangladeshi territory could, for example, lead to a refugee exodus similar in scope to the 1971 crisis. In these circumstances India could be required to provide security assistance to its large neighbour.

This chapter will focus on the evolution of India's security relationships with Sri Lanka and the Maldives, which are important to India's maritime security and its broader strategic role in the Indian Ocean. Both are positioned close to the east-west trade routes across the northern Indian Ocean and both have the potential to contribute to India's ability to project power throughout the region. India conducted military interventions in both Sri Lanka and the Maldives during the 1980s, essentially as an expression of its Monroe Doctrine. India's intervention in the Maldives in 1988 to stave off an attempted coup by foreign mercenaries was widely seen as a positive example of how India might act as a benign security provider to the region. In contrast, its intervention in Sri Lanka between 1983 and 1990 was seen by many as a failed attempt to impose hegemony. The episode involved a toxic mix of largely imagined fears of US plots, Indian internal security concerns, and an overestimation by India of its own military capabilities. The national trauma of India's failed intervention in Sri Lanka has had a considerable impact on its Indian Ocean strategy and fostered a more cooperative approach to regional relations. Both these episodes shine a light on India's strategic preoccupations and potential strengths and weaknesses as it seeks to extend its power in the Indian Ocean.

India's failed intervention in Sri Lanka

India's relationship with Sri Lanka is a difficult one and seems likely to remain so for the foreseeable future. It is inescapably dominated by the fact of more than 1,000 years of resistance by the indigenous Sinhalese to attempts by Dravidian South Indians, mostly Tamils, to impose demographic, cultural and economic hegemony over the island. Sinhalese nationalists see the recent 26-year civil war—which ended with the decisive military defeat of Sri Lankan Tamils in 2009—as merely another manifestation of resistance to Dravidian hegemony. Fear of domination by India is an ever-present factor in Sinhalese strategic calculations. This has led to claims that the Sinhalese are a majority with a minority complex, while the Tamils are a minority with a majority complex. While ethnic Tamils represent only 18 per cent of Sri Lanka's population of around 21 million people, they represent more than 80 per cent of the combined population of Sri Lanka and Tamil Nadu (the Tamil Indian state which is separated from northern Sri Lanka only by the narrow Palk Strait). In contrast, the Sinhalese community represents more than some 74 per cent of the population of Sri Lanka but only a small minority of a combined Sri Lanka/Tamil Nadu. Stephen Cohen calls the Sinhala/Tamil dispute a 'paired minority conflict' in which each side feels the threatened party.[7]

Sri Lanka has never been ruled from India. During the colonial era it was ruled by the Dutch, and then the British, but separately from its Indian colonies. Nevertheless, India perceives Sri Lanka as sitting squarely within its South Asian sphere of influence. In 1971, India deployed forces to help defeat a leftist insurgency in southern Sri Lanka, and it again deployed military forces in 1987—ostensibly to separate the warring Sinhalese and Tamil communities.

India has also tried to limit Sri Lanka's external relationships. It forcefully dissuaded Sri Lanka from joining the US-sponsored SEATO pact in the early 1950s. India effectively created a 'bottom line' to the relationship in the 1980s when it made clear that it would not permit Sri Lanka to form security relationships with other states that India saw as a threat to its interests. While this is now tacitly accepted by Sri Lanka, Colombo has not accepted India's asserted right to intervene in its domestic affairs.

India and the Sinhala–Tamil conflict

Over the last several decades the India–Sri Lanka relationship has been dominated by Sri Lanka's civil war and its aftermath. Longstanding grievances of the Tamil community over political autonomy and language rights intensified into a full-scale separatist insurgency in the 1970s, with many Tamils seeking an independent homeland in the north and east of Sri Lanka. In July 1983, after a series of ethnic riots left thousands of ethnic Tamils dead, Indira Gandhi decided that a settlement to the conflict could only be brought about through Indian intervention. New Delhi adopted a policy of strategic coercion against the Sri Lankan government, involving support for Tamil insurgents, threats of invasion, as well as the positioning of India as a mediator between the warring parties. This strategy evolved into full-scale military intervention in 1987.

Many Indians supported the Sri Lankan Tamils' fight for a separate homeland. But the primary objective of New Delhi during the 1980s was to end the civil war through forcing a political settlement that gave the Tamils limited autonomy but not a separate state. According to J. N. Dixit, India's high commissioner to Sri Lanka during this period, the Indian government had three key motivations in taking action in Sri Lanka.[8] *First*, for domestic political reasons, New Delhi had to be seen as doing something to support their Tamil ethnic brothers in Sri Lanka. *Second*, there were concerns that the creation of an independent Tamil state in Sri Lanka could lead to the secession of Tamil Nadu state from India. There had been a strong separatist movement in Tamil Nadu dating from India's independence, although a reorganisation of Indian states along linguistic lines in the 1950s had weakened it considerably. But in 1983, Indian military forces were already fighting the Maoist 'Naxalite' insurgency, as well as large-scale separatist insurgencies in Kashmir and its northeast states, and another major separatist conflict was brewing with Sikhs in the Punjab. New Delhi took the view that it could not risk yet another internal conflict. *Third*, there were fears that the United States would use the conflict as an opportunity to gain another strategic foothold in South Asia. Many in the Indian security establishment believed that the United States was trying to use the conflict as an opportunity to form an alliance with Sri Lanka just as it had with Pakistan. As Rajiv Gandhi saw it: 'The hostilities opened up opportunities for others to fish in troubled waters and to cause problems in our part of the world'.[9] These fears were reinforced by exaggerated or inaccurate intelligence provided by India's external intelligence agency, the Research and Analysis Wing (RAW), and its diplomats in Sri Lanka,which contributed to an overreaction to the Sri Lankan conflict.

Since the late 1970s, when the Tamil conflict intensified, the Sri Lankan government under President Jayawardene had sought foreign military assistance from all comers. As Jayewardene later commented: 'I would accept help from the Devil itself to break the back of the terrorists'.[10] Jayewardene even suggested at one stage that Sri Lanka might seek US protection from Indian invasion, although Washington gave no indication that it would support Sri Lanka in that event.[11] Sri Lanka obtained limited military assistance from several countries, including Britain, China, Pakistan and Israel,[12] but the United States refused to provide any military assistance. Nevertheless, the RAW perceived a growing US 'presence' in Sri Lanka, primarily from a radio broadcast facility operated by the Voice of America and fears that the United States intended to use Trincomalee as a naval base.

The Voice of America (VoA) issue involved US plans to expand a broadcast facility in Sri Lanka used for VoA radio broadcasts to South and Central Asia. New Delhi saw these broadcasts as an infringement of India's sovereignty and claimed that the facilities would be used for signals intelligence and/or for military communications. No evidence was ever provided in support of these assertions. As the US ambassador, James W. Spain, recalled telling J. N. Dixit: 'Stop this nonsense. The VoA facility here is not for eavesdropping on India. If we wanted to spy on your security installations, we have other ways'.[13] President Jayewardene later claimed that New Delhi had refused his suggestions that they inspect the VoA facility to prove to themselves that it was not being used for nefarious purposes.[14] All in all, it seems unlikely that the United States would require either signals intelligence or military communications facilities in Sri Lanka given its existing facilities in Diego Garcia and it appears that New Delhi was not interested in testing its own claims in this respect.

Of even greater concern to New Delhi was the possibility that the US Navy would gain access to the huge port of Trincomalee in northern Sri Lanka, which was formerly Britain's principal naval base in the northeast Indian Ocean. India's suspicions were raised by an increasing number of goodwill visits by the US Navy to the port and Sri Lankan proposals to contract out the refurbishment of oil storage tanks and modernisation of port facilities at Trincomalee, which the RAW claimed were being awarded to US front companies.[15] But there is little evidence that the US had any real interest in developing a material strategic presence in Sri Lanka. The establishment of a major US base at Trincomalee would seem implausible given the political instability of Sri Lanka, although it is possible that the US would want to be in a position to preclude a Soviet presence in light of the Soviet intervention in Afghanistan at that time. In fact, US strategic interest in Sri Lanka was very limited—Washington was highly ambivalent about the amount of political support it was prepared to offer the Sri Lankan government in the conflict, preferring to see a regional solution agreed between India and Sri Lanka. The

United States saw the need for stability and maintenance of the *status quo* in South Asia, including recognition of India's role as a regional stabilising power, as a higher priority than its relationship with the Sri Lankan government.[16]

India's compellence strategy in Sri Lanka

As has been discussed previously, Indira Gandhi responded to the 1983 ethnic riots in Sri Lanka by elaborating, through Bhabani Sen Gupta, the so-called 'Indira Doctrine' as a new and quite muscular form of India's Monroe Doctrine. This effectively placed the Sri Lankan government on notice of India's limits in relation to the conflict. Gandhi then placed R. N. Kao in charge of planning India's strategy. Kao had been the long-time head of the RAW, including during the Bangladesh War, and was now Gandhi's national security advisor. Kao put together what could be called a 'compellence' strategy for the purpose of imposing a political settlement on the conflict, which included three key elements:

- threats of conventional military intervention against Sri Lanka with the possibility of partitioning the country;
- covert military support for Tamil insurgent groups in Sri Lanka; and
- positioning India as a mediator between the warring parties.

Rajiv Gandhi, who took office in October 1984 following his mother's assassination, largely followed the core elements of his mother's strategy, though after some hesitation.

New Delhi first sought to pressure the Sri Lankan government into settling the conflict through threatening to use force to partition Sri Lanka between the largely Tamil north and the Sinhalese south. Gandhi instructed India's Southern Army command to begin planning for Operation *Buster,* involving an Indian army landing on Sri Lanka's west coast to be followed by a thrust to Trincomalee in the east, effectively slicing Sri Lanka in two. Further airborne and seaborne operations were planned and publicly rehearsed over the next several years. In April 1986, Exercise *Tri Shaktri* practised using airborne troops from the 54 Infantry Division to secure airheads in Sri Lanka in conjunction with seaborne landings by the 340 Independent Infantry Brigade (both these units fulfilled those roles in 1987). S. D. Muni, a former Indian diplomat, claims that New Delhi did not bring these plans to fruition prior to 1987 for fear of damaging its relationship with the United States.[17] But New Delhi nevertheless saw the threat of partition as a useful coercive tool, even if it was the opposite of what it actually wished to achieve.

New Delhi also sought to coerce Colombo through supporting the Tamil insurgents. Indira Gandhi believed that if the Sri Lankan government was politically unable to come to a settlement itself, India could use an insurgency to force the Sri Lankan government to accept Indian intervention to impose an external political settlement. In some ways this strategy echoed India's creation of and support for the *Mukti Bahini* insurgents in the early 1970s, which destabilised Pakistan's rule over East Pakistan/Bangladesh and justified India's military intervention in December 1971. Gandhi reportedly told Kao to 'repeat the success of the Bangladesh operation in Sri Lanka'.[18]

From mid-1983, on the instructions of Gandhi, RAW began funding, arming and training several Tamil insurgent groups. RAW also attempted to create its own pet insurgent group, called the Tamil Eelam Liberation Organisation (later subsumed by the LTTE—Liberation Tigers of Tamil Eelam). Centralised training was provided at RAW's Special Frontier Force Training Facility at Chakrata, north of New Delhi, and RAW also operated training facilities in Tamil Nadu and elsewhere in India.[19] At least 1200 Tamil insurgents were trained by RAW between September 1983 and July 1987.[20] In addition, Sri Lankan Tamil groups were permitted to operate dozens of their own training camps in Tamil Nadu. According to a February 1986 report by the Tamil Nadu director general of police, there were some 49 camps in Tamil Nadu run by Sri Lankan Tamil militants, training thousands of cadres.[21] It has been claimed that by the end of 1985 the numerical strength of Tamil insurgents equalled or surpassed the numbers of the Sri Lankan Army.[22] Insurgents were trained in most aspects of guerrilla warfare, including the use of anti-aircraft missiles, as well as diving and underwater sabotage.[23] Light arms and supplies (but not anti-aircraft missiles) were delivered by the Indian Air Force to insurgents in Tamil Nadu for export to Sri Lanka within 48–72 hours.[24] Whether through inexperience or design, RAW made little attempt to keep track of the identity of the insurgents it was training or the weapons it was providing.

The third element of Gandhi's strategy was to position India as the essential mediator between the warring sides. India used its role as sponsor of the Tamil insurgent groups to pressure them to negotiate with the Sri Lankan government, for instance at Indian-sponsored peace talks at Thimpu in Bhutan in July 1985. But the Sri Lankan government refused to endorse the basic principles insisted on by the Tamil parties as a basis for political settlement and Tamil groups walked out of negotiations. While India continued to pressure Tamil groups, for instance by using the Tamil Nadu police to disarm militants, the LTTE made it clear that it would not accept anything less than an independent Tamil state.

The 1987 Accord

By early 1987, the Indian government had concluded that a political settlement would need to be imposed on the warring parties through military intervention. The principal architect of India's 1987 intervention was its high commissioner in Colombo, J. N. Dixit. In some ways, including his imperial *hauteur* in dealing with lesser powers, Dixit might be seen as Lord Curzon's intellectual heir, and in fact the Colombo newspapers called him India's 'Viceroy' to Sri Lanka. Dixit presented to President Jayewardene the terms of an Accord under which the Sri Lankan government would formally agree to the deployment of Indian forces to Sri Lanka. At the same time, RAW stepped up training of Tamil insurgents to increase pressure on Colombo. The Sri Lankan government responded to Indian demands by taking the offensive against Tamil insurgents, hoping to gain a quick military victory before India intervened. The issue came to a head in May 1987, when government forces were on the point of retaking the insurgents' capital of Jaffna in northern Sri Lanka. When the Indian Air Force dropped supplies to the insurgents and Rajiv Gandhi threatened further intervention, Jayewardene agreed to India's demands. It appears that India was determined to take all necessary action to impose the Accord on Sri Lanka in the event of dissent. According to one report, in the event that it was not accepted by the Sri Lankan Cabinet or Sinhalese nationalists sought to move against President Jayawardene, New Delhi had contingency plans to seize key points in Colombo and detain officials in the Sri Lankan government and armed forces. This was to be executed by Indian marine commandos already deployed in Colombo city and aboard a frigate, INS *Himgiri*, anchored in Colombo harbour.[25]

Although the principal purpose of the Accord was to provide a legal basis for the placement of Indian peacekeeping forces in Sri Lanka, India also tried to use it to formalise certain special prerogatives. In a side letter to the Accord, India obtained undertakings prohibiting any extra-regional security presence in Sri Lanka. Among other things, Sri Lanka agreed to work with India to ensure that so-called 'foreign' military and intelligence personnel would not prejudice relations with India, that it would not allow Trincomalee *or any other ports in Sri Lanka* to be made available for military use by any other country in a manner prejudicial to India's interests, that India would have special rights to operate the Trincomalee oil tank facilities and that Sri Lankan territory would not be used for foreign broadcasting services for military or intelligence purposes. One Indian official reportedly commented that under these arrangements, 'the strategic harbour of Trincomalee is now effectively in Indian control and no longer capable of becoming another Diego Garcia'.[26] Certainly Indian leaders were in no doubt about the overall significance of these arrangements. According to a senior Indian journalist, C. Narendra Reddy, Rajiv Gandi told a Congress Party meeting before he left for Colombo that following these agreements, 'Sri Lanka would come under the Indian Orbit like Bhutan'.[27]

Washington, which had been coordinating its Sri Lanka policy with New Delhi, endorsed the Accord within hours of its signing.[28] As one senior Sri Lankan government minister commented, 'What went on between Colombo and Washington was no secret to India because the US kept New Delhi well informed of whatever discussion Colombo had with Washington about the Sri Lankan problem'.[29] Jayewardene complained that 'America won't lift a finger to help me without asking India'.[30]

The intervention was doomed from the start. India had imposed an 'agreement' to which neither the Sri Lankan government nor the Tamil insurgents had genuinely agreed, but India was not prepared to apply sufficient force to impose its will on both sides. It was clear that the intervention would be strongly opposed by large parts of the Sinhalese community and its announcement led to widespread rioting in Colombo and the imposition of a nationwide curfew. On arriving in Colombo to sign the Accord, Rajiv Gandhi was greeted by small-arms fire at Colombo airport as Sri Lankan authorities tried to control demonstrators. The Sri Lankan prime minister and much of his cabinet refused to attend the signing ceremony and Gandhi was later attacked and assaulted by a sailor in the Sri Lankan guard of honour. The LTTE also denounced the Accord, with its leader, Prabhakaran, commenting: 'This agreement did not concern the problem of the Tamils. This is primarily concerned with Indo–Sri Lankan relations. It also contains within itself the principles, the requirements for making Sri Lanka accede to India's strategic sphere of influence'.[31]

Indian troops deployed in the north of Sri Lanka were initially greeted with enthusiasm by the Tamil population. But by early October 1987 the peacekeeping presence had deteriorated into a counterinsurgency campaign. The LTTE and other insurgent groups refused to disarm and the Sri Lankan government also failed to implement many aspects of the Accord. Indian forces, which ultimately numbered some 80,000 troops plus elements of the Indian Navy and Air Force, soon found themselves in a full-scale conflict with Tamil insurgents that included an assault on the Tamil stronghold at Jaffna—ironically, the very thing that the Indian intervention was supposed to prevent. The Indian forces were unprepared for a counterinsurgency operation against a determined and experienced opponent and were hamstrung by continued assistance being provided to the insurgents from India. The Indian Navy came to an arrangement with the LTTE under which it turned a blind eye to trafficking of supplies across the narrow Palk Strait that separates Tamil Nadu from Sri Lanka.[32]

By early 1989 it was clear that the Indian presence could not be sustained. India's position was not helped when the Sri Lankan government began supplying the LTTE with weapons, ammunition and funding to fight the Indian forces.[33] A new Indian government under Prime Minister V. P. Singh finally withdrew the last Indian troops in March 1990, with some 1200 dead and several thousand wounded.[34] India's military disaster was capped by the assassination of Rajiv Gandhi by an LTTE suicide bomber in May 1991. The Sri Lanka adventure, which became known as 'India's Vietnam', blunted India's taste for military interventions for some years.

The India–Sri Lanka security relationship post intervention

The events of 1983–90 left a legacy of bitterness and mistrust between India and Sri Lanka that continues today. The intervention only confirmed the suspicions of Sinhalese nationalists about India's hegemonistic ambitions. The failure of the intervention and Gandhi's assassination also led New Delhi and most of the Indian public to lose all sympathy for the Tamil insurgents. India was left hamstrung in its dealings with Sri Lanka for some two decades, officially adopting a non-interventionist stance while being quietly sympathetic to the

Sri Lankan government's struggle. New Delhi's primary concern now became combating the destabilising presence of LTTE insurgents in and around Sri Lanka, including their connections with India's domestic insurgents. The focus of India's Sri Lanka policy also shifted from political intervention to economic engagement as the most effective tool for influencing its neighbour. In line with the Gujral Doctrine (discussed in Chapter 2), India approved a Free Trade Agreement giving considerable tariff concessions to Sri Lanka, which led to considerable growth in trade and investment. By 2007–8 Sri Lanka had become India's largest trading partner in South Asia and India had become the second largest investor in Sri Lanka.

Colombo also demonstrated a preparedness to place limits on its external relationships to accommodate India. It did not contest the veto by Indian high commissioner, Nareshwar Dayal, of a plan to lease oil tanks in Trincomalee to a Singapore company. The oil tanks were then offered to India on a no-strings-attached basis that would, in effect, allow India to veto use of the port by others.[35] This was seen by Colombo as a way of giving India a further stake in ending the Tamil insurgency. Under a 35-year agreement, the state-owned Indian Oil Corporation has acquired control over and refurbished some 20 oil tanks at Trincomalee, which are currently used to supply fuel to northern Sri Lanka from Indian refineries.[36]

Despite the sometimes 'desperate' requests of the Sri Lankan government, for a long time after 1990 the Indian government was reluctant to provide any assistance beyond some intelligence sharing and limited coordination in the interdiction of LTTE supply lines across the Palk Strait.[37] But New Delhi became increasingly concerned to avoid a repeat of its stance on Myanmar which, it believed, opened space for China and Pakistan to gain greater influence there. Colombo used these concerns as leverage for greater economic and military support.[38] The terms of a Defence Cooperation Agreement were finalised in 2004; this aimed to formalise the supply of equipment, training, exchange of intelligence and joint maritime patrols and was intended to formally supercede the 1987 Accord. Although the agreement was not signed for Indian domestic reasons, it was nevertheless largely implemented. In an echo of the 1987 Accord, India also demanded that Palaly airbase near Jaffna be for the exclusive use of the Indian Air Force. This demand was seen in Colombo as insulting and symptomatic of India's hegemonistic mindset; in any event, no formal agreement on the subject was reached.[39]

From 2006 there was a substantial increase in Indian military assistance to Colombo, which led it to play a significant, if largely undisclosed, role in the destruction of the LTTE. India took responsibility for much of the training of government forces—one Indian government report claimed that in 2007 up to 53 per cent of the training of the Sri Lankan military was carried out by India.[40] This was a major factor in transforming it into a much more effective fighting force. India also provided considerable intelligence assistance. The Indian Navy and Sri Lankan Navy conducted coordinated patrols to interdict LTTE supply routes across the Palk Strait and Indian Navy aircraft flew regular reconnaissance missions over Sri Lankan waters and far beyond in the northeast Indian Ocean. Between September 2006 and October 2007 Indian maritime surveillance and US satellite intelligence located eight LTTE cargo ships in international waters, allowing them to be destroyed by the Sri Lankan Navy. The destruction of these so-called 'floating warehouses', several of which were found some 3,000 km southeast of Sri Lanka in the vicinity of Australia's Cocos Islands, represented a major blow to the LTTE's war-fighting capabilities and was a significant factor in the defeat of the LTTE.

India also supplied what it called 'defensive' arms to Colombo, a phrase that was sometimes broadly interpreted. Arms transfers reportedly included 5 Mi17 helicopters, an Offshore Patrol Vessel and five other naval vessels, ground-based radars (along with crew) to protect Sri Lanka airbases, Russian shoulder-fired IGLA ground-to-air missiles and automatic anti-aircraft guns.[41] But New Delhi also refused many of the 'shopping lists' for weapons provided by Colombo during this period. According to an Indian security official: 'We kept refusing weapons ... They were pretty upset about that, but we didn't see weapons like tanks, planes, MBRLs [multi-barrelled rocket launchers] as counterinsurgency weapons at all'.[42]

In light of domestic political constraints on Indian military assistance to Colombo, the Indian government had no choice but to tolerate the acquisition of arms from China and Pakistan required by the Sri Lankan government to prosecute the civil war, although New Delhi tried to limit the types of weapons being transferred, particularly those it deemed a potential threat to India. In 2007 Sri Lanka complained that the Indra-II 2-D radar systems previously supplied by India were inadequate to detect low-flying aircraft being used by the LTTE for attacks on Sri Lankan bases and sought systems from both China and Pakistan that could fulfil their requirements. India vetoed these acquisitions on the grounds that they would be placed too close to Indian airspace and instead supplied Colombo with advanced Indian 3-D radar systems.[43] Indian national security advisor, M. K. Narayanan, publicly warned Colombo that:

> It is high time that Sri Lanka understood that India is the big power in the region and ought to refrain from going to Pakistan or China for weapons, as we are prepared to accommodate them within the framework of our foreign policy.[44]

Similarly, Indian foreign minister, Pranab Mukherjee, commented that Colombo had been told that India would 'look after your security require-ments, provided you do not look around. We cannot have a playground of international players in our backyard'.[45]

The United States also provided limited assistance to the Sri Lankan govern-ment, taking pains to avoid offending Indian sensibilities. The US provided coastal maritime surveillance radar systems to Sri Lanka in 2007. Although India initially objected to the placement of the US radars in northern Sri Lanka at Trincomalee, Jaffna and Mannar, New Delhi eventually backed off following an undertaking that Indian maritime radar systems could also be installed in the area.[46] When Sri Lanka requested US assistance in developing an integrated air defence system in 2007, the US only agreed to help provided that India had full transparency of the project.[47]

There was considerable political coordination between Colombo and New Delhi in the lead-up to the destruction of the LTTE in 2009. In 2006, an Indian–Sri Lankan joint committee was established to coordinate positions on the Tamil conflict, comprising three key Indian officials—National Security Advisor M. K. Narayanan, Foreign Secretary Shivshankar Menon and Defence Secretary Vijay Singh—and three Sri Lankans, including two brothers of the Sri Lankan president.[48] This ensured that New Delhi was kept well apprised of developments. New Delhi made public calls for a negotiated settlement but was unable to persuade either side to come to the negotiating table or, perhaps, it preferred there to be no negotiated solution.[49]

The contemporary India–Sri Lanka security relationship

The destruction of the LTTE in 2009 removed many political roadblocks in the India-Sri Lanka relationship, but it also significantly reduced India's leverage in Sri Lanka. Colombo no longer requires India's assistance against the LTTE and Sri Lanka's growing economic relationship with China, in particular, provides it with other options. President Mahinda Rajapaksa has resisted New Delhi's pressure for Colombo to come to a political settlement with the Tamil community, demonstrating the real limitations to India's influence over Sri Lanka's domestic affairs. For a long time New Delhi helped Colombo fend off Western-led criticism of the Sri Lankan government's conduct in destroying the LTTE. But in May 2012, India voted with the United States and others in favour of a resolution in the UN Human Rights Council calling for an investigation of war crimes committed by Sri Lankan government forces in 2009. This represented a considerable change in the relationship. These tensions have held up finalisation of the India–Sri Lanka Comprehensive Economic Partnership Agreement which would involve considerable expansion of Sri Lanka's access to the Indian market.

Since 2009 India has given considerable emphasis to enhancing military-to-military relations, particularly naval cooperation. India has offered 1400 training places to the Sri Lankan armed forces. In September 2011, Indian and Sri Lankan navies held the large-scale SLINEX exercises involving asymmetric attacks of small vessels, something in which the Sri Lankan Navy has particular expertise. The Sri Lankan Navy, which is less influential and has less access to resources than the huge Sri Lankan Army, has been relatively more receptive to cooperation with India. As Sri Lanka's former chief of navy, Vice Admiral Thisara Samarasinghe, commented in 2010, 'Our relationship with India is a role model for co-operation between two navies on a common problem'.[50] There are numerous common interests, including concerns that the LTTE will regroup in Tamil Nadu and resume the armed struggle across the Palk Strait and the problem of smuggling and illegal fishing (mostly by Indian fisherman). In addition to regular naval patrols, the Indian Navy conducts manned and unmanned aerial surveillance of waters around Sri Lanka. An annual security dialogue at defence secretary level commenced in 2012.

Many in India's security community fear that India's influence in Sri Lanka will be marginalised by China. Certainly the Chinese economic presence in Sri Lanka is growing, including several high-profile infrastructure projects. (Although India is also funding several major infrastructure projects, mostly in the north of Sri Lanka, such as the rehabilitation of Kankasanthurai (KKS) port.) The biggest symbol of Chinese influence in Sri Lanka has been the development of a new hub port at Hambantota on the country' southern tip, which has led to a chorus of protests from Indian analysts. But, as discussed in Chapter 10, Hambantota probably has less strategic significance than might appear. Indian analysts are also concerned about the development of a Chinese-operated satellite ground station in Kandy, which could substantially enhance China's satellite surveillance capabilities in the Indian Ocean. There are also numerous other infrastructure and resource projects being undertaken by Chinese companies in Sri Lanka which do not have a direct security aspect but are indicative of increased Chinese political influence.

Although the Rajapaksa regime finds the China relationship useful in balancing some of the pressures it faces from India and the West over the Tamil issue, the China factor should not be overstated. Colombo balances Indian and Chinese interests in Sri Lanka, as shown when India and China were awarded equal-sized offshore hydrocarbon exploration licenses in the Mannar Basin. According to former Sri Lankan diplomat Jayantha Dhanapala, although 'there are elements in America and India who would like to raise the China bogey … this is not a zero sum game where our relationship with China is at the expense of our relationship with India. We cleverly balanced the relationship'.[51] Colombo is also mindful of New Delhi's sensitivities towards what it would regard as a hostile security presence in Sri Lanka. In December 2010, Sri Lankan defence secretary Gotabhaya Rajapaksa ruled out Sri Lanka entering into a defence cooperation with Pakistan, and Colombo is also well aware of the strength of India's reaction if it ever allowed Sri Lankan territory to be used by China. As President Mahinda Rajapaksa commented: 'I know that China is not interested in putting a naval base here. I will not allow this country to be used against any other country'.[52]

India and the Maldives

India also regards the island state of the Maldives as falling squarely within its South Asian sphere of influence. The Maldives are located off the southern tip of India and is comprised of some 2000 low-lying coral islands stretching some 800 km from north to south. Although it has a population of only

300,000 its location is important to India's strategic aspirations. The east-west shipping routes across the Indian Ocean pass the Maldives and the former British air and naval base on the island of Gan provides a potential base to dominate the central Indian Ocean. The Maldives is also a potential source of security threats to India: its sparse population and numerous uninhabited islands make it a possible haven for terrorists, pirates and smugglers and there are fears that its Muslim population could become radicalised. India's role as an effective security guarantor of the Maldives was confirmed in the late 1980s, when India intervened to prevent an attempted coup by foreign mercenaries. Over the last decade or so India has taken an increasingly prominent role in promoting political and economic stability, as well as effectively taking responsibility for the Maldives' external security.

Operation Cactus: India's 1988 intervention in the Maldives

A defining moment in the India–Maldives strategic relationship occurred in 1988 when India intervened in the Maldives to prevent an attempted coup by mercenaries, organised by a Maldivian businessman.[53] In November 1988, a force of some 80–200 mercenaries, largely drawn from a Sri Lankan Tamil insurgent group, the People's Liberation Organization of Tamil Eelam (PLOTE), infiltrated the Maldivian capital of Malé and took control of key points in the city. The rebels failed to capture the Maldivian president, Abdul Gayoom, who took refuge in the Maldives National Security Service headquarters. Gayoom personally, or through the Maldivian ambassador to the United Nations, requested military assistance from several countries, including India, the United States, Britain, Pakistan, Sri Lanka, Malaysia and 'other' Asian states.[54] The Sri Lankan military placed 85 commandos on standby at its Ratmalana airbase at Colombo, and Malaysia reportedly alerted its navy (although it is three to four days' sailing from the Maldives).[55] The US Marine detachment at Diego Garcia was also placed on alert but the US State Department ruled out direct intervention, and worked with Britain to help coordinate a response from India.

New Delhi responded to the crisis with uncharacteristic speed and decision, seeing it as India's prerogative and responsibility. On the same day as Gayoom's request for assistance, the Indian Air Force airlifted some 300 paratroops from Agra to Malé, landing on the nearby island of Hulhule which was still under the control of Maldivian security services. Additional Indian troops were transported by air and sea from Cochin and Indian Air Force Mirages were deployed over Malé in a show of force. The Indian troops took control of Malé within several hours and rescued President Gayoom. A group of insurgents with 27 hostages managed to escape on board a merchant ship. The following day, with US assistance, Indian maritime patrol aircraft were vectored onto the ship, which then tracked it until two Indian naval vessels reached the area. Sea King helicopters from INS *Godavari* dropped depth charges to deter evasion and Indian Marines operating from Sri Lanka boarded the ship and returned the rebels to Malé for trial. Most of the Indian troops were withdrawn from the Maldives after order had been restored, with around 150 troops remaining for a year after the attempted coup.[56]

India's intervention in the Maldives was a model for the benign security role that India could play in the Indian Ocean. It was undertaken at the express invitation of a nominally democratic Maldivian government, and India was careful to avoid the appearance of military occupation. India also undertook the intervention alone, demonstrating its ability to airlift troops over long distances and successfully intercept the plotters at sea. India showed that it could execute a combined services operation in an efficient and timely manner.[57] The decision of the United States not to mount a rescue mission—which almost certainly would have had to come from Diego Garcia—was a wise one. US intervention would have evoked bitter memories in New Delhi. Instead, the forbearance of the United States gave a clear signal of its acceptance of India's leading role in South Asia.

India received international praise for the operation. President Reagan expressed his appreciation for India's action, calling it 'a valuable contribution to regional stability'.[58] Margaret Thatcher reportedly commented: 'Thank God for India: President Gayoom's government has been saved. We could not have assembled and dispatched a force from here in good time to help him'.[59] Lee Kwan Yew saw it as essentially a peacekeeping operation of the type that the United States conducted globally and Australia conducted in the South Pacific.[60] According to the Indian cabinet secretary, B. G. Deshmukh, '*Operation Cactus* enhanced India's prestige enormously and showed our efficiency and capability to mount a successful operation at short notice. There was universal acknowledgement of our role as a police force in the area …'.[61] But the intervention nevertheless caused some disquiet among India's neighbours in South Asia and further afield. According to the Sri Lankan *Island* newspaper: 'It would be ostrich-like to ignore the fear of smaller nations in South Asia about current developments providing opportunities for what has been described as the spread of Indian hegemonism'.[62]

The contemporary India–Maldives security relationship

Since 1988 the bilateral security relationship has been close. India provides equipment and training to the Maldivian armed forces and the Indian Navy has effectively assumed responsibility for maritime security. The Maldivian government partially hedges its reliance on India through playing an active role in international fora such as the United Nations, the Commonwealth, SAARC and NAM, promoting collective action to protect small and vulnerable states.[63] It has also sought economic assistance from a variety of sources, including China. Although Indian officials periodically express concerns that the Maldives might fall under the influence of Pakistan or China, the Maldives has steered clear of any security links that would be of real concern to India.

A deterioration in Maldives' security environment in recent years has increased its dependence on India for security. Maldives now faces threats from Islamic radicalisation, piracy, economic crisis and political instability and, not least, an existential threat from inundation by rising sea levels. There is growing concern over the activities of Lashkar-e-Taayba (LeT) in the islands, particularly given that numerous Maldivians had been either killed or captured fighting for the LeT in northwest Pakistan.[64] President Mohamed Nasheed has acknowledged that Maldivians had received training with Al Qaida in Pakistan and that there was a Maldivian connection in the 2008 terrorist attacks in Mumbai.[65] The LeT also attempted to set up an Indian Ocean base on an uninhabited island in the Maldives for, amongst other things, weapons storage.[66] The Maldivian government has also become increasingly concerned about threats from Somali-based piracy and the vulnerability of isolated tourist islands to attack from pirates or terrorists.[67]

In August 2009 India effectively brought the Maldives into its security net through a comprehensive security agreement which included the stationing of Indian aircraft and naval vessels in the Maldives and the construction of a maritime surveillance system.[68] India has transferred a fast patrol boat to the Maldives and provides extensive training to the Maldivian security forces. India has also built a system of 26 coastal surveillance radars across the Maldives archipelago which is networked with the Indian coastal radar system, allowing India's Southern Naval Command to 'overlook inclusion of the Maldives into the Indian security grid'.[69]

According to some reports, the security agreement allows India the use of Gan Atoll in the southernmost group of islands in the Maldives. Like Diego Garcia, which lies a further 700 km south, Gan can potentially be used to dominate the central Indian Ocean. The British established a naval and air base there during World War II and after their departure, in 1976, Iran, the Soviet Union and Libya all tried to acquire use of the base, which was only prevented through Indian pressure on the Maldivian government. While there have been reports of Indian plans to base Dornier reconnaissance aircraft at Gan it is not clear whether India intends to establish a permanent presence there.[70] However, a senior Indian naval official was reported as commenting: 'It is important for us to station assets there. That does not mean taking it over. In fact, we have flown our aircraft from there. We want to station there now'.[71] Another official commented that Gan 'could eventually provide the Indian Navy with a listening post to monitor the movements of Chinese vessels as they sail to and from Africa, ferrying oil and gas'.[72]

New Delhi has also encouraged trilateral security cooperation among India, Sri Lanka and the Maldives. The former Maldives foreign minister Ahmed Shaheed also proposed a 'pluralistic regional security community', beginning with a triangular dialogue among India, Sri Lanka and the Maldives.[73] In 2012, the Sri Lankan Coast Guard was invited to participate in the India–Maldives *Dosti* exercises and the Indian Navy is reportedly keen on promoting interoperability among the navies. Trilateral discussions have also been held on poaching, piracy and maritime terrorism. While there is good reason for the three to cooperate, this will be limited in the short term by the sometimes difficult political relations between New Delhi and Colombo and political instability in the Maldives. Nevertheless, India and Sri Lanka have shared interests in ensuring the stability of the Maldives, and this may include, for example, an interest in ensuring that the Maldives does not form external relationships that would be the source of regional tensions.

The United States has also increased security assistance to the Maldives. In 2009, in response to the deteriorating economic and security situation, US President Obama authorised the extension of security assistance.[74] This has focused on the Maldives' counter-piracy and counterterrorism capabilities and includes training, equipment and intelligence support, regular high-level visits, US Navy ship visits, expert exchanges, conferences and Joint-Combined Exercise Training. It is not clear whether US assistance is now coordinated with India. The Maldives ambassador to the US, Abdul Ghafoor Mohamed, reportedly believed in 2010 that Malé would 'be able to address any concerns' that New Delhi might have about it.[75]

Although China's economic influence is growing quickly, there is no evidence of any plans to establish a security presence in the Maldives. It seems the Maldives takes the view that Delhi should be able to differentiate between its economic relationship with China and its security relationship with India.[76] China provides considerable aid and is the largest source of tourism to the Maldives and the opening of a Chinese embassy in Male, immediately prior to the SAARC Summit in November 2011, was interpreted by some as a reminder to SAARC members of China's legitimate role throughout South Asia. When a $500 million package of Chinese loans to the Maldives was announced in September 2012, the Maldives government went out of its way to downplay its strategic significance. According to the former Maldivian foreign minister, Dr Ahmed Shaheed, 'Nothing will change the fact that we are only 200 miles from Trivandrum [India]'.[77] Nevertheless, the magnitude of the deal for a country of some 300,000 people will substantially increase China's political influence. Some, for example, believe that Chinese interests were involved in the recent cancellation of an Indian contract to develop and operate Malé's international airport. But there is no evidence that the Maldives is trying to explicitly leverage a possible security dimension to its relationship with China. As Maldivean president Nasheed commented in February 2011: 'There is not enough room in the Indian Ocean for other non-traditional friends. We are not receptive to any installation, military or otherwise, in the Indian Ocean, especially from un-traditional friends. The Indian Ocean is the Indian Ocean'.[78]

In coming years it seems likely that India will increasingly be required to assist in the stabilisation of the country. A framework agreement for development and cooperation was signed in November 2011 as part of a package to help develop the Maldivian economy, for instance in the areas of banking and financial infrastructure. India also agreed to extend a $100 million standby credit facility to help stabilise the fiscal position. Political instability is also testing India's role. In February 2012, President Mohamed Nasheed was forced to resign under pressure from elements in the Maldivian security forces. A year later Nasheed sought political asylum in the High Commission to evade arrest by the new government and was persuaded to leave some 10 days later. These events created some difficult choices for New Delhi. Unlike 1988, there was no foreign involvement in these events or any formal request from the Maldives government that would justify an Indian intervention. India has made the best of a bad situation by being the first to recognise the new government under Mohamed Waheed. Subsequently, India tried to take a relatively hands-off stance over the dispute, allowing events to take their course although insisting that any new elections must be free and fair. Indian 'hawks' such as B. Raman claimed that India's approach to the dispute undermined what he calls India's role as 'the sole arbiter of political fortunes in the Maldives', allowing other actors such as the Commonwealth and UN to take a role in internal peace-making. Others might see India's approach as representing a relatively mature balance between fulfilling the obligations of regional leadership while seeking to avoid being drawn into domestic disputes as far as possible.

There are no real indications that the new government under President Waheed will be materially less friendly to India. In September 2012, Indian defence minister A. K. Antony announced further Indian training of Maldivian naval and air force personnel and the extended deployment of an Indian helicopter squadron. However, the rise of Islamist fundamentalism and the presence of radical Islamic elements amongst Waheed's supporters does raise the possibility of a future Maldives government dominated by elements friendly to Pakistan. Such a development would probably represent a significant test for India's special role in the islands.

India's relationships with Sri Lanka and the Maldives and its role in the Indian Ocean

How do India's relationships with Sri Lanka and the Maldives shed light on its broader ambitions in the Indian Ocean? India sees both Sri Lanka and the Maldives as falling squarely within its South Asian sphere of influence and its security relationships with each have been intense. The development of those relationships over the last several decades may demonstrate an evolution of India's approach to a regional leadership role.

India's intervention in Sri Lanka in the 1980s showed a disastrous blend of overconfidence, bad intelligence and a lack of will in playing the role of regional hegemon. It also demonstrated the consequences of the miscalculation of strategic threats (in that case, a largely imagined belief that the United States had strategic ambitions in Sri Lanka) which are used to justify otherwise unnecessary and risky actions. But since that time India has followed a policy of restraint with respect to Sri Lanka that has generally been more fruitful. This has included a focus on economic integration, the provision of limited and relatively discrete military assistance to end its civil war and a willingness to cooperate with the United States in promoting stability. Although relations with Colombo remain strained by the Tamil ethnic issue, Sri Lanka appears to have accepted an implicit understanding of some necessary limitations to its strategic freedom *vis a vis* India. The continued legal validity of the 1987 Accord and the side letter raises interesting questions which neither New Delhi nor Colombo appear to want to publicly address.

Some have compared the Sri Lanka–India relationship with Finland's relationship with the Soviet Union during the Cold War, as a lesson of how small countries can coexist with a giant neighbour.[79] In that case, the Soviet Union allowed Finland to determine its own political and economic affairs in return for an understanding that Finland would not participate in Western military alliances. Finland was thus prepared to cede some sovereignty in exchange for non-interference in its internal affairs. While this analogy highlights the need of small countries to follow a policy of self-restraint and reassurance towards one's big and powerful neighbour, such arrangements may only work where there is a preparedness to refrain from interference in the subordinate state's internal affairs—which has not been the case in Sri Lanka. But Sri Lanka does appear to have implicitly accepted India's position that it would not allow Sri Lanka to form significant security relationships with states that might threaten its interests. Although Sri Lanka seeks economic relationships with China and others it is unlikely to allow China to develop a material security presence. In other words, Sri Lanka is likely to follow a policy of self-restraint and reassurance towards India and will not threaten India's dominant security role in the northeast Indian Ocean. In short, the strategic relationship between India and Sri Lanka is a complex one. While Colombo is keen to demonstrate its strategic independence from its huge neighbour, it will almost inevitably partly rely on Indian assistance for external security and perhaps on occasion even for internal security.

India's security relationship with the Maldives has generally been less fraught, perhaps reflecting the extreme asymmetries in size and the absence of ethnic conflict affecting India. India's intervention in the Maldives to procure political stability has been held up as a model of benign regional leadership—and a model which might be used further afield in the Indian Ocean. India's relatively restrained approach has allowed it to bring the Maldives within India's maritime security net with a minimum of controversy. While India's role inevitably brings pressures to act as arbiter in Maldives' internal political disputes, New Delhi's reaction to the political instability in the Maldives in 2012 again points to a policy of restraint. For its part, the Maldives appears to be willing to accept its dependence on India for security. As the former Maldives foreign minister, Ahmed Shaheed, warned, small states in the region should resist the temptation to form balance of power coalitions with outside powers. According to Shaheed, the acceptance by small South Asian states such as the Maldives of a form of 'finlandization' was necessary for regional peace and order in South Asia.[80] It remains to be seen to what extent other states in the Indian Ocean region may be prepared to grant such a role to India.

Notes

1 2009 estimates. CIA World Factbook—India. Online: www.cia.gov/library/publications/the-world-factbook/ (accessed 10 October 2013).
2 2009 estimates at international exchange rates. CIA World Factbook. Online: www.cia.gov/library/publications/the-world-factbook/ (accessed 10 October 2013).
3 Barry Buzan, Ole Waever and Jaap de Wilde (1998) *Security: A New Framework for Analysis*, Boulder, CO: Lynne Rienner Publishers, pp. 10–11.
4 Razeen Sally (2010) 'Regional economic integration in Asia: The track record and prospects', ECIPE Occasional Paper No. 2.
5 'Don't allow differences to stop South Asian integration: NSA' (2012) *The Economic Times*, 9 March.
6 There is also a maritime boundary dispute which has been referred to international arbitration for resolution.
7 Stephen P. Cohen (2001) *India: Emerging Power*, Washington, DC: Brookings Institution, p. 199.
8 J.N. Dixit (1989) 'IPKF in Sri Lanka', *USI Journal*, Vol. 119, No. 49, July, pp. 249–50.
9 *Foreign Affairs Reports* (New Delhi), Vol. 36, July–Oct: 1987, p. 208.
10 'Mossad comes to Sri Lanka' (1984) *Tamil Times*, June, p. 4.
11 Phillip Towle (1979) *Naval Power in the Indian Ocean*, Canberra: Australian National University, p. 65.
12 Israeli intelligence agencies were providing training to both the Sri Lankan armed forces and the Tamil insurgents.
13 Desmond Ball (1996) *Signals Intelligence (SIGINT) in South Asia: India, Pakistan, Sri Lanka (Ceylon)*, Canberra: Australian National University, p. 98.
14 Rohan Gunaratna (1993) *Indian Intervention in Sri Lanka: the role of India's intelligence agencies*, Colombo: South Asian Network on Conflict Research, p. 14.
15 According to India's then deputy high commissioner in Colombo, Rajendra Abhyankar, Indian oil companies were also concerned that a commercial operator of the Trincomalee oil tank farm might use them to store oil which could be sold on the Indian spot market. Interview with author, 29 April 2013, Mumbai.
16 See generally J. Manor and G. Segal (1985) 'Causes of conflict: Sri Lanka and Indian Ocean strategy', *Asian Survey*, Vol. 25, No. 12, December, pp. 1165–85.
17 S.D. Muni (1993) *Pangs of Proximity: India and Sri Lanka's Ethnic Crisis*, New Delhi: Sage Publications, p. 69.
18 Gunaratna, *Indian Intervention in Sri Lanka*, p. 7.
19 The Special Frontier Force played a central role in training the Bangladeshi *Mukti Bahini* insurgents in 1971.
20 M.R. Narayan Swamy (1995) *Tigers of Lanka: From Boys to Guerrillas*, Delhi: Konark, p. 107; Krishna, *Postcolonial Insecurities: India, Sri Lanka, and the Question of Nationhood*, New York: Oxford University Press, 2000, p. 123.
21 Jain Commission Interim Report, *Growth of Sri Lankan Tamil Militancy in Tamil Nadu*, Chapter I 'Phases I & II (1981–1988)', Section 3, paragraph 7.11.
22 Swamy, *Tigers of Lanka*, p. 112.
23 Swamy, *Tigers of Lanka*, p. 110; and S. D. Muni, *Pangs of Proximity*.
24 Swamy, *Tigers of Lanka*, p. 111.
25 Rajesh Kadian (1990) *India's Sri Lankan Fiasco: Peace Keepers at War*, New Delhi: Vision Books, p. 18.
26 Dilip Bobb (1987) 'High stakes gamble', *India Today*, 15 December, p. 81.

27 C. Narendra Reddy (1987) 'Expectations of Indian government', *Indian Express*, 1 August.
28 Washington was well informed about India's support for Tamil insurgents. Among other things, the head of RAW in Chennai, K.V. Unnikrishnan, who was the chief liaison with the LTTE and other insurgent groups, was on the CIA's payroll.
29 Amal Jayawardene (1995) 'Sri Lanka's foreign policy under J.R. Jayewardene and Ranasinghe Premadasa—1977–93' in Mahina Werake and P.V.J. Jayasekera, *Security Dilemma of a Small State, Part 2: International Crisis and External Intervention in Sri Lanka*, Kandy: Institute for International Studies, pp. 204–31 at p. 239.
30 *The Sunday Times* (Colombo), 9 August 1987.
31 Quoted in Kadian, *India's Sri Lankan Fiasco*, p. 26.
32 As a result, the Indian Navy suffered no casualties or damage to any vessels in Operation *Pawan*.
33 C.A. Chandraprema (2012) *Gōta's War: the crushing of Tamil Tiger Terrorism in Sri Lanka*, Colombo: Ranjan Wijeratne Foundation, p. 183.
34 In doing so, the Indian government overruled elements of the Indian military that proposed to retain control of Trincomalee port until the Sri Lankan government had fulfilled its obligations under the Accord. Interview with Rajendra Abhyanka, 29 April 2013, Mumbai.
35 According to a senior Sri Lankan diplomat, K. Godage (2005) 'Why won't India show her hand?' *Sunday Island*, 6 February; and Jyoti Malhotra (2000) 'Lanka offers free access to Trincomalee, India mulls over it', *Indian Express*, 12 May.
36 Rahul Bedi (2003) 'US closes in on South Asia's 'strategic jewel', *AsiaTimes Online*, 7 January. Online: www.atimes.com/atimes/South_Asia/EA07Df02.html (accessed 10 October 2013).
37 Chandraprema, *Gōta's War*, p. 248.
38 International Crisis Group (2008) 'Sri Lanka's return to war: limiting the damage', *Asia Report* No. 146, 20 February.
39 Gokhale, *Sri Lanka*, p. 122.
40 Ministry of External Affairs, BSM Division, 26 February 2007.
41 International Crisis Group (2007) 'Sri Lanka's return to war', p. 16; and Rahul Bedi, 'Sri Lanka turns to Pakistan, China for military needs', *IANS*, 6 February.
42 Quoted in International Crisis Group, 'Sri Lanka's return to war', p. 15.
43 'India begins supplies radars to Sri Lanka' (2007) *India Defence*, 8 June.
44 'Chinese arms, radar for Sri Lanka military' (2007) LankaNewspapers.com, 5 June.
45 Express News Service (2008) 'Won't stop military cooperation with Lanka: Pranab', *Indian Express*, 24 October.
46 US Embassy Colombo cable to US State Department (2007) 'Indian Navy reportedly lifts objections to US-provided maritime radar', 13 June. Online: www.cablegatesearch. net/cable.php?id=07COLOMBO838 (accessed 10 October 2013).
47 US Embassy Colombo cable to US State Department (2007) 'Sri Lanka requests US military team to assess air defense following LTTE air attack', 1 April. Online: www. cablegatesearch.net/cable.php?id=07COLOMBO516 (accessed 10 October 2013).
48 Gotabaya Rajapaksa (2011) 'Key factor in defeating terrorism was political leadership', speech in Colombo, 6 January.
49 Nirupama Subramanian (2011) 'How India kept pressure off Sri Lanka', *The Hindu*, 17 March.
50 Sergei DeSilva-Ranasinghe (2012) 'Post-war posture', *Jane's Defence Weekly*, 9 May, pp. 27–32 at p. 27.
51 Sergei DeSilva-Ranasinghe (2009) 'Sri Lanka—The New Great Game', *The Diplomat*, 28 October.
52 Ravi Velloor (2010) 'A man who loves his country', *Straits Times*, 17 March.
53 According to one report, Libya assisted in the attempted coup with the backing of the Soviet Union. 'Libya backed Maldives coup' (1988) *Intelligence Digest*, 7

December p. 8. While Libyan involvement is possible, the complicity of the Soviet Union seems unlikely.

54 S. Bilveer, 'Operation Cactus: India's 'Prompt Action' in Maldives', *Asian Defence Journal*, Vol. 2, No. 89, pp. 30–3.

55 Anonymous (1988) 'Maldives—The coup that failed', *Asiaweek*, 18 November, pp. 37–8.

56 Gayoom was 'grateful but alarmed' at the presence of the Indian troops and urged them to be recalled as soon as possible. Hewitt, *The new international politics of South Asia*, p. 257.

57 The operation may not have ended so successfully. According to one Indian army officer, in a potentially disastrous error, some Indian military planners initially confused the target country with Mauritius and only discovered that they were using the wrong maps shortly before the aircraft carrying the Indian troops took off. Dalit Singh (1990) 'Military Intelligence not up to the mark', *Illustrated Weekly of India*, 14 October, pp. 30–2.

58 *Asian Defence Journal*, December 1988, p. 131.

59 Sandy Gordon (1996) *Security and Security Building in the Indian Ocean*, Canberra: Strategic and Defence Studies Centre, pp. 55–6.

60 Sunanda K. Datta-Ray (2009) *Looking east to look west: Lee Kuan Yew's Mission India*, Singapore: Institute of Southeast Asian Studies, p. 262.

61 B.G. Deshmukh (2004) *A Cabinet Secretary Looks Back*, New Delhi: HarperCollins, p. 197.

62 Quoted in *Straits Times*, 7 November 1988, p. 5.

63 Dr. P. Sahadevan (1999) 'Maldives', in Dipankar Banerjee, *Security in South Asia: Comprehensive and Cooperative*, New Delhi: Manas, pp. 202–47.

64 US Embassy New Delhi cable to Department of State (2009) 'Indian officials to visit Maldives to raise concerns about stability there', 26 June. Online: www.cablegatesearch.net/cable.php?id=09NEWDELHI1334 (accessed 10 October 2013).

65 Jyoti Malhotra (2009) 'There's a Maldivian link to 26/11', *Business Standard*, 25 October.

66 Balaji Chandramohan (2011) 'Indo–Maldives relations continue to blossom', *Atlantic Sentinel*, 22 November.

67 Manu Pubby (2009) 'India bringing Maldives into its security net', *Indian Express*, 13 August.

68 Sujan Dutta (2009) 'Indian Navy eyes Maldives—counter to China's 'String of Pearls' plan', *The Telegraph* (India), 20 August.

69 Pubby, 'India bringing Maldives into its security net'.

70 Sergei DeSilva-Ranasinghe (2011) 'China–India rivalry in the Maldives', *The Jakarta Post*, 17 June.

71 Dutta, 'Indian Navy eyes Maldives'.

72 Rahul Bedi (2009) 'India strengthens military co-operation with the Maldives', *Jane's Defence Weekly*, 21 August.

73 Dr Ahmed Shaheed (2009) 'Building a framework for India–Maldives security co-operation: an oceanic agenda for the future', Open Society Association, 22 August.

74 US Embassy Colombo cable to State Department (2010) 'Maldives assistance overview: US and other donors', 13 January. Online: www.cablegatesearch.net/cable.php?id=10COLOMBO26 (accessed 10 October 2013).

75 US Secretary of State cable to US Embassy Colombo (2010) 'Maldives ambassador's Washington consultations', 26 February. Online: www.cablegatesearch.net/cable.php?id=10STATE18437 (accessed 10 October 2013).

76 Raja Mohan (2012) *Samudra Manthan: Sino–Indian Rivalry in the Indo–Pacific*, Washington, DC: Carnegie Endowment for International Peace, p. 146.

77 'Maldives says China to grant Maldives $500 million loan' (2012) *South Asia Monitor*, 5 September.
78 'Maldives not in favour of Chinese naval expansion in Indian Ocean' (2011) *Times of India*, 26 February.
79 Amal Jayawarden (1990) 'Finland vs. Sri Lanka: use and misuse of the analogy', in Shelton U. Kodikara (ed.), *South Asian strategic issues: Sri Lankan perspectives*, New Delhi: Sage Publications, pp. 116–25 at p. 120. Indeed, President Jayawardene was expressly advised to apply the lessons of Finland during the negotiation of the 1987 Accord with India.
80 T.V. Paul (2010) 'State capacity and South Asia's security problems', in T.V. Paul (ed.), *South Asia's Weak States: Understanding the Regional Security Predicament*, Stanford, CA: Stanford Security Studies, pp. 3–29, at p. 24.

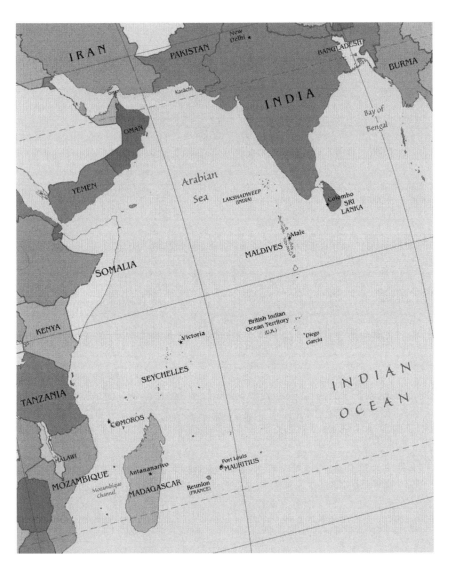

Map 4.1 The Southwest
Adapted from the University of Texas Libraries collection.

4   The Southwest Indian Ocean

This chapter examines India's strategic role in the southwest Indian Ocean, the main gateway to the Atlantic Ocean. It is sometimes called the 'Latin Quarter' due to the preponderance of French spoken in its many island states and territories. India is keen to demonstrate its role as a maritime security provider throughout the southwest, for instance in combating Somali-based piracy and helping police the huge exclusive economic zones (EEZs) of the islands. India has sought to develop a security presence through the provision of training, equipment such as patrol boats, aircraft and coastal surveillance radar systems and security advisors. The Indian Navy also provides offshore patrolling and hydrographic surveys in several states and is now also seeking to establish a small security presence in the region. A major focus of maritime security in the southwest is on the Mozambique Channel, which is the key route for shipping between the Middle East and the Atlantic Ocean.

The southwest is a part of the Indian Ocean where India has the opportunity to build a leading role, if not a sphere of influence. This chapter will look at India's three key security relationships in the area: with Mauritius, Seychelles and France. Mauritius is effectively a client state and acts as India's key security partner in the region. In contrast, the strategically placed Seychelles has for decades successfully balanced the demands of major powers, while also relying on India as a sort of benign guarantor. India is also developing a cooperative security partnership with France, which has the strongest military presence in the region.

The willing subordination of Mauritius

In many ways Mauritius is the 'Little India' of the Indian Ocean: a confidential US diplomatic report judged that Mauritius has 'willingly subordinated' itself to India.[1]

During the colonial era, Mauritius was used by the Dutch, the French and then the British as a staging point for shipping between the Atlantic and Indian Oceans. With no indigenous population, the European colonists imported slaves from Africa and indentured labour from India to work its sugar cane plantations. Today, some 70 per cent of the island's population is of Indian descent, and the Indian diaspora clings tenaciously to Mother India. The remaining population is mostly of African descent, with a very small white French community. India effectively assumed responsibility for the security of Mauritius after the departure of the Royal Navy in 1974, helping to establish the Coast Guard and providing equipment and training to security forces. New Delhi quickly came to consider Mauritius as one of its closest international partners and a potential safe haven in case of political troubles in India.[2] A turning point in India's role in Mauritius occurred in the 1980s, when India secretly intervened to ensure the continuing political ascendancy of the majority Hindu community. Importantly, India appears to have acted more or less in cooperation with the United States. An examination of these events provides some important insights into India's perceptions of its role in the region and its willingness to cooperate with others.

In the early 1980s, the southwest was the scene of great rivalry and intrigue when the Soviet Union and the United States jostled for influence over the small and politically weak Indian Ocean island states. Simultaneously, an embattled South African regime was actively destabilising governments that it considered hostile and suborning those that could be bought. This created considerable instability, and several island states, including the Seychelles, Comoros and Madagascar, were the subject of coups involving foreign powers or mercenaries. Mauritius struggled to maintain its parliamentary democracy in the face of this turmoil. As the Mauritius Times commented, 'Mauritius is the only important island left in the Indian Ocean that is not in the pocket of any superpower … It would be sheer folly to dismiss the likelihood of a coup in Mauritius'.[3]

In June 1982, Prime Minister Seewoosagur Ramgoolam, Mauritius' leader from independence and a close friend of India, lost power to the main Mauritian opposition party, the MMM. The departure of Ramgoolam led to a period of instability and opened the door to other influences. Anerood Jugnauth, a London-trained barrister of Indian descent, became prime minister, and Paul Berenger, a firebrand socialist of white French descent, was appointed finance minister. Indira Gandhi swung her support behind Jugnauth and Berenger, hoping to earn their support for India and its policies in the Indian Ocean. Days after their election victory, Gandhi made a 'triumphant' visit to the island, showcasing India's special relationship with Mauritius and New Delhi's approval of the new government. Among other things, Mrs Gandhi granted Mauritius a special taxation treaty that has since allowed Mauritius to develop itself as an offshore financial centre and the primary route for foreign investment into India.

But ideological and personality differences surfaced in the new government within months. Many Hindus were unhappy about Berenger's ties with Libya's Muammar Gaddafi, who was seen as an Arab radical and a fellow traveller of the Soviet Union.[4] There was also disquiet over symbolic attempts by the Berenger to promote French Creole as Mauritius' national language over the English favoured by the Indian community, and this became a proxy for the increasing communal tensions. Hindu leaders were particularly frustrated that they had less economic and political power than the Franco–Mauritians despite their majority numbers. Some believed that Berenger intended to overthrow Jugnauth and establish a dictatorship in which high-caste Hindus would be excluded from power. Berenger's increasingly autocratic behaviour seemed to indicate that a coup was not too far away.

For New Delhi, Berenger's growing power raised concerns about the position of the Indian community. Over the previous decades there had been considerable discrimination against the Indian diaspora throughout the Indian Ocean region—at the hands of whites in South Africa and black Africans in East Africa. The entire Indian community had been expelled from Uganda in 1972 and in Sri Lanka the Tamil conflict was about to erupt into civil war. Beyond the Indian Ocean region, official discrimination occurred even where the Indian community represented a majority of the population. In Guyana, the majority Indian ethnic community had been excluded from power since independence. In Fiji, constitutional restrictions prevented a majority Indian ethnic community from gaining power. Against this backdrop, New Delhi was concerned that a Berenger-led government in Mauritius would favour the Creole and Muslim minorities, potentially provoking a refugee exodus of Hindus to India.[5]

Both New Delhi and Washington were also concerned about the geopolitical implications of Berenger taking power, if for different reasons. New Delhi was concerned that Berenger's apparent ambitions for the social and political transformation of Mauritius would cause it to drift out of India's sphere of influence and that it would lose its only unquestioning supporter in the Indian Ocean. The United States was worried that Berenger would give the Soviet Navy access to Port Louis and that he would aggressively prosecute Mauritius' territorial claims over Diego Garcia. General Vernon Walters, the legendary Deputy Director of the CIA, took a close interest in Mauritius, cultivating personal links with key Hindu community leaders such as Harish Boodhoo.[6] Each of the CIA and RAW kept Jugnauth apprised of Berenger's foreign links, including secret meetings between Berenger and Mikhail Orlov, the Soviet ambassador to the Seychelles and regional representative of the KGB.[7] Although there is no publicly available evidence of active collusion between New Delhi and Washington, there does appear to be something of an alignment of interests in relation to Mauritius. Since the Soviet intervention in Afghanistan, Indira Gandhi had been making considerable efforts to improve relations with the United States, and, according to one commentator, by 1982 was downplaying Diego Garcia as a bilateral issue in private talks with Washington.[8]

In February 1983, when Jugnauth travelled to New Delhi to request assistance in the event of a coup led by Berenger, Mrs Gandhi assured him of Indian support, telling him that, 'Within five hours a contingent of my air force will be in Mauritius'.[9] The power struggle came to a head a few weeks later. The government disintegrated, with Berenger and most of the cabinet resigning, leaving Jugnauth with only a small number of mostly Hindu followers. The collapse of the government heightened communal tensions and Jugnauth feared for his safety amid reports of the formation of a workers' militia. Hindu leaders exploited communal fears about Berenger, while Berenger's supporters accused them of being in league with New Delhi.[10]

Plans for intervention: Operation Lal Dora

Indira Gandhi responded to the crisis by ordering the Indian Army and Navy to prepare an expeditionary force, to be called Operation *Lal Dora*, to stop a possible coup against Jugnauth.[11] Mauritius was well beyond the airlift capabilities of the Indian Air Force, and instead the Indian Navy was to land two battalions from the army's 54 Rapid Reaction Division in Port Louis, the capital of Mauritius. The navy planned to transport the troops from its naval base in Bombay with two days preparation, followed by around five days' sailing time. The navy then had no specialised amphibious lift capability, but the troops were to be transported on a makeshift fleet of warships that carried a handful of helicopters but would need to operate without any fixed wing air cover.[12] The 54 Division troops waited on the Bombay docks while the navy hurriedly loaded stores and equipment.

While the navy and army made their preparations in Bombay, senior military and intelligence officers met with Mrs Gandhi in the War Room in South Block in New Delhi. Present at the meeting was the National Security Advisor, R. N. Kao. The navy was represented by Admiral O. S. Dawson, chief of naval staff, and the army by Lieutenant General S. K. Sinha, then vice chief of army. It became apparent that the army and navy had quite different views about the operation, including over command of the Task Force. General Sinha told Mrs Gandhi that he did not have confidence in the planned operation.[13] Apart from the question of command, Sinha had major concerns about army's ability to conduct an amphibious operation of this nature and the possibility of US intervention. The army's previous experience with an amphibious landing had been disastrous. In December 1971, in Operation *Beaver,* a force of Gurkhas was landed near Cox's Bazaar in Bangladesh to stop retreating Pakistani troops from escaping into Burma. The operation turned into a fiasco when the landing force could not find the correct beach and several Gurkhas drowned when they were ordered to disembark with full equipment into deep water. Sinha, a Gurkha himself, was deeply aware of the army's lack of amphibious experience.

Sinha, perhaps driven by fears of US intervention in the planned operation, also appears to have taken the initiative of consulting with the US about its views on the Mauritian crisis. According to B. Raman, a former head of the counterterrorism division of RAW, the Indian intelligence services became aware that Sinha had leaked Jugnauth's request for assistance and the details of the War Room meeting to the US Embassy.[14] Several months later, in May 1983, against longstanding army tradition, Mrs Gandhi controversially ordered that Sinha be passed over in his expected promotion to army chief and he took early retirement. Many later believed that Sinha was passed over because of his opposition to Indira Gandhi's plans for the Indian Army to conduct an assault on Sikh militants sheltering in the Golden Temple in Amritsar.[15] But, according to Raman, Sinha was passed over because of his leaks about the Mauritius crisis.

With the military commanders unable to agree on execution of the operation, Operation *Lal Dora* was put on hold. The most obvious reason was the army's distinct lack of enthusiasm for the operation, but Gandhi may have merely intended Indian preparations for the operation to be a signal of India's determination to support Jugnauth. The Indian Mission in Port Louis subsequently spread the word that the Indian Navy was 'surrounding Mauritius'.[16] At the suggestion of Kao, Mrs Gandhi sent N. F. Suntook, then head of RAW, to Port Louis to deal with the crisis at a political level.[17] Suntook had been due to retire from RAW at the end of the month and was requested to delay his retirement by a couple of weeks. Suntook's mission to Mauritius was never publicly disclosed, and indeed his abrupt disappearance a few days prior to his scheduled retirement party provoked some bizarre accusations in the Indian media that he had defected to Washington.[18]

In Port Louis, Suntook was assisted by Prem Singh, the Indian high commissioner. Since his appointment in 1982, Singh had already become well known for his highly partisan support for Jugnauth against Berenger.[19] He was later accused of having played a virtual pro-consul role in Mauritian politics, which led to his recall in 1986. Suntook and Singh worked with Harish Boodhoo and other Hindu and Muslim leaders to persuade them to swing their support behind Jugnauth, apparently providing some leaders with financial incentives to help in their decisions.[20] The efforts of Jugnauth and his Indian backers to build a new Hindu coalition were successful. Jugnauth formed a new Hindu-based political party which gained the numbers to form a new government in parliament. Several months later, Jugnauth, again likely with financial assistance from New Delhi, convincingly won elections against Berenger. Jugnauth's re-election in 1983 effectively ended any question of the political supremacy of the Hindu community or any question of India's special role in Mauritius. Jugnauth immediately appointed Major General J. N. Tamini, an Indian Army officer on secondment to RAW, as the Mauritian national security advisor, a post that he then occupied for more than a decade. Since then it has been accepted that the post will be filled by an Indian appointee, usually a RAW officer.[21]

But India was not the only actor in this drama, and there is reason to believe that Jugnauth may have owed some other debts. Despite its close links with India, the new government under Jugnauth also took a distinctly pro-Western turn in its foreign policy. Gaetan Duval, a well-known conservative, was appointed as the new deputy prime minister. Duval took charge of foreign policy, stating that Mauritius considered itself 'a staunch ally of the West'.[22] Jugnauth moved to break Mauritius' links with the Soviet Union and Libya, refusing to receive the Soviet ambassador, Nicolai Pankov, who was thereupon recalled to Moscow, and he also expelled the entire Libyan diplomatic mission for their activities with local Muslims. Jugnauth also backpedalled on his opposition to Diego Garcia and lifted an embargo on the supply of labour to the US base.[23] Relations between Mauritius and South Africa also improved—Duval was known to be particularly close to South Africa and was a frequent visitor there. Jugnauth stated that Mauritius would be 'realistic' in its relations with Pretoria and South Africa was allowed to open a trade office.[24] Mauritius' economic ties with South Africa were a cause of continuing disagreement with India, which came to a head during Rajiv Gandhi's visit to Port Louis in July 1986 when Jugnauth refused demands that Mauritius join in a mandatory trade boycott of South Africa.

Since the events of 1983 India has continued to support the Hindu-majority political parties, ensuring that power has alternated between Anerood Jugnauth and Navin Ramgoolam (the son of Seewoosagur Ramgoolam). Berenger has assumed power only for a brief period during that time, in spite of Indian objections.[25] Berenger's sensitivity towards India has caused him to describe bilateral relationship as 'umbilical and sacred'[26] while Jugnauth describes the connection in terms of 'blood relations'.[27]

The contemporary India–Mauritius security relationship

India now has a comprehensive role in the security of Mauritius. New Delhi supplies a RAW officer to act as national security advisor to the Mauritian prime minister, an arrangement that seems to elicit little comment in Port Louis. India also supplies the commander of the Mauritian Coast Guard and equips and trains the Coast Guard and Police Helicopter Squadron.[28] Since 2003 the Indian Navy has also provided maritime security through periodic patrols of the Mauritius EEZ; since 2009 this includes hydrographic surveys and anti-piracy patrols.[29] India has also installed a radar coastal surveillance system throughout the Mauritian island chain, including five stations on the islands of Mauritius, and one each on Rodrigues, Saint Brandon and the Agalega islands.[30]

Their economic relationship is almost as close as the security relationship. India is Mauritius' major trading partner and the level of bilateral trade between them doubled between 2010 and 2011. A Preferential Trade Agreement has been under negotiation which, if finalised, could give Mauritius' struggling textiles industry access to the huge Indian market. Mauritius is also the primary gateway for international investment into India, largely due to a highly favourable double tax treaty put in place in 1982 by Indira Gandhi. In the decade to January 2010, Mauritius was the source of 43 per cent of global foreign direct investment in India, largely reflecting the so-called 'Mauritian route' used by US, European and other offshore investors for making tax-free investments into India. On the back of the tax treaty, Mauritius has developed an extremely profitable offshore financial services industry which is now an important source of income and employment to the country.

Mauritius has also long been a haven for Indian money, not all of it legitimately acquired. In recent years, the Indian Finance Ministry has become concerned about the extent to which the tax treaty is used for money laundering by wealthy Indians who 'round trip' money through Mauritius to avoid paying tax in India or disclosing the source of their income. In 2012, New Delhi adopted new anti-tax avoidance rules and began pressuring Port Louis to make changes to the tax treaty, including giving Indian tax authorities access to account information. The tax treaty has now become a point of contention in the relationship. The Mauritian government is concerned that changes to the treaty could do major damage to Mauritius' role as an offshore banking centre for India. It could also significantly reduce the competitive advantage of Mauritius as an investment conduit as compared with its major commercial rival, Singapore. Despite the special relationship, many in the Indian security community remain highly suspicious of any Chinese economic interests in Mauritius. There was some alarm in 2009 at the announcement of a Chinese-financed special economic zone and the expansion of Mauritius' airport, which was intended to be part of a Chinese policy of using Mauritius as a platform to service Southern Africa.

Another issue that has been the subject of discussion between New Delhi and Port Louis over the last few years has been proposals by India to use the remote Agalega Islands, which are located around 1,000 km north of the main island of Mauritius. Since 2006 there have been reports of discussions between the Mauritian and Indian governments over the long-term lease of the islands to the Indian government, ostensibly for tourism.[31] It has been speculated that India intends to upgrade an airstrip on North Agalega to service Indian manned and unmanned surveillance aircraft.[32] This would significantly improve India's air surveillance capabilities throughout the western Indian Ocean, including the Mozambique Channel.

While the Mauritian government may not have any great objection in principle to Indian use of the airstrip on North Agalega—particularly to conduct anti-piracy operations—there are concerns about where it might lead.[33] Any Indian military presence on the Agalegas would also bring back uncomfortable memories for Mauritians of the US occupation of Diego Garcia—and particularly for Mauritian prime minister, Navin Ramgoolam, son of 'Old Man' Sir Seewoosagur Ramgoolam who agreed to the separation of the Chagos Islands from Mauritius in the 1960s. Mauritius' claim to sovereignty over the Chagos (and their huge EEZ) and the claims of the Chagos islanders has since become a patriotic touchstone. As a result, any deal with India over the Agalegas will likely ensure that the 300 Creoles who live in the Agalegas are seen to benefit from arrangement. Despite these sensitivities, a confidential US diplomatic report concluded that, 'The Mauritian public seems to accept that India can have its way as long as the islands remain Mauritian. This is indicative of Mauritius' willing subordination to India … ' The report concluded that the 'new bottom line is that if India wants something from Mauritius short of territory—they are likely to get it'.[34]

In July 2012, the Mauritian foreign minister, Arvin Boolell, reportedly offered India the use of the Agalega Islands in return for retention of the tax treaty, commenting that India could use the North and South Agalegas for tourism, marine studies or 'building a strategic presence in the Indian Ocean'. According to Boolell, there was 'no problem on the issue'.[35] Boolell later 'clarified' that there was not actually any connection between the Agalegas and the tax treaty.[36] Nevertheless, India has now agreed to fast-track finalisation of the trade agreement.[37] There are also expectations that India's Finance Ministry can be persuaded to back off from some of its tougher positions on the tax treaty. Deals on the tax treaty, the trade agreement, and perhaps on the Agalegas, will likely take time to play out. Any Indian use of North Agalega is also likely to occur only gradually, perhaps beginning with Indian investment in the airstrip and other infrastructure on the islands.

The Seychelles plays a balancing game

The Seychelles is also important to India's southwest Indian Ocean strategy, but its relationship with India is quite different to that of Mauritius. The tiny island state, with a population of just 86,000, achieved independence from Britain in 1976, and since that time has been courted by many powers wanting to use it for military purposes. Its location between Madagascar and the Persian Gulf, about 1,600 km east of Kenya, makes it an excellent base from which to project power throughout the entire western Indian Ocean. The Seychelles is well aware of its strategic importance—as its president told a US military official, it is 'an aircraft carrier in the middle of the Indian Ocean without the planes'.[38]

The Seychelles has for decades successfully balanced the interests of many powers, including the United States, the Soviet Union, France, South Africa, Tanzania, North Korea and now China. During the Cold War, the Seychelles was led by President Albert René, a dictator who had a fondness for Marxist rhetoric but who also tried to maintain a broadly non-aligned stance. Through the 1980s, Victoria, the Seychelles capital, became a magnet for international intrigue and organised crime, a sort of Casablanca of the Indian Ocean, where drug runners, spies and plotters rubbed shoulders in hotel bars. The United States maintained a small intelligence and satellite tracking station near the capital, while Soviet 'fishing boats' used the port as a centre for their regional activities. President René's close advisors included various international 'businessmen' of dubious reputation, some of whom had close links with Pretoria (although the Seychelles was officially hostile towards the apartheid regime). René also relied on both India and France as benign protectors who could help it resist the pressures from the Superpowers and protect his rule.

During this period, René became the target of numerous plots planned by Seychellois exiles, disgruntled elements in his regime, criminals and assorted anti-communists in Pretoria, London, Washington and even Sydney.[39] This included a famous coup attempt in 1981 by a group of white mercenaries led by Colonel 'Mad' Mike Hoare at the behest of South African security services. The plot was uncovered when the mercenaries, disguised as a drinking club called the Ancient Order of Frothblowers, flew in to Victoria airport with bags full of weapons. When their arms cache was discovered by an alert customs officer, a gunfight ensued and most of the mercenaries fled to Johannesburg aboard a hijacked Air India plane which had made the mistake of landing at the airport during the excitement.[40]

Beset by the plots of both friends and foes, in 1982, President René sought a commitment from Indira Gandhi to intervene to protect him. According to René, India was 'the awkward grandfather of the region. India would like to play a big role, but it has a complex, that people will say they're being imperialistic. ... India should say 'we're not going to let that nonsense go on'.[41] Although Gandhi declined to give a public commitment, in the following years India assumed a protective security role in Seychelles, providing helicopters, training and technicians to the tiny Seychelles air force and paying frequent visits to Port Victoria with warships.

India's role as a benign security guarantor to the Seychelles was crystallised in 1986 over a series of coup attempts against René led by his minister of defence, Ogilvy Berlouis. The Berlouis plot, codenamed Operation *Distant Lash*, involved up to 30 mercenaries and 350 Seychellois. Despite claims that Washington was behind the plot, the Reagan administration was in fact ambivalent about any moves against René, fearing that the Seychelles could be destabilised by the installation of a new leader. It seems more likely that South African intelligence had a hand in it.[42] When Berlouis was about to move against René in June 1986, Rajiv Gandhi personally ordered the Indian Navy to help. Coincidentally, an Indian destroyer, the INS *Vindhyagiri,* was already en route to Port Victoria on a scheduled visit and it was instructed to report an engineering defect on arrival that would require an extended stay. An Indian naval officer was sent to the Seychelles on a commercial airline to ostensibly take charge of repairing the ship, and an 'engineering team' of 20 sailors was readied for dispatch on another flight. In the meantime, René removed himself to the presidential palace under the protection of his 50-strong North Korean bodyguard. The INS *Vindhyagiri* stayed at Port Victoria for almost two weeks, making use of its Sea King helicopter to provide public displays of commando assaults, while training its 4.5-inch gun on the city. Also present in Port Victoria was a Soviet patrol boat, the *Zoroaster,* whose commander was junior to the *Vinghyagiri*'s captain. At one stage the *Zoroaster* was dispatched on patrol in response to a false report that two Royal Naval vessels were en route in support of the Berlouis coup. By mid-June the planned coup had been averted. An Indian intelligence officer in Port Victoria at the time commented that the Indian naval presence 'served the purpose'.[43]

India helped to quash another attempt to unseat President René two months later. The plot was uncovered in late August 1986 while René was attending a meeting of the Non-Aligned Movement in Harare with Rajiv Gandhi and other leaders of non-aligned states. Gandhi was tipped off about the plot by Moscow and lent René his own plane, *Air India 001,* to return to the Seychelles.[44] According to a credible report, on landing in the Seychelles, René, disguised as an Indian woman wearing a sari, was met at the airport by the Indian high commissioner and taken to safety at the commissioner's residence.[45] The key plotters, officers of the Seychelles army, were then arrested or forced into exile in London. An Indian frigate, INS *Godavari*, which was then returning to India from New York, was diverted to Port Victoria, although it arrived too late to see any action.

By the late 1980s, threats of coups against the Seychelles government had mostly receded and the India–Seychelles security relationship focused on training the Seychelles security forces.[46] India built the Seychelles Defence Academy in 1989 and has largely managed it since then. The Indian Navy has assisted with maritime security in the Seychelles EEZ under a 2003 defence cooperation agreement, and in 2005 gifted an offshore patrol vessel to the Seychelles, reportedly in a hurried effort to pre-empt offers of Chinese assistance.[47]

In 2010, India increased its security role, focusing on the assistance it could provide in combating piracy. India's renewed interest was likely prompted by the May 2010 visit of Seychelles president James Michel to Beijing, where the Chinese reportedly offered to supply an offshore patrol vessel. In June 2010 Prime Minister Singh announced that India would be writing off almost half of Seychelles' debt to India and in the following months Foreign Minister S. M. Krishna and Defence Minister A. K. Antony visited Victoria. Antony sought to better institutionalise previously *ad hoc* defence cooperation. India agreed to supply to Seychelles a second offshore patrol vessel as well as maritime surveillance aircraft (one Dornier and two helicopters). India also provides training to Seychelles Special Forces for VIP protection, commando operations and diving and has provided a maritime security advisor, a military advisor and naval advisor to the Seychelles president.[48] The Indian Navy conducts anti-piracy patrols and hydrographic surveys in Seychelles waters and India is also constructing a coastal surveillance radar system.[49]

But the Seychelles continues to play the field to get what it can. The United States maintains a considerable military presence there, including deployments of P3 Orion and Reaper UAV aircraft with support personnel, ostensibly used for anti-piracy purposes but also for counterterrorism operations in Somalia and elsewhere. In 2009, President Michel reportedly invited the US to establish its Africa Command in Victoria.[50] The United Arab Emirates has also gifted five patrol boats to the Seychelles as part of an anti-piracy assistance package. Michel has also not been backward in playing the China card, accepting Chinese offers of limited training to the small island nation's defense forces and a turboprop surveillance aircraft. Following a visit of the Chinese defence minister in December 2011, China was invited to use Port Victoria for the operational turn-around of PLAN vessels on anti-piracy patrols in the northwest Indian Ocean, which would add to PLAN's use of Karachi, Salalah and Djibouti for resupply. Michel later assured New Delhi that no military facilities would be given to China and that India would remain the Seychelles' 'main development partner.'[51] Despite the games that the Seychelles plays with other powers, India seems to have maintained a key strategic role in the islands.

France as a security partner in the southwest

India's role in the southwest Indian Ocean is buttressed by the growing security partnership with France, which is the strongest power in and around the Mozambique Channel. The Mozambique Channel is the key shipping route between the Middle East and the Atlantic Ocean, and is a focus for India's strategic ambitions in the southeast. India is also developing a close security relationship with Mozambique on the African side of the channel (which will be discussed in Chapter 5), and is seeking to develop a security role with Madagascar on the eastern side.[52] A cooperative relationship with France is an important way of extending India's security role in the Mozambique Channel and throughout the southwest. The French *department* of Reunion, about 200 km west of Mauritius, is the headquarters for the French South Indian Ocean armed forces, which includes two frigates and several patrol vessels and a detachment of the Foreign Legion at Mayotte inside the Mozambique Channel. France's security presence in the southwest is supported by its large base at Djibouti.[53] Far to the south, France also owns Antarctic territories, which include Kerguelen Island, the St Paul and Amsterdam islands and the Crozet Islands, and has a scientific base on Kerguelen Island with a small military presence.[54] France exercises considerable political influence throughout the southwest through its leading role in the Indian Ocean Commission, which acts as a conduit for significant development assistance from the European Union.

During the Cold War, India had special regard for France due to its semi-autonomous strategic posture within the western alliance, and this continues to be a factor in the relationship. According to one Indian analyst:

> French attitudes towards Indian Ocean politics were totally different from other powers. It has supported the idea of [the] peace zone proposal. In the post-colonial world, France consistently emphasized its role as an ocean power. Its strategy is based on its own perception of an independent 'Great Power'.[55]

Indeed, during the 1970s, the RAW and the French and Iranian security services attempted to establish a cooperative signals intelligence programme to monitor the entire western Indian Ocean region—probably for both US and Soviet traffic. But the relationship has not been entirely without irritations and during the 1980s there was a degree of friction over the politically restive Tamil community in Reunion, which represented around 25 per cent of the population. Concerned about growing Indian influence, France initially refused

India's requests to open a consulate in Reunion, although it allowed one to be opened in 1986. For a while there was also a degree of low-level competition between India and France for strategic influence in Mauritius, reflecting French cultural influence there and its physical proximity to Reunion. France was not invited to be a member of the Indian Ocean Region—Association for Regional Cooperation (IOR-ARC) upon its formation in 1997, despite its requests. Although Australia, South Africa and Singapore reportedly supported French membership, it was resisted by India, likely due to concerns about a potentially influential competitor to the organisation. After several unsuccessful attempts to gain membership, France has had to settle for the status of dialogue partner.

Despite these irritations, over the last decade or so there has been a convergence of Indian and French strategic perspectives on the Indian Ocean as part of a broader pattern of Indo–French defence cooperation in the Indian Ocean and globally. France is comfortable with an expanded Indian maritime security presence in the southwest, including India's growing role in policing the area against pirates. India has invited France to be a member of IONS— thereby recognising France as a 'legitimate' littoral state. Since 1993, India and France have held annual bilateral naval exercises which have grown in size and complexity, including Exercise *Varuna 2011* involving Indian and French carrier groups in the Arabian Sea. France now sees India as a key partner in providing logistical support for the deployment of the French fleet and naval aviation in peacetime and a potential partner in regional crisis prevention.[56] India clearly benefits from a cooperative partnership with France in extending its own influence in the southwest, and the relationship may be a model for its growing relationships with other middle powers in the Indian Ocean.

India's role in the southwest

While the southwest Indian Ocean is not the most strategically significant part of the Indian Ocean, it is important to India's broader regional role in that it is the area where India has the opportunity to build a leading role, if not a sphere of influence, in quiet cooperation with other powers. As will be discussed in later chapters, there are constraints on the development of India's role in other parts of the Indian Ocean that are less evident in the southwest.

India's three key security relationships in the area, with Mauritius, Seychelles and France, offer different models for security relationships in the Indian Ocean, ranging from 'willing subordination' in the case of Mauritius, to a sort of vague and benign guarantor relationship in the case of the tiny Seychelles and a cooperative security partnership with France, which currently has the strongest military presence in the region. These relationships are examples of the flexibility that India will need to demonstrate in the future as it extends its influence beyond South Asia throughout the Indian Ocean.

Notes

1 A. Srivathsan (2011) 'U.S. saw Indian "hidden agenda" in Mauritius', *The Hindu*, 2 April.

2 During the controversial Indian general elections of 1977, Indira Gandhi kept an AN-12 long-range aircraft on standby at Sarsawa Air Force Base ready to fly her to Mauritius in case her life was endangered. Dilip Bobb (1980) 'Blunting the edge', *India Today*, 1 September, p. 85.

3 *The Mauritius Times*, 23 June 1978, quoted in P.K.S. Namboodiri, J.P. Anand and Sreedhar (1982) Intervention in the Indian Ocean, Delhi: ABC Publishing, p. 260.

4 Both Libya and the Soviet Union were providing funding to the MMM party. Sir Anerood Jugnauth, interview with author, 12 May 2012. At the same time, the CIA provided support to Ramgoolam.

5 Selig Harrison and K. Subrahmanyam (1989) *Superpower Rivalry in the Indian Ocean: Indian and American perspectives*, New York: Oxford University Press, p. 263. The experience of the Fijian Indians has also had a direct political impact on Mauritius. Paul Berenger claims that he lost the 1987 general elections in Mauritius as a result of the 1987 coup in Fiji, which had heightened fears about the position of the Indian community in Port Louis. Author interview with Paul Berenger, May 2012.

6 Boodhoo met with Walters both in Mauritius and Washington, DC. Interview with author, May 2012.

7 According to Jugnauth advisor, Satteeanund Peerthum (2012) Author interview, May.

8 Ashok Kapur (1982) *The Indian Ocean: Regional and International Power Politics*, New York, Praeger, p. 210.

9 S. Peerthum (1998) 'L'ingérence néocolonialiste', in *L'Express*, 'Portrait d'une nation', 12 March, p. 56.

10 Malenn D. Oodiah (1989) *Mouvement Militant Mauricien: 20 ans d'histoire, 1969–1989*, Port-Louis: s.n., p. 146.

11 Lal Dora means 'red thread' in Hindi. It is commonly used in the Hindu *puja* ritual and other Hindu rituals and invokes the blessings of the Hindu gods. For a detailed discussion of Operation *Lal Dora*, see David Brewster and Ranjit Rai (2013) 'Operation Lal Dora: India's aborted military intervention in Mauritius', *Asian Security*, Vol. 9, No. 1, pp. 62–74.

12 India's sole aircraft carrier at that time, INS *Vikrant*, was then in the process of being refitted for new Sea Harrier aircraft and was not operational.

13 Lt General S.K. Sinha (2012) Interview, February.

14 B. Raman (2007) *The Kaoboys of R&AW: Down Memory Lane*, New Delhi: Lancer, p. 120. Although Raman does not name Sinha as the officer behind the leaks, there can be little doubt as to whom he is referring.

15 Shortly after these events, Mrs Gandhi requested Sinha to begin planning an assault on the Golden Temple, which was subsequently implemented in the highly controversial Operation *Bluestar* in 1984. However, Sinha strongly advised Mrs Gandhi against such a course of action, fearing (correctly) for its impact on army morale.

16 Prem Singh (2012) Interview, May.

17 Raman, *The Kaoboys of R&AW*, p. 119.

18 The Indian home minister, P.C. Sethi, was forced to deny these allegations in parliament. V. Balachandran (2010) 'The day media turned a patriot into a traitor', *Sunday Guardian*, 19 September.

19 According, to Kishan S. Rana, who was a later Indian high commissioner to Mauritius. Kishan S. Rana (2003) 'Island diplomacy', *Indian Express*, 7 June; and Kishan S. Rana (2006) *The 21st Century Ambassador: Plenipotentiary to Chief Executive*, New Delhi: Oxford University Press, p. 74.

20 Peerthum, 'L'ingérence néocolonialiste.'
21 The current Mauritian national security advisor is Shantam Mukherjee, appointed in December 2010. Vel Moonien (2010) 'Arrivée de Shantam Mukherjee, le nouveau conseiller du PM en matière de sécuritié', *L'Express*, 9 December.
22 C. Legum (ed.) (1985) *Africa contemporary record: annual survey and documents*, London: Collings, p. B221.
23 *Times of India*, 17 May 1983.
24 'Mauritius: a change in direction?' (1983) The South African Institute of International Affairs, Brief Report No. 53, December.
25 Rana, 'Island Diplomacy'. According to one source, the Indian government helped to engineer Berenger's electoral defeat in 2005 which ended his brief term as prime minister.
26 Amit Baruah (2003) 'India–Mauritius ties "umbilical and sacred"', *The Hindu*, 22 November.
27 'India–Mauritius ties more than diplomatic: Jugnauth' (2009) *The Hindu*, 3 December.
28 Ashwin Kanhye (2011) 'L'Inde offre $10 M pour la surveillance de notre ZEE', *Le Matinal*, 31 March.
29 Sudha Ramachandran (2007) 'India's quiet sea power', *Asia Times*, 2 August; 'Indian Ship to patrol Seychelles, Mauritius' (2009) *Deccan Chronicle*, 24 November.
30 'India to supply coastal security equipment to Mauritius' (2009) *Indo–Asian News Service*, 6 November; 'Indian Navy activates listening post, monitoring station in Madagascar, Indian Ocean' (2007) *India Defence*, 7 July. The Indian Space Research Organisation also operates a satellite tracking station.
31 Sidhartha (2006) 'India acquiring global footprint', *Times of India*, 25 November 2006; Sidhartha (2006) 'India eyes island in the sun', *Times of India*, 25 November 2006.
32 Steven J. Forsberg (2007) 'India stretches its sea legs', *United States Naval Institute Proceedings*, Vol. 133, No. 3, March, p. 38–42.
33 Author interview with senior Mauritian government minister, May 2012.
34 Srivathsan, 'US saw Indian "hidden agenda" in Mauritius'.
35 Sidartha (2012) 'Mauritius offers India two islands in effort to preserve tax treaty', *The Economic Times*, 6 July.
36 'Minister clarifies Mauritius island offer' (2012) *The Times of India*, 7 July.
37 'India, Mauritius to fast-track PTA' (2012) *The Hindu*, 6 July.
38 'Seychelles: General Ward, US Africa Command visit 19 August helps cement new, closer relationship', 8 September 2009. Online: www.cablegatesearch.net/cable.php?id=09PORTLOUIS271&q=india%20security%20seychelles (accessed 10 October 2013).
39 In 1986 an associate of the former Seychelles president Mancham recruited a Sydney organised crime figure, Peter Drummond, to put together a six or seven-man assault team to attack a prison in the Seychelles, free the political prisoners and take control of the main island. The coup was planned for October 1986, but in the meantime Drummond was arrested by Australian police on murder charges. Andrew Keenan (1988) 'Cut-price plan for islands coup', *Sydney Morning Herald*, 13 May.
40 For an entertaining account of the attempted coup, see Mike Hoare (1986) *The Seychelles Affair*, New York: Bantam.
41 Harrison and Subrahmanyam, *Superpower rivalry in the Indian Ocean*, p. 263.
42 David Hebditch and Ken Connor (2005) *How to Stage a Military Coup: From Planning to Execution*, London: Greenhill, p.155; and Stephen Ellis (1996) 'Africa and international corruption: the strange case of South Africa and Seychelles', *African Affairs*, pp. 165–96 at p. 189.
43 David Brewster and Ranjit Rai (2011) 'Flowers are blooming: the story of the India Navy's secret operation in the Seychelles', *The Naval Review*, Vol. 99, No. 1, pp. 58–62.

44 'Seychelles: The Game of Nations' (1987) *Africa Confidential*, Vol. 28, No. 22, 4 November. René may also have been told of the planned coup by the South African security services, which sought to cultivate all sides in Seychelles in order to cement its own influence.

45 Donald Taylor (2005) *Launching out into the Deep: the Anglican Church in the history of the Seychelles to 2000 AD*, Victoria: Board of Church Commissioners, p. 648, and additional information provided by the author.

46 Harrison and Subrahmanyam, *Superpower Rivalry in the Indian Ocean*, p. 263.

47 Ramachandran, 'India's quiet sea power'.

48 Media briefing by Ministry of External Affairs, 27 April 2012.

49 'Securing footprints' (2012) *Strategic Affairs*, May, p. 68.

50 'Seychelles: General Ward, US Africa Command visit 19 August helps cement new, closer relationship'.

51 Mohan, *Samudra Manthan*, p. 140.

52 Earlier reports (including by this author) that the Indian Navy had opened an electronic monitoring facility in northern Madagascar were inaccurate. While India has been in negotiations with Madagascar to establish such a facility, the Madagascan government has been under pressure from China not to proceed with such a move.

53 See generally, Christian Bouchard and William Crumplin (2012) 'The *Marine nationale* in the southwest and southern Indian Ocean', paper presented at Royal Australian Navy Sea Power Conference, Sydney, February.

54 In the 1980s, Paris reportedly considered transferring nuclear testing activities to Kerguelen from Mururoa in the Pacific. Keith Suter (1989) 'Kerguelen: A French mystery', *Newsletter of the Antarctic Society of Australia*, No. 16, March, pp. 5–10. France may also store 'military-related equipment' on the island. Bertil Lintner (2010) 'Australia's strategic little dots', *Asia Times*, 25 June.

55 Vidhan Pathak (2006) 'France and Francophone Western Indian Ocean Region— Implications for Indian Interests', *Journal of Indian Ocean Studies*, Vol. 14, No. 2, August, pp. 186–203 at p. 198.

56 Gilles Boquérat (2003) 'French interests in the Indian Ocean and the relevance of India', *Journal of Indian Ocean Studies*, Vol. 11, No. 2, August, pp. 234–46 at p. 243.

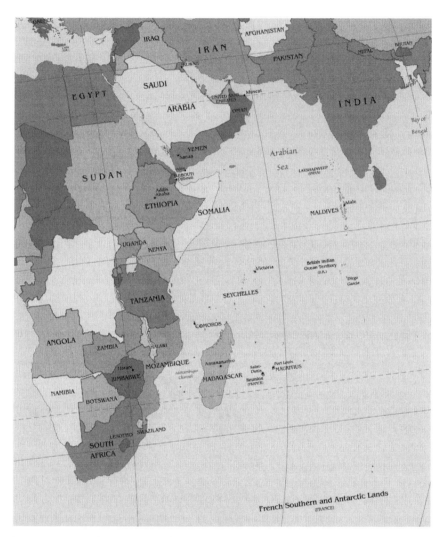

Map 5.1 East and Southern Africa
     Adapted from the University of Texas Libraries collection.

5 East and Southern Africa

As part of its growing role in the Indian Ocean region, India is also expanding its economic, political and strategic influence in continental Africa. India exerted considerable political influence there during the period of decolonisation, including in the fight against white regimes in Southern Africa. India's main security interests are now in East and Southern Africa, where it is expanding its economic influence and promoting its role as a maritime security provider in the western Indian Ocean. India considers South Africa to be its key strategic partner in sub-Saharan Africa. But while there are some strategic commonalities between India and South Africa, this has not always translated into common perspectives.

India's strategic ambitions in Africa

Africa forms the western 'wall' of the Indian Ocean and is a potentially important area for the expansion of India's strategic influence. Saul Cohen, the noted geostrategist, argued that in the post-colonial and post-apartheid era, the entire eastern half of the African continent might gravitate geostrategically to South Asia.[1] If that is occurring, it is occurring slowly and partially.

India's strategic interests in continental Africa are primarily economic—to develop dependable sources of energy and other resources and gain access to a huge market for Indian products. India also sees the expansion of its role in Africa as an important part of enhancing its global status, including garnering support for India's claims for a permanent seat in the UN Security Council. For decades India has made a large commitment to UN peacekeeping operations in Africa as a way of promoting its international status and showing its commitment to the United Nations. Its direct security interests in continental Africa are now relatively limited, with Islamic terrorism being a key concern.

India's principal strategic focus in Africa is in the east and south of the continent, as part of its broader ambitions in the Indian Ocean region. India's key security objectives in this respect include fostering a partnership with South Africa, developing India's role as a maritime security provider in East Africa, and precluding the development of a Chinese security presence in the region. India's interest in East and Southern Africa also reflects its historical links with former British colonies and the large resident Indian communities that date from colonial times. India has given particular focus to South Africa as its key strategic partner in Africa and a potentially important security partner in the Indian Ocean. South Africa has the largest economy and most capable military in sub-Saharan Africa and its location makes it the gateway between the Indian and Atlantic oceans. While many in New Delhi still see South Africa as a 'natural' strategic partner, the relationship has been slow to develop and South Africa's strategic perspectives often diverge from those of India.

India's strategic role in the newly independent Africa

In the decades after its independence India had a high political profile in Africa. In many ways Africa represented a natural constituency for the newly independent country seeking to extend its international influence. During the years of decolonisation, India exerted considerable political and ideological influence in Africa as a role model and a leader of the Non-Aligned Movement. India's early victory in gaining independence from Britain made it a natural ideological ally for African nationalists fighting for independence. Mahatma Gandhi was said to have inspired a whole generation of African leaders in their own independence campaigns and some of them to use nonviolent means. For India, the newly independent states of Africa also represented a large pool of potential supporters for its non-aligned policies and its desire to be seen as an international leader. But while India's anti-colonial stance gave it considerable status in Africa, Nehruvian also limited India's role. As Mohan commented, India viewed:

> Africa through the lone prism of Third World solidarity and non-alignment. Africa was not seen as a neighbour, but as a rhetorical item on India's exalted global agenda. Africans became fellow travelers in the struggle against imperialism, neocolonialism and racial discrimination.[2]

India's ability to develop a broader strategic role in Africa during the twentieth century was subject to several constraints. As in other parts of the Indian Ocean region, India's influence was limited by financial weakness and inward-looking economic policies. Its commitment to decolonisation through nonviolent means made it relatively reluctant to provide military assistance to national liberation movements, unlike competitors such as China, Pakistan and the Soviet Union. Another major constraint on India's role in East Africa, and one that still partly exists today, was the large Indian ethnic population that was often deeply resented by black African nationalists. These communities grew from migrant workers imported by imperial Britain, and formed a merchant or middle class sitting between the white colonists and the black Africans. Although Nehru distanced himself from Indian ethnic groups, advising them to identify with their adopted countries and not seek any economic privileges, the treatment of these communities was still a continuing source of irritation in India's relations in the region. Following independence, Kenya, Tanganyika (now Tanzania) and Uganda both placed considerable economic and political restrictions on the local Indian communities. The problem was most acute in Uganda, where the eccentric and bloody dictator, Idi Amin, summarily deported some 60,000–70,000 South Asians in 1972. India adopted a relatively soft line regarding Amin's actions, partly because there was little it could do, and New Delhi largely treated the Indian exiles as Britain's problem. While protesting Britain's decision to restrict entry to many Indian Ugandans, India also enacted emergency regulations to prevent the inflow into India of deportees holding British passports. Paradoxically, India's relationship with Uganda improved considerably after the Indian community was expelled, and as will be discussed later, India began providing military assistance to Amin within a few years.

The Indian communities elsewhere in East Africa also suffered considerable official discrimination. New Delhi was particularly concerned about 200,000 Indians in Kenya who were subjected to so-called 'Kenyanisation' policies that included institutional discrimination and deportation. Any attempts by New Delhi to mitigate these policies generated considerable hostility in Nairobi. In 1968, President Kenyatta refused to even meet with the visiting Indian minister of state for external affairs, B. R. Bhagat, who had been sent to Nairobi with a personal message from Indira Gandhi.[3] In 1972 Kenyatta informed Indira Gandhi that he would 'kick every Indian out of Kenya' unless she supported his bid to have a UN agency located in Nairobi.[4] As a result of these discriminatory policies, around half of the Indian community left Kenya, leading to a somewhat cool relationship between India and Kenya that continued for many years. The issue was different in South Africa, where official discrimination by the white regime inspired India to provide considerable political and moral support to those fighting against apartheid. But this also left some suspicions about India's motivations among some black South Africans.

While India was at the forefront of political campaigns against colonialism, its ideological emphasis on achieving national liberation through non-violent means made it reluctant to provide military support for nationalist liberation groups, especially in British colonies. The steady withdrawal of Britain from the continent, especially after Harold Macmillan's 'Wind of Change' speech in 1960, appeared to make British decolonisation inevitable and achievable with a minimum of violence. India's opposition to the more radical groups within the Non-Aligned Movement during the 1960s contrasted with China's radical anti-imperialist line and Beijing's willingness to give material support to liberation movements that gave it considerable influence among many African leaders. Countering the influence of China, and to a lesser extent Pakistan, became a major aim of India's Africa policy.[5]

India's security involvement in Africa during the decolonisation period mainly involved the provision of limited military assistance to several newly independent states in East and Southern Africa. This was mostly in the form of training or help in the establishment of local military academies. RAW also helped to establish intelligence and security services in several African states, including Uganda, Mozambique, Zimbabwe, Zambia, Malawi and Botswana, often using retired RAW officers.[6] One little-known relationship involved the provision of military support to Idi Amin's regime in Uganda, even after Amin's despotic rule and territorial ambitions over neighbouring states had become evident. India had a close relationship with Uganda from its independence in the 1960s and although the relationship understandably soured after Amin expelled much of the country's Asian community, India resumed civilian and military support a few years later. After Israeli commandos destroyed most of the Ugandan Air Force on the ground during the 1976 Entebbe raid, Amin was on the hunt for a new air force. In October 1977, following a personal request from Amin, Indian prime minister Morarji Desai agreed to provide the Ugandan Air Force with spares (and, perhaps, pilot training) for their new MiG-21 aircraft being supplied by the Soviet Union. Desai also agreed to supply the Ugandan Army with light weapons, ammunition and TATA trucks in return for cotton and other commodities.[7] Ironically, technical personnel supplied by the Indian government filled many posts that had been vacated by the deported South Asians.[8]

India's military support for Amin was extraordinary not only because of his treatment of South Asians only a few years before but also because of the reason for Amin's arms purchases. In a microcosm of Cold War rivalries, Amin (who was principally backed by the Soviet Union) was at that time threatening to invade and annex large portions of Kenya (which received considerable US military assistance) and Tanzania (which was backed by China). The following year, the Ugandan Army actually invaded Tanzania, which responded by overthrowing Amin a few months later. Desai's reasons for providing military support to Amin are difficult to discern. It may have been a matter of Cold War alignments, but Amin's close ties with the Indian industrial conglomerate, TATA, may have also been a factor.[9] Indian military support to Uganda continued after Milton Obote took power from Amin in 1979.

From the late 1960s, India also provided limited training to nationalist insurgents, initially focusing on the Portuguese colonies and later on the white regimes in Southern Africa. India generally avoided providing assistance to national liberation movements in British colonies, reflecting either a wish to avoid conflict with Britain or a judgment that it would relinquish its colonies in a peaceful manner. But Portugal, which had earned New Delhi's ire over its refusal to give up its Indian colony at Goa, showed every intention of hanging on to its African possessions. India provided limited material support and training to small numbers of insurgents in Portuguese Angola, the Frente Nacional de Libertação de Angola (FNLA) and later the Movimento Popular de Libertação de Angola (MPLA); in Mozambique, the Frente de Libertação de Moçambique (FRELIMO); and in Guinea Bissau, the Partido Africano da Independência da Guiné e Cabo Verde (PAIGC). But, in general, India preferred to distance itself from the insurgent groups, providing financial aid through UN-administered funds, the OAU Liberation Committee, the

Non-Aligned Solidarity Fund for the liberation of Namibia, and later the AFRICA Fund. India's choice of partners among rival national liberation movements was often influenced by Soviet alignments and/or rivalry with China or Pakistan. These (often arbitrary) decisions about which insurgent groups would be given support and those that would not continue to affect some of India's relationships in the region.

India and the struggle against apartheid South Africa

As decolonisation proceeded during the 1960s and 1970s, India's security role in Africa became increasingly focused on the conflicts involving the remaining white-ruled states in Southern Africa. India took a leading role in mobilising international political opposition against Rhodesia and South Africa. But again, its role was limited by financial constraints and its unwillingness to become too closely involved in armed conflict.

The ideological opposition of India's elite to South Africa's apartheid system dates back to well before India's own independence. Mahatma Gandhi's experience in being thrown out of a train carriage in South Africa is believed to have sparked his commitment to anti-colonialism. India raised the issue of the unjust treatment of the Indian community under the apartheid regime before the UN General Assembly in its first meeting in October 1946 and a month later imposed a trade embargo against South Africa. India officially severed diplomatic ties in 1954, at the request of South Africa.

While there is a considerable degree of truth in the accepted narrative of India's unyielding moral support for decolonisation and opposition to the White South African regime, India's strategic calculations were sometimes more complex. Concern about the international status of India and Indians was a significant factor in India's early opposition to apartheid. Prior to India's independence, Mahatma Gandhi and other Indian South Africans had campaigned against the application of apartheid rules to the Indian community on the basis that it was unfair to lump Indians with the 'Kaffirs', and some in the African National Congress (ANC) long believed that India was primarily concerned with discrimination against the Indian community. During the 1950s and 1960s, at least, there were differing views within the Indian government over the South African 'problem'.[10] India's permanent representative to the UN, Sir Benegal Narsing Rau, saw discrimination against the South African Indian community as less of a human rights issue and more of a problem for India's international image and suggested that the acceptance by South Africa of a few high-caste Indians as equals could redress the problem. Similarly, in 1960 an Indian ambassador was reported as commenting that the issue was 'all about show'.[11]

While New Delhi imposed a formal trade embargo on South Africa from 1946, it also tolerated covert trade when its national interests so required. Continuing commercial trade included the supply of South African diamonds to Bombay's large diamond-cutting industry through London and the export of Indian spice to South Africa through Maputo.[12] India purchased South African arms where necessary, including artillery pieces during and after the 1971 Bangladesh war. In 1978, South Africa also acquired around a hundred Indian Army Centurion tanks through the secondary market.[13] During the 1980s, South Africa supplied an Indian defence manufacturer with materials to manufacture 20 million detonators per year.[14] According to Hussein Solomon, a South African strategic analyst, several other forms of military technology sold to India were kept classified by both parties.[15] Sanctions-avoiding trade was often facilitated through traders in Mauritius or Singapore.

New Delhi also sought to limit South Africa's capabilities as a potential regional competitor in the Indian Ocean. India's opposition to South Africa's 1955 Simons Town security agreement with Britain and British arms sales to South Africa was not only a reflection of India's policy of isolating the White regime but also driven by concerns that South African military strength might pose a challenge to India's own position in the Indian Ocean.[16] Overall, India's opposition to the White regimes in Southern Africa was seen as an opportunity to take a leading international role on an issue which had the moral support of much of the international community.

From the early 1970s India took an active role in assisting insurgent groups and the so-called 'Frontline' Black African states that opposed the White regimes in South Africa, Southwest Africa and Rhodesia. In March 1970, India announced that it would give African states any assistance required, including military support, to liberate Rhodesia from White rule, but in practice little support was forthcoming. In 1978, Indian foreign minister A. B. Vajpayee publicly invited requests for arms by liberation movements in Southern Africa.[17] India provided aid, including military training and arms, to the ANC in South Africa, the South West African People's Organisation (SWAPO) in Southwest Africa/Namibia and the Zimbabwe African People's Union (ZAPU) in Rhodesia/Zimbabwe and funded the establishment of representative offices in New Delhi for the ANC (in 1967) and SWAPO (in 1981).[18]

From the late 1970s, the Desai government also provided military assistance to the 'Frontline States' through the deployment of army and air force training teams to Zambia and Botswana.[19] The Zambian armed forces were then fending off attacks from White Rhodesian forces against Black Zimbabwean insurgent bases on Zambian territory, and Botswana was establishing armed forces in a belated attempt to respond to military incursions by South Africa. It is likely that Indian Army teams also trained ZAPU insurgents based in Zambia and Botswana. RAW was also active in these countries, including training ANC and SWAPO cadres in Zambia and India.[20] India's assistance to liberation movements in Southern Africa in the early 1980s was coordinated by one of India's most senior diplomats, V. Natwar Singh, who was high commissioner to Zambia (1980–2), and who later became India's foreign minister. India's relationship with Robert Mugabe in Zimbabwe was not so warm. India had backed Joshua Nkomo's Soviet-aligned Zimbabwe African People's Union (ZAPU) while China and Pakistan backed Mugabe's Zimbabwe

African National Union—Patriotic Front (ZANU PF), which took power in Rhodesia/Zimbabwe in 1980. Zimbabwe continues to have a close security relationship with China, often to the exclusion of India.

By the early 1980s India found that it needed to take a more active role in order to maintain credibility with their African counterparts. Rajiv Gandhi took the lead in negotiating a compromise between the African states and Britain in the CHOGM summit in October 1985, in which South Africa was given six months to start dismantling apartheid before the imposition of economic measures against it. Gandhi also sought to take a lead in negotiating international aid to the Frontline States, sponsoring the establishment of the AFRICA Fund to strengthen the economic and technical capabilities of the Frontline States. India contributed some $40 million to the fund and assisted in raising an aggregate of $476 million by 1989.

The Frontline States also tried to draw India into the Mozambique civil war. During the 1980s, South Africa conducted a successful campaign to destabilise Mozambique through support for the Resistência Nacional Moçambicana insurgents (known as RENAMO or MNR). By 1985, the MNR controlled up to 80 per cent of Mozambique territory, including the strategic Beira road, rail and pipeline corridor, the key supply route between the Mozambique port of Beira and landlocked Zimbabwe. In September 1986, the Frontline States asked India to provide technical assistance and security forces to protect the Beira Corridor, a suggestion that Indian officials 'treated with circumspection'.[21] Zimbabwe President Robert Mugabe asked for the deployment of a squadron of Indian Air Force Mig-21 aircraft with Indian pilots to provide air cover for the corridor: half the aircraft were to be based in Harare and half in Chimoio, Mozambique. Mugabe suggested that this would initially be facilitated by Indian Air Force personnel already deployed in Botswana. According to one report, Rajiv Gandhi was sympathetic to the idea, particularly as it would involve India supplanting Pakistan as a military partner to Zimbabwe.[22] But Gandhi evidently decided that deployment of the Indian Air Force to Mozambique was too much of a reversal of India's public stance against the overseas deployment of Indian forces or carried too much risk of India being sucked into a Southern African quagmire. The following year, India also reportedly refused to sell MiG-21 aircraft to Zimbabwe, probably for similar reasons.[23]

It appears that New Delhi may have decided instead to secretly provide assistance to Mozambique through providing what has been called 'a small naval presence' in Mozambique waters.[24] The MNR was being supplied in northern Mozambique from the Comoros Islands, with supplies coming from South Africa, Saudi Arabia and Oman, and in southern Mozambique by South African naval units. There were no significant encounters with Indian and South African forces in the Mozambique Channel during this time. In September 1986, South African Strike Craft relying on signals intelligence tracked down the Indian destroyer, INS *Godavari,* to Kosi Bay, just south of the Mozambican border, whereupon they exchanged naval courtesies and went their separate ways.[25] By June 1987 India had become embroiled in the Sri Lankan civil war and soon after South Africa ceased its support for the MNR, which led to the end of the insurgency.

India's contemporary strategic role in East Africa

Over the last decade or so, New Delhi has tried to move past the limitations of the decolonisation era to broaden its strategic role, particularly in East Africa. This reflects India's historical links with the region, as well as a wish to enhance its role in the Indian Ocean. The acceptance by East African states of an Indian naval presence in their waters would be an important legitimisation of India's regional role.

India's has had strong economic links with East Africa since the colonial era, partly as a product of the large Indian merchant communities. Today it is the second largest exporter to Kenya (after China) and the largest to Tanzania. But while local Indian communities present an economic opportunity, their presence still has the potential to strain political relationships. The Indian communities in Kenya (over 100,000, including 15,000 Indian citizens), Tanzania (90,000), Uganda (12,000), Mozambique (20,000) and Zimbabwe (15,000), though much reduced from colonial times, still wield economic influence far out of proportion to their numbers.[26] While India has historically distanced itself from these communities, Indian domestic political imperatives may increasingly force New Delhi to become involved. In January 2008, a wave of political violence targeted Gujarati merchants in the western Kenyan city of Kisumu and led to the destruction of some 90 per cent of Indian-owned properties and the flight of thousands of ethnic Indians. Following demands by Narendra Modi, then chief minister of Gujarat State, the Indian Navy was 'quietly deployed' for a possible evacuation of Indian citizens. The Indian government did not proceed with an evacuation after deciding that Indians were not in immediate danger and that their evacuation could render them more vulnerable and strain bilateral relations.[27] However, incidents such as this may become more frequent in future years as Indians become more vocal and have increased expectations regarding New Delhi's responsibility to protect persons of Indian origin. The local Indian communities may therefore continue to constrain India's relations in East Africa in the event of political instability.

Over the last decade, New Delhi has been trying to raise its security profile in East Africa as part of an expanded role in the Indian Ocean. India has cooperation agreements and training programmes through which it provides limited defence aid to Kenya and Tanzania, but it has not so far had much success in positioning itself as a maritime security provider in their waters. India has long had a cordial relationship with Tanzania. But Kenya, the most powerful state in East Africa, has historically been aligned with the United States and its relations with India have sometimes been cooler.

In recent years, India has been successful in positioning itself as a maritime security provider to Mozambique to help police the Mozambique Channel against maritime terrorism and piracy. This presents an opportunity for India to prove its credentials as a benign maritime security provider in East Africa and to build a regular naval presence in the Mozambique Channel. At the invitation of the Mozambique government, the Indian Navy deployed off Maputo to help provide maritime security for the African Union summit in 2003 and again in 2004 when Maputo hosted the World Economic Forum. Over the last few years, the tempo of the relationship has increased considerably with numerous visits at Prime Ministerial or senior Minister level. In 2010 Indian prime minister Manmohan Singh identified defence and security cooperation as one of the 'four pillars' to a partnership between India and Mozambique.[28] There are now several security agreements in place, including a 2006 defence cooperation agreement and a 2011 MOU that deals with maritime patrols along the Mozambican coast, training, supply of defence equipment and services (the Mozambique Air Force uses Russian equipment) and the rehabilitation of military infrastructure.[29] A 2012 security agreement provides for antipiracy patrols by the Indian Navy in the Mozambique Channel, including Mozambique waters. This followed a January 2012 MOU among South Africa, Mozambique and Tanzania, pursuant to which the South African Navy patrols Mozambique and Tanzanian waters.

India's relations with post-apartheid South Africa

India has long regarded South Africa as a potential key security partner in sub-Saharan Africa, a view which contributed to its fight to see the installation of a Black majority government. In the 1940s, K. M. Panikkar identified South Africa, along with Australia and Britain, as the putative members of a new Indian Ocean security council to be headed by an independent India. While visions of cooperation were submerged by India's opposition to apartheid, they resurfaced with the end of the White regime. With the demise of the apartheid regime in 1994, many believed that the door would be opened to a new era of strategic partnership between these two regional powers. India's relationship with South Africa is potentially quite different to India's relationships elsewhere in Africa—although far smaller in population than India, South Africa is effectively a regional hegemon in sub-Saharan Africa. A partnership with South Africa could provide several benefits: *first*, helping expand India's economic and strategic influence in continental Africa, *second*, as a useful 'South-South' political partner on global issues, and *third*, supporting India's leadership role in the Indian Ocean. But while there are some strategic similarities between India and South Africa, it should not be assumed that this necessarily translates into common strategic interests.

India invested heavily in its relationship with the ANC during the Apartheid era and in the early post-apartheid years the Black-majority government of South Africa also prioritised closer relations with India. A 'strategic partnership' (India's first ever) was announced during President Mandela's visit to New Delhi in April 1997, which was intended to signal the development of broad institutional links to influence global decision-making on trade, investment and security issues. But the relationship has not prospered as hoped. Although there are some commonalities in strategic perspectives, the partnership has produced few concrete results. The economic relationship remains comparatively weak, political cooperation is patchy and the prospects for sustained security cooperation are limited.

New Delhi would like to see South Africa become India's principal economic partner in Africa. South Africa has the largest economy in Africa by some way and there are hopes that India could gain the benefit of South Africa's relationships in Southern Africa and further afield. But the economic relationship remains relatively weak and unbalanced. From a very low base during the apartheid era, bilateral trade reached $7 billion in 2011, with the trade balance in South Africa's favour. While trade is growing in absolute terms, South Africa's share of India's imports has fallen in recent years. A Preferential Trade Area (PTA) agreement that has been under negotiation since 2003 would provide India with improved trade access to South Africa and its Sourthern African partners. Unresolved issues include exports of pharmaceuticals to South Africa and restrictions on foreign investment in India. India blames South Africa for dragging its feet in negotiations on the deal, citing the 'low level of ambition' by Southern African states.[30] Indian officials have also expressed unhappiness at South Africa blocking a proposed merger of Indian and South African telecommunications companies, pointing to apparently laxer rules being applied to Chinese proposals.[31] India's experience stands in contrast to South Africa's economic relationship with China, which is now South Africa's largest trading partner, with bilateral trade worth $45 billion in 2011 (up 77 per cent on the previous year). China has also become a major investor in mining and financial services. Although there are considerable complementarities in the Indian and South African economies that could lead to greater economic engagement, they are also very much economic competitors in the remainder of Africa. In coming years there may be increased investment by Indian companies seeking to use South Africa as a bridgehead into the rest of Africa, but it seems unlikely that there will be a broader economic partnership in Africa.

It has also been assumed in New Delhi that commonalities in their strategic circumstances would lead to common political perspectives. South Africa is regarded in New Delhi as a potential key South–South political partner in the international system, helping to balance both the United States and China on international issues. But while there is considerable scope for cooperation on global issues, there are also important limitations.

The IBSA Dialogue Forum, which was established by India, Brazil and South Africa in 2003, reflects India's desire to bring South Africa into a South–South global partnership. The IBSA grouping is specifically intended to encapsulate the strategic commonalities between India, South Africa and Brazil—all of them developing economies, regional powers and democracies—which distinguish them from authoritarian China and Russia. The grouping is seen by its members as a potentially useful way to leverage their power in international fora, including helping them to secure positions and appointments in organisations such as the IMF and the UN, ostensibly as 'bridge-builders' between North and South. The IBSA dialogue has also included security on its agenda and has resulted in the biennial IBSAMAR naval exercises among India, South Africa and Brazil.

But while South Africa has been a relatively enthusiastic participant in IBSA as a way of extending its influence among larger states, it has been careful not to be confined to a relationship with India. Hopes in New Delhi that the IBSA grouping might reinforce a special relationship with Pretoria have been set back by the 2011 entry of South Africa into the competing BRICS (Brazil, Russia, India, China, South Africa) grouping. India reportedly opposed South African proposals to include China in the IBSA Dialogue.[32] After a concerted campaign by South Africa, including visits by South African President Zuma to all of the member countries, China then extended an invitation for South Africa to join the BRICS grouping—what has been called a 'strategically timed, diplomatic master stroke' by China in extending its influence in South Africa and Africa.[33] South Africa's participation in BRICS may represent something of a loss to New Delhi—it seems that Pretoria did not wish to be corralled into an Indian-sponsored grouping that did not include its major trading partner, China. The China-centric nature of BRICS has also overshadowed India's traditional role as an ideological leader of the global South and the strength of BRICS now has the potential to render IBSA irrelevant. India has declined China's suggestions that IBSA should be dissolved or at least hold joint summits with BRICS, opting to retain its own forum.[34] While Pretoria's desire to develop its relationship with China is primarily driven by economic factors, it also sees a relationship with China as an important counterweight to the power of the United States and Europe in the international system.[35] This makes South Africa an unlikely partner in attempts by India to constrain China's influence in the Indian Ocean region.

Nor have commonalities in their strategic circumstances necessarily led to shared perspectives in security issues. While New Delhi has developed a more mature relationship with the United States in recent years, South Africa's leadership tends to use anti-Western rhetoric that is sometimes reminiscent of another era. The still-close connection of South Africa's leadership to their freedom struggle is, for example, reflected in quite different views about terrorism. This is India's primary security concern on continental Africa, including concerns about the use of South Africa as a safe haven by Islamic terrorist groups. But Pretoria has been reluctant to cooperate in this area. This partly reflects the history of the ANC, which was itself labelled a 'terrorist group', and South Africa is consequently reluctant to fight what might be regarded as 'national liberation groups'. As a result, South Africa has refused India's requests to establish a joint working group on terrorism and has been hesitant to cooperate with others on terror-related issues.[36]

Nuclear issues have also been a considerable irritant.[37] South Africa, which gave up its own nuclear weapons in 1994 and joined the Nuclear

Non-Proliferation Treaty, was highly critical of India's nuclear tests in 1998.[38] Although South Africa supported India's special waiver from Nuclear Suppliers Group rules in 2008, South African diplomats were reportedly unhappy about the increasing nuclear cooperation between the United States and India, a non-NPT signatory, while Iran, an NPT signatory, is the subject of international condemnation for its nuclear programme. Despite rumours that South Africa may offer uranium to India, there has been no agreement, nor any attempt by South Africa to amend the legislation that would prohibit such an arrangement.[39]

The arms supply relationship has also not been smooth. While India hoped that South Africa would become a major customer for Indian arms, it has struggled to make significant sales, partly due to the relatively low level of foreign purchases by the South African armed forces. Although India emerged as a major customer of South Africa's large defence industry, in 2005, Denel, the South African state-owned defence company, became embroiled in a corruption scandal and has since been blacklisted from Indian defence tenders.

Potential for security cooperation in the Indian Ocean

New Delhi also hoped that South Africa would become an important partner in the Indian Ocean. Delhi has long recognised South Africa as a key Indian Ocean power and sees considerable value in military cooperation, particularly with the South African Navy, in legitimising an expanded regional role for India. There are active defence interactions between India and South Africa, including regular high-level military delegations, a Joint Committee on Defence Cooperation and several defence agreements.[40] The relationship between the Indian and South African navies is particularly cordial and from 2006 they have held annual staff talks separately from the other armed services. There have been several exchanges of ship visits and India has assisted with submarine training. Since 2008, India, South Africa and Brazil have participated in the biennial IBSA maritime (IBSAMAR) exercises off the Cape of Good Hope, which have included anti-air and anti-submarine warfare, visit-board-search-seizure operations and anti-piracy drills. At South Africa's request, the IBSAMAR exercises also include officers from other SADC states. India has also participated in other exercises with South Africa and other Southern African states, including Exercise *Blue Crane* in South Africa, involving forces from some 12 Southern and East African countries. India also maintains good defence relationships elsewhere in Southern Africa, maintaining army and/or air force training teams in Zambia, Botswana, Namibia and Lesotho.[41]

While there is a desire by both the Indian and South African navies for greater cooperation, in practice this will be constrained by the South Africa Navy's limited capabilities and South Africa's overwhelming strategic focus on continental Africa. During the early years of the Cold War, South Africa was seen by the United States and its allies as a key maritime security partner against the Soviet Union—effectively the maritime guardian of the gateway between the Indian and Atlantic oceans and with responsibility for security of SLOCs to the Middle East. But international sanctions degraded the South African Navy's capabilities and the wars and insurgencies in Southern Africa during the 1970s and 1980s inevitably focused the navy on coastal security and counterinsurgency operations. But apartheid South Africa still exercised significant influence of sorts in the southwest Indian Ocean, including sponsoring coups or attempted coups in the Seychelles and Comoros during the 1980s and maintaining considerable political influence in Mauritius.

The end of apartheid led to a fundamental shift in South Africa's strategic perspectives towards building cooperative economic and security relationships with its continental neighbours. Southern Africa and Africa as a whole is South Africa's highest strategic priority. South Africa refocused its attentions on its immediate neighbours in the Southern African Customs Union and a broader grouping of neighbours that form the Southern African Development Community (SADC). The SADC is the most economically powerful grouping in Africa and is itself dominated by South Africa. Although it is primarily focused on economic development, the organisation also facilitates regional defence cooperation, which South Africa naturally dominates. South Africa is also committed to Africa-wide cooperation, as demonstrated by its role in establishing the African Union in 2002 as the successor to the Organisation of African States. In recent years South Africa has begun to assume security responsibilities elsewhere in continental Africa.

Post-apartheid South Africa also took tentative steps to join a broader Indian Ocean grouping, seeing it as a way of forming broader international connections and particularly as a way of promoting the South Africa–India relationship. In November 1993, even before the change to Black majority government, the White South African foreign minister, Pik Botha, mooted the possibility of joint South Africa–Indian initiatives in the Indian Ocean region.[42] South Africa was a founding member of the Indian Ocean Region-Association for Regional Cooperation (IOR-ARC) in 1997 but is now only a lukewarm supporter. Among other things, India strongly opposed South Africa's proposals to include South Africa's SADC partners in the grouping.[43] Pretoria remains concerned that IOR-ARC may detract from South Africa's focus on Southern Africa, and South Africa's SADC partners reportedly share these concerns.[44] In coming years, South Africa's relationships in the Indian Ocean are therefore likely to be focused on key SADC states and with bilateral relationships with major powers such as France and India.

While the South African Navy remains by far the most capable navy in Africa, it has limited interest in pan-Indian Ocean security issues. There have been significant reductions in naval spending over the last two decades, and only around 7 per cent of South Africa's defence budget is allocated to the navy's operational requirements. The closure of the navy's base at Durban in the mid-1990s and the consolidation of its remaining vessels in Cape Town some 1200 km to the southwest appeared to signify its withdrawal from the Indian Ocean. South Africa's naval horizons seemed limited to coastal security of its own waters and those of its immediate neighbours. South Africa declined invitations from the EU and NATO to participate in anti-piracy operations off the Horn of Africa, apparently due to budget constraints and a view that South Africa had insufficient interest in the problem.[45]

But there are tentative signs of a renewed willingness of South Africa to involve itself in maritime security in East Africa. Since 2010, as part of Operation *Copper,* South African vessels with support from Special Forces have conducted anti-piracy patrols in the Mozambique Channel, based out of the port of Pemba in northern Mozambique. In January 2012, South Africa entered into a tripartite maritime security agreement with Mozambique and Tanzania and announced the reopening of the Salisbury Island naval base at Durban as a base from which to combat piracy. The Mozambique defence minister, Filipe Nyusi, has advocated extending this arrangement to Kenyan waters.[46] As discussed previously, in 2012 the Indian Navy agreed to commence anti-piracy patrols in the Mozambique Channel, apparently without prior consultation with South Africa. Although Pretoria may see an Indian naval presence in the waters of one of its SADC partners with a degree of unease, it may well seek to develop a cooperative arrangement in the event of an extended deployment of the Indian Navy. As India expands its maritime security role in Africa, it might be seen in Pretoria as a competing influence over South Africa's neighbours.

Notes

1 Saul B. Cohen (1973) *Geography and Politics in a World Divided*, New York: Oxford University Press, p. 65.
2 C. Raja Mohan (2003) *Crossing the Rubicon*, London: Palgrave Macmillan, p. 233.
3 Anirudha Gupta (1974) 'Ugandan Asians, Britain, India and the Commonwealth', *African Affairs*, Vol. 73, No. 292, pp. 312–24.
4 John W. McDonald and Noa Zanolli (2008) *The Shifting Grounds of Conflict and Peacebuilding: Stories and Lessons*, Lanham, MD: Lexington Books, p. 113.
5 A.K. Dubey (1990) *Indo–African Relations in the Post-Nehru Era (1965–1985)*, Delhi: Kalinga, p. 14.
6 Raman, *The Kaoboys of R&AW*, p. 182.
7 *The Standard* (Kenya), 22 September 1977; *The Standard* (Kenya), 5 October 1977.
8 Tony Avirgan and Martha Honey (1982) *War in Uganda: the legacy of Idi Amin*, Westport, CR Hill, p. 25
9 Between 1974 and 1978, Uganda was one of the largest export customers for TATA vehicles. Mahmood Mamdani (1983) *Imperialism and Fascism in Uganda*, Nairobi: Heinemann, p. 90.
10 See Hussein Solomon (2012) 'Critical reflections of Indian foreign policy: between Kautilya and Ashoka', *South African Journal of International Affairs*, Vol. 19, No. 1, pp. 65–78.
11 Hussein Solomon and Sonja Theron (2011) 'Behind the veil: India's relations with apartheid South Africa', *Strategic Review for South Africa*, Vol. 33, No. 1, pp. 102–19.
12 'Anti-apartheid India found to have SA links' (1988) *The Star*, 23 September, p. 15.
13 Although this may have occurred without Indian government sanction.
14 Solomon, 'Critical Reflections of Indian Foreign Policy'.

15 Ibid.
16 Nandhini Iyer (1985) *India in the Indian Ocean: Groping for a policy, 1947–70*, New Delhi: ABC Publishing, p. 69.
17 Shanti Sadiu Ali (1980) 'India's Support to African Liberation Movements' in R. R. Ramchandani (ed.), *India and Africa*, New Delhi: Radiant, p. 64. From 1977 to 1978 the Desai government increased spending on African liberation movements from Rs.5 million to Rs.31 million.
18 India reportedly provided aid and arms to ZAPU from at least 1974. Jan Pettman (1974) *Zambia: Security and Conflict*, New York: St Martin's Press.
19 According to Zambia's President Kenneth Kaunda during a visit to New Delhi in September 1980. A. Appadorai (1981) 'Non-alignment: some important issues', *International Studies*, Vol. 20, No. 1, pp. 3–11 at p. 9.
20 B. Raman, *The Kaoboys of RAW*, p. 183.
21 *The Economist*, 13 September 1986, p. 30.
22 'India jets poised to aid Mugabe' (1986) *The Observer (London)*, 31 August, p. 13. Pakistan helped establish the post-independence Zimbabwe Air Force and from 1983 to 1986 the Zimbabwe Air Force was led by a Pakistani officer.
23 Amit Gupta (1990) The Indian Arms Industry: A lumbering giant', *Asian Survey*, Vol. 29, No. 9, pp. 846–61, p. 858.
24 Maggie Jonas (1987) 'Tide turns against MNR', *New African*, May, p. 20; and David Robinson (2006) 'Curse on the land: a history of the Mozambiquan civil war', doctoral thesis, The University of Western Australia.
25 According to a former senior South African naval officer. Email to author 21 February 2012.
26 Numbers from India, High Level Committee on the Indian Diaspora (2001) *Report of High Level Committee on Indian Diaspora*, New Delhi: Ministry of External Affairs.
27 'Kenya violence: centre not to evacuate Indians' (2008) *Business Standard*, 4 January.
28 'India offers $500m credit line to Mozambique' (2010) *The Hindu*, 1 October.
29 'India and Mozambique to cooperate on maritime security, anti-piracy efforts' (2011) *Defenceweb*, 30 June.
30 Pearl Sebolao (2010) 'South Africa: India's developmental model an inspiration to country', *Business Day*, 31 August.
31 Elizabeth Sidiropoulous (2011) 'India and South Africa as partners for development in Africa?', *Chatham House Briefing Paper*, March.
32 Philip Alves (2007) 'India and South Africa: shifting priorities', *South African Journal of International Affairs*, Vol. 14, No. 2, pp. 87–109, n. 43.
33 Sanusha Naidu (2011) 'South Africa joins BRIC with China's support' *East Asia Forum*, 1 April. Online: www.eastasiaforum.org/2011/04/01/south-africa-joins-bric-with-china-s-support/ (accessed 10 October 2013).
34 Rajeev Sharma (2011) 'BRIC vs. IBSA = China vs. India?' *The Diplomat*, 2 March.
35 Adam Habib (2009) 'South Africa's foreign policy: hegemonic aspirations, neo-liberal orientations and global transformation', *South African Journal of International Affairs*, Vol. 16, No. 2, August, pp. 143–59, at p. 152.
36 Elizabeth Sidiropoulous, 'India and South Africa as partners for development in Africa?', p. 90.
37 Ruchita Beri (2003) 'India's Africa policy in the post-Cold War era: an assessment', *Strategic Analysis*, Vol. 27, No. 2, pp. 216–32.
38 Stephen Cohen, *Emerging Power India*, p. 246.
39 See Joelien Pretorius (2011) 'Africa–India nuclear cooperation: pragmatism, principle, pos-colonialism and the Pelindaba Treaty', *South African Journal of International Affairs*, Vol. 18, No. 3, December, pp. 319–9.

40 Including the Memorandum of Understanding concerning Cooperation in the Field of Defense Equipment (1996); Agreement on Defense Co-operation (2000); and Agreement on Supply of Defense Equipment (2003).

41 Zambia since the 1970s, Botswana since 1978, Namibia since 1995 and Lesotho since 2001.

42 *Business Day*, 23 November 1993.

43 Greg Mills (1998) *South Africa and Security Building in the Indian Ocean Rim*, Canberra Papers on Strategy and Defence, No. 127, Canberra: Australian National University.

44 Ruchita Beri (2012) 'South Africa and the IOR-ARC: shifting priorities', in Vijay Sakhuja (ed.), *Reinvigorating IOR-ARC*, New Delhi: Indian Council of World Affairs, pp. 60–71 at p. 64.

45 Deane-Peter Baker (2012) 'The South African Navy and African maritime security', *Naval War College Review*, Vol. 65, No. 2, pp. 145–65.

46 Agencia de Informacao de Mocambique (2012) 'Mozambique: anti-piracy patrols should move further north', 10 July.

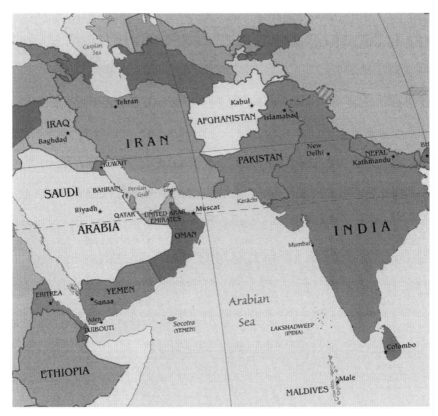

Map 6.1 The Northwest
Adapted from the University of Texas Libraries collection.

6   The Northwest Indian Ocean

This chapter examines India's strategic role in the northwest Indian Ocean, focusing on its security relationships in and around the Persian Gulf. These relationships form part of a larger story of India's strategic relations in West Asia and the Arab world that goes well beyond its role in the Indian Ocean.

The northwest quadrant of the Indian Ocean is critical to India. Access to energy is the most vital strategic concern, but India also has other important security concerns in the region, including terrorism and piracy. Given its size and proximity, one might expect that India would be a natural security provider and hegemon in the northwest. But India's ability to project power in the area, particularly into the crucial Persian Gulf, is severely constrained by Pakistan's relationships in the region in security terms. Over the last 50 years, India has made several attempts to develop long-term strategic partnerships inside the Gulf, but it remains largely locked out from the region in security terms. In many ways, the northwest is the strategic 'hub' of the Indian Ocean and the failure of India to have a major security role there may undermine any claim it might make to be the 'leading' power of the Indian Ocean.

British India's empire in the northwest Indian Ocean

For much of the colonial era, Britain was the pre-eminent power in the northwest Indian Ocean—and that power was largely maintained and administered through India. Britain's strategic imperatives were driven by a combination of concerns over external threats to British India and the protection of British rule over the subcontinent. As the *The Times* of London argued at the turn of the twentieth century, 'British supremacy in India is unquestionably bound up with British supremacy in the Persian Gulf. If we lose control of the Gulf we shall not rule long in India'[1] Britain's key objectives in the northwest Indian Ocean were to protect the security of the sea lanes between Britain and India and to check attempts by continental powers to develop overland access routes to the Indian Ocean (by Czarist Russia to the Gulf through Persia/Iran and by Imperial Germany to the Gulf through Mesopotamia/Iraq). In the early twentieth century an additional strategic objective was added—the imperative to secure oil reserves in the Persian Gulf.

Britain pursued its strategic objectives by establishing a system of indirect rule over the northwest that allowed it to exclude potentially hostile powers from the region, while limiting its involvement in local affairs. During the nineteenth century, the British Indian government created a regional empire of protectorates and protected states through treaties with local rulers under which the British viceroy to India took responsibility for defence and external affairs.[2] These treaties gave the viceroy the same rights and powers as he exercised over the princely states on the Indian subcontinent. Through this system, the British Indian government gained effective control over the external affairs of Kuwait, Bahrain, the Trucial States (now UAE), Qatar, Muscat and Oman (including Zanzibar) and British Somaliland, while Aden and its hinterland was formally annexed as Indian territory. Persia and Mesopotamia also fell within a British Indian sphere of influence through resident consuls that held considerable, if largely informal, power. The affairs of the entire Persian Gulf were overseen by the political resident at Bushehr in southern Persia, who reported to the Indian government. Although direct military intervention in local affairs was generally kept to a minimum, Indian Army troops (or local forces using troops recruited from India) were stationed at key locations, including at Aden, Muscat and Bahrain, while ships of the Royal Indian Marine patrolled the waters of the Gulf. India also played a dominant economic role in the region. Bombay merchants controlled the pearling trade (the main export from the Gulf prior to the discovery of oil) and the Indian rupee was the principal currency throughout the Gulf (and it remained legal tender in several countries until the 1960s). There were large Indian merchant communities in trading centres such as Kuwait, Bahrain, Oman and Aden.

In the early twentieth century, the British Indian government hoped to consolidate control over the Gulf through Indian colonisation of the area. When the Indian Army occupied Mesopatamia (now Iraq) during World War I, the creation of a permanent Indian administration became one of Delhi's prime objectives in the Middle East. Charles Hardinge, the British viceroy, believed that British Indian control over the Gulf, combined with Indian immigration to Mesopotamia, could make it a 'second Egypt'. One Indian government official reported that the area was capable of accommodating up to 25 million Indian immigrants.[3] But, after some debate, London opposed the 'Indianisation' of Mesopotamia. Although these plans might now be dismissed as imperialist dreams from another era, the millions of Indian guestworkers now in the Persian Gulf are a reminder of India's demographic power in the region.

While in some ways India represents a natural hegemon in the northwest, its strategic links with the region were largely amputated at independence. Its inward-looking economic policies, socialist rhetoric, and an attachment to non-alignment undermined its strategic role in this region as it often did elsewhere in the Indian Ocean. Regimes that were concerned about an expansionist Soviet Union or threats from local revolutionaries could expect to receive no help from

New Delhi. At the same time, Pakistan was able to effectively marginalise India as a major strategic player through developing its own alliance relationships. In many ways British India's imperial role was inherited by Pakistan, whose close security links with the Gulf are, in a sense, the continuation of Greater India's links with the region.

Pakistan's role in the northwest Indian Ocean

The partition of India and establishment of Pakistan in 1947 was a strategic disaster for India—not only on the Indian subcontinent but also in the broader region. The terrible bloodletting of the population transfers during Partition and the accession of Muslim-majority Kashmir to India have resulted in what appears to be permanent enmity between India and Pakistan. The dreams of some, including Muhammad Jinnah, the founding father of Pakistan, that India and Pakistan could jointly enforce a sort of Monroe Doctrine over the subcontinent were utterly destroyed.[4] Instead, virtually from its establishment Pakistan sought to internationalise its dispute with India, leading the United States and China to become major strategic actors in South Asia. The enmity between India and Pakistan, including wars in 1947, 1965, 1971 and 1999 and several near wars, kept India strategically preoccupied in South Asia and unable or unwilling to project its influence beyond. Only in the last couple of decades has India's growing dominance over Pakistan allowed it to begin to transcend this preoccupation. This book will not try to untangle the toxic relationship between the two countries but will confine itself to analysing the extent to which Pakistan acts as a constraint on India's broader ambitions in the Indian Ocean.

Since its creation, Pakistan's strategic perspectives have been predominantly land orientated, focused on the threat posed by India over the subcontinent's northwest plains as well as on threats from domestic insurgencies. As a result, the Pakistan Navy has received relatively few resources and, since at least 1971, has represented an ever-decreasing threat to India. Any qualitative advantage that Pakistan may have had in the decades following independence has been severely eroded and the Indian Navy is now substantially larger and more capable than the Pakistan Navy in virtually all respects. The Pakistan Navy is now a modest but effective coastal defence force roughly one-fifth the size of India's in terms of naval combat vessels. Although Pakistan's submarines previously represented a potent threat to India, the fleet is now aging. Pakistan has also commenced the development of a nuclear-powered submarine in an attempt to match India's nuclear submarine programme, but this is likely to take many years to come to fruition. India's economic growth and military modernisation programme has allowed it to pull away from Pakistan and set its sights on broader horizons. While the maritime balance could theoretically change if Pakistan acquires significant new capabilities (for example, Anti Access Area Denial systems capable of sinking aircraft carriers), the Pakistan Navy is increasingly seen more as a potential source of non-conventional threats to India, particularly following its suspected involvement in the 2008 Mumbai terror attacks.[5]

While any conflict between India and Pakistan will almost inevitably be land based, the Indian Navy could play an important secondary role in such conflicts, including by blockading Pakistan's ports, which represent a major strategic vulnerability. Pakistan is highly dependent on imports for energy and food and some 97 per cent of its external trade is by sea. Its main port at Karachi is close to India and has shallow approaches and a long channel that could be easily mined. India used this to its advantage during the 1971 war when it blockaded Karachi. The Indian Navy also threatened a blockade during the 1999 Kargil conflict which, according to some, was an important factor in convincing Pakistan to withdraw its forces from Kashmir.[6] Pakistan has since developed ports at Gwadar and Ormara to provide greater strategic depth and make Pakistan less vulnerable to blockade. As will be discussed later, Pakistan would see the possible development of a Chinese naval presence at Gwadar in western Pakistan as altering the naval balance in its favour.

The relative decline of Pakistan as a naval threat has allowed the Indian Navy to devote fewer resources to Pakistan and more to its capabilities elsewhere in the Indian Ocean. Pakistan has historically not played a significant role in much of the Indian Ocean region—India's victory over Pakistan in 1971 crystallised its role as the dominant naval power in South Asia and the secession of Bangladesh removed Pakistan as a military threat in the east. While Pakistan's relationships with Islamic-majority countries in Southeast Asia (Malaysia and, to a lesser extent, Indonesia) still somewhat constrain India's regional role, Pakistan's influence there is waning. But Pakistan's security relationships in the northwest Indian Ocean continue to represent a major obstacle to an expanded role for India. To a significant extent, Pakistan has inherited India's pre-independence role as a security provider in the northwest.

India's strategic weakness in the northwest in the years following independence was reinforced by US Cold War strategies that helped promote Pakistan's role. The CENTO alliance, which joined the US and Pakistan together with Iran, Iraq and Turkey, was intended to be an anti-Soviet grouping but also provided a political and military structure for its members to support Pakistan in its dispute with India. This became evident during the 1965 Indo–Pakistan war, when Saudi Arabia, Jordan and Iran provided Pakistan with military and material support. During the 1971 Bangladesh War Pakistan again received considerable military support from several countries in the northwest, including Saudi Arabia and Jordan. While Iran also provided military assistance it was a little more circumspect, either out of a degree of sensitivity regarding its relationship with India or possibly for fear of Soviet retaliation. Although the 1971 war was a major military victory for India in South Asia, it represented a significant political defeat for it in much of the Arab world—not least because of the widely held perception that India had conspired with the

Soviet Union to dismember Pakistan. The war damaged most of India's relationships in the region and further focused Pakistan's energies on building security relationships in the Gulf. The political and military nexus which Pakistan developed with many Gulf Arab states after 1971 has had a profound impact on India's role in the Gulf.

Pakistan's principal strategic partner in the northwest is Saudi Arabia, where Pakistan acts as a major source of military training and manpower. Through the 1970s and 1980s there were up to 15,000 Pakistani troops stationed in Saudi Arabia, acting as a sort of Praetorian Guard to the Saudi regime, and Pakistan now reportedly keeps two army divisions on standby for deployment to Saudi Arabia.[7] Pakistan also maintains active army, naval and air force training presences elsewhere in the Gulf, including Bahrain, the United Arab Emirates (UAE) and Oman, and is the source of many personnel serving in the security forces of the Gulf states. As a counterpoint to India's MILAN naval exercises held in the northeast Indian Ocean (discussed in Chapter 7), the Pakistan Navy sponsors the biennial AMAN exercises in the Arabian Sea, which in 2011 included participants and observers from 47 countries from the Indian Ocean region and elsewhere. The Pakistan Navy is also an active participant in regional security initiatives, including the US-sponsored international naval task forces which operate in the Persian Gulf and Arabian Sea, which Pakistan has led on several occasions.[8]

The United States values the Pakistan Navy as a partner in the region because of its local knowledge and close working relationships with the Gulf Arab states.[9] USCENTCOM, the US military command whose area of responsibility includes the Middle East, has good reason to maintain cordial relations with the Pakistan military, and this has constrained an expansion of India's regional role despite overall improvements in India–US strategic relations. As will be discussed in Chapter 9, US–Indian relations are complicated by the administrative split between USCENTCOM and US Pacific Command (USPACOM), which has primary responsibility for the military relationship with India. While this reduces potential operational frictions arising from US military support for Pakistan, it has also inhibited India–US military cooperation in the northwest Indian Ocean.[10]

Of even greater significance than Pakistan's conventional security presence in the region is its role as a nuclear power. Saudi Arabia is suspected of helping to fund Pakistan's nuclear weapons programme from the 1980s, which enabled Pakistan to become a declared nuclear weapons state in 1998. As a *quid pro quo*, Pakistan may now provide a form of nuclear umbrella for Saudi Arabia and there are claims that Pakistan has agreed to transfer nuclear weapon technology or nuclear weapons to Saudi Arabia in the event that Iran acquires nuclear weapons.[11] Although Pakistan's dysfunctional polity has contributed to an overall decline in its influence and India's economic influence in the region is growing, Pakistan's role in providing a type of nuclear deterrent for the Gulf Arab states could effectively prevent India from developing a major role in the region.

India's search for regional partners: Egypt and Iraq

One of India's key strategic objectives in the northeast Indian Ocean over the last 60 years has been to find a strategic partner to help it overcome its strategic isolation. Since independence, India has had little influence with conservative Islamic monarchies in the Gulf. Through the Cold War India tried to reduce its strategic isolation by developing strategic partnerships with secular or socialist regimes such as Egypt and Iraq that shared some ideological perspectives and/or a security relationship with the Soviet Union. While these relationships provided some benefits to India, including helping to secure oil supplies during times of crisis, India has had little lasting success in forming partnerships in the region.

For several decades, India's strategic role in West Asia was anchored by its relationship with Egypt under the leadership of President Nasser. India and Egypt both had leading roles in the Non-Aligned Movement. From the early 1950s they provided mutual diplomatic support over several issues, including the 1956 Suez crisis, the Kashmir dispute, India's annexation of Goa in 1961 and Egypt's military intervention in North Yemen in 1962. Their shared relationship with the Soviet Union also led India to provide training and maintenance services to the Egyptian Air Force and Navy. But Egypt's break with the Soviet Union and its strategic realignment towards the United States led to a breakdown in the relationship in the late 1970s.

Through the 1970s and 1980s India also had a close security relationship with Saddam Hussein's Ba'athist regime in Iraq. India found a friend in the secular and socialist-leaning regime, which had a much more flexible stance towards India than other conservative Arab regimes. There was also a strong personal relationship between Hussein and Indira Gandhi, who he referred to as 'Sister Indira'.[12] The relationship developed in the late 1960s in line with their respective relationships with the Soviet Union and the link was formalised when Iraq entered into a Friendship Treaty with the Soviets in 1972, a year after the India–Soviet Friendship Treaty. The relationship helped guarantee oil supplies to India at favourable prices, and in return India provided considerable security assistance, much of it to the Iraqi Air Force (IQAF). From independence the IQAF had been the most politically influential of Iraq's armed forces and it had played a leading role in installing the Ba'athist regime through a series of coups in the 1960s. In later years, Saddam Hussein is said to have been particularly fearful of potential coups against him from within the IQAF.[13]

From the late 1960s onwards, India had up to 120 Indian air force instructors deployed in Iraq at any one time, as well as accepting Iraqi pilots for training at home.[14] The security relationship was expanded in 1975 when the Indian Army sent training teams and the Indian Navy established a naval academy in Basra. According to one account, Indian pilots flew support missions for the IQAF in Hussein's 1975 offensive against Kurdish separatists, although they were under instructions not to fly beyond the front lines in Kurdistan.[15] India continued to provide considerable military assistance to

Iraq throughout the Iran–Iraq war (1980–8). In addition to training, India provided technical assistance to the IQAF through a complicated tripartite arrangement involving France, including converting Iraqi MiG-21 and Hunter aircraft to carry French-made missiles.[16] India also worked with Iraq and France to jointly develop the 'Adnan' AWAC aircraft based on the Soviet Il-76 transport (of which some three aircraft were produced, none of which became operational).[17] This was an important project for Iraq, which had no AWAC aircraft for its air war with Iran. A significant Indian Air Force presence was maintained in Iraq until 1989.[18]

But Hussein's invasion of Kuwait in August 1990 turned the Iraq relationship into a liability. While most of the Arab world mobilised against Iraq under the leadership of the United States, India responded with studied ambiguity. India was constrained from taking any effective role in the conflict by its relationship with Iraq, its non-aligned rhetoric and concerns for the welfare of some 180,000 Indian workers trapped in Iraq and Kuwait. In August 1990, the Indian foreign minister, I. K. Gujral, was infamously pictured in Baghdad in a warm embrace with Hussein while negotiating the evacuation of Indian workers. India took care not to openly condemn Iraq and was instead reduced to making deliberately ambiguous statements about Iraqi actions. The Gulf War ended India's close relationship with Iraq and served to demonstrate how little strategic influence India had in the Persian Gulf. As Rajiv Gandhi commented, India was 'reduced to hapless spectators' of the conflict.[19]

India and the Persian Gulf after the Cold War

Since the end of the Cold War, several developments have helped India increase its influence in the Persian Gulf. India's move away from its attachment to nonalignment and more recent improvements in US–India relations have opened the door for a greater security role for India. The liberalisation of India's economy allowed it to expand trading and investment links with the Gulf beyond energy supply, and there has been a recognition of shared interests in combating Islamic extremism. In 2005 India sought to give greater coherence to its regional strategy by launching a 'Look West' policy, intended to act as a counterpoint to its 'Look East' policy in East Asia. India's key security objectives in the Gulf now include energy security, ensuring the safety of Indian migrant workers and the maintenance of regional stability.

India's most immediate strategic interest in the Persian Gulf is energy. India is highly reliant on imported oil and gas; in 2010 it imported around 70 per cent of its oil requirements, much of that from the Gulf. Reliance on imports will increase considerably in coming years as the gap between demand and domestic production grows. Some analysts claim that India faces a 'Hormuz Dilemma' in the Strait of Hormuz similar to China's 'Malacca Dilemma' in the Malacca Strait. India's concerns are heightened by the development of the port of Gwadar some 600 km east of the Strait of Hormuz and the potential for China to establish a naval presence there. This creates an imperative for

India to take an active role in security of the Strait of Hormuz or to develop good security relationships with the states located on or near the Strait.

In recent years, India has developed considerable economic interests in the Gulf. In 2008–9, India's trade with the six Gulf Arab states (Saudi Arabia, Kuwait, Bahrain, UAE, Qatar and Oman) *excluding oil,* totalled $86.9 billion, surpassing its trade with the European Union ($80.6 billion), ASEAN ($44.6 billion) and the United States ($40.6 billion).[20] Economic relationships are dominated by trade in energy and Indian migrant labour, but are broadening to include gems, food and manufactured products. The UAE acts as India's regional economic hub—and India is the UAE's largest trading partner. This includes wide-ranging trade and investment ties: as of 2007, some 3,300 Indian companies had offices or manufacturing facilities in UAE.[21]

Indian migrant labour is also a major economic and demographic factor in the region. In 2004 there were some 3.6 million Indian workers in the Gulf (including around 1.5 million in Saudi Arabia and 1 million in UAE and 450,000 in each of Kuwait and Oman).[22] These numbers may now be closer to 5 million. Indian nationals now comprise significant proportions of the local populations: in 2000, Indians constituted some 32 per cent of the population of UAE, more than 20 per cent of the population of Bahrain and Qatar and in excess of 10 per cent of the population of Kuwait and Oman.[23] Remittances from Indian workers in the Gulf are a major foreign exchange earner for India—in 2003 amounting to some $17.4 billion or around 3 per cent of India's GDP. But the presence of millions of Indian nationals is also a significant strategic constraint for India. As India discovered following Saddam Hussein's invasion of Kuwait in 1990, the imperative to ensure the welfare of huge numbers of Indian nationals can trump otherwise strategically optimal positions. Indian migrant workers also have a domestic security impact for India. Over several decades many Indian workers have returned to India bringing with them Wahabist Islamic beliefs, which in many communities is altering the more tolerant Sufi Islamic traditions that are prevalent in India.

India's relationship with Saudi Arabia, the most powerful Arab state in the area, has improved in recent years, if from a low base. From the 1960s Saudi Arabia became one of the key political, financial and military backers of Islamabad, assisting Pakistan in the 1965 and 1971 wars with India and during the Soviet–Afghani war. But relations have improved since the 1990s, largely due to a convergence of economic interests, which has led to limited security cooperation. An MOU on information sharing was signed in January 2006, reflecting some common interests in counterterrorism. The Saudis have also expressed interest in joint training and naval cooperation in the Arabian Sea and the Gulf and in September 2012 a Joint Committee on Defence Cooperation was established. India recognises that a productive political and security relationship with Saudi Arabia could act as a counterweight to Pakistan in the Islamic world. In the past few years the Saudis have been taking a more even-handed approach to the India–Pakistan conflict, urging that it be settled peacefully, and Riyadh has proposed that India be granted observer status at the Organisation of the Islamic Conference (although this was blocked by Pakistan). Nevertheless, New Delhi continues to be concerned about Saudi military support for Pakistan, Saudi financing of Islamist groups in Kashmir and the growth of Wahabist influence throughout South Asia.[24]

India is also developing limited security relationships with several smaller Gulf Arab states, including Oman, Qatar and UAE. They share a common interest in combating jihadist terrorism and some may also see India as a partial hedge against the larger Gulf powers and their overwhelming reliance on the United States for security. Some might also see India as a potential source of support for the ruling regimes against domestic opposition.

India is a major customer of LNG from Qatar, which has some of the world's largest gas reserves, and in 2008 they signed a security agreement which, according to some reports, includes Indian security guarantees. For some years the Qatari regime has followed a somewhat quixotic foreign policy line, including forging links with Israel. It also has a very close security relationship with the United States—among other things, it is the site of USCENTCOM forward headquarters. The agreement with India, which was reportedly entered into following 'persistent' Qatari efforts, relates to maritime security and intelligence sharing. According to one report, Qatar wanted more 'comfort' than was provided by its security arrangements with the United States. Indian officials described the security agreements as being the most far reaching that India has signed with any country and were 'just short of stationing troops [in Qatar]'.[25] Another official added that 'We will go to the rescue of Qatar if Qatar requires it, in whatever form it takes'.[26] According to Raja Mohan, although Qatar was keen to see India develop a semi-permanent naval presence, India was cautious about taking action that might upset others in the region.[27] However, US diplomats privately downplayed the significance of the arrangement, calling it more symbolic than substantive.[28]

India's closest security relationship in the Gulf is with Oman, which for decades has used India to partially balance its relationships with its larger neighbours. Some compare the benevolent dictatorship of Oman's Sultan Qabus with Singapore's Lee Kwan Yew, and certainly Oman's regional role and its foreign policy approach can in some ways be compared with those of Singapore. Like Singapore on the Malacca Strait, Oman sits at the key chokepoint of the Strait of Hormuz and, like Singapore, Oman pursues an omni-directional but broadly pro-Western foreign policy. As Oman's deputy prime minister, Sayyid Fahd bin Mahmoud Al Said, reportedly explained in a confidential interview with a US official: Oman sees India as a reliable partner that contributes to regional stability and security. It wants to encourage India to engage in the region diplomatically and politically as part of a balance of power, but it does not believe that India requires a military presence in the region.[29]

Oman has cultivated a close relationship with India since gaining effective independence from Britain in 1971. India supported Oman's admission to the United Nations despite the opposition of the majority of Gulf Arab states and in turn Oman was the only Arab state to not condemn India over the

Bangladesh War. The relationship has a significant, if limited, security component. India has deployed small naval and army training teams to Oman almost continuously since 1971.[30] Over the past several decades there have been numerous security agreements on a wide range of matters and there are annual naval and air exercises and regular military-to-military talks. The Indian Air Force uses Oman's Thumrait air base (which is operated by the US Air Force) in support of anti-piracy efforts and the Indian Navy uses port facilities at Salalah. An undersea pipeline to supply India with natural gas has been under discussion for many years, although there are considerable questions about its feasibility. There are also some frustrations in the relationship, including New Delhi's reluctance to provide Oman with access to Indian defence technology due to concerns over the possibility of leakage to Pakistan. India also has concerns about the political stability of Oman after the death of the sultan and the possibility of a renewal of the Dohar insurgency.

But while Oman has good security links with India, these are still overshadowed by its links with both the United States and Pakistan. Oman has a close security relationship with the United States, which includes allowing access to airfields and ports and the pre-positioning of equipment. Oman has also long relied on Pakistan, which is located just across the Gulf of Oman, for security assistance and as a major source of manpower for its army. But its relationship with Pakistan is also somewhat complicated by Pakistan's Islamist policies.[31] In short, while Oman does not see India as a principal security provider, it wants to keep India engaged in the region.

Despite a relative paucity of local security partners, India is seeking to develop a direct maritime security presence in the region. Since October 2008 the Indian Navy has continuously deployed one or two vessels in anti-piracy patrols in the Gulf of Aden, off Somalia. As will be discussed in Chapter 9, India has declined to participate in the US-sponsored Combined Task Force 151 (CTF 151), to which some 20 countries have contributed naval assets, and barely coordinates its activities with other navies conducting anti-piracy operations in the region. Nevertheless, the anti-piracy deployment is a way of demonstrating India's ability to provide public goods to the region.

India's attempts to develop a strategic partnership with Iran

India's most potentially important relationship in the Persian Gulf is with Iran. In some ways Iran represents a 'natural' strategic partner that could unlock India's regional role. India's relationship with Iran over the last 60 years followed a quite different trajectory from its relationships with the Gulf Arab states. India and Iran have deep cultural connections, not least through centuries of rule of the Indian subcontinent by the Persianised Moghuls—some claim that New Delhi's political elite are still imbued with the Persian cultural tradition. According to Indian prime minister Narasimha Rao, there was 'more in common between secular India and Shi'a Iran than with an increasingly Wahhabized Arab world'.[32] While there are currently severe constraints on India's ability to develop the relationship, a change in Iran's theocratic regime could allow for a closer strategic partnership. This would have significant consequences for India's role in the Gulf and the northwest Indian Ocean.

India has attempted to develop a strategic alignment with Iran on more than one occasion. In the early 1970s, India and Iran developed a strategic partnership that might have changed the whole regional balance of power. The relationship was prompted by Iran's ambitions to play an expanded security role after the British withdrawal from the Persian Gulf and was consistent with US policy of encouraging its allies throughout the world to take greater responsibility for regional security. In pursuing these ambitions, the Shah of Iran sought to develop a partnership with India as the dominant power in South Asia. The Shah hoped to stabilise South Asia following the Bangladesh War to secure Iran's eastern flank and allow it to focus its attention on the Gulf. The Shah also hoped to encourage India to reduce its dependence on the Soviet Union and ensure that the Soviet navy did not gain access to Indian facilities. Finally, the Shah sought India's agreement that it would stay out of the Persian Gulf. For its part, India was attracted to a partnership with Iran, not only by cheap oil and investment money but also by the possibility of reduced US influence in the Gulf. As a prominent Indian analyst commented, 'in India's perception, the Shah's aspiration to make Iran the dominant regional power in the Persian Gulf did not entirely jell with America's strategic interests in the region'[33] (i.e. New Delhi believed that Tehran would increasingly diverge from Washington's perspectives). One might also see the relationship as the congruence of influence of two middle regional powers that both wished to stabilise regional security while minimising the role of extra-regional powers.

Iran quickly became India's largest oil supplier, and by the mid-1970s Iran was supplying 75 per cent of India's imported oil, 20 per cent of that at pre-oil embargo prices. Iranian–Indian security ties also unfolded in a series of secret accords, laying the groundwork for military collaboration, the establishment of a joint arms industry and nuclear cooperation. India agreed to assist Iran's nuclear power programme. The Shah also hoped to build up a joint arms industry based on Iranian money and Indian know-how and manpower that could challenge Western arms suppliers and any future Arab arms industry.[34] There were also plans to share intelligence. In 1975 and 1976 the RAW, SAVAK, the Iranian intelligence service and SDECE, the French intelligence service, formed a joint project to establish electronic monitoring stations to collect maritime intelligence in the Indian Ocean region. The idea was that the Iranians would provide the money, the French the equipment and India would operate the stations. Two stations were established on the east and west coasts of India and two more were planned as part of Indian diplomatic missions elsewhere in the region. According to B. Raman, a former senior officer of RAW, these were not established due to objections from the Indian foreign ministry, despite host country knowledge and approval.[35]

Iran's maritime security objectives were initially focused on the protection of Iranian shipping in the Persian Gulf. During the 1970s there was a massive expansion of Iran's naval capabilities and it constructed several new naval bases, including a major naval base at Chahbahar, giving the Iranian navy direct access to the Indian Ocean. India responded with remarkable equanimity, apparently seeing Iran's regional naval ambitions as consistent with India's interests.[36] Iran also took responsibility for Oman's security, deploying troops, aircraft and naval forces to put down an insurgency in Oman's Dhofar region. At the same time, at Iran's request, India scaled back on its relationship with Oman, withdrawing a small naval training team and an offer to supply Indian-built Gnat fighters.[37] Indira Gandhi reportedly decided that India had neither the desire nor the capacity to intervene in intra-mural quarrels in the Gulf.[38]

Iran also looked to establish a naval presence in the Indian Ocean proper. Iran was granted port access to Mauritius in 1972 in return for an undisclosed aid commitment, which provoked little comment from New Delhi, although India did block an Iranian proposal to lease the former British naval and air base at Gan in the Maldives.[39] In 1974 the Shah visited South Asia, Southeast Asia, Australia and New Zealand and proposed a regional collective security system among the Indian Ocean littoral states that would allow the United States and Soviet Union to reduce their presence. The Shah proposed that both Iran and India should increase their naval roles, including by conducting joint patrols of the Indian Ocean.[40] Any concerns that New Delhi may have had about Iran's efforts to take the mantle of an Indian Ocean naval power were outweighed by the perceived benefits of the partnership on India's position in the northwest Indian Ocean. New Delhi may have also concluded that despite the Shah's talk, in practice Iran's naval presence in the Indian Ocean was unlikely to extend much past the Gulf of Oman.

But Iran's ambitions to become a major regional naval power quickly receded following the overthrow of the Shah and the Iraqi invasion of Iran in 1980. The fall of the Shah also effectively doomed the strategic partnership with India. The new regime had little interest in relations with Delhi, and Delhi was wary that Tehran would seek to export militancy to India's Shi'a population. The loss of the partnership was a major blow for India and significantly narrowed its options in the region.

But strategic convergences between them became apparent again within a decade. With the end of the Cold War and the collapse of the Soviet Union, both India and Iran had an interest in the stability and prosperity of the newly independent Central Asian republics. From the mid-1990s, both were also strongly opposed to the Pakistan-backed Taliban regime in Afghanistan. Tehran instituted a 'Look East' strategy, aimed at reducing Iran's economic dependence on the West and promoting relationships with India, Southeast Asia, Japan and China.[41] In turn, India saw a chance to diversify energy supplies and its relationships in the northwest Indian Ocean. A relationship with Iran was also popular among those in New Delhi who saw it as a symbol of India's strategic autonomy.

Between 2000 and 2003 there was increasing convergence on a number of issues, which culminated with the announcement of a new 'Strategic Partnership' in January 2003. Although the partnership primarily focused on economic cooperation, it also had significant strategic overtones. The partnership was driven by common concerns about Afghanistan, the possibility of India using Iran as a trade corridor to Central Asia, and Iran's desire to develop India as a gas customer, including plans for a gas pipeline to India.[42] Iran also saw a relationship with India as a way of helping break its international isolation.

In the strategic dimension, much of the focus of the strategic partnership was on Central Asia and Afghanistan. From the end of the Cold War, India found that attempts to expand its influence in Central Asia were checked by Islamabad, which saw them as part of an Indian strategy to 'encircle' Pakistan. But for India, Iran presents an alternative bridge into Central Asia. In Afghanistan, both India and Iran provided economic and other support to the Northern Alliance (pre 2001) and then the Karzai regime against the Pakistani-supported Taliban. A cooperative relationship with Iran may also have assisted in improving India's relations with Persian-speaking Tajikistan, which included the Indian Air Force gaining access to Tajikistan's Farkhora air base to support operations in Afghanistan.[43]

The most ambitious Indo–Iranian plan involves cooperation in the development of a North–South transportation corridor from the Indian Ocean to the Central Asian republics via Afghanistan, and to Russia via the Caspian Sea. This included Indian assistance in developing the Iranian port of Chahbahar and the construction of a highway and rail link from there to the city of Zaranj in western Afghanistan. The Afghani portion of the highway was completed in 2009 by India's quasi-military Border Roads Organisation, but the rail project has not yet commenced. The most significant aspect of the project for India's strategic position in the Indian Ocean is the development of the port of Chahbahar. Chahbahar is located on the Gulf of Oman, *between* Gwadar and the Strait of Hormuz and an Indian presence there would have considerable security implications for the Persian Gulf. In August 2012 Iran approved a $100-million Indian project to expand container facilities at the port pursuant to a trilateral agreement with India and Afghanistan. The port would be operated by the Indian state-owned Jawaharlal Port Trust. Washington announced its support for the project—the need for new transport routes to Afghanistan as an alternative to Pakistan apparently overcoming its desire to isolate Iran.[44] While India's interests in Chahbahar appear to be purely commercial, there are also unsubstantiated claims that the Indian Navy will be granted access rights to the port, which would provide it with easy access to the Strait of Hormuz and potentially allow it to outflank Gwadar. India also has unusually large consulates in Iran, including at Zahedan, near Iran's borders with Pakistan and Afghanistan, and at Bandar Abbas, on the Strait of Hormuz, which may be used for intelligence purposes, including signals intelligence.[45] There are long-standing claims that India is also supporting the separatist insurgency in Pakistan's Baluchistan province, on the border of Iran, as tit for tat for Pakistan's support for Kashmiri separatists.

The 2003 Indo–Iranian Strategic Partnership also included a plan for regular security dialogues and links between the national security councils in each country.[46] There have been sporadic reports of relatively low-level defence cooperation both before and after the 2003 accord, including Indian assistance in the maintenance of Russian-sourced equipment such as tanks and artillery and training of Iranian naval engineers. In March 2003, the Indian and Iranian navies held a symbolic naval exercise in the Arabian Sea, coinciding with US preparations for the Iraq war, and again in 2006, during US President Bush's visit to the region. According to Christine Fair, a US analyst, these were intended as a signal by Delhi to Tehran that Delhi's policies would not be dictated by Washington.[47] Over the last two decades, India has on several occasions considered cooperating with Iran in civilian nuclear technology and Washington claims that at least two senior Indian nuclear scientists have provided assistance. Washington has also expressed concerns about reports that India was providing Iran with assistance in its satellite and space programme.[48] But overall, defence cooperation has remained largely symbolic and India has failed to implement a number of agreements. A 2006 US congressional report concluded that Indo–Iranian cooperation was too sporadic and low-level to represent a major strategic alliance—instead, the cooperation represented a 'manifestation of generally good Indo–Iranian relations and an opportunity to mutually enhance their potential to project power in the region'.[49] Nevertheless, it is likely that a degree of security cooperation is continuing. As the Indian national security advisor, M. K. Narayanan, commented in 2008, there is a 'great deal taking place between India and Iran that is not in the public realm'.[50]

There have been several unsubstantiated (and probably inaccurate) reports of a secret defence pact between the two countries, including reports by *Janes* that India would be allowed to use Iranian military bases in the event of any outbreak of tensions with Pakistan.[51] These reports generated considerable alarm in Islamabad, creating the prospect that, in the event of conflict with India, Iran would no longer provide Pakistan with strategic depth (as it did in the 1965 and 1971 wars), and might even be the source of a second front. Even the *possibility* of Indian access to Iranian facilities would be a strategic nightmare for Pakistan, causing a division of Pakistani forces between its eastern and western borders. This speculation highlights the potential significance of defence arrangements between India and Iran on the balance of power in West Asia.

But the 2003 Strategic Partnership failed to develop in many areas. The election of the conservative Mahmoud Ahmadinejad as Iranian president in August 2005 led to a cooling of the relationship. At around the same time, at the urging of the United States, India voted against Iran on an International Atomic Energy Agency resolution regarding Iran's nuclear programme, which was seen by some as sealing the fate of any putative alliance. New Delhi was then negotiating its own break-through nuclear deal with the United States, and some believe that Washington made the deal and the broader relationship conditional on Indian support for the United States over the Iran nuclear issue. Washington may also have convinced New Delhi that a nuclear Iran with a medium-range missile deliver system would represent a direct security threat to India.[52] Since 2005, India has voted several times against Iran in IAEA resolutions to refer the Iranian nuclear programme to the UN Security Council.

It is clear that the relationship will be subject to considerable constraints for the foreseeable future, most particularly because of the hostile relationship between Iran and the United States. As a result, India's relationship with Iran is possibly the biggest area of potential friction between India and the United States in the Indian Ocean. New Delhi understands clearly the likely impact of a close relationship with the present regime in Tehran, but it also wishes to keep the Iran option open. The US-led oil boycott of Iran announced in early 2012 again put India in a difficult position given its dependence on Iranian oil and its other interests in Iran. New Delhi came to an arrangement with Washington under which it agreed to partially reduce purchases from Iran. Saudi Arabia offered to supply Iran's share to India, although over-reliance on Saudi oil would also be a potential source of concern for New Delhi.[53] While India has so far been able to balance these conflicting interests *vis a vis* its relationship with the United States, any military action by the United States against Iran could have the potential to cause significant damage to the relationship.

India has also been sensitive to the impact of its relationship with Iran on its other relationships in the region. In particular, a close relationship with Iran could endanger Indian access to crucial Israeli defence technology.[54] Equally significant is India's growing relations with Saudi Arabia and other Gulf Arab states. The Saudi opening to India under Saudi King Abdullah bin Abdul-Aziz al-Saud since 2006 may be partly motivated by a desire to pre-empt an Indian–Iranian strategic partnership in the Gulf. Any partnership with an Iran that was openly hostile to the Gulf Arab states would have a major impact on India's relations with them.

India's role in the northwest

The northwest quadrant of the Indian Ocean is critical to India due to its proximity to South Asia and India's reliance on energy imports. But it is also an area in which India faces considerable obstacles to expanding its strategic influence. While India might be expected to be a natural security provider there, its ability to project power in the area is severely constrained by Pakistan. India will need to overcome these constraints if it is to stake a claim to be the 'leading' power of the Indian Ocean.

Since independence, India has made several attempts to build long-term partnerships with several middle powers in the northwest, including Egypt, Iraq and Iran. For various reasons, none of these have been successful. India's economic influence has grown considerably over the last decade or so and its security relationships with Gulf states are improving. But Pakistan's relationships in the region and the Islamic factor will make it difficult for it to develop a significant security role in the Persian Gulf.

Despite these constraints, a strategic relationship with Iran presents considerable opportunities for India in the long term. In the event of change in Iran's ruling regime, India would be sorely tempted to develop a new strategic partnership with the country. This could provide India with much-needed strategic leverage in the Persian Gulf *vis a vis* the United States and Gulf Arab states and potentially provide an opportunity to establish a direct military presence there. Needless to say, it would also have significant implications for the balance of power between India and Pakistan.

Notes

1 Quoted in Lovat Fraser (1911) *India Under Curzon and After*, London: William Heinemann, pp. 112–13.
2 The difference between 'Protectorates' and 'Protected States' involved some unclear distinctions about the extent to which British India could intervene in the state's internal affairs. See generally, James Onley (2009) 'The Raj Reconsidered', *Asian Affairs*, Vol. 40, No. 1.
3 Robert Blyth, *The Empire of the Raj, Eastern Africa and the Middle East 1858–1947*, London: Palgrave Macmillan, pp. 134, 137.
4 *Star of India*, 11 January 1941. According to Jinnah, the Hindus could guard the coastlines in the south and west, while the Muslims could guard the land frontiers. *The Leader*, 14 March 1941.
5 'Pakistan Navy frogmen trained Kasab, other terrorists: Headley' (2010) *The Times of India*, 19 July.
6 Gurmeet Kanwal (1999) 'Pakistan's military defeat', in Jasjit Singh (ed.), *Kargil, 1999: Pakistan's Fourth War for Kashmir*, New Delhi: Knowledge World, p. 220.
7 Bruce Riedel (2011) 'Saudi Arabia: nervously watching Pakistan', Brookings Institute, 28 January 2008; Syed Saleem Shahzad, 'Pakistan ready for Middle East role', *Asia Times*, 2 April.
8 As of late 2012, Pakistan has commanded CTF 151 three times and CTF 150 on six occasions.
9 Holmes, Winner and Yoshihara (2009) *Indian Naval Strategy in the Twenty-first Century*, Abingdon: Routledge, p. 151.
10 For example, USCENTCOM reportedly vetoed Indian attempts to participate in CTF150 (presumably to the exclusion of Pakistan), as it preferred to have Pakistan as a participant. Cohen and Dasgupta (2010) *Arming without Aiming*, Washington, DC: Brookings Institution Press, p. 175.
11 Arnaud de Borchgrave (2003) 'Pakistan, Saudi Arabia in secret nuke pact: Islamabad trades weapons technology for oil', *The Washington Times*, 22 October; Riedel (2012) 'Saudi Arabia'; *Hugh Tomlinson*, 'Saudi Arabia to acquire nuclear weapons to counter Iran', *The Times*, 11 February.
12 Pranay Sharma (2011) 'Sailing up the Tigris: for India's new envoy to Iraq, a quiet renewal', *Outlook India*, 4 July.
13 Matthew M. Hurley (1992) 'Saddam Hussein and Iraqi air power: just having an airforce isn't enough', *Airpower Journal*, Vol. 6 No. 4, pp. 4–16.
14 David Nicolle and Tom Cooper (2004) *Arab MiG-19 and MiG-21 units in combat*, Oxford: Osprey, p. 78.

15 Jim Hoagland (1975) 'Syrian–Iraqi dispute flares: Damascus accused of aiding Kurds Syria, Iraq Split over aid to Kurds', *Washington Post*, 27 February, p. A16. Soviet pilots were also used to fly ground strikes.

16 Tom Cooper and Farzad Bishop (2000) *Iran–Iraq War in the air, 1980–1988*, Atglen, PA: Schiffer, p. 6.

17 James Smith, (1991) 'Developments in the Indian Air Force', *Jane's Intelligence Review*, November, p. 523. During the late 1980s Iraq may have also contributed to India's indigenous 'Project Guardian' AEW system based on H-2175 and H-2176 aircraft, which was later abandoned.

18 According to Indian Air Marshall Philip Rajkumar, 'The Indian Air Force in Iraq'. Online: www.bharat-rakshak.com/IAF/History/1990s/Rajkumar-Iraq.html (accessed 10 October 2013).

19 Attar Chand (1991) *Rajiv Gandhi: his Mind and Ideology*, New Delhi: Gian, p. 409.

20 Geoffrey Kemp (2010) *The East Moves West: India, China and Asia's Growing Presence in the Middle East*, Washington, DC: Brookings Institution, p. 42.

21 Pradhan (2009) 'India's Economic and Political Presence in the Gulf: A Gulf Perspective', in Gulf Research Centre, *India's Growing Role in the Gulf: Implications for the Region and the United States*, Dubai: Gulf Research Centre.

22 Anisur Rahman (2008) 'Indian manpower in the Gulf: Strategic and economic dimensions', in Rajendra M. Abhyankar, *West Asia and the Region: Defining India's Role*, New Delhi: Academic Foundation, pp. 203–22.

23 High Level Committee on the Indian Diaspora (2001) *Report of High Level Committee on Indian Diaspora*, New Delhi: Ministry of External Affairs.

24 Prabeer Hazarika (2005) 'India faces secret Saudi–Pakistan defence alliance', *India Daily*, 23 March.

25 'India, Qatar ink defence pact' (2008) *The Financial Times*, 11 November.

26 'India: PM vows to defend tiny Qatar 'if needed'' (2008) *ADN Kronos International*, 12 November; 'India, Qatar to ramp defence, economic, energy ties (roundup, combining different series)' (2008) *Thaindian News*, 10 November.

27 Mohan (2012) *Samudra Manthan: Sino–Indian Rivalry in the Indo–Pacific*, Washington, DC: Carnegie Endowment for International Peace, p. 163.

28 US Embassy Doha cable to US State Department (2008) 'First-ever Indian PM visit to Qatar aims to spark better ties', 18 November. Online: www.cablegate search.net/cable.php?id=08DOHA810 (accessed 10 October 2013).

29 US Embassy Muscat cable to US State Department (2010) 'Oman—Government's Number Two gives his views of the region', 22 February. Online: www.cablegate search.net/cable.php?id=10MUSCAT99 (accessed 10 October 2013).

30 But India declined to respond to Omani calls for military assistance during the Dhofar War (1960–75), on the grounds of not wishing to become involved in intramural Arab conflicts. The Dhofar insurgents were supported by the Soviet Union and South Yemen, one of India's socialist friends in the region.

31 Pakistan was also suspected to have been involved in an attempted coup plot against Sultan Qaboos in 1994, which, according to one report, led to enhanced intelligence cooperation arrangements between Oman and India. Bansidhar Pradhan (1999) 'Indo–Omani relations: political, security and socio-cultural relations', in A.K. Pasha (ed.), *India and Oman: History, State, Economy and Foreign Policy*, New Delhi: Gyan Sagar, pp. 72–90, at p. 85.

32 B. Raman (2008) 'India's strategic thrust in S.E. Asia—before and after 9/11', *South Asia Analysis Group*, Paper No. 2643, 26 March.

33 Bhabani Sen Gupta (1983) 'India's relations with the Gulf countries', in Alvin Z. Rubinstein (ed.), *The Great Game: Rivalry in the Persian Gulf and South Asia*, New York: Praeger, p. 158.

34 The Economist (1979) *Foreign Report*, Issue 1569, 31 January, p. 2.

35 B. Raman (2007) *The Kaoboys of R&AW*, New Delhi: Lancer, pp. 43–5. The operation was dropped after the overthrow of the Shah in 1979 and the election of Mitterand in 1981.
36 R.M. Burrell and Alvin J. Cottrell (1974) *Iran, Afghanistan, Pakistan: Tensions and Dilemmas*, Beverly Hills, CA: Sage, p. 23.
37 Ann Schulz (1977) 'The Gulf, South Asia and the Indian Ocean', in Mohammed Mughisuddin (ed.), *Conflict and Cooperation in the Gulf*, New York: Praeger, pp. 13–27 at p. 17; Alvin J. Cottrell (1978) 'Iran's Armed Forces under the Pahlavi Dynasty', in George Lenczowski (ed.), *Iran under the Pahlavis*, Stanford, CA: Hoover Institution Press, p. 410.
38 'Iran and India: Big Man locally' (1974) *The Economist*, 4 May, p. 52.
39 Itamar Rabinovich and Haim Shaked (eds) (1978) *From June to October: the Middle East between 1967 and 1973*, New Brunswick, NJ: Transaction Books, p. 367.
40 R.K. Karanjia (1977) *The Mind of a Monarch*, London: Allen & Unwin, p. 252.
41 Jalil Roshandel (2004) 'The Overdue 'Strategic' Partnership between Iran and India', in Robert Hathaway (ed.), *The 'Strategic Partnership' between India and Iran*, Washington, DC: Woodrow Wilson Centre, p. 17.
42 One proposal involves the construction of a 2,670 km natural gas pipeline from Asaluyeh in Iran to India across Pakistan. The Indian security community has significant concerns about the potential leverage that such an arrangement would give to Pakistan.
43 K. Alan Kronstadt and Kenneth Katzman (2006) 'India–Iran Relations and US Interests', Congressional Research Service, 2 August, p. CRS-6.
44 Press Trust of India (2012) 'US supports India, Iran and Afghan pact on Chabahar port', 28 August.
45 Donald L. Berlin (2004) 'India–Iran relations: A deepening entente', Honolulu, HI: Asia Pacific Centre for Security Studies, October.
46 'India and Iran expand links' (2003) *Jane's Intelligence Digest*, 29 January.
47 C. Christine Fair (2007) 'Indo–Iranian ties: thicker than oil' in Henry Sokolski (ed.), *Gauging US–Indian Strategic Cooperation*, Carlisle, PA: Strategic Studies Institute.
48 Fair, 'Indo–Iranian ties', pp. 286–8.
49 Kronstadt and Katzman, 'India–Iran relations and US interests', p. CRS-5.
50 Indo Asian News Service (2008) 'India says treat Iran with respect ahead of Ahmadinejad visit', 20 April. Online: www.thaindian.com/newsportal/uncategor ized/india-says-treat-iran-with-respect-ahead-of-ahmadinejad-visit_10040097.html (accessed 10 October 2013).
51 'Strategic Shift in South Asia' (2003) *Jane's Intelligence Weekly*, 28 January.
52 'India and Iran: end of an alliance' (2005) *Jane's Intelligence Digest*, 5 October.
53 Sergei DeSilva-Ranasinghe (2012) 'India's Iranian sanctions predicament', *FDI Strategic Weekly Analysis*, Vol. 3, No. 4, 8 February.
54 'Tel Aviv worried about New Delhi's ties with Iran' (2003) *The Times of India*, 11 September.

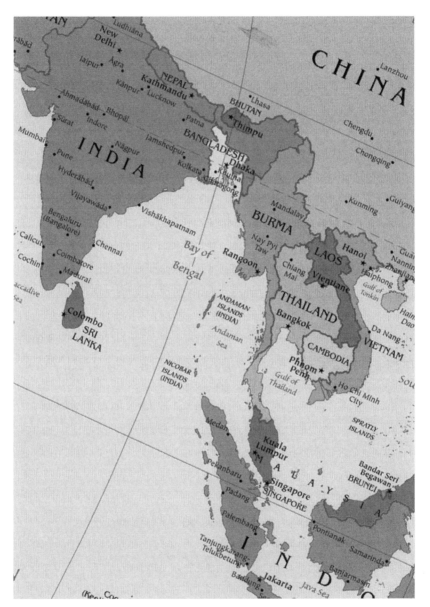

Map 7.1 The Northeast
Adapted from the University of Texas Libraries collection.

7 The Northeast Indian Ocean

India is the dominant naval power in the northeast and is generally regarded as a net security provider to the region. India has several security imperatives in and around the northeast. *First*, it represents a key space for the defence of India against potential threats that may emanate from or through the Southeast Asian archipelago. *Second*, the ability to control the sea lines of communication that cross the Bay of Bengal and Andaman Sea and enter the Pacific Ocean through the Malacca Strait would provide India with a bargaining chip in dealing with rival powers, particularly China. *Third*, the area is affected by numerous non-state security issues that may either directly threaten India's interests or otherwise require it to act as a regional maritime security provider, including piracy and smuggling, maritime terrorism, the activities of separatist movements and territorial disputes over offshore energy resources. *Fourth*, is the desire by India to expand its strategic role in Southeast Asia and further into the Pacific in order to balance China's growing influence.

India has been relatively successful in recent years in developing its role in the northeast Indian Ocean in a cooperative and relatively benign manner. India has focused on expanding its influence into archipelagic Southeast Asia through Singapore, which historically recognised India as a natural security provider to the region. India will also need to develop other larger partners in the region, some of whom have been more hesitant in recognising India's regional security role.

India's leading security role in the northeast Indian Ocean

India's leading security role in the northeast is a function of its geographic advantages and relative capabilities. Geographically, the Bay of Bengal and Andaman Sea is a semi-enclosed bay, surrounded by land on three sides. The western side is dominated by the Indian subcontinent and the eastern side by Southeast Asia (Myanmar, Thailand, Malaysia and Indonesia). India's dominance is reinforced by a relatively low level of strategic interest in the Indian Ocean by some states and the lack of naval capabilities of others. Only Myanmar represents a contested strategic space in this region. India has significant concerns over Myanmar's relationship with Beijing, which could potentially provide China with direct naval access to the region. But recent developments appear to indicate that Myanmar is more interested in playing off its neighbours for its own advantage than allowing itself to be dominated by any one of them.

India has dominated the northeast since at least 1971, when the separation of Bangladesh from Pakistan removed any realistic challenge to its position. India's successful naval blockade of Bangladesh severely inhibited Pakistan's ability to defend the territory and was an important reminder of some of the strategic consequences of control over the bay. Other challengers to India's predominance in the northeast over the last 70 years have been fleeting or illusory. Japan dominated the area during World War II after its forces occupied most of Southeast Asia and the British Eastern Fleet was evacuated to Africa, leaving India's entire eastern seaboard virtually defenceless. India was only saved from invasion by Japan's other military commitments and its limited interest in conquering India. In the 1960s, India's position in the northeast Indian Ocean was also briefly challenged by Indonesia. Indonesian president Sukarno infuriated New Delhi by suggesting that the Indian Ocean should be called the 'Indonesian Ocean'[1] and then threatened to seize the Andaman and Nicobar islands from India. As a result, during the 1965 Indo–Pakistan war, most of the Indian fleet was deployed in the Bay of Bengal to protect the Andaman Islands from Indonesia.[2] While any challenge from Indonesia is now history, India remains extremely sensitive towards any possible extra-regional naval presence in the Bay of Bengal/Andaman Sea. This was played out in India's intense reactions to the 'incursion' of the USS *Enterprise* into the area in 1971 and to unsubstantiated claims about a Chinese military presence in Myanmar in recent times.

Over the last decade or so, India has given much attention to improving its capabilities in the northeast Indian Ocean. There has been a considerable rebalancing of resources from the Indian Navy's Western Naval Command to its Eastern Naval Command, reflecting reduced perceptions of conventional maritime threat from Pakistan and increased threat perceptions in relation to China. The Western Naval Command, based in Mumbai, was traditionally regarded as the 'sword arm' of the Indian Navy, with a senior ranking commander and significantly more capable fleet than the other command. But the status of the Eastern Naval Command has been now equalised and it is now the larger fleet in terms of major warships, which will include the Indian Navy's new aircraft carrier and its entire nuclear submarine fleet. The build up of the Eastern Fleet will also include the planned construction of a major new base south of Visakhapatnam on India's east coast, with capacity for two aircraft carriers and nuclear submarines. According to Lawrence Prabhakar, an Indian naval analyst, the proposed base will have 'comprehensive anti-air, anti-submarine and amphibious capability, meaning a greater allocation of priority to the emergent Chinese naval force posture in the Myanmar region'.[3]

India strategic position in the northeast Indian Ocean is underpinned by its control of the Andaman and Nicobar Islands, a 720 km-long island chain which runs north-south through the Andaman Sea near the western end of the Malacca Strait. As K. M. Panikkar once commented, possession of the Andaman and Nicobar Islands gives India strategic bases 'which if fully utilised in coordination with air power can convert the Bay of Bengal into a secure area'.[4] The islands also form a natural base for India to project power into the Malacca Strait and beyond into the South China Sea, and have been described by a Chinese naval writer as constituting a 'metal chain' that could lock the western end of the Malacca Strait tight.[5] Since the mid-1990s, India has developed extensive military facilities in the Andaman and Nicobar Islands, including facilities to service elements of the Eastern Fleet and air bases for surveillance and strike aircraft. The operational radius of aircraft based in, or staging through, the Andaman and Nicobars encompasses the Malacca Strait and large portions of the South China Sea. India is undertaking a major development of military infrastructure, which includes runway upgrades and the development of port infrastructure for use by major vessels. In addition, the 3,500-strong army brigade based there is being expanded to divisional strength.[6] A new fleet replenishment base and naval air station is being developed on Great Nicobar, at the northern end of the Malacca Strait. However, the Indian Air Force has not yet permanently deployed frontline strike aircraft in the islands.

India's leading role in the northeast is reinforced by relatively benign perceptions within the region. Over the last two decades, the Indian Navy has actively developed cooperative security relationships in the region, for instance through conducting joint naval patrols, bilateral exercises and hosting the biennial MILAN 'gathering' of navies at Port Blair in the Andaman Islands. MILAN is not primarily intended as a naval exercise but rather an opportunity to increase military to military relationships with Southeast Asian navies as well as selected regional navies from Japan, Australia and New Zealand. The absence of the United States and China from the MILAN meetings is a none-too-subtle reminder of India's assertion of regional leadership. The Indian Navy has made considerable efforts to prove itself the leading provider of public goods to the region, providing maritime security in areas such as piracy, smuggling, refugees, terrorism and separatism. The Indian Navy has also demonstrated its capacity to provide humanitarian assistance and disaster relief, as demonstrated after the 2004 Tsunami, the 2007 Cyclone Sidr in Bangladesh and 2008 Cyclone Nargis in Myanmar.

India's maritime security ambitions in the Malacca Strait

A focal point of India's maritime security ambitions in the northeast Indian Ocean is its ambitions in the Malacca Strait, which is identified by the Indian Navy as part of its 'primary area of interest'.[7] An ability to exert negative control over the Strait would have major significance for India's strategic role in the region, and indeed the entire Indian Ocean. Some claim that the Strait represents for India a rough counterpart to the strategic importance of the

Panama Canal to the United States.[8] Others place it at the mid-point in an 'arc of rivalry' between India and China stretching from the Persian Gulf to the Sea of Japan.[9] Kaplan describes the Strait as being as strategically significant in coming decades as was the Fulda Gap during the Cold War.[10]

The Malacca Strait is the primary chokepoint for sea traffic between the Indian and Pacific oceans and one of the world's busiest waterways, including a projected 140,000 ship movements per annum by 2020. It is transited by around one-third of global trade and the bulk of energy supplies from the Middle East to East Asia. The Strait, which is some 550 nautical miles long and whose navigable routes narrow to less than one nautical mile, is considered to be particularly prone to commercial piracy and terrorist attacks. While there have been concerns about piracy in the past, instances of piracy is much reduced in recent years. The potential for terrorism has also been of concern, although no attacks have eventuated. Two other narrow straits through the Indonesian archipelago, the Lombok and Sunda straits, also represent chokepoints for trade between the Indian and Pacific Ocean.

While India's position in the Andaman and Nicobar Islands provides it with a considerable measure of control over the western approaches to the Strait, India has also sought to develop an active security role inside the Strait. In 2002, at the request of the United States, India provided naval escorts for high-value commercial traffic through the Strait as part of US-led Operation *Enduring Freedom*. India's participation in the operation was supported by Singapore (which hosted Indian naval vessels), and India is believed to have consulted Malaysia and Indonesia as well as the Philippines and Australia on the initiative. In 2006, the chairman of the US joint chiefs of staff, General Pace, commented that the United States was 'very comfortable' with India's assistance in providing security in the Strait.[11]

Security in the Strait is complicated by legal and political issues surrounding its status. The Strait is largely within the territorial waters of Indonesia, Malaysia and Singapore and under international law foreign naval vessels have a right of transit only. Foreign naval vessels may 'escort' other transiting vessels while transiting themselves, but, at least according to the littoral states, may not conduct armed 'patrols'. Indonesia and Malaysia are particularly jealous in safeguarding their sovereignty and are highly sensitive to the presence of any external maritime security providers in the Strait. In light of sensitivities about any perceived internationalisation of the Strait, some have argued for an extended definition of the 'Malacca Strait' to include Thailand and India as 'littoral' states and allow the creation of a composite security system of joint patrols throughout the relevant waters.[12]

Since the turn of this century there has been some controversy over moves by the United States and others to take a role in providing maritime security in the Strait. In 2004, the United States announced its Regional Maritime Security Initiative under which it proposed to provide security in the Malacca Strait in partnership with littoral states. This was strongly opposed by Indonesia and Malaysia, which construed it as proposing the deployment of US forces in the Strait. Indonesia and Malaysia have also refused to participate in the Japanese-sponsored multilateral ReCAAP initiative involving the voluntary exchange of information on piracy and other security threats in the Strait. In light of these controversies, India publicly distanced itself from the United States over the Regional Maritime Security Initiative and has insisted that any initiatives must be subject to the unanimous consent of littoral states.[13] At the same time, India has consistently lobbied littoral states for an active role in Strait security.

Singapore has generally encouraged India's offers to take a security role, but Indonesia has been more ambivalent. In 2005, an Indonesian Foreign Ministry spokesman publicly rebuffed Indian requests for a security role, telling the Indian chief of naval staff, Admiral Arun Prakash, that responsibility for safety in the Malacca Strait lay with Indonesia, Malaysia and Singapore only.[14] But the Indonesian military may take a more benign view of an Indian presence. In March 2009, in a meeting of the ASEAN Regional Forum, an Indonesian military spokesman reportedly requested India to take part in maintaining security in the Malacca Strait, on the basis that 'all approaches to the strait will be more secure for international shipping'.[15] Similarly, the Indonesian defence minister Purnomo Yusgiantoro was reported in 2010 as commenting that Indonesia had 'no reservations at all' about India maintaining security in the Malacca Strait.[16] In contrast, Malaysia has generally opposed any Indian role in the Strait, although it has consented to an Indian role in the 'Eye in the Sky' project to provide air surveillance over the Strait.[17]

In brief, there seems little prospect that the littoral states will agree to giving India a direct security role in the Strait in the current security environment, where there are few immediate security threats to be resolved. Any such role would also be regarded very adversely by China. But if the littoral states come under increased pressure to take action on Strait security, they might allow India to participate in Strait security on their terms. Any security role for India would be significant, not only for Strait security, but also in legitimising India's claims to be a benign security provider to the region as a whole.

India's engagement with archipelagic Southeast Asia

An important element in India's strategic interest in the northeast Indian Ocean is its strategic ambitions in Southeast Asia. India is driven not only by an imperative to balance China's growing regional influence but also by its aspirations to expand its strategic space into the region. Southeast Asia has historically not been able to either wholly provide for its own security or exclude extra-regional powers. As a result, since the 1960s most Southeast Asian states have relied on US strategic predominance to maintain a *Pax Americana*, while also balancing the interests and roles of other key extra-regional powers—including China, Japan and Australia. For more than a decade, several Southeast Asian states have also been encouraging India to play a greater role in the region. But India is overcoming decades of indifference and disengagement as it seeks to build regional influence.

India has profound cultural and religious ties with Southeast Asia, dating back thousands of years. The region's main religions, Hinduism, Buddhism and Sufi Islam, were largely derived from or through India, and India's strong cultural influence continues to be reflected in Southeast Asia's art, language and mythology. India also played an important role in the region during the colonial era. Until 1867, British imperial possessions on the Malay peninsula were administered from Calcutta and India was the source of its administrators, merchants and workers. Many colonial-era legacies, including Indian communities and institutions, live on in the region. But, as elsewhere in the Indian Ocean region, India's inward turn in the years following independence severely undermined its influence. India effectively discouraged investment and trading links, and failed to utilise the local Indian merchant communities that could have formed the basis of close economic relationships. Nehru had particular contempt for Western-leaning governments of Southeast Asia and discouraged attempts to engage with them over their political or security concerns.[18] However, he was not willing to counter the growing US strategic and cultural influence in Southeast Asia through developing India's own presence in the region.

During the 1960s there were several proposals for India to join in collective defence arrangements to counter Chinese-sponsored subversion and fill a power vacuum it was feared would arise following the British withdrawal east of Suez. Although some in the region saw India as a potential security guarantor, consistent with its principles of non-alignment, India refused to participate in any regional security arrangements. Several Southeast Asian states also saw India as potentially playing an important economic role in the region and some, like Singapore, reportedly tried to encourage India to join ASEAN upon its formation in 1967. This was motivated not only by a desire to increase India's stake in the region but also, perhaps, with a view to helping balance Indonesia's role within that grouping. India, apparently uninterested in developing economic links in the region and suspicious of a possible security dimension to ASEAN, declined any tentative approaches regarding its participation.[19]

India's apparent lack of interest in the region during the 1960s and its persistent downplaying of regional security concerns may have seemed 'callous, incredible and unrealistic' to Southeast Asians.[20] But during this period the Indians saw themselves as hardly capable of providing for their own security, let alone acting as a regional security provider. As the junior Indian foreign minister, B. R. Bhagat, argued in the Indian parliament in April 1968:

> If there was a defence agreement [with Southeast Asia] it would only mean India committing her manpower to the defence of areas which is beyond our capacity at present ... If we dispersed our efforts and took on responsibilities that we are not capable of shouldering, it would not only

weaken our own defence but would create a false sense of security and might even provoke a greater tension in the area.[21]

During the latter years of the Cold War, India's alignment with the Soviet Union was held in deep suspicion by some Southeast Asian countries and reinforced India's political estrangement from the region. India's support for Vietnam and its occupation of Cambodia led to claims that India was part of a communist-inspired Moscow-Hanoi-Delhi axis. There were also suspicions that India was providing logistical support for the Soviet Navy in the northeast Indian Ocean. Indonesia was particularly sensitive to the possibility of Indo–Soviet naval cooperation. In 1974, to allay Jakarta's concerns, Indian foreign minister Swaran Singh expressly promised that India would not provide the Soviet Navy with facilities in the Andaman Sea.[22] In the mid-1980s, an Indonesian military commander claimed that there had been numerous sightings of Soviet submarines near Sabang in Aceh and that they came from the Indian base at Nicobar Island.[23] Whether or not this was true, the waters around Sabang were a preferred loiter area for Soviet submarines.[24]

Some have argued that claims of Indo–Soviet naval cooperation were merely a disinformation campaign by US and Pakistani intelligence agencies.[25] But India does appear to have provided limited assistance to the Soviets, at least during the 1970s. According to the French naval historian, Coutau-Bégarie, between 1971 and 1976 the Soviet Navy was given limited access to the port of Visakhapatnam on India's east coast and Port Blair in the Andamans pursuant to a formal access arrangement. This was allowed to expire by the Desai government in 1977 despite an attempt by Soviet Admiral Gorshkov to secure its extension. But fears of large-scale operational cooperation between the Indian and Soviet Navies were largely misplaced.[26] Indo–Soviet naval cooperation was principally focused on the provision of Soviet equipment and training to India's Eastern Fleet, based at Visakhapatnam.[27] Soviet concerns over technology security led to a rather odd compartmentalisation of the Indian Navy between its Eastern Fleet, which relied on Soviet equipment, training and doctrine, and the Western Fleet, which largely used British equipment and was still heavily influenced by traditions inherited from the Royal Navy.

In the late 1980s, India's naval expansion plans and its military interventions in Sri Lanka and the Maldives renewed the concerns of several ASEAN states about India's ambitions in region. Singaporean prime minister, Goh Chok Tong, publicly questioned India's intentions in Southeast Asia. The Malaysian defence minister, Tengku Rithauddeen, commented that:

We would still like to see an Indian assurance that it will not use force against neighbouring countries ... [Malaysia] hoped that New Delhi would not go to the extent of flexing its military muscle beyond the Indian Ocean or attempt to control the gateway to the Straits of Malacca.[28]

The Indonesian chief of naval staff visited New Delhi to raise concerns about a proposed new base at Great Nicobar Island, which may have contributed to those plans being shelved.[29] Several Southeast Asian states increased their naval spending. The Royal Thai Navy cited alleged incursions into Thai waters by Indian submarines as reason for joint exercises with Japan and to justify its modernisation programme, although this may well have been more part of a procurement strategy than reflecting real threat perceptions.[30] Malaysia built a deep-water naval base at Lumut on its northwestern coast. Some in New Delhi claimed that these concerns were deliberately inspired by Canberra, either to obstruct India's efforts to improve relations in Southeast Asia or to justify increases in Australia's defence spending.[31]

The end of the Cold War and India's Look East policy

It is only in the last two decades that India has really sought to comprehensively engage with Southeast Asia. In the depths of India's post-Cold War economic and political crisis in 1992, the Rao government launched the 'Look East' policy which was designed to expand economic, political and security ties with Southeast Asia. India also saw its inclusion in Southeast Asian political, economic and security groupings as an important way to avoid the marginalisation of India in the post-Cold War international landscape. India's most immediate motivation was the need to expand trade and investment links with Southeast Asia in the face of a major economic crisis. But while there was a great deal of enthusiasm in Southeast Asia for building economic relationships with India, the economic engagement has developed much more slowly than was initially hoped. India's legacy of Nehruvian economic policies meant that it took a decade or more for substantive economic engagement between Southeast Asia and India.

Despite the rhetoric, India has been relatively slow to reduce protectionist barriers to trade with Southeast Asia, reflecting fears that Indian markets would be swamped with cheap goods. It took until 2009, after six years of negotiations, to conclude a multilateral ASEAN-India Free Trade Agreement that was largely confined to manufactured goods and allowed India to continue to protect agricultural products. Multilateral agreements on trade in services and investment are still being negotiated. India has finalised comprehensive bilateral free-trade arrangements only with Singapore and Malaysia, although other bilateral trade agreements are under negotiation. In negotiating trade arrangements, New Delhi has often allowed domestic political considerations, particularly in the agricultural sector, to trump longer term strategic and economic considerations. India's approach contrasts sharply with the more generous approach shown by China in negotiating trade agreements in the region.

As a result of India's hesitations in opening its economy, the economic relationship currently represents only a fraction of its potential. The volume of trade and investment flows between ASEAN and India is still relatively low compared with that of ASEAN's other main economic partners, although it is growing. As of 2011, India was ASEAN's seventh largest trading partner after Australia. Bilateral trade between India and ASEAN states grew 32 per cent from US$49 billion in 2009–10 to US$57 billion in 2010–11 and is expected to reach around $70 billion in 2012. Investment flows are also well below their potential. Between 2008 and 2010 India was the seventh largest source of foreign direct investment (FDI) in ASEAN, comprising some 2.4 per cent of total FDI in ASEAN.[32] There have been significant increases in Indian investment in ASEAN over the last couple of years, led by investment by Indian power companies in the Indonesian coal sector, while ASEAN member states accounted for about 10 per cent of India's total FDI inflow in 2011.

At the political level, India's policy has been to recognise and promote the 'centrality' of ASEAN in the region, which has caused it to focus on support for ASEAN-based organisations. As Indian prime minister Manmohan Singh commented in 2012, 'We believe that ASEAN centrality is essential in the evolving regional architecture for peace, stability, development and prosperity'.[33] Raja Mohan argues that a strong ASEAN represents a vital national interest for India, helping to insulate Southeast Asia from great power rivalry which would work to India's detriment.[34] India became a full dialogue partner to ASEAN in 1995 and an annual India–ASEAN summit has been held since 2002. In 2005 India was included in the first East Asia Summit. India has also sponsored new subregional organisations. India together with Thailand sponsored the establishment of the BIMSTEC grouping in 1997 to promote technical and economic cooperation among states in the northeast Indian Ocean region (including Malaysia, Thailand and Myanmar).[35] In 2000, India, again with Thailand, founded the Mekong Ganga Cooperation group to promote greater east-west transport connectivity between South Asia and Indochina. While both groupings are symbolically important, neither has played a significant role in extending India's strategic influence.

India has also been a strong supporter of ASEAN-centred security arrangements. India joined the ASEAN Regional Forum (ARF) in 1996 and effectively acceded to two ASEAN-sponsored security treaties: the Nuclear Weapons Free Zone Treaty (through announcing in 2000 that it would abide by the Treaty Protocol—as a non-NPT state it could not formally accede to it) and the Treaty of Amity and Cooperation (formally acceding in 2003). India also participated in the first meeting in 2010 of the defence ministers of ASEAN plus Australia, China, India, Japan, New Zealand, Russia, South Korea and the United States (known as ADMM + 8). But while India will likely continue to support the 'centrality' of ASEAN institutions, ASEAN has only a limited role in regional security, meaning that security engagement mostly occurs at the bilateral level.

Alongside multilateral engagement with the region, India has also engaged on a bilateral basis with key states bordering the northeast Indian Ocean. India's most successful engagement in the region has been with Singapore, with which it has developed a comprehensive relationship in the economic, political and security dimensions. However, India has also sought to develop closer relations with Indonesia, Malaysia and Thailand, with varying degrees of success. While India's post Cold War engagement with Southeast Asia was initially focused on economic and political links, most ASEAN states have, to a greater or lesser degree, welcomed an increased regional security role for India, particularly in maritime security. India is generally seen as a benign security presence and a potentially important regional counterweight to China and ASEAN has acknowledged India's 'important role in maintaining the peace, stability and prosperity of the region'.[36]

Many Southeast Asian states see India as potentially playing an important role in helping to ensure a balanced distribution of power in the region, alongside other key extra-regional powers, the United States, China, Japan and Australia. For some years Vietnam has been encouraging India to establish a naval presence there as part of its strategy of partnering with major powers to balance China and as a way of internationalising its territorial dispute with China in the South China Sea.[37] Indonesia, and more recently Malaysia and Thailand, have encouraged greater political and economic engagement by India in Southeast Asia as a way of balancing China. Singapore, in particular, has consistently welcomed and encouraged a balanced role for external security providers on the basis that competition between major regional powers 'must be squarely confronted and cannot be wished away'.[38] Singapore's conception of a 'balance of power' involves a multipolar balance that provides freedom to smaller states. As Singapore's prime minister Lee Hsien Loong has argued, Singapore's concept of a balance of power:

> Depends on the competing interests of several big powers in the region, rather than on linking the nation's fortunes to one overbearing power. The big powers can keep one another in check, and will prevent any one of them from dominating the entire region, and so allow small states to survive in the interstices between them.[39]

India's security partnership with Singapore

Singapore acts as India's strategic anchor in the eastern reaches of the Indian Ocean and the hub of India's economic, political and strategic relationships in Southeast Asia.[40] Lee Kuan Yew, Singapore's founding father and national visionary, was a great advocate for an expanded role for India in the region and this view is more or less shared by Singapore's current leaders. When India announced its Look East policy in 1992, Singapore responded with enthusiasm and quickly positioned itself as India's *de facto* regional sponsor. Despite some scepticism about the ability of India to deliver on economic reforms, the Singaporeans have shown considerable patience with India's systemic problems. Singapore now unquestionably plays a pivotal role in India's ambitions: it is India's regional advocate, its economic and political gateway into Southeast Asia and its most enthusiastic security partner. As Indian defence minister

Pranab Mukherjee commented in 2006, Singapore has become 'the hub of [India's] political, economic and security strategy in the whole of East Asia'.[41]

Since gaining independence in 1965, Singapore has been the most active of the Southeast Asian states in drawing external powers into the region, and has made several attempts to encourage India to take a security role in Southeast Asia. In the years following its independence, Singapore saw itself in a precarious strategic position, threatened by Communist Chinese-supported internal subversion, a hegemonic Indonesia and a potentially revanchist Malaysia. In what was probably his first act as leader of an independent Singapore in August 1965, Lee Kwan Yew made a request to Indian prime minister Lal Bahadur Shastri for assistance in training the newly established Singapore Army, to which New Delhi did not respond. In following years Lee continued to lobby New Delhi to take over Britain's role as a 'protecting' power for Singapore. Lee believed that India's presence was necessary to deter Malaysia's plans to continue to control Singapore after independence and to guarantee against Indonesia going 'berserk'. At the same time, Malaysia actively campaigned in New Delhi against any Indian assistance to Singapore.[42] In May 1968, following the announcement of the withdrawal of the Royal Navy from Singapore, Lee proposed to Indira Gandhi that the Indian Navy should take over its regional security role, including using Singapore's naval dockyard facilities for the building and repair of ships.[43]

Attempts to develop an Indian security role in the region were revived after the end of the Cold War. In 2003, India and Singapore entered into a comprehensive defence cooperation agreement which has facilitated annual defence policy dialogues, joint exercises, intelligence sharing and cooperation in defence technology. Over the last decade or so, the Indian and Singapore armed forces have developed a close relationship. The army and air forces have conducted annual exercises since 2004. The Singapore Air Force was given long-term use of the Indian Kalaikunda air base and India has agreed to the stationing of Singaporean army personnel and equipment at its Babina and Deololli firing ranges. While such arrangements are of obvious benefit to Singapore, which possesses few training areas of its own, India also benefits from being able to conduct extended training with Singapore forces. The use of Indian territory by foreign defence forces represents a major policy shift for India, which, from independence, fiercely opposed foreign military bases anywhere in Asia. Maritime security is at the core of the security relationship, particularly given the position of Singapore at the head of the Malacca Strait. The Singapore and Indian navies exercise together frequently, mostly in the Bay of Bengal but also in the South China Sea. Indian naval vessels are frequent visitors to Changi Naval Base, and the development of a semi-permanent Indian logistical presence seems not beyond the realms of possibility.[44]

From India's perspective, Singapore's size, economic role and geographic position make it an almost ideal partner for extending its influence in Southeast Asia. Singapore's role as a trading and services hub gives India an expeditious way of expanding its economic presence in the region. Singapore's clear-sighted approach to its own needs and those of the region allows the relationship with India to develop without the historical or ideological baggage that could be a factor in some of India's other relationships. But India's role in Singapore's security should also be put in perspective—while the relationship with India is growing, Singapore primarily relies on the United States and its partners in the Five Power Defence Arrangement (FPDA), particularly Australia, as its key external security partners, and that is unlikely to change in the foreseeable future.

India's other strategic relationships in archipelagic Southeast Asia

Other states in archipelagic Southeast Asia, such as Indonesia, Malaysia and Thailand, also see India's engagement in Southeast Asia as helpful in providing a useful balance to China. But while they have been more or less tolerant of India's strategic ambitions in the northeast Indian Ocean, they been cautious about seeing an expanded security role for India east of the Andaman Islands. This may inhibit the expansion of India's security role in Southeast Asia.

India's relationship with Indonesia, though relatively undeveloped, may be key to its strategic role in Southeast Asia in coming years.[45] New Delhi has long perceived Indonesia, the dominant state in archipelagic Southeast Asia, as the linchpin of any strategy to constrain Chinese influence in Southeast Asia.[46] Indonesia is important in several ways. It is by far the largest state in Southeast Asia and is regarded as *primus inter pares* in ASEAN. It represents a large market for Indian exports as well as a major supplier of resources. A close relationship with Indonesia will significantly enhance India's role in the region as well as helping India develop its other relationships across Southeast Asia. Indonesia's historical concern about China also makes it a potentially important partner in balancing China's economic, political and strategic influence.

In recent years Indonesia has adopted a more active foreign policy, showing impatience with the 'golden cage' of ASEAN and seeking to develop bilateral relationships with major powers beyond it. Although ideological differences between Indonesia and China have been reduced, Sino–Indonesian relations remain strained by fears of Chinese assertiveness and, to some degree, by continuing resentment in Indonesia against its economically powerful Chinese ethnic minority. Indonesia's relations with the United States have improved and Jakarta has indicated that it would like to see a continuing US security role in Southeast Asia as a counter to China's rising power. As Indonesia's strategic posture evolves, it is also likely to see India as an attractive security partner. The growth of China's power in the region will only increase Indonesia's need for balancing partnerships. Both India and Indonesia are now prepared to cooperate with the United States in a number of areas, including the creation of 'balanced' regional institutions. A relationship with India would fit well with Indonesia's hopes to extend its reach beyond ASEAN towards other major powers and, ultimately, to sit alongside India at the top table in a multipolar regional order. Indonesia may also see benefit from India playing an active maritime security role in the region.

Despite these reasons for closer relations, to date engagement in the security dimension has been more symbolic than substantive. A 2001 *Defence Cooperation Agreement* provides for the supply by India of training and defence equipment and the development of the Indonesian defence industry, but both Jakarta and New Delhi see it in broader symbolic terms. While Indian assistance in defence technology and training could be of value to Indonesia in light of India's expertise in Russian equipment, there has been little real progress in this area. Indonesia has unsuccessfully sought to acquire Indian radar systems and BrahMos cruise missiles.[47] In October 2012, after prevaricating for some years, India agreed to provide training and support for Indonesia's Russian-built Su-30 aircraft.[48] India's Pipavav shipbuilder also has plans to build naval corvettes in Surabaya, which could also prompt greater cooperation between the Indian and Indonesian navies in the provision of training and technology. However, India's ability to become a significant supplier of defence technology and services to Indonesia is likely to be constrained by both the small size of Indonesia's defence acquisition budget and India's limitations as an arms supplier.

In 2002, New Delhi's concerns about possible links between the secessionist Free Aceh Movement (*Gerakan Aceh Merdeka*) and Pakistan and the use of islands in the Nicobar Island group for gunrunning led to the *IndIndocorpat Agreement*, under which the Indian and Indonesian navies undertake biennial 'coordinated' naval patrols in the Six-Degree Channel at the northern entrance to the Malacca Strait. Although token in practical terms, such joint action, particularly at the entrance of the Malacca Strait, has considerable symbolic value. India has also proposed that the two navies enter into a formal maritime domain information-sharing arrangement.

Jakarta does not appear to have significant concerns about the growth of Chinese influence in the Indian Ocean. New Delhi raised concerns with Jakarta over possible Chinese involvement in the development of a port facility in the Palau Weh islands in Aceh province, a contract which was later awarded to Malaysian interests. But concerns about a Chinese naval presence in the Indian Ocean are not high on Indonesia's agenda; instead, its security concerns about China are focused on the South China Sea, including a possible dispute with China over the oil-rich waters adjacent to Indonesia's Natuna Islands. But Indonesia is likely to show increasing interest in Indian Ocean security as it grows as an economic power. In May 2011, the Indonesian Navy conducted a long-range operation to Somalia to help free an Indonesian ship from pirates. Although the operation tested the limits of the Indonesian Navy's capabilities, it might also be seen as an example of Indonesia's expanding interests across the Indian Ocean.

Indonesia's size and its geographical position as gatekeeper between the Indian and Pacific oceans may make it an indispensible regional partner for an India. A broad-based strategic partnership between India and Indonesia could transform India's role in Southeast Asia. But, while bilateral trade is growing very quickly, both India and Indonesia are subject to significant internal constraints which make any political or security engagement slow and hesitant. The development of a broad-based relationship with Indonesia would require a major political, economic and security commitment by New Delhi that has so far not been forthcoming.

India's security relationships with Thailand and Malaysia are also evolving slowly. Thailand's views about maritime security in the Indian Ocean are broadly convergent with India's and it is increasingly accepting of India's leading role in the Bay of Bengal/Andaman Sea. Thailand also sees India as a useful counterweight to Chinese influence in Myanmar. However the security relationship is relatively undeveloped. Bilateral cooperation from the late 1990s focused on enhancing east-west trade connectivity between India, Thailand and Indochina. India and Thailand worked together to co-sponsor the BIMSTEC and the Mekong Ganga Cooperation groupings, both of which were intended to position India and Thailand as regional leaders in the Bay of Bengal/Indochina. Over the last decade or so, India provided assistance to combat Islamic separatists in Southern Thailand in return for Thailand taking action against Indian separatists who were using Thailand as a supply route for arms. Since 2006, the Indian and Thai navies have also conducted symbolic 'coordinated patrols' in the Andaman Sea, which are primarily intended as a confidence-building measure. An MOU on Defence Cooperation was signed in January 2012 and an annual Defence Dialogue has been established. However, closer security cooperation will likely be limited by Thailand's political instability and its very limited naval capabilities in the Andaman Sea.

Malaysia, through its political and economic influence and its geographical position, is also important to India's strategic ambitions in the region, but the relationship is more complicated. India provided Malaya/Malaysia with considerable diplomatic support in the years following the latter's independence and during the *Konfrontasi* era with Indonesia, but relations have sometimes been strained in the last few decades as Malaysia began emphasising its ties with Muslim countries, including Pakistan. There are now several irritations in the relationship, including political unrest among the Indian ethnic community in Malaysia (representing some 8 per cent of the population), unhappy about their economic and political marginalisation.[49] Malaysia's relatively close links with China has also led it to be cool about including India in East Asian regional groupings—Malaysia opposed holding a separate ASEAN–India summit and quietly supported China's attempts to exclude India from the first East Asian Summit in 2005.

Malaysia has also been somewhat cautious about India's strategic ambitions in the region. Malaysia has had concerns about the level of Chinese influence in Myanmar and the potential for a Chinese naval presence in the northeast Indian Ocean.[50] But Kuala Lumpur has not been enthusiastic about India's attempts to promote itself as the leading maritime security provider in the Andaman Sea and gain a role inside the Malacca Strait. Unlike some of its neighbours,

Malaysia considers that it has an active role to play in Indian Ocean security, as indicated by the deployment the Royal Malaysian Navy to the Gulf of Aden since 2008 as part of the Combined Military Forces. Malaysia has declined to hold regular bilateral naval exercises or conduct 'coordinated patrols' with the Indian Navy similar to the patrols the Indian Navy conducts with Indonesia and Thailand and, as discussed previously, it has also opposed India's attempts to gain a security role in the Malacca Strait. But there is some cooperation in respect of shared defence platforms. Since 2007 the Indian Air Force has provided training for the Malaysian Air Force's Russian-built SU-30 MKM aircraft, primarily in Malaysia. There is also an agreement to cooperate in maintenance and training for the French-designed Scorpene submarines being deployed by the Malaysian and Indian navies.

The political and economic relationship seems to be on the upswing. There are long-standing links between Indian and Malaysian small to medium-sized enterprises which could make the India–Malaysia economic relationship qualitatively different to India's economic relations with other Southeast Asian states, and there are expectations of a significant increase in two-way direct investment. It is possible that as economic links develop Kuala Lumpur will become more comfortable with an Indian security presence in its immediate area.

Myanmar: contested space or a buffer state?

The only real challenge to India's supremacy in the northeast over the last couple of decades has been through Myanmar. Myanmar represents a direct security threat to India through its use as a sanctuary by insurgents active in India's Northeast states. Much has also been made of Chinese strategic penetration of Myanmar and the potential for it to be used as a base for China's strategic ambitions in the Indian Ocean. Some see Myanmar as essentially a 'contested space', vied over by India and China as a strategic 'prize'. But it is probably more accurate to see Myanmar as a buffer state. Barry Buzan, a noted regional theorist, calls it, an 'insulator state', in effect 'insulating' South Asia from both Southeast Asia and China.[51] This implies that, although Myanmar may lean one way or another, it is unlikely to allow itself to be permanently incorporated into any sphere of influence.

During the colonial era, the British rulers of India regarded Myanmar as a buffer state between India and China and for that reason wanted to control it, just as they hoped to control Afghanistan, which acted as a buffer state between India and Russia. While Britain took advantage of China's internal preoccupations to conquer Myanmar and attach it to British India in the 1880s, it essentially remained a buffer state. In the decades following independence, Myanmar demonstrated a 'prickly' neutralism against all comers. Although it was administered from New Delhi until 1937, Myanmar falls somewhat outside of India's strategic concept of South Asia. India has not sought to exercise any hard form of Monroe Doctrine over Myanmar but is clearly sensitive to any 'external' influences there. While some in New Delhi might aspire to bring Myanmar into an Indian sphere of influence, a more realistic ambition would be for Myanmar to adopt policies that promote economic development, settle its internal conflicts, and allow it to better resist external domination.

Myanmar's role in the Indian Ocean is constrained by its economic weakness and its preoccupation with internal threats. The lion's share of Myanmar's military resources is devoted to its army, which is fighting numerous separatist insurgencies. Myanmar's small brown-water navy is essentially constabulary and focused on arms and other types of smuggling. These internal preoccupations mean that there is little chance that the Myanmar Navy will be a material factor in the regional maritime balance for the foreseeable future. Nevertheless, Myanmar is the cause of considerable concern to India, first, as a source of regional instability, including acting as a safe haven for separatist groups in India's northeast states, and second for its potential to facilitate a Chinese presence in the Indian Ocean.

India has had a relatively cool relationship with Myanmar since its independence in 1948. Among other things, there was considerable resentment in Myanmar over Indian migrants, who dominated administration and trade during the colonial era. Although most Indians community have since fled Myanmar, a lasting enmity towards the Indian community continues to affect relations. This was a significant factor in India's support for democratic protests against the Burmese junta in September 1988 and its support for Burmese exile groups for years afterwards. George Fernandes, Indian defence minister from March 1998 to 2004 was a strong supporter of Burmese exile groups, even allowing one group to set up an office in his home.[52] This led to an antagonistic relationship with the Burmese military junta for much of the 1990s.

Separatist insurgencies in Northeast India and Myanmar

The most immediate security issue between India and Myanmar is the ethnic-based separatist insurgencies in India's Northeast states and western Myanmar. Many separatist groups live on both sides of the border and both India and Myanmar have attempted to use these insurgencies as strategic leverage against the other, from time to time supporting or condoning insurgencies in the other's territory.

During the 1990s, RAW provided assistance to several separatist groups active in Myanmar in order to place pressure on the Myanmar regime and in an attempt to use the separatist groups to help police India's border. This included financial and military support to the Kachin Independence Army (KIA), the most important of the insurgent groups in northern Myanmar, as *quid pro quo* for the KIA's assistance in counter-insurgency operations against the Naga insurgents operating in India's Nagaland and Manipur states.[53] RAW also provided assistance to Arakanese insurgent groups in an attempt to secure India's eastern borders with Myanmar. According to RAW deputy chief, B. B. Nandi, "These rebels served India's interest much better than [Myanmar's] military regime'.[54] RAW may have also used Arakanese separatists for intelligence gathering on Chinese activities along the coast and islands.[55]

RAW's support for separatist groups in Myanmar led to considerable tensions with the Indian Army, which was fighting a multiple insurgency (often with the same groups) on the Indian side of the border. Indian arms provided to insurgent groups in Myanmar often found their way across the porous border to Indian separatist groups.[56] To some army officers this recalled RAW's role in India's failed intervention in Sri Lanka, which had resulted in considerable casualties for the army. From the mid-1990s, the Indian Army took the lead in trying to develop a more cooperative relationship with the Myanmar military (known as the *Tatmadaw*), to combat the insurgencies on both sides of the border. According to the former chief of India's Eastern Army Command, General H. R. S. Kalkat, India's Myanmar policy should be 'better left to the army. We are soldiers and they are soldiers and our blood is thicker than the bloods of bureaucrats and politicians'.[57] Tensions between the Indian Army and RAW became public in February 1998 when, in Operation *Leech*, Indian forces arrested 34 and killed six Myanmar insurgents in the Andaman Islands after the insurgents were lured to a scheduled rendezvous with their Indian liaison officer. RAW's deputy chief B. B. Nandi then offered to testify on behalf of the insurgents in court because he felt they were victims of treachery.[58] RAW may still provide support to some Myanmar insurgent groups.[59]

Since the 1990s there has been intermittent and largely ineffective cooperation between India and Myanmar in cross-border counterinsurgency operations. Over this period, and particularly since 2006, India provided intelligence and limited training and equipment. India supplied helicopters, avionics upgrades of Myanmar's Russian and Chinese-made fighter planes, and British-built BN-2 Islander maritime surveillance aircraft, as well as artillery and ammunition. Training has been provided at India's Kochi Naval air base and India's Counterinsurgency and Jungle Warfare School in Mizoram. This assistance was either intended to bolster the Tatmadaw's counterinsurgency capabilities or was given as *quid pro quo* for promises to take on insurgent groups.

The failure of both India and Myanmar to take effective action against separatist insurgents sheltering in their territories continues to be a significant irritant in the relationship. Certainly India's efforts to purchase cooperation have not succeeded. As a senior Indian intelligence officer commented, 'Although we have been giving the military regime weapons and vehicles, the junta is not reciprocating in the same manner. We have been pressing for a crackdown on camps inside Myanmar, but Myanmar has turned a deaf ear to us'.[60] The Tatmadaw is suspected of having significant commercial interests in the smuggling activities undertaken by Indian separatist groups and are reluctant to interrupt that trade. Bertil Lintner, a noted Myanmar analyst, described a 2011 offensive by the Tatmadaw against Indian separatists as a 'phantom operation' claiming that it is in the interest of Myanmar to maintain a 'buffer of instability' with India.[61]

During the 1960s, China used the ungoverned areas of northern Myanmar to provide material support to Indian separatist groups operating in Northeast India, although this was considerably reduced in the late 1970s. In recent years there have been renewed claims of covert Chinese and Pakistani support for Indian separatist groups operating from Myanmar territory.[62] Lintner argues that China has a greyer role in supplying arms to Indian insurgents, with Chinese authorities turning a blind eye to the arms trade run by former Chinese army officers and private arms dealers in retaliation for India's support for the Dalai Lama.[63]

India's principal long-term strategic concern with Myanmar stems from China's strategic influence there. For several decades following independence there was considerable antagonism towards China. But Myanmar's international isolation after the military junta took power in 1988 led it to turn to China and the relationship was reinforced by China's international isolation following Tiananmen Square in June 1989. For China, Myanmar is an attractive strategic partner on its periphery. Among other things, the relationship can help India off balance in the northeast Indian Ocean, just as the China–Pakistan relationship creates pressure on India from the west. The relationship is primarily economic but also has a significant security dimension. Between 1988 and 1992 almost 60 per cent of Myanmar's national budget was reportedly spent on military modernisation, much of this in acquiring arms from China.[64]

For India, one of the most worrying features of the relationship was the possible development of a Chinese presence in the northeast Indian Ocean. There is no doubt that China is trying to develop a non-military presence in the Indian Ocean, through what it calls its 'bridgehead strategy' of connecting Yunnan province with the Indian Ocean through Myanmar. This includes the development of a road/rail/river corridor using the Irrawaddy river and oil and gas pipelines between the Burmese port of Sittwe and Yunnan province. Over the last two decades there have been numerous claims of Chinese involvement in the development or upgrading of several commercial ports or naval facilities, as well as the establishment of a Chinese signals intelligence facility on Myanmar's Great Coco Island. But fears about a covert Chinese military presence appear to have been misplaced. As will be discussed in Chapter 10, in 2005 the Indian Navy conceded that there was no Chinese intelligence facility on Great Coco Island and nor were there any Chinese naval bases anywhere in Myanmar. In fact, the Indian Navy has good institutional relationships with its Tatmadaw counterparts, including arrangements for berthing of Indian ships at Myanmar ports and conducting joint naval manoeuvres.[65]

A major shift in Myanmar's strategic alignment now appears to be underway. Since March 2011, a reformist government under President Thein Sein has made considerable steps towards democracy and national reconciliation, including bringing opposition leader Aung San Suu Kyi into the political process and attempting to resolve various ethnic conflicts. These moves were closely connected with the reversal of US policy from isolation of the Myanmar regime towards one of engagement. The United States has taken the lead in facilitating the opening of Myanmar's society and economy to the outside world, and its new status in the international system was clearly signalled by the visit of President Obama in November 2012.

At the same time, Myanmar has partly distanced itself from China. This began in September 2011 with the suspension by President Sein of the unpopular Myitsone dam project, which had been sponsored by China and was intended to be a major source of cheap electricity to southern China. According to one observer, Yun Sun, the cancellation of the dam project 'fundamentally shook Chinese leaders' trust and confidence in Myanmar as a partner'.[66] Sun believes that the opening of Myanmar to the West was a result of several miscalculations by China, including an overestimation of its political and economic influence. The deterioration of its strategic relationship with Myanmar represents the most significant set-back for China in the Indian Ocean region for many years.

India has very much taken a back seat in this realignment. Given its historical strains with Myanmar's regime, New Delhi may well have considered it prudent to allow the United States to take the leading role. In any event, it is further evidence of a much more relaxed attitude towards US influence in the region and an implicit partnership in opposing China's regional influence. Myanmar's opening also likely signals considerable economic opportunities for India, including reviving New Delhi's dreams of improving east-west trade connectivity between India and Southeast Asia through Myanmar. This would be of considerable economic benefit to India's Northeast states, which also hope to gain transport access through Myanmar to the Indian Ocean port of Sittwe. This would potentially have considerable strategic consequences for India and mitigate its reliance on communications with its Northeastern states via the narrow 'chicken's neck' area around Bangladesh.

The long-term implications of Myanmar's strategic realignment are not yet clear. Myanmar could well revert to the isolationist 'prickly neutralism' that characterised the first four decades of its independence, although the current signs are that it will move closer to the ASEAN economic and political model. Either result will likely continue to reduce China's influence in Myanmar and remove a potential challenge to India's predominant strategic position in the northeast Indian Ocean. But the 'normalisation' of Myanmar could also represent an important opportunity for India in developing its regional relationships, allowing, for example, the potential activation of sub-regional groupings such as BIMSTEC and Mekong-Ganga Cooperation, which in the past have been hampered by Myanmar's isolationism and pariah status.

India's role in the northeast

India is the dominant naval power in the northeast Indian Ocean and is generally regarded as a net security provider to the region. Among other things this gives India the ability to control the sea lines of communication that cross the Bay of Bengal/Andaman Sea and transit the Malacca Strait. The development of a security role within the Malacca Strait itself remains a long term objective.

But India has been relatively slow in developing security relationships in Southeast Asia. Although India has close historical links there, its inward turn following Independence severely undermined its influence in the region, which means that India is still making up for much lost ground. While there is now a broad consensus among ASEAN states in favour of India playing a more active security role in Southeast Asia, there is no clear understanding among them as to what that role should be. This reflects a systemic failure of coordination among ASEAN states as well as the failure of India to meld its bilateral defence relationships states into a coherent regional strategy. As a result, each of India's defence relationships with ASEAN states is largely driven by particular dynamics and circumstances of bilateral relationships. India has developed a close defence relationship with Singapore, which acts as its 'hub' in the region. Elsewhere, India's moves have been slow and hesitant. Some in New Delhi hope to work with Vietnam to establish an Indian naval presence in the South China Sea, but India is likely to be cautious about taking any action that could lead to a possible confrontation with China. India also aspires to develop defence relationships with Indonesia, Thailand and Malaysia, but here again the rhetoric has often exceeded the reality. If India is to build a major strategic role in the region it will need to prove itself a useful partner to these key states. This will require a much greater and more consistent commitment to the entire region than has been evident over the last decade or so.

Notes

1 Which led to a debate in the Indian Parliament in 1963. Raj Narain Misra (1986) *Indian Ocean and India's Security*, Delhi: Mittal, note 85.
2 According to the Indian chief of naval staff, Vice Admiral Bhaskar S. Soman. Rangit Rai (2010) 'Why the Indian Navy did "sweet Fanny Adams" in the 1965 War', *The Naval Review*, Vol. 98 No. 4, November, pp. 379–84.
3 Sudha Ramachandran (2006) 'India navy drops another anchor', *Asia Times*, 17 October.
4 K.M. Panikkar (1945) *India and the Indian Ocean: an Essay on the Influence of Sea Power on Indian History*, London: George Allen & Unwin, p. 96.
5 Zhang, Ming (2006) 'The Malacca dilemma and the Chinese navy's strategic choices', *Modern Ships*, No. 274, October, p. 23.
6 Rajat Pandit (2010) 'Strategically-important A& n Command to get a boost', *Times of India*, 6 February.
7 Indian Navy (2007) *Freedom to Use the Seas: India's Maritime Military Strategy*.
8 James Holmes *et al.* (2009) *Indian Naval Strategy in the Twenty-first Century*, Abingdon: Routledge, p. 154.
9 Gurpreet Khurana (2009) 'China–India maritime rivalry', *Indian Defence Review*, Vol. 23, No. 4.
10 The most likely invasion route of the Soviet Union into West Germany. Kaplan (2009) 'Center stage for the twenty-first century', *Foreign Affairs*, Vol. 88, No. 2, p. 25.
11 'Indian Navy awaits regional nod for patrolling Malacca Straits' (2006) *India Defence*, 7 June.
12 Rajeev Sawhney (2006) 'Redefining the limits of the Straits: a Composite Malacca Straits Security System', *RSIS Commentaries* No. 37, 18 May.

13 Gurpreet S. Khurana (2008) 'The Malacca Straits "conundrum" and India', in N.S. Sisodia (ed.), *Changing Security Dynamics in Southeast Asia*, New Delhi: Institute for Defence Studies and Analyses, pp. 125–42 at p. 134.

14 Rakesh Sinha (2005) 'Jakarta says no to Indian patrol in Malacca Straits', *Indian Express*, 13 July.

15 'Indonesia asks India to help maintain Malacca Strait security' (2009) *Xinhua*, 5 March.

16 P.S. Suryanarayana (2010) 'Indonesia to 'learn' from India's defence sector', *The Hindu*, 18 June.

17 Suryanarayana (2008) 'India, Malaysia to step up defence ties'; and 'Indian Air Force chief to visit Malaysia; boost in military ties', *India Defence*, 17 August.

18 J.N. Dixit (2004) *Makers of India's Foreign Policy: Raja Ram Mohun Roy to Yashwant Sinha*, New Delhi: HarperCollins, p. 12.

19 Kripa Sridharan (1996) *The ASEAN Region in India's Foreign Policy*, Aldershot: Dartmouth Publishing, p. 49.

20 Kripa Sridharan (2001) 'Regional Perceptions of India', in Frederick Grare and Amitabh Mattoo (eds), *India and ASEAN: The Politics of India's Look East Policy*, New Delhi: Centre de Sciences Humaines, pp. 67–89 at p. 74.

21 Indian Parliament, Lok Sabha debates, 1968.

22 *The Statesman*, 12 August 1974.

23 Yang Razali Kassim (1986) 'India angered by claim over Soviet subs', *Straits Times*, 13 October. Which was strongly denied by Indian officials, although they did not directly answer the allegations.

24 Derek da Cunha (1990) *Soviet Naval Power in the Pacific*, Boulder, CO: Lynne Rienner, p. 177.

25 B. Raman (2002) *Intelligence: Past, present and future*, New Delhi: Lancer Publishers, p. 46.

26 Hervé Coutau-Bégarie (1983) *La puissance maritime sovietique* [Soviet Sea Power], Paris: Economica.

27 There may have been isolated instances of operational coordination. According to Soviet Admiral Zuyenko, a squadron of Indian minesweepers working to clear mines in Bangladesh after the 1971 war were placed under Soviet operational command. *Los Angeles Times*, 26 December 1972. This was denied by Indian authorities. There are also claims of the operational coordination of Indian and Soviet ASW forces in detecting American submarines in the Arabian Sea and the Bay of Bengal.

28 Michael Richardson (1989) 'East Asia and Western Pacific brace for Indian ascendency', *The International Herald Tribune*, 4 October.

29 G.V.C. Naidu (1991) 'The Indian Navy and Southeast Asia', *Contemporary Southeast Asia*, Vol. 13, No. 1, June, p. 81.

30 Sandy Gordon with Desmond Ball, Paul Dibb and Amin Saikal (1996) *Security and Security Building in the Indian Ocean Region*, Canberra: Strategic and Defence Studies Centre, p. 81.

31 S.K. Bhutani (1995) 'India–Australia Bilateral Relations', in Dipkar Banerjee (ed.), *Towards an Era of Cooperation: An Indo–Australian Dialogue*, New Delhi: Institute for Defence Studies and Analyses, p. 376.

32 ASEAN Statistical Yearbook (various years). Online: www.asean.org/resources/.

33 Manmohan Singh (2012) speech at Tenth India–ASEAN Summit, Phnom Penh, November.

34 C. Raja Mohan (2012) 'An uncertain trumpet? India's role in Southeast Asian security', paper presented at RSIS South Asia Programme Workshop, Singapore, 30 November.

35 The Bay of Bengal Initiative for MultiSectoral Technical and Economic Cooperation organisation.

36 ASEAN Secretary General, Yong Ong (2004) 'Advancing the ASEAN–India partnership in the New Millenium', address in New Delhi, 18 October.

37 The India–Vietnam relationship is beyond the scope of this book. For a discussion of the relationship, see David Brewster (2009) 'The strategic relationship between India and Vietnam: The search for a diamond on the South China Sea?', *Asian Security*, Vol. 5, No. 1, January, pp. 24–44.

38 Goh Chok Tong (2005) 'Constructing East Asia', speech to Asia Society, 15th Asian Corporate Conference, Bangkok, 9 June.

39 *Straits Times*, 6 November 1984.

40 See generally, David Brewster (2009) 'India's security partnership with Singapore', *The Pacific Review*, Vol. 22, No. 5, December, pp. 597–618.

41 Pranab Mukherjee (2006) address to the 5th IISS Asian Security Summit, 3 June.

42 Datta-Ray (2009) *Looking East to Look West: Lee Kuan Yew's Mission India*, Singapore: Institute of Southeast Asian Studies, p. 87.

43 Dr V. Suryanarayan (2008) 'India–Singapore relations: an overview', Chennai Centre for China Studies, C3S Paper No. 140, 2 April.

44 C. Raja Mohan (2008) 'India's geopolitics and Southeast Asian security', *Southeast Asian Affairs*, pp. 43–60.

45 See generally, David Brewster (2011) 'The evolving security relationship between India and Indonesia', *Asian Survey*, Vol. 51, No. 2, March/April, pp. 221–44.

46 Mohammed Ayoob, *India and Southeast Asia: Inidan Perceptions and Policies*, New York: Routledge, p. 36.

47 'Indonesia and Malaysia keen on buying BrahMos' (2007) *Frontier India Strategic and Defence*, 13 April; Amitav Ranjan (2004) 'India says not yet to Indonesian plea', *India Express*, 21 April.

48 Manu Pubby (2012) 'India to train, support Indonesian Sukhoi fleet', *The Indian Express*, 17 October.

49 Dr V. Suryanarayan (2008) 'Malaysian Indian Society in Ferment', *South Asia Analysis Group*, Paper No. 2880, 14 October.

50 Bertil Lintner (1994) 'Enter the Dragon', *Far Eastern Economic Review*, 22 December, p. 24.

51 Barry Buzan and Gowher Rizvi (1986) *South Asian Insecurity and the Great Powers*, New York: St Martin's Press.

52 Renaud Egreteau (2003) *Wooing the Generals: India's New Myanmar Policy*, Delhi: Authorspress, p. 125.

53 Andrew Selth (1996) 'Myanmar and the strategic competition between China and India', *Journal of Strategic Studies*, Vol. 19, No. 2, pp. 213–30.

54 Subir Bhaumik (2011) 'Arakanese rebels freed from Indian jail', *AsiaTimes*, 21 May.

55 Egreteau, *Wooing the Generals*, p. 153.

56 'Shake-up for Indian spies' (2000) *Jane's Foreign Report*, 28 June.

57 Bhaumik, 'Arakanese rebels freed from Indian jail'.

58 Ibid.

59 In 2011, the Tatmadaw accused India of supplying the Kachin Independence Army with food, which was not denied by the KIA. Joseph Allchin (2011) 'India flexes diplomatic, military muscle in Myanmar', *Eurasia Review Newsletter*, 18 October.

60 'India breaks silence on Myanmar, hedges its bets' (2007) BDNew24.com, 27 September. Online: http://ns.bdnews24.com/details.php?id=76312&cid=1 (accessed 10 October 2013).

61 Ratnadip Choudhury (2011) 'Bertil Linter: Myanmar will not cooperate with India in crossborder insurgencies', *Tehelka*, 28 September. Online: www.tehelka.com/story_main50.asp?filename=Ws280911Myanmar.asp (accessed 10 October 2013).

62 Anirban Bhaumik (2011) 'China wooing NE insurgents in Myanmar', *Deccan Herald*, 2 October.

63 Choudhury, 'Bertil Lintner'.

64 J. Mohan Malik (1994) 'Sino–Indian rivalry in Myanmar: implications for regional security', *Contemporary Southeast Asia*, Vol. 16, No. 2, September, pp. 137–56.
65 C. Raja Mohan (2012) *Samudra Manthan: Sino–Indian Rivalry in the Indo–Pacific*, Washington, DC: Carnegie Endowment for International Peace, p. 179.
66 Yun Sun (2012) 'China's strategic misjudgement in Myanmar' *Journal of Current Southeast Asian Affairs*, Vol. 31, No. 1, pp. 73–96, at p. 87.

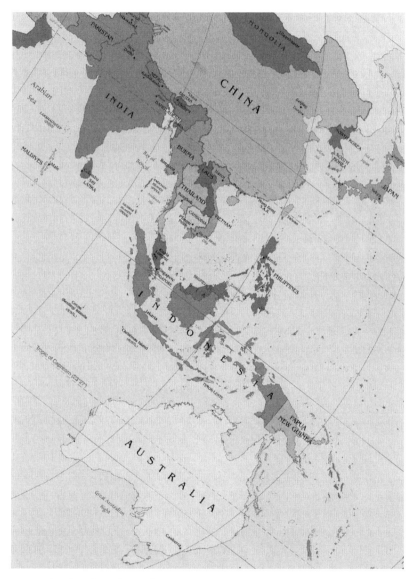

Map 8.1 The view from Australia
Adapted from the University of Texas Libraries collection.

8   Australia

The southeastern quadrant of the Indian Ocean, which is dominated by Australia, represents a secondary area of strategic interest for India. India currently has few direct security interests in the area, although this may grow in coming years as its economic relationship with Australia grows. But Australia is a potentially important partner for India's strategic ambitions in the Indian Ocean. After India, it has the most capable navy of any of the Indian Ocean states and is an active security provider in much of the region. India and Australia also share many interests in the Indian Ocean and Southeast Asia and there are considerable opportunities for security cooperation. Although Australia has shown enthusiasm for developing the security relationship, India has been relatively cautious.

Australia's strategic perspectives on the Indian Ocean

For most of its history, Australia has looked north and east, towards the Pacific rather than the Indian Ocean. There are good reasons for this: most of Australia's population and industry lie on the Pacific Ocean, and its economic relationships are dominated by East Asia. Australia has also long perceived security threats as emanating from its north and not the west. Even before it gained independence from Britain, Australia was preoccupied by prospects of 'hordes' of Asians wanting to occupy the largely empty continent. These concerns were reinforced by Japan's invasion of Southeast Asia in the early 1940s and Chinese-sponsored subversion in the region during the Cold War.

But Australia is a major Indian Ocean state too. By traditional definition, more than 14,000 km of Australia's coastline is on the Indian Ocean, more than any other littoral state.[1] Australia also has by far the largest area of maritime jurisdiction in the Indian Ocean, including an EEZ aggregating 3.88 million square kilometres and an extended continental shelf of 2.02 million square kilometres. With the development of its vast mineral and energy resources in Western Australia over the last few decades, Australia has begun paying much more attention to the Indian Ocean.

Canberra has long relied on great and powerful friends for its security: first via its imperial links with Britain and then with the United States under the

ANZUS alliance. These alliances have allowed Australia to make only a relatively small contribution to maritime security in the Indian Ocean, where it has largely relied on the Royal Navy and then the US Navy to secure its sea lines of communication to the Middle East and Europe. But Australia has been an active contributor to the security of the broader region. Since the beginning of the twentieth century, Australia has sent numerous expeditionary forces to Africa, the Middle East and West and Southeast Asia as part of British Imperial forces and US-sponsored coalitions. Major military deployments over the last two decades have included to Kuwait, Somalia, East Timor, Iraq, Afghanistan and the Gulf of Aden. Indeed, the Australian Army is largely structured as an expeditionary force for coalition operations. These arrangements have generally worked to Australia's satisfaction, helping to ensure that a friendly power retained predominance in the Indian Ocean region—for which Australia paid what it considered to be an acceptable premium on its 'insurance policy'. Australia has had no desire to sponsor the establishment of a local security order: indeed, for decades it has worked assiduously to draw the US further into the Indian Ocean region and keep it there.

Australia was first forced to focus seriously on the Indian Ocean with the withdrawal of British forces east of Suez from the late 1960s. Canberra worked hard to draw Washington's attention to the Indian Ocean by playing up a supposed, and largely illusory, Soviet naval threat.[2] Through the 1970s Australia was one of the staunchest supporters of the US military presence in the region. In what has been described as a 'charade', Australia adopted the rhetorical objective of a balance of forces between the United States and the Soviet Union at the 'lowest practical level', while at the same time working non-publicly to ensure US superiority.[3] While Australia paid lip service to the Indian Ocean Zone of Peace proposal promoted by India (more so under centre-left than conservative Australian governments), calling it a 'fine ideal', at the same time it worked to secure or enhance the US military commitment in the region.[4] Australia's support for US presence in the Indian Ocean even contributed to its support for Indonesia's takeover of Portuguese East Timor in 1975.[5] The United States was also encouraged to establish military facilities in Australia: a US communications facility was opened on North West Cape in 1967 that became a vital link in communications with US nuclear submarines transiting the Indian Ocean, and US space-tracking and communications facilities were also opened in central Australia. In 1970 Australia unsuccessfully proposed that the US Navy use the new naval base near Perth as a home port. Until recently, however, Australia has generally resisted the presence of US combat troops on its territory.

One of the greatest tests for Australia's Indian Ocean strategy came in 1977 when, in a diplomatic surprise, the Carter administration called for an agreement with the Soviet Union involving the 'complete demilitarisation' of the Indian Ocean. Talks on what was to become known as the Naval Arms Limitation Treaty (NALT) almost led to a freeze on the level of US and Soviet naval deployments in the Indian Ocean. While India saw the talks as being consistent with the aims of its Indian Ocean Zone of Peace proposal, Australia saw the proposal as highly adverse to its strategic interests. According to Australian prime minister Malcolm Fraser, it 'raised serious concerns about the viability of the ANZUS Treaty'.[6] Canberra lobbied Washington hard over the proposal. According to the Australian ambassador to Washington, Alan Renouf, Australia's primary concern was to ensure that Washington did not agree to any limitations on its capacity to assist Australia in case of threat, including any freeze on the deployment of land-based strike aircraft or restrictions on US military facilities in Australia.[7] Australia also wanted the proposed treaty to define the Indian Ocean to exclude the Timor and Arafura seas to the north of Australia or any of the seas to Australia's south.[8] The refusal of the United States to limit its ability to establish military facilities in Australia was one of the key unresolved issues with the Soviet Union when the talks collapsed in early 1978.[9] The Soviets believed that Australia exercised a negative influence on the talks and had some responsibility for their suspension.[10] Australia's role in influencing the direction of the US–Soviet talks (and, perhaps, in helping bring them to an end) has been called 'an outstandingly successful Australian diplomatic effort'.[11]

The Soviet intervention in Afghanistan in December 1979 only reinforced Australia's desire to secure US predominance in the Indian Ocean. The Soviet action in Afghanistan was viewed (incorrectly) by the Fraser government as the first step in a strategy to gain access to a 'warm water' port on the Indian Ocean. Canberra had long been concerned over ambiguities in the application of the ANZUS treaty to the Indian Ocean and in 1980, at Australia's request, Washington formally acknowledged that Australia's west coast and Indian Ocean territories were covered by the treaty.[12] At the same time, Australia sought to better integrate itself with US military activities in the Indian Ocean. At Australia's instigation, the first large-scale ANZUS *Sandgroper* exercise was conducted in the Indian Ocean as a manifestation of the extended reach of the ANZUS alliance. Australian personnel serviced US aircraft transiting to the Indian Ocean via Singapore, and Australia and the United States began operating joint reconnaissance patrols out of the Cocos Islands, Diego Garcia and Singapore.[13] By the late 1970s, Australian ASW aircraft were making frequent use of US facilities at Diego Garcia for reconnaissance flights to track Soviet vessels, with Australian aircraft reportedly comprising around 25 per cent of all air surveillance missions from Diego Garcia.[14] Australia also permitted the United States to stage 'unarmed' B-52 bombers through Darwin to conduct 'training and surveillance' over the Indian Ocean. From 1981, Australia also sought to demonstrate an independent contribution to the ANZUS alliance in the Indian Ocean through the rotation of P-3 Orion maritime surveillance aircraft through the Australian airbase at Butterworth, Malaysia.[15] But Australia deflected US requests that it provide troops for the US Rapid Deployment Force (now CENTCOM), expressing concerns about regional reactions.[16] Nevertheless, by the early 1980s Australia had achieved its post-British era strategic objectives in the Indian Ocean, involving an increased US military presence in the region and the effective extension of the ANZUS defence perimeter in the Indian Ocean to Diego Garcia, but not as far as the Persian Gulf.

During the mid-1990s, Australia demonstrated a fleeting interest in Indian Ocean multilateralism as part of the short-lived 'Look West' policy. As discussed previously, in 1997 Australia joined with India and South Africa to sponsor the establishment of IOR-ARC with the primary aim of promoting regional trade. Although Australia argued that the grouping should be inclusive, India insisted on the exclusion of Pakistan and other key Islamic states such as Saudi Arabia, Indonesia and Malaysia. Australian attempts to explore possible frameworks for regional security cooperation were also rebuffed.[17] The form of IOR-ARC was very much influenced by Australia's positive experience in the establishment of APEC in the 1980s—i.e. the promotion of 'open regionalism' and voluntary trade liberalisation. But attempts to emulate APEC were a mistake, primarily due to the considerable developmental differences between Indian Ocean states and their lack of experience in regional cooperation. Within a couple of years it had become clear that IOR-ARC's approach to trade liberalisation had failed and Australia, India and other key members lost interest. Over the last several years Australia and India have attempted to revive interest in the grouping, including placing maritime security issues such as anti-piracy efforts on the agenda. But while IOR-ARC could become a useful low-level forum for regional coordination, there is little likelihood that it will become a significant actor in regional security.

Australia's defence resources in the Indian Ocean

The Indian Ocean is gradually assuming considerable importance in Australian defence planning. Over the last several decades Australia has gradually rebalanced its defence resources from its population centres in the southeast towards the Indian Ocean and the north. This was initially prompted not by a desire to project power into the Indian Ocean but by a greater emphasis on continental defence and self-reliance. The so-called 'Defence of Australia' policy, adopted in 1986, involved a move away from Australia's long-standing policy of 'forward defence' in Asia and a greater focus on defending territory and economic interests from direct attack. In 1987, the Royal Australian Navy announced that it would become a two-ocean navy through moving around half its existing fleet to the Indian Ocean. The Royal Australian Air Force developed two 'bare bases' (i.e. bases which have no deployed units but can be used in contingencies) in Western Australia and an existing bare base in central Australia was upgraded to host strike aircraft. These moves were intended to facilitate the deployment of air and naval resources to the west and north in the event of conflict, to defend the so-called 'air-sea gap' between Australia and Southeast Asia.

Although the Defence of Australia policy has been largely abandoned, the gradual rebalancing of defence resources north and west has continued, reflecting demographic and economic changes. Over the last two decades in particular there has been a demographic shift in Australia's population towards Western Australia as it developed into a major resources exporter. Some of the world's largest iron ore reserves are located in Western Australia, and the development of its offshore oil and gas reserves mean that Australia is likely to become the largest LNG exporter in the world within the next decade.[18] In 2011, a Force Posture Review recommended, among other things, the development of infrastructure at the northwest ports of Exmouth, Dampier, Port Headland and Broome to allow greater use by warships; the upgrading of the airbase at Exmouth for greater use by maritime surveillance and strike aircraft; and the upgrading of a small airfield on Cocos Island.[19]

Australia's island possessions in the Indian Ocean, Christmas Island and the Cocos Islands have come under increased scrutiny as part of a renewed focus on the Indian Ocean. The islands have been under Australian jurisdiction since the 1950s, when they were transferred from British colonial administration, and they have long been on the periphery of Australia's strategic considerations. Australia does not maintain a military presence on Christmas Island (which is located some 360 km south of Jakarta).[20] An airfield at Cocos Island (located a further 900 km southwest) is used as an occasional staging facility for the Australian and US military flights to the central Indian Ocean and Australia also reportedly maintains signal intelligence facilities there. Some question whether Australia could defend the islands against military attack due to their remoteness from the Australian mainland.[21] But the islands' location also potentially helps Australia to project air power into the South China Sea, the straits through the Indonesian archipelago or the Andaman Sea/Bay of Bengal, which could become particularly important if bases in Singapore or Malaysia were not available. The replacement of Australia's P-3 Orion surveillance fleet, which occasionally uses the Cocos for refuelling, with P-8 Poseidon aircraft could provide an opportunity to upgrade the airfield for joint use by Australian and US forces. In 2011, Australian defence minister Stephen Smith confirmed that there may be greater use of the Cocos Islands in the future by Australian and US forces.[22]

In recent years Australia has drawn even closer to the United States as an alliance partner in both the Pacific and Indian Oceans and is in the process of operationalising the alliance beyond what was ever considered necessary during the Cold War. In conjunction with the so-called US 'pivot' towards Asia, the Australian government announced the rotational deployment of up to 2,500 US Marines to Darwin for parts of the year to train with the Australian Defence Force. The US will also be granted greater access to Australian air bases and will pre-position fuel, ammunition and equipment in northern Australia and there will likely be increased use of Fremantle by the US Navy. There has been speculation over home porting a US carrier task group in Fremantle, although it would require significant investment in infrastructure.[23] As will be discussed later, Washington expects Australia to take greater security responsibilities in the Indian Ocean in partnership with India.

Australia now has considerable security commitments in the Indian Ocean region. As at May 2012, Australian Defence Force personnel were deployed in nine operations in countries in the Indian Ocean region, including Afghanistan, Bahrain, Iraq, South Sudan and East Timor, and around a third of the Royal Australian Navy was deployed in the Indian Ocean.[24] Australia's 2009 Defence White Paper stated: 'Over the period to 2030, the Indian Ocean will join the Pacific Ocean in terms of its centrality to our maritime strategy and defence planning'.[25] But Australia still had trouble coming to grips with the idea of the Indian Ocean as a region in strategic terms. Although Canberra has a unified policy framework for the Pacific Ocean and another for the Antarctic and the Southern Ocean, there is no equivalent for the Indian Ocean as a whole.[26] Australia's grand strategy in the Indian Ocean will likely include encouraging the continuation of US predominance for as long as possible, while developing a secondary partnership with India. Although Australia may be tempted to translate its grand strategy in the Asia Pacific—regional engagement within the umbrella of an established US regional alliance system—into the Indian Ocean, it is questionable whether this approach would work and Australia may well need to take a quite different strategic approach.[27]

The development of the Australian–India strategic relationship

In coming years it will likely be in the interests of both Australia and India to develop a good working relationship in the India Ocean. But the political and strategic relationship between Australia and India has not been close for most of their history as independent states. During the Cold War and after, the relationship was largely characterised by long periods of indifference interspersed with occasional political irritation.[28] Australia and India share a language, British colonial heritage and institutions and a democratic tradition, all of which could underpin a shared strategic outlook. However, in practice the colonial link has served to divide just as much as it has united them. Australia's Anglo-Saxon heritage led it to identify closely with Britain and then the United States as essentially benign international forces. In contrast, India saw its colonial heritage as an alien intrusion and for many years also saw any US strategic presence in the region in neo-imperialist terms. Differing ideas of identity and nationalism also find expression in very different perspectives on strategic alliances. As has been discussed, many in New Delhi see security alignments as inconsistent with their ideas of 'independence'. In contrast, Australia has often assumed that security alignments are virtually a prerequisite for its national independence and certainly a means of enhancing its regional influence. Many would consider a goal of strategic autonomy for Australia about as realistic or desirable as a goal of economic autonomy.

These differing perspectives have led many in New Delhi to see Australia as politically suspect and strategically inconsequential. During the Cold War, Australia did not figure materially in New Delhi's calculations of Indian Ocean security: rather, it was often considered as merely a US stooge and a site of

US military facilities.[29] In contrast, Canberra frequently considered India as difficult to deal with and too close to the Soviets. New Delhi's opposition to the US presence in the Indian Ocean was often perceived as unbalanced and favouring the Soviet Union. This is well demonstrated by the complaints of Australian prime minister Malcolm Fraser in 1976 to Chinese premier Hua Guofeng, describing India's stance as 'unreal ... They condemn the United States in her efforts to build a support base, Diego Garcia, in the Indian Ocean, necessary to preserve the balance, but they do not condemn the build-up of the Soviet Union in the Indian Ocean'.[30] It appears that Fraser could not comprehend why New Delhi did not perceive the obvious benefits of the *Pax Americana* in the Indian Ocean.

India's naval expansion plans briefly became a matter of concern to some in the Australian defence establishment in the late 1980s. While India was not perceived as presenting a direct threat to Australia, some believed that India might provoke a competitive arms build-up in Southeast Asia that would work to Australia's disadvantage.[31] In March 1990, the Australian chief of air staff, Air Marshall David Evans, criticised India's plans to an audience in Beijing, commenting that, 'Perhaps it is no more than excessive nationalism that compels India to seek an almost dominant role in the Indian Ocean'.[32] K. Subramanyam, the influential Indian strategist, dismissed the Australian claims, stating, 'The idea of a threat from India to Australia, or anywhere else, is ridiculous and hilarious. The only possible threat to Australia would be on the cricket pitch'.[33] Some in New Delhi saw Australia as just attempting to justify increases in its own defence spending or obstructing India's efforts to improve relations with ASEAN.[34] Indian chief of naval staff, Admiral O. S. Dawson, reportedly saw Australian concerns in terms of a white nation trying to prevent the rise of an indigenous Asian naval power.[35] The 1990 sale by Australia to Pakistan of 50 Mirage III jets and spares for a seemingly knock-down price of A$36 million also strained the relationship. Although the jets were considered to be obsolete by Australia, they were in fact suitable for front-line deployment by Pakistan, and possibly significantly increased Pakistan's capabilities during a period of heightened India–Pakistan tensions.[36]

Canberra sought to defuse the controversy over India's regional ambitions. Australian defence minister, Kim Beazley, commented that India 'has never and does not threaten Australia', and ascribed India's objectives as related to its international status rather than any specific military objectives.[37] He never-theless described India's posture as 'intriguing' and as posing 'possibilities for extensively increased Indian influence at the major eastern Indian Ocean chokepoints'.[38] Beazley presciently acknowledged that, while the expansion of India's maritime capabilities eroded Australia's capability advantage at a more important level, the increased regional interest in maritime affairs provided greater scope for Australia to participate in efforts to promote regional security.[39]

While any concerns about India's strategic ambitions disappeared quickly with the end of the Cold War, it took a long time for the relationship to improve. Indeed, India's Pokhran II nuclear tests in 1998 caused damage to the relationship which is still being repaired. Australia responded harshly to India's nuclear tests, motivated by concerns about the stability of South Asia, convictions about the sanctity of nuclear non-proliferation norms and to some extent by domestic political considerations.[40] Prime Minister John Howard characterised the tests as 'a grotesque status symbol'[41] while Foreign Minister Alexander Downer called them 'outrageous acts'.[42] Canberra suspended ministerial contacts, non-humanitarian aid and defence-related cooperation and its defence attaché was withdrawn from New Delhi. India responded with similar suspensions of cooperation. New Delhi took particular offence at Australia's reaction to the tests, seeing it as a case of Australia either doing the bidding of the United States or trying to curry favour with Washington through outdoing US opposition. New Delhi saw hypocrisy in the Australian stance in condemning India's desire to provide for its own security while sheltering under the nuclear umbrella of US extended deterrence. Some even sought to explain Australia's reaction to the tests on the basis of racism.[43] While some in Canberra believe that Australia was unfairly singled out by New Delhi, there is little doubt that Australia placed itself, along with Japan, at the forefront of international opposition to India's actions. The affair demonstrated a particular indifference by Australia to India's security perspectives and their relationship.

A new security partnership?

From the nadir of 1998, the relationship between Australia and India has improved markedly, and the security engagement has now gained momentum. Australia moved quickly to try to normalise relations following India's Pokhran II nuclear tests, with Australian prime ministers and senior ministers making numerous visits to New Delhi over the following years. The increased political engagement has led to several bilateral agreements on security-related matters, including a 2003 agreement on terrorism, a 2006 memorandum of understanding on defence cooperation, a 2007 defence information sharing arrangement and agreements on intelligence dialogue, extradition and terrorism in 2008. In April 2007, the first-ever trilateral naval exercises were held between the United States, Japan and India in the Western Pacific, and in August 2007 the annual India–US Malabar naval exercise was transformed into large-scale multilateral exercises in the Bay of Bengal involving three carrier battle groups and other ships from the United States, India, Japan, Australia and Singapore. Australia's 2009 Defence White Paper flagged the 'strong mutual interest' of Australia and India in enhancing maritime security cooperation in the Indian Ocean, commenting that, 'As India extends its reach and influence into areas of shared strategic interest, we will need to strengthen our defence relationship and our understanding of Indian strategic thinking'.[44]

In November 2009, Australia and India announced a Joint Declaration on Security Cooperation, intended to set out shared strategic perspectives and create a framework for the further development of bilateral security cooperation. At the same time, Prime Minister Rudd told an audience in New Delhi that India and Australia were 'natural partners' and should become 'strategic partners'.[45] The Security Declaration is a non-binding declaration of principles and understandings in security matters and establishes a bilateral framework for further cooperation in security matters.[46] Australia also has similar security declarations with Japan and South Korea. Although the Australia–India Security Declaration contained little new of substance, it is a notable step in establishing a framework for the further development of the security relationship, including the formalisation of regular consultations and dialogues between foreign ministers, senior military and diplomatic representatives and joint working groups on maritime security operations and counter-terrorism and immigration. In conjunction with the Security Declaration, Australia and India entered into cooperation arrangements in intelligence, law enforcement, border security, terrorist financing and money laundering. Australia has also sought to encourage greater interaction between the defence forces.

Both Australia and India have been cautious about allowing the relationship to be perceived as anything that might resemble a coalition against China. In early 2007 Japanese prime minister Shinzo Abe proposed the so-called 'Quadrilateral Initiative', under which India would join a formal security dialogue with Japan, the United States and Australia. Some saw the proposal as essentially suggesting the extension of the US–Japan–Australia trilateral security dialogue to include India. However the proposal did not proceed. Chinese official and semi-official sources reactive negatively to the initiative and the Malabar naval exercises of 2007, claiming that they resurrected 'a Cold-War mentality' and marked 'the formation of a small NATO to resist China'.[47] In May 2007 China issued diplomatic demarchés to India, Japan, the United States and Australia requesting explanations of the Quadrilateral proposal. During the course of 2007, Australia, India, the United States and even Japan had become increasingly hesitant about the initiative. Canberra saw the proposal as undefined and unduly provocative and declined to participate in meetings on the initiative after May 2007, although its withdrawal was only announced in early 2008. The Indian government also faced significant domestic political pressure against any perceived alliance involving the United States. The proposal lost any momentum in late 2007. In December 2011, following the change in the Australian policy on uranium exports to India, Australia also proposed that India should join with it and the United States in a separate Trilateral Security Dialogue. Australian foreign minister Kevin Rudd was reported as commenting that Australia had received a positive response from India on the proposal, although this was later denied.[48]

India's nuclear status has also been a continuing irritant. Although Australia supported approval of the US–Indian nuclear deal by the Nuclear Supplier's Group in August 2008, for domestic political reasons it continued to refuse to supply uranium to India for several years. While India did not need Australian uranium, having secured supplies elsewhere, Australia's refusal to supply uranium was taken by New Delhi as indicating a lack of commitment to the relationship and a refusal to acknowledge India's great power status. But a change in Australia's uranium policy in 2011 and the ongoing negotiation of uranium supply arrangements has largely removed this impediment to the relationship.

The economic relationship is another growing factor in the security relationship. A weak economic relationship has contributed to the lack of political alignment over the last 60 years, but now India is becoming one of Australia's largest customers for resources and energy. This is driven by a general desire to expand Australia's export markets and also balance Australia's economic relationship with China. India is now Australia's fourth largest export customer after China, Japan and South Korea, although the balance of trade is heavily in favour of Australia. Bilateral investment also remains relatively low. Although an Australia–India Free Trade Agreement has been proposed, negotiations have not yet commenced and it seems unlikely that any agreement will be finalised quickly. A greater degree of economic interdependence could have a positive effect on the security relationship.

Australia and India as partners in the Indian Ocean?

What are the opportunities and constraints in a strategic partnership between Australia and India in the Indian Ocean? How will Australia deal with a growing role for India as US predominance declines? To what extent will India be prepared to take into account Australia's interests?

Many Australian analysts see the strategic interests of Australia and India as 'essentially congruent' and there is certainly considerable scope for cooperation in the political-security arena.[49] Over the last couple of years Australia and India have worked together to try to resuscitate IOR-ARC, and they share an interest in seeing the development of 'balanced' multilateral economic, political and security institutions in Southeast Asia. There may also be scope for cooperation on particular issues such as nuclear non-proliferation and disarmament.[50] There is considerable scope for maritime security cooperation. Commonly cited areas include maritime policing (piracy and maritime terrorism, illegal fishing, people trafficking, etc.) and Humanitarian and Disaster Relief (HADR), anti-terrorism, local capacity building and maritime domain awareness. While Southeast Asia would be a natural focus for cooperation given their common interests in that region, there is also the potential for cooperation elsewhere—for example, among the Indian Ocean islands.

India and Australia, along with the United States and Japan, were key players in the multilateral naval response effort to the 2004 Indian Ocean tsunami. This displayed India's capabilities as an HADR provider to the region and was a major turning point in Indian thinking about the potential for cooperation with other key maritime democracies in both the Indian and Pacific oceans.

Assistance in building the capacity of ASEAN states to provide maritime security is another potential area for cooperation. To date, India has largely focused its capacity-building efforts in Southeast Asia on Vietnam, providing, for instance, training, spare parts for Soviet-vintage patrol craft and aircraft maintenance, while Australia has focused capacity-building efforts on Indonesia and the Philippines. Indonesia, which has numerous requirements in maritime security, would provide a potential focus for cooperation between India and Australia in regional capacity building.

Another potentially important area for cooperation is in maritime intelligence, surveillance and reconnaissance (ISR). In recent years India has made major investments in maritime ISR capabilities. Australia already has considerable maritime ISR capabilities throughout the eastern Indian Ocean in areas which abut or overlap with areas of strategic interest to India, including operating P-3C Orion maritime surveillance aircraft through Malaysia's Butterworth air base. There are substantial opportunities for cooperation between India, Australia and key security partners in Southeast Asia in enhancing maritime domain awareness. In coming years, both India and Australia will acquire Boeing P-8 maritime aircraft as the backbone of their maritime ISR capabilities, which may create opportunities for cooperation in training and maintenance. It has been suggested that India and Australia could jointly sponsor a regional maritime domain partnership which would involve collaboration with Southeast Asian states in intelligence sharing, maritime domain awareness and coordinated patrolling.[51] A regional arrangement co-sponsored by India and Australia and including Southeast Asian maritime states could be a useful way of advancing ISR cooperation while also satisfying Indian political sensitivities about regional security partnerships that do not necessarily involve direct reliance on the United States.

Despite the potential for cooperation there are several possible sources of difficulty in building a security relationship. One is the inherent problem of building a productive relationship between an emerging power with great power aspirations such as India and an active middle power such as Australia. Australia is neither a major power (such as Japan) inherently important to India nor a small, useful 'gateway' state (such as Singapore). While there has been some recognition of the potential for security cooperation, there is arguably no mutual understanding that each is a crucial element in the other's security. This is compounded by a view of some in New Delhi that Australia is not an 'independent' strategic actor due to its relationship with the United States. Why deal with Canberra when one can deal with Washington? There is still relatively little imperative in New Delhi to engage with Australia or any real sense that India should take Australia's opinions into consideration, particularly when making judgments about China or the Indian Ocean.[52] In short, other than as a potential energy supplier, Australia will find it difficult to make itself an indispensible partner to India.

India is also particularly demanding of recognition of its major power status, including its leading role in the Indian Ocean. But Australia may not easily accede to the idea of 'India's Ocean'. While Australia is keen to cooperate with India as a major regional power, it will seek to extend US predominance in the Indian Ocean for as long as possible, while also maintaining its position as one of the major naval powers on the littoral. Some in Australia may not always be as confident as the United States that a powerful India will necessarily be a benign presence in the Indian Ocean.[53] Australia's likely objective will be to mould India's ambitions in the Indian Ocean, so that India does not disregard the legitimate security concerns of littoral states and extra-regional powers. As Bergin and Bateman commented:

> The relationship with India must be one of equal partners. This might be hard. India seems reluctant to treat Australia on an equal basis. This will create problems should India extend its reach and influence into areas of common strategic interest.[54]

Australia and India also have quite different instincts in security collaboration, which will likely inhibit the development of the relationship. If strategic autonomy is part of India's DNA, then collaboration is part of Australia's. As an independent state it has only ever conducted military operations as part of an international coalition, and the Australian Defence Force is largely built around an assumption of coalition operations. In contrast, India's instinct is to oppose multilateral security cooperation except under the clear banner of the United Nations. Cooperation, particularly operational cooperation, carries with it an ideological taint that India's strategic autonomy will be undermined. India's instincts against cooperation may have a considerable impact on its relationship with Australia. Although the Indian Navy is keen to work with the Royal Australian Navy, New Delhi has only recently agreed in principle to hold bilateral naval exercises, after years of lobbying.

A further important area of difference is China. While some might see the 'China threat' as a key factor in the relationship, there are considerable differences between Australian and Indian perceptions of China. While Australia is concerned about China's assertiveness in the South China Sea, Australian analysts have tended to treat Indian claims about the nature and extent of Chinese involvement in the Indian Ocean region with a degree of scepticism.[55] They tend to see any Chinese presence in the Indian Ocean less in terms of an encirclement of India and more as an expression of China's legitimate interests in protecting its key trading routes to the Middle East and Europe.[56] From Australia's perspective, the prospect of heightened naval rivalry in the eastern Indian Ocean or the South China Sea would be viewed seriously. Whereas India may see strategic benefit in having the capability to control China's sea lanes of communication, Australia arguably may have a greater interest in ensuring that China's security dilemma in the Indian Ocean is not worsened. It may, for example, be in Australia's interests to facilitate China's role as a responsible stakeholder in the Indian Ocean.

Where does that leave prospects for security cooperation in the Indian Ocean region? As noted above, there are numerous shared interests and opportunities for security cooperation. But a closer relationship will require sustained political will in both Canberra and New Delhi to overcome considerable differences in their strategic cultures. Australia has already recognised India as an important security partner in the Indian Ocean, but India is only beginning to recognise Australia as a useful partner. For India, Australia in some ways represents a difficult case. India has no direct security interests in the southeast Indian Ocean and Australia's close relationship with the United States creates political unease in New Delhi. On the other hand, Australia, whose naval power ranks second only to India among the littoral states, could be a useful partner for India in leveraging its reach. Apart from the potential benefits of cooperation in Southeast Asia and elsewhere, New Delhi could find that a good working relationship with Australia might ease the way for India's longer-term strategic aspirations in the Indian Ocean.

Notes

1 Australian conceptions of the Indian Ocean's boundaries commonly differ from international definitions. Most international definitions of the Indian Ocean place its eastern limit at Tasmania at the southeastern corner of Australia. But Australian authorities regard all the seas to the south of Australia from Tasmania up to Cape Leeuwin on Australia's southwest point as being part of the Southern Ocean. The International Hydrographic Organisation has proposed a northern limit to the 'Southern Ocean' at 60° South, which Australia has objected to. Differing conceptions of these boundaries are more than just a cartographical curiosity. During 1978 negotiations of a US–Soviet Naval Arms Limitation Treaty, which would have limited the deployment of US military forces in the Indian Ocean, Australia successfully argued that the Indian Ocean did not extend past Cape Leeuwin.

2 Even Washington then believed that Australian concerns were overstated. Henry S. Albinski (1981) 'Australia and the Indian Ocean', in Larry W. Bowman and Ian Clark (eds), *The Indian Ocean in global politics*, Boulder, CO: Westview, pp. 59–86 at p. 61.

3 Henry Albinski (1982) *Australian–American Security Relationship: A Regional and International Perspective*, Brisbane: Queensland University Press, p. 128.

4 Report of the Committee on Foreign Affairs, Defence and Trade on Australia and the Indian Ocean, Australian Senate, 1976, p. 137. For a discussion of Australian policy during this period, see Kim C. Beazley and Ian Clark (1979) *The Politics of Intrusion: the Super Powers and the Indian Ocean*, Sydney: Alternative Publishing Cooperative.

5 Among other things, Australia wanted to ensure that Indonesia would not restrict the passage of US nuclear submarines through the Ombai-Wetar straits near Timor and other waterways through the Indonesian archipelago, as the alternative passage of US warships around the south of Australia would significantly delay US force projection into the Indian Ocean in periods of crisis. Albinski, 'Australia and the Indian Ocean', p. 63.

6 Damien Murphy (2009) 'Reds out from under the beds', *Sydney Morning Herald*, 31 December.

7 Alan Renouf (1986) *Malcolm Fraser and Australian Foreign Policy*, Sydney: Australian Professional, p. 113.

8 Indeed, Australia formally requested that the United States excise the entire coast of Western Australia from the proposed treaty. Cabinet Minute, Foreign Affairs and Defence Committee, Canberra, 3 November 1977. Decision No. 4277 (FAD). Australian National Archives.

9 Richard N. Haass (1987) 'Arms control at sea: the United States and the Soviet Union in the Indian Ocean 1977–78', *The Journal of Strategic Studies*, Vol. 10, No. 2, pp. 231–47.

10 Albinski, 'Australia and the Indian Ocean', p. 63. Canberra also reportedly declined to help when the Soviets asked them to intervene to restart the talks. Albinski, *Australian–American Security Relationship*, p. 128.

11 Albinski, 'Australia and the Indian Ocean', p. 63.

12 The treaty expressly covers 'an armed attack on the metropolitan territory of any of the Parties, or on the island territories under its jurisdiction, in the Pacific' [Article V]. It was argued by Canberra that the word 'Pacific' as used in the treaty referred to a World War II definition of the *Pacific theatre*, which extended into the Indian Ocean.

13 William T. Tow (1978) 'ANZUS: a strategic role in the Indian Ocean?', *The World Today*, Vol. 34, No. 10, pp. 401–8.

14 Albinski, 'Australia and the Indian Ocean', p. 70.

15 During the 1980s, so-called Operation *Gateway* primarily focused on 'prosecuting' Soviet submarines before and after they transited the Malacca Strait, after which the RAAF would hand surveillance responsibility over to the US Navy. RAAF Orion aircraft continue to conduct maritime surveillance activities out of Butterworth as part of the Five Power Defence Arrangement with Malaysia.

16 Richard Leaver (1983) 'Australia and the Indian Ocean', in P.J. Boyce and J.R. Angel (eds), *Independence and Alliance: Australia in World Affairs 1976–80*, Sydney: George Allen and Unwin, p. 275.

17 Sandy Gordon with Desmond Ball, Paul Dibb and Amin Saikal (1996) *Security and Security Building in the Indian Ocean Region*, Canberra: Strategic and Defence Studies Centre, Ch. 6.

18 Brian Robins (2011) 'Qatar gas challenge', *Sydney Morning Herald*, 30 November.

19 Mark Dodd (2012) 'Defence urged to shift presence to the north', *The Australian*, 31 January, p. 2.

20 Although in the mid-1970s the US had installed a Sonar Surveillance System array terminating at Christmas Island, which was of major importance to anti-submarine warfare operations. Desmond Ball (1980) *A Suitable Piece of Real Estate: American Installations in Australia*, Marrickville: Southwood Press, p. 121.

21 See Ross Babbage (1988) *Should Australia plan to defend Christmas and Cocos Islands?* Canberra, Strategic and Defence Studies Centre, pp. 1–3.

22 John Kerin (2011) 'Cocos base under review', *Australian Financial Review*, 21 November.

23 Nick O'Malley (2012) 'Perth naval base 'plan' would cost too much: study author', *National Times*, 2 August.

24 Sergei DeSilva-Ranasinghe (2012) 'Fact sheet: The Indian Ocean and Australia's national interests', Future Directions International Strategic Analysis Paper, 29 May.

25 Australian Government (2009) *Defending Australia in the Asia Pacific Century: Force 2030*, Canberra: Commonwealth of Australia, p. 37.

26 Sam Bateman and Anthony Bergin (2010) *Our Western Front: Australia and the Indian Ocean*, Australian Strategic Policy Institute, March, p. 33

27 Andrew Phillips (2012) 'Australia and the challenges of regional order building in the Indo–Pacific Age', submission to Australian Senate Enquiry, April.

28 For a fuller discussion of the Australia–India strategic relationship in general, see Meg Gurry (1996) *India: Australia's Neglected Neighbour? 1947–1996*, Griffith: Centre for the Study of Australia–Asia Relations; and Brewster (2012) *India as an Asia Pacific Power*, London: Routledge, Ch. 8.

29 K. Subrahmanyam (1988) 'Strategic Developments in the Indian and South Pacific Ocean regions', in Robert H. Bruce, *Australia and the Indian Ocean: Strategic Dimensions of Increasing Naval Involvement*, Perth: Centre of Indian Ocean Studies, pp. 79–95.
30 Confidential transcript of discussions, reported in *Keesing's Contemporary Archives*, London: Keesings, 1976, p. 27939.
31 Tim Huxley (1992) 'India's naval expansion and Australia', *Contemporary South Asia*, Vol. 1, No. 33, pp. 407–23.
32 S.K. Bhutani (1995) 'India–Australia bilateral relations', in Dipankar Banerjee (ed.), *Towards an Era of Cooperation: an Indo–Australian Dialogue*, New Delhi: Institute for Defence Studies and Analyses, p. 376.
33 Brian Ridge (1988) 'India—a threat to Australia?', *Defender*, Winter, pp. 37–42, at p. 38.
34 S.K. Bhutani, 'India–Australia bilateral relations', p. 376.
35 Raju G.C. Thomas (1989) 'The sources of Indian naval expansion', in Robert H. Bruce (ed.), *The Modern Indian Navy in the Indian Ocean: Developments and Implications*, Perth: Centre for Indian Ocean Regional Studies, pp. 95–107 at p. 98.
36 See generally, Graeme Cheeseman (1992) *Selling Mirages: The Politics of Arms Trading*, Canberra: Strategic and Defence Studies Centre. It was suggested that the low cash price may have been part of a contra deal in which Australia received US equipment at a discount. Bronwyn Young (1990) 'Government cops plenty of flak over Indian Mirage sale', *Australian Financial Review*, 27 April, p. 3.
37 Kim Beazley (1990) 'Australian defence and the Indian Ocean', in Robert H. Bruce (ed.) *Indian Ocean Navies*, Perth: Curtin University of Technology, p. 146.
38 Kim C. Beazley, 'The Two Ocean Navy', in Bruce, *Australia and the Indian Ocean*, pp. 9–20 at p. 11.
39 Beazley, 'Australian defence and the Indian Ocean', p. 147.
40 The Howard government was seeking to outflank the Labour opposition on the anti-nuclear issue in the weeks leading up to a Federal election.
41 Hamish McDonald (1999) 'Nuclear posturing—out on a street-cred limb', *Sydney Morning Herald*, 8 February.
42 Alexander Downer (1998) 'Australian response to India's nuclear tests', Media Release, 14 May.
43 Man Mohini Kaul (2002) 'Australia–India relations: a critical survey', in D. Gopal (ed.), *Australia in the Emerging Global Order: Evolving Australia–India Relations*, New Delhi: Shipra, pp. 220–34.
44 Australian Government, *Defending Australia in the Asia Pacific Century*, p. 96.
45 Kevin Rudd (2009) 'From fitful engagement to strategic partnership', address to the Indian Council of World Affairs in New Delhi, 12 November.
46 For a detailed discussion of the Australia–India Security Declaration, see David Brewster (2010) 'The Australia—India Security Declaration: the Quadrilateral redux?', *Security Challenges* Vol. 6, No.1, Autumn, pp. 1–9.
47 Sun Cheng (2008) 'A comparative analysis of Abe's and Fukada's Asia diplomacy', *China International Studies*, No. 10, Spring, pp. 58–72.
48 Rob Taylor (2011) 'Australia backs security pact with US, India', *The Australian*, 30 November.
49 See, for example, Rory Medcalf and Amandeep Gill (2009) 'Unconventional partners: Australia–India cooperation in reducing nuclear dangers', *Lowy Institute Policy Brief*, October.
50 Ibid.
51 Commander Shishir Upadhyaya (2009) 'India and Australia relations: scope for naval cooperation', *National Maritime Foundation*, 4 December.
52 Gregory R. Copley (2009) *Such a Full Sea: Australia's Options in a Changing Indian Ocean Region*, Melbourne: Sid Harta Publishers, p. 127.

53 Sandy Gordon (2010) 'Strategic interests of the major Indian Ocean powers: an Australian perspective', in H. Singh, *Pentagon's South Asia Defence and Strategic Yearbook, 2010*, New Delhi: Pentagon Press.

54 Bateman and Bergin, *Our Western Front*, p. 35.

55 See, for example, Andrew Selth (2007) 'Chinese military bases in Burma: the explosion of a myth', Regional Outlook Paper No. 10, Brisbane: Griffith University.

56 Although Australia was quick to quash attempts by China to establish a signals intelligence facility in East Timor to monitor shipping in the Wetar Strait, which the US Navy uses as a corridor between the Pacific and Indian Oceans. According to leaked US diplomatic cables, in 2007 China proposed building and operating the facility free of charge, ostensibly to help monitor illegal fishing, although it insisted that the facility be staffed by Chinese technicians. East Timorese officials rejected the proposal after consulting with Australia and the United States. Philip Dorling (2011) 'Chinese bid to set up East Timor spy base', *Sydney Morning Herald*, 10 May.

9   The United States

The United States will likely remain the predominant military power in the world for decades to come, but its relative strength is declining in the face of the rise of China and India. Washington has responded to the rise of China's power by refocusing its military capabilities away from West Asia and towards the Pacific, which will place considerable strains on its resources in the Indian Ocean. The United States has identified India as an essential strategic partner in the Indian Ocean, with the potential to take over many security responsibilities in the region. For its part, India sees limited cooperation with the United States as a useful means of achieving its long-term goals in the Indian Ocean, but is hesitant in cooperating too closely.

America's strategic dilemma in the Indian Ocean

The United States is facing a strategic dilemma in the Indian Ocean. Following a decade of major land-based military deployments in West Asia battling Islamic jihadists, the United States has recognised that the growing power of China represents a greater strategic threat. This will require a long-term rebalancing of US defence resources towards East Asia, which will place considerable strains on its ability to secure its interests in the Indian Ocean.

Despite the imperatives created by the rise of China, most US analysts believe that the Indian Ocean region will become more important to the United States in coming years. Key security issues include the continuing importance of the Middle East for energy, the potential for nuclear proliferation throughout the region, and a continuing jihadist threat, particularly from the many fragile or failing states in the region. The US Navy's 2007 strategic concept paper, *A Cooperative Strategy for 21st Century Seapower*[1] identified the Pacific and Indian oceans (and not the Pacific and *Atlantic* oceans, as has historically been the case) as the two oceans where US combat power will be 'continuously postured' in coming years. Robert Kaplan has argued that the Indian Ocean has a particular significance for the United States as a world power, especially in light of the long-term decline of its military superiority, claiming that the United States must plan an elegant decline in the Indian Ocean, where 'Indispensability, rather than dominance, must be its goal'.[2] Others argue that the Indian Ocean will become relatively less important with the decline of the jihadist threat and the current technological revolution in extraction of gas and oil which will make the United States considerably less dependent on Middle East oil. This may give the United States more strategic room to manouevre—in other words, the United States may not always feel compelled to protect energy sources for others.[3]

The US Rebalance to East Asia

The dilemma faced by the United States in the Indian Ocean has been brought to a head with the rise of China as a military power and its increasing assertiveness in the Western Pacific. The global economic crisis is compelling the United States to make major cuts in defence spending and wind down its commitments in Afghanistan, while focusing relatively more on East Asia. A new US strategy in Asia was announced in November 2011 as a 'Pivot' or 'Rebalance' towards Asia. This signifies that in the post-Afghanistan world there will be a greater *relative* focus of US defence resources in East Asia than in other regions of the world. Much of that focus will involve the US Navy. For example, the current 50/50 split of naval resources between the US Pacific and Atlantic fleets will become 60/40 by 2020. At the same time there will be major cuts in overall US defence spending, including major cuts in US ground forces (more than 100,000 troops will be cut from the army and Marine Corps) and large cuts in spending on the navy and air force.

In addition to reducing the number of US combat troops deployed in the Indian Ocean region, the Rebalancing strategy will also involve a qualitative change in the US strategic commitment to the region—away from a focus on large-scale land-based insurgencies (such as those in Iraq and Afghanistan over the last decade) and towards an offshore maritime-based role. After having 'boots on the sand' for more than a decade, the United States is now looking at a very different role. As Admiral Jonathan Greenert, the US chief of naval operations, commented in November 2011, the US Navy is now ready to provide the 'offshore option' to US strategic requirements.[4] This will likely involve much greater reliance on stand-off strike capabilities (including UAVs) and much less on ground forces.

There are concerns that these reductions could create a capability gap for US power in the Indian Ocean. New Delhi is particularly concerned that a reduced US commitment to counterterrorism could lead to a greater terrorist threat against India, and that a rushed withdrawal from Afghanistan could spark renewed civil war and increased Pakistani influence. The ability of the United States to respond to crises may be partially ameliorated by the shift in US defence resources from the northwest Pacific (Japan, South Korea) towards the southwest Pacific. In 2012, the US announced the relocation of 4,500 US marines to Guam from Okinawa, the rotation of marines through Darwin in northern Australia, the basing of at least four Littoral Combat Ships in Singapore and the rotation of troops through the Philippines. While these deployments were primarily motivated by increased tensions in the South China Sea, they will also provide the US with greater flexibility to move resources throughout the whole Indo–Pacific from Korea to the Middle East. Unlike the large permanent bases in Japan and South Korea, the deployments in the southwest Pacific are smaller, more flexible and more expeditionary in nature.

India as a regional security partner

But the United States hopes that much of any capability gap in the Indian Ocean will be filled by its friends and allies. This primarily means India, although Washington hopes that Australia and countries such as Indonesia can also assume greater responsibilities for regional security. The evolving US strategy will include facilitating local partners such as India to take the lead in various security tasks while retaining certain 'lynchpin' capabilities to influence regional security.[5]

Over the last decade or so the United States has encouraged the expansion of India's naval ambitions and capabilities throughout much of the Indian Ocean region. India is largely seen in Washington as a *status quo* power and net security provider, in contrast to China and Pakistan, which are treated as sources of instability. While US pronouncements have gone out of their way to avoid any suggestion of an alliance with India, there is a great deal of optimism that India will work in cooperation with the United States in providing security to the region. Washington believes that India's strategic interests are broadly aligned with the United States and that India will play an important role in 'burden sharing' (if not outsourcing) certain maritime security needs in the Indian Ocean. According to a 2002 Pentagon report, the US military sees India as a capable partner that can take on more responsibility for low-end operations in Asia such as peacekeeping, search and rescue, disaster relief and high-value cargo escort, allowing the US to focus on high-end operations. The Indian military is seen as an important partner in the Indian Ocean region because of its relatively sophisticated military capability, its proximity to unstable areas and its experience in peacekeeping operations. A security relationship with India may also provide training opportunities and, potentially, facilities to expand US power projection.[6]

A key factor in US efforts to cooperate with India has been a desire by the United States to build India as a regional counterweight to China. According to Kaplan, leveraging allies like India and Japan against China helps provide a mechanism for the US 'to gradually and elegantly cede great power responsibilities to like-minded others as their own capacities rise'.[7] China also plays a big role in India's motivations for cooperation with the United States. As a former senior Indian military official commented: 'India principally wants the [United States] to partner it in shaping the strategic space in the region, which could otherwise be usurped by other regional players'.[8] Many would argue that a key US strategic concern in the Indian Ocean should be to avoid or mitigate the prospects of strategic competition between India and China. Indeed, Kaplan suggests that the United States may ultimately play a balancing role or even to act as an 'honest broker' in relation to Sino–Indian naval rivalry in the Indian Ocean, commenting that:

> The United States will remain the one great power from outside the Indian Ocean region with a major presence there—a unique position that will give it the leverage to act as a broker between India and China in their own backyard.[9]

Alternatively, Washington may see Sino–Indian rivalry in the Indian Ocean region as not being contrary to its interests, and at least in the short term is driving India closer to the US. On several occasions over the last few years US officials have actively stoked public concerns in India over China's intentions in the Indian Ocean. Admiral Mike Mullen told the Indian press in July 2010 that China was taking 'a much more aggressive approach' in the Indian and Pacific oceans, and 'from my perspective, we need to work with India in that regard'.[10] Similarly, an undiplomatic jest by a Chinese naval officer to his US counterpart that the United States should take responsibility for security in the eastern Pacific and China should take responsibility for maritime security in the western Pacific and the Indian Ocean was dutifully reported to the Indian press by USPACOM's Admiral Keating.[11] While on a 2011 visit to New Delhi, US secretary of state, Hillary Clinton, described the China naval expansion as 'frightening'.[12] While these comments may be intended to draw Indian public opinion closer to the United States, they could also have unintended consequences.

The US strategy of encouraging India to become a regional naval power in the Indian Ocean has been compared with Britain's strategy in the late nineteenth and early twentieth centuries when it found itself challenged by the growth of German naval power. Britain then forged partnerships with emerging naval powers, the United States in the Western Hemisphere and Japan in the Pacific, allowing them a measure of regional hegemony, while Britain concentrated its resources in the North Atlantic against Germany.[13] This analogy, while far from perfect, captures some of the factors present in US thinking and the dilemma it faces in responding to the Chinese threat in East Asia. For its part, India's willingness to cooperate with the United States in achieving its ambitions to become the dominant power in the Indian Ocean is also not as paradoxical as it may seem. As the former US secretary of state, Dean Acheson, once conceded, the United States in developing its sphere of influence in the Western Hemisphere in the nineteenth century relied on Britain, the then superpower, to enforce the Monroe Doctrine until the United States was sufficiently strong to do so itself.[14] Similarly, India has reasons to cooperate with the United States in enforcing a Monroe Doctrine in the Indian Ocean region while it builds its national power.[15]

Enhanced US–Indian naval cooperation in the Indian Ocean fits well with a more cooperative approach promoted by the United States in order to leverage its naval power throughout the world. This strategy, which has been described as positioning the United States as an 'administrator' for the international security system, recognises the global strain on US naval resources and the value of long-term naval partnerships. The US Navy's 2007 *Cooperative Strategy* emphasises the need for the US Navy to establish partnerships in order to leverage its presence in the Pacific and Indian Oceans, and notes that, although US forces can be surged, 'trust and cooperation cannot be surged'.[16] The US Navy's prioritisation of improved integration and interoperability with partner navies and enhanced maritime domain awareness has reportedly been well received among Indian naval strategists.[17] Over the last several years the US Navy has promoted its Global Maritime Partnership initiative for cooperation among friendly navies to combat non-state security threats, in which the US encourages other states to assume leadership roles in addressing local and regional problems regardless of US involvement. India responded favourably, if tentatively, when invited to join the initiative in 2006.[18]

There are many good reasons for military cooperation between the United States and India, but the relationship is sometimes a difficult one. If some in Washington quietly hope that India will become a key ally, a Japan as it were of the Indian Ocean region, they are likely to be disappointed. From India's perspective, the relationship appears to be more of an alignment of convenience; it is also constrained by India's concerns about strategic autonomy and the somewhat difficult history between the two states.

The US and India in the Indian Ocean during the Cold War

Over the last 20 years the relationship between the United States and India in the Indian Ocean region has evolved from one of restrained rivalry towards one of strategic alignment. During the Cold War, the relationship was often strained and distant. While Washington was not hostile to India and did not see it as representing any real threat to US regional predominance, from at least the early 1970s it saw India as more or less aligned with Moscow and potentially willing to facilitate a Soviet military presence in the area. New Delhi's concerns about the United States were primarily focused on the effect of US support for Pakistan in undermining India's ability to dominate the subcontinent. But it also saw the US military presence in the Indian Ocean as a constant threat to India's ability to achieve its destiny in the region.

As discussed previously, many trace the beginnings of strategic friction between India and the United States in the Indian Ocean to the deployment of the USS *Enterprise* into the Bay of Bengal in the closing days of the Bangladesh War, an incident whose emotional impact far outweighed whatever political symbolism was intended by the United States. Indian suspicions about the United States were further confirmed by the development of Diego Garcia as a US military base, which became a focal point of India's opposition to the US presence in the Indian Ocean throughout the Cold War and after. The Indians saw Diego Garcia as an unsinkable aircraft carrier moored off India's coast, giving the United States the ability to intervene at will in the affairs of

South Asia. In some ways the US presence on Diego Garcia might be compared to the Soviet Union's attempts to build a military presence in Cuba in the early 1960s—but unlike the Americans, India did not have the ability to do anything about it.

The fall of the Shah of Iran in 1979 and the Soviet intervention in Afghanistan later that year, combined with a significant increase in Soviet naval activity, brought Cold War rivalries squarely into the Indian Ocean. Through the late 1970s and early 1980s, the Soviet Union and United States jostled for influence among the small and weak states in the region, often vying for access to port and air facilities or seeking to pre-empt their rival. New Delhi saw this rivalry as bringing the prospect of nuclear war to the region and precluding India from its destiny of becoming the leading power in the Indian Ocean. India responded to the increased US presence in several ways. The Indian Navy adopted major expansion plans and New Delhi sought to rally other Indian Ocean littoral states to support the IOZOP proposal that would severely limit US forces in the region. But New Delhi found that it was largely powerless to alter the military balance in the Indian Ocean.

While US–Indian strategic relations in the Indian Ocean were frequently strained—certainly in public rhetoric—from the early 1980s there was also a degree of strategic convergence. Several factors prompted a desire by New Delhi to improve relations with the United States, including the Soviet military presence in Afghanistan (which India did not publicly condemn, despite profound concerns); ideological shifts in New Delhi; and from the late 1980s, the winding down of the Cold War. The need to gain a free hand to intervene in Sri Lanka may have been another significant factor in New Delhi's softening towards the United States.[19] As a result, even from the early 1980s India was reportedly willing to subordinate its concerns about US military bases in the Indian Ocean in order to allow for improvements in the overall relationship.[20] At the same time, Washington was prepared to demonstrate greater consideration for India's regional prerogatives and interests. As discussed in Chapter 3, the US provided considerable political support for the Indian interventions in Sri Lanka in 1987 and the Maldives in 1988, in effect signalling a partial acceptance of the Indian Monroe Doctrine in South Asia.

During the 1980s the United States also began providing India with limited but strategically important defence technology and training. The Reagan administration decided to provide limited assistance to India in an effort to *enhance* its strategic autonomy (which they defined as freedom from Soviet influence). From the early 1980s India had sounded out the purchase of a range of US defence technology, including F-5 aircraft, super computers, night-vision goggles and radars. Although there was considerable resistance in Washington to the transfer of defence technology to a non-ally, especially one associated with Moscow, from 1984 Washington approved the supply of selected technology to India, including gas turbines for naval frigates and engines for prototypes for India's light combat aircraft.[21] There were also unpublicised transfers of technology, including the engagement of a US company, Continental

Electronics, to design and build a new VLF communications station at Tirunelveli in Tamil Nadu, which was commissioned in the late 1980s.[22] This provided the Indian Navy with the ability to communicate with (submerged) submarines throughout the Indian Ocean, which was particularly significant for the Indian Navy's Charlie-class nuclear-powered cruise-missile attack submarine (leased from the Soviet Union in 1988). In 1990–1, the United States also supplied India with electronic warfare and passive intelligence equipment worth $400 million, which the Indian military ordered after seeing the superiority of US technology in the First Gulf War.[23] Limited training was also provided: in 1986–7, US and British special forces also helped train a new Indian Marine Special Force, which was established in the lead up to the Sri Lanka intervention to conduct amphibious reconnaissance, raids and counterterrorist operations in a maritime environment.[24] While these instances of security cooperation point to a limited strategic convergence, only the end of the Cold War removed the political and psychological obstacles that prevented significant improvements in the relationship.

The post-Cold War strategic relationship

The end of the Cold War led to a fundamental change in India's strategic relationship with the United States that in many ways has underpinned its emergence as a major power.

The US–Indian economic relationship, which had been severely dampened by India's protectionist policies, surged with the liberalisation of the Indian economy in the early 1990s. The political relationship between India and the United States also improved considerably, although there were still major irritations from the Clinton administration's statements about human rights violations in Kashmir and the pressure it placed on India to give up its nuclear weapons ambitions. While India's nuclear tests in 1998 caused a major rupture in the relationship when the United States and its regional allies responded with punitive economic sanctions, the development also led to an intense and sustained political engagement. In the following years, India pursued the US relationship aggressively, with Prime Minister Vajpayee calling India and the United States 'natural allies' whose relations 'constitute the key element in the architecture of tomorrow's democratised world order'.[25] The United States demonstrated its credentials as a useful diplomatic partner when it supported India during the 1999 Kargil crisis, which went a long way to dispelling a decades-long view that the United States would always support Pakistan over the Kashmir dispute. India was able to return the gesture when it offered its 'unconditional and unambivalent support' to the United States following 9/11.[26] India offered Indian military facilities in support of the Afghanistan campaign and in 2002 provided naval escorts for US shipping through the Malacca Strait.

US efforts to engage with India accelerated under the Bush administration, which made every effort to tell India of its importance. In March 2005 the

Bush administration announced that it would 'help India become a major world power in the 21st century', adding: 'We understand fully the implications, including the military implications, of that statement'.[27] A senior US official in New Delhi commented: 'India as a global power is in an early, formative phase. The United States' job for the next five to ten years is to promote, assist and shape that process'.[28] Much to the delight of Indian commentators, a Central Intelligence Agency report called India 'the most important swing state in the international system'.[29]

The 2007 Indo–US civilian nuclear agreement provided a foundation for a comprehensive security relationship. Under the agreement, the United States effectively recognised India as a *de facto* nuclear weapons state and allowed India access to civil nuclear and US defence technology.[30] Washington's willingness to rewrite the international non-proliferation regime in India's favour signalled a major commitment to New Delhi. Although the nuclear agreement is yet to be fully implemented, it has facilitated a further expansion of the military-to-military relationship and opened the door for the supply of US defence technology to India.

The Bush administration was relatively open about placing its relationship with India in the context of China. According to US secretary of state, Condoleezza Rice:

> I really do believe that the US–Japan relationship, the US–South Korean relationship, the US–Indian relationship, all are important in creating an environment in which China is more likely to play a positive role than a negative role. These alliances are not against China; they are alliances that are devoted to stable security and political and economic and, indeed, values-based relationships that put China in the context of those relationships, and a different path to development than if China were simply untethered, simply operating without that strategic context.[31]

The Obama administration has continued much of the rhetoric about the India relationship, with President Obama calling India 'an indispensible partner'[32] and the relationship as, 'One of the defining partnerships of the twenty-first century'.[33] However the Obama administration is widely seen in New Delhi as less sympathetic towards India than Republican administrations. Many in New Delhi recall the Clinton administration's 'meddling' over Kashmir and nuclear weapons and there are suspicions about the current administration's approach towards China. In some respects, during his first term of office Obama adopted a more accommodating approach to China than the Bush administration, particularly in southern Asia where he sought greater cooperation from Beijing over Afghanistan and Iran. A joint US–Chinese statement made during President Obama's visit to China in November 2009 incensed New Delhi by apparently recognising a legitimate strategic role for China in South Asia, including suggestions that it may play some sort of honest broker role between India and Pakistan.[34]

The Obama administration has also sought to move the US–India relationship away from a focus on China and into a worldwide partnership that looks more at common interests beyond South Asia. In November 2010 President Obama announced US support for India's permanent membership of the UN Security Council and indicated US support for bringing India into various non-proliferation groupings, including the Nuclear Suppliers Group, the Wassenaar Agreement (export controls on dual-use technologies), the Australia Group (which deals with chemical and biological weapons proliferation) and the Missile Technology Control Regime. In recent years there has also been considerable discussion of the shared interest the United States and India have in protecting the 'global commons' (that is, freedom to use the seas, the air, space and even cyberspace).[35]

While encouraging India to develop strategic perceptions closer to those of the United States, Washington has not, in general, expected public support from New Delhi in international fora in the manner of the diplomatic support expected from US allies. According to Bronson Percival, a former US State Department official, US policy was to support India without an expectation of immediate returns or automatic reciprocity.[36]

US–Indian military cooperation in the Indian Ocean region

The US–Indian strategic relationship now has a strong focus on military-to-military cooperation, particularly in the naval sphere. Washington's focus has been on assisting the build-up of India's conventional naval and air force capabilities to complement the US presence in the Indian Ocean. A 2005 defence agreement provides for intelligence sharing and training, technology transfers and missile defence cooperation. Strategic dialogue has been institutionalised through the Defence Policy Group, a consultative mechanism jointly chaired by the US under secretary of defense for policy and the Indian defence secretary. This sits over the executive steering groups for military-to-military dialogue and the Defence Procurement and Production Group.

One of the most productive areas in the US–India strategic relationship has been in military exercises. The United States and India began conducting joint military exercises in 1992, and these have since increased significantly in frequency, scale, complexity and jointedness. India conducted more than 50 military exercises with the United States between 2003 and 2010, significantly more than with any other country. In the year to April 2011 there were some 56 'cooperative events' among US and Indian military services.[37] The US and Indian navies hold four major annual bilateral exercises: *Malabar*, the premier fleet exercise; *Habu Nag* (naval aspects of amphibious operations); *Spitting Cobra* (explosive ordnance destruction); and *Salvex* (diving and salvage). US and Indian Marine forces engage through the annual Exercise *Shatrujeet*, a company-sized ground field exercise. US and Indian special forces participate in several other exercises, including an exclusive special forces exercise, Exercise *Varja Prahar*. Army-to-army engagement is centred on Exercise *Yudh Abhyas*, and air forces engagement through Exercise *Cope India*. In 2010, USPACOM and the Indian Integrated Defence Staff (IIDS) conducted an inaugural joint exercise between defence staffs, based on an HADR scenario.

Malabar, the principal naval exercise, has an important symbolic and practical role in US–Indian naval cooperation. In 2007, the exercise, which had previously been conducted on a bilateral basis, was expanded to include three carrier battle groups and other ships from India, the United States, Japan, Australia and Singapore. The presence of two US carrier task forces in the Bay of Bengal was particularly symbolic for New Delhi, where the USS *Enterprise* incident of 1971 is still remembered darkly. Exercise *Malabar 2007* was also seen by many as having particular strategic significance, involving US allies and friends in a putative maritime *entente* aimed at containing China. In the wake of the controversial 2007 exercises in the Bay of Bengal, the multinational component of these exercises has been shifted out of the Indian Ocean—with the result that Malabar exercises in the Indian Ocean have been bilateral US–India affairs.[38] There is still considerable sensitivity in New Delhi about containing the scope and symbolism of the Malabar exercises. In 2013 New Delhi refused permission to the Indian Air Force to participate in *Malabar* and rebuffed US attempts to include Japan as another participant in the exercises.

The US has proposed several agreements with India to facilitate cooperation and interoperability of their armed forces that are highly controversial in India. These include a Logistics Support Agreement that would facilitate increased use of shared logistical services, a Basic Exchange and Cooperation Agreement for Geospatial Cooperation (BECA), which provides for mutual logistical support and enables exchanges of communications and related equipment, and a Communications Interoperability and Security Memorandum of Agreement (CISMOA) that requires equipment supplied to India be compatible with American systems. Although the United States has signed similar agreements with many of its allies, these agreements remain highly controversial in India due to their perceived implications for the integration of India into the US global military network. As of 2013 they had not been finalised.

The United States has for some time promoted itself as an arms supplier to India with the objectives of both improving India's power projection capabilities, particularly in the maritime sphere, and eventually supplanting Russia as India's primary defence supplier. However, progress on defence trade has been relatively slow, reflecting US legal hurdles and the ponderous nature of the Indian defence acquisitions process. While an End-User Verification Agreement was signed in 2009, other agreements required under US domestic law for the transfer of sensitive defence technology are still under negotiation. Between 2004 and August 2011, India had concluded defence contracts with the United States valued at $8.26 billion, including the purchase of six C-130J Hercules, three Boeing 737 VIP jets, ten Boeing C-17 Globemasters and twelve Boeing P-8I Poseidon maritime reconnaissance aircraft.[39] Other reported sales included the *USS Trenton* (a 16,000-tonne amphibious landing ship), Harpoon Block II missiles[40] and General Electric aircraft engines for India's Tejas lightweight fighter. However, in 2012 US suppliers were passed over when the $10 billion-plus contract to acquire 126 multi-role combat aircraft was awarded to Dassault of France. Importantly, India and the United States have very different views on how military supply fits into the broader relationship. For the United States a military supply relationship, which necessarily includes enhanced interoperability and institutional relationships, is a normal way of building a broader security relationship. The use of US-supplied equipment creates linkages up and down the chain of command through training and other joint activities. In contrast, many in New Delhi regard unfettered access to US defence technology as an end in itself, as well as a litmus test of a broader strategic partnership.[41] New Delhi sees the United States as just one of several competing suppliers which include Russia and Israel and many in the Indian military do not expect that the use of US-supplied equipment will have a significant effect on training or doctrine.[42]

The Hawaii-based US Pacific Command (USPACOM) has a leading role in the military relationship. But while US–Indian military-to-military relations are reportedly excellent, the Indian Ministry of Defence tries to keep a tight reign on contacts. US diplomats see the Indian civilian leadership as going slow on the relationship despite the enthusiasm of the Indian armed forces. According to one US diplomatic cable in 2009:

> The uniformed leadership of all three services—in particular the Navy—appreciate their improving ties with the US military, but bureaucratic inertia and recalcitrant officials in the Ministry of External Affairs and the Ministry of Defense (sic) continue to complicate attempts to improve the relationship.[43]

Although, an Indian liaison officer was temporarily posted to USPACOM headquarters in the wake of the 2004 Tsunami (a position only previously offered to Japan, South Korea and Australia), the Indian Ministry of Defence has not allowed an officer to be posted there on permanent assignment, claiming that it does not seek such a relationship with US combatant commands. This is largely driven by New Delhi's preoccupation with status and its wish to be regarded as a global power that deals direct with Washington rather than relegated to the status of a regional power that deals with regional commands. There are also concerns that the Indian military are becoming too close to the United States. In April 2011, apparently at the instruction of Indian defence minister, A. K. Antony, all unsupervised contact between armed forces officials and foreign defence delegations was disallowed. Antony was reportedly 'uncomfortable' with the growing military to military relationship.[44] He is concerned about the political costs of US ties and does not want the US relationship to be at the cost of 'traditional' security relationships.[45]

US–India military to military relationships are also complicated by US bureaucratic divisions relating to the Indian Ocean. The Area of Responsibility of USPACOM, which has primary responsibility for the India relationship, ends at the India–Pakistan border. This means that in operating in the Indian Ocean, the Indian military needs to deal with USPACOM, USCENTCOM and, increasingly, the Stuttgart-based USAFRICOM. The arrangement is seen by the US as beneficial in reducing potential operational frictions arising from US military support for Pakistan, but Indian military officials see it as involving an irrational division of India's strategic spheres in South Asia and the broader Indian Ocean region.[46]

India–US naval cooperation

Of all the Indian armed services, the Indian Navy is the most comfortable with the US relationship, although it recognises that it must act within the constraints imposed by New Delhi. According to the Indian Navy's 2007 strategy document: 'While the option of formal alliances is not available. ... we can however reach out to our maritime partners or collaborate with friendly nations to build deterrence'.[47] The central role of naval cooperation in the security relationship was formalised in the 2006 *Framework for Maritime Security Cooperation*, which commits India and the United States to 'comprehensive cooperation in ensuring a secure maritime domain'. Expanding navy-to-navy ties proved to be a politically low-cost way of strengthening the overall strategic relationship during the high profile controversies over the civil nuclear deal.[48]

The US Defense Department has identified antipiracy cooperation, HADR cooperation and cooperation in maritime domain awareness as among the key areas of military-to-military engagement in the Indian Ocean.[49] According to the US 2010 Quadrennial Defense Review, the US will also seek to enhance Indian capabilities in long-range maritime surveillance, maritime interdiction and patrolling, air interdiction, and strategic airlift. Sea lane protection is identified by both the US and Indian militaries as the most promising field of service-to-service cooperation. An oft-cited, if short-lived, example of naval cooperation occurred in 2002 when at the request of USPACOM the Indian Navy contributed offshore patrol vessels for several months to the US-led Operation *Enduring Freedom*, to escort 'high-value' non-combatant shipping (e.g. oil tankers) transiting through the Malacca Strait. The US request was clearly driven by a desire to expand India's strategic footprint beyond South Asia (in contrast to which USCENTCOM ignored Indian offers of assistance in Afghanistan). US military officials saw India's participation as potentially legitimising an expanded military role in Southeast Asia. New Delhi recognised it as an opportunity to demonstrate its value as a security partner to the United States in the months following 9/11, as well as advancing its case as a maritime security provider in the Malacca Strait.[50] In May 2002, the Indians suggested that joint naval patrols be extended to Hormuz, but the US turned down the proposal, citing 'jurisdictional' constraints between USPACOM and USCENTCOM.[51] It is possible that New

Delhi thought that it could use the opportunity to create a wedge between US–Pakistani cooperation in the Arabian Sea. For its part, the United States would have wanted to avoid being 'wedged'.

India has been less enthusiastic in recent years about participating in US-sponsored anti-piracy efforts in the western Indian Ocean. Since October 2008, the Indian Navy has deployed one or two vessels in anti-piracy patrols off Somalia. Despite being touted by a recent US Department of Defence report as being evidence of the development of the US–Indian military relationship, in fact there is very little cooperation of an operational nature. India has refused to join the US-sponsored Combined Task Force 150 (maritime counterterrorism operations) or Combined Task Force 151 (anti-piracy operations), to which some 20 countries have contributed naval assets. Although CTF 151 was established as a counter-piracy task force under a 2008 UN Security Council resolution, the Indian government has been reluctant to join CTF 151 for several reasons, including its sponsorship by the United States and the participation in the task force of the Pakistan Navy. India separately provides escort services to Indian and other flagged vessels. While India participates in the Shared Awareness and Deconfliction (SHADE) meetings with the Combined Maritime Forces and other independently operating maritime security providers, in practice Indian naval operations are barely coordinated with CTF 151. The Indian Navy made the deployment only after overcoming opposition from the Indian Foreign Ministry, which, according to some, repeatedly turned down requests from the navy to conduct interceptions.[52]

Another significant area of cooperation is in humanitarian assistance. The 2004 Tsunami which devastated much of the northeast Indian Ocean led to the creation of an informal coalition or 'core group' of India, the United States, Japan and Australia, coordinated by the United States, to provide disaster relief. The Indian Navy's experience in the tsunami led it to see the significant political-diplomatic value of contributing to international disaster relief operations and an understanding of its own limitations in that area. With the encouragement of the United States it has enhanced its amphibious operations capabilities, for instance through the acquisition of the amphibious landing ship, USS *Trenton* (now INS *Jalashva*). The successful experience of the Indian, US, Japanese and Australian navies cooperating during the 2004 Tsunami was also credited by many with inspiring the multilateral *Malabar 2007* naval exercises in the Bay of Bengal. There was also reportedly operational cooperation between US and Indian navies during civilian evacuations in Lebanon in 2006.

Maritime domain awareness (MDA) is another key area for potential cooperation between India and the United States and its allies in the Indian Ocean. According to the Indian Navy's *Maritime Military Strategy* 'this singular factor—MDA—has the potential and capability to widen the gap between the capabilities of the Indian Navy and other regional maritime forces in the IOR'.[53] India has traditionally had weak capabilities in Intelligence, Surveillance and Reconnaisance (ISR) capabilities; these are now being enhanced with considerable assistance from both Israel and the United States.[54] Of greatest significance to India's ISR capabilities will be the delivery of up to 24 Boeing P-8i MMA aircraft, beginning in around 2013. These will be equipped with modern anti-submarine warfare, anti-surface warfare, and ISR sensors, capable of broad-area, maritime and littoral operations and designed to work with the Global Hawk broad-area maritime surveillance UAVs which are also being acquired by India.[55] The United States hopes that these combined systems may also be operated by key partners such as Australia, Japan and Singapore. Lawrence Prabhakar, a prominent Indian naval analyst, has suggested that India might join a multilateral cooperative MDA system similar to the proposed 'Pacific Pool' of Global Hawk UAVs (a proposed common regional fleet of Global Hawks operated out of Guam by the United States, Australia and other Pacific allies).[56] While India would receive many operational benefits from such an arrangement in the Indian Ocean, it seems highly unlikely that this would be politically acceptable to New Delhi given its aversion to multi-lateral security cooperation, especially anything that might smell of reliance on the United States. Nor is it feasible that New Delhi would agree to pub-licly operate defence assets out of Diego Garcia. Nevertheless, the Indian and US navies have been quietly exchanging information on declared merchant traffic in the northwest Indian Ocean for some years.

Indian perspectives on security cooperation

Despite the commonalities in interests between India and the United States in the Indian Ocean and elsewhere, there are still many constraints on the relationship. New Delhi certainly now has a much more relaxed view of US presence in the Indian Ocean and even South Asia than was previously the case. While New Delhi formally continues to challenge Britain's claim to the British Indian Ocean Territory, Indian rhetoric about Diego Garcia has softened considerably over the last decade or so in line with improvements in US–Indian relations and, perhaps, a grudging acceptance of the stabilising role that Diego Garcia cur-rently plays in the region. But improvements in the US–India relationship may also place some implicit constraints on the use of Diego Garcia by the United States, which may be more circumspect in using Diego Garcia as a primary base of operations where there are significant Indian sensitivities (for example, strikes against Iran).

Even in South Asia, within India's core sphere of influence, New Delhi may see Washington as a potentially useful security partner. Over the last decade, India and the United States have worked closely together in Afghanistan. As discussed previously, in Sri Lanka, India and the United States provided assis-tance to Colombo in the destruction of the LTTE, and since that time have worked together to maintain pressure on Colombo to reach a political settlement with the Tamil community. In the Maldives, the United States provides training and equipment to the Maldives security forces without criticism. New Delhi has also apparently been happy to take a back seat in Myanmar, where

Washington has taken the lead in engaging with the military government and encouraging it to reduce its reliance on China.

Despite these changed perceptions, India's political culture still remains a major obstacle to US–Indian security cooperation. Indian public perceptions of the United States have moved well beyond the 'bogey-man' image that was cultivated by Indira Gandhi and other leaders during the Cold War. Many wealthy and middle-class Indians now have educational and familial links with the United States and US culture has penetrated Indian society, particularly among younger generations. The unusually warm welcome that President Obama received in his November 2010 visit to India demonstrated the extent of positive feelings for the United States among the general population. According to a 2013 opinion poll, Indians had the warmest feelings towards the United States compared with any other country. In the same poll, 72 per cent thought that the United States would be a good partner for India in the Indian Ocean.[57]

But the relationship continues to be controversial in India, particularly for those of a leftist or Nehruvian strategic perspective who regard the relationship in zero sum terms, essentially seeing cooperation with the United States as involving co-option or coercion. The United States is still widely perceived by the Indian elite as a potentially unreliable strategic partner that may ultimately seek to dominate India. Although there is a general appreciation of the importance of improved relations with the United States there is an almost visceral fear of India being entrapped and losing its strategic autonomy. This can operate at many levels. Apparently simple arrangements for access to logistical services or to facilitate interoperability in communications are held in deep suspicion by some as being part of a US strategy of making India reliant upon it. Any agreements with the United States relating to security or military-related issues are treated with an extraordinary degree of caution and suspicion. Even having the *capability* to act jointly is resisted by New Delhi for fear that it would compromise India's strategic autonomy. The Indian defence minister A. K. Antony has reportedly denied any prospect of Indian and US forces ever operating together and senior Defence Ministry officials have completely ruled out actual joint operations with the US because they are tantamount to becoming part of a military alliance.[58] As a result of these political considerations, strategic cooperation with the United States is often kept beyond the public gaze, and to the greatest extent possible, far from India's shores.

The level and type of cooperation between India and the United States differs in the various subregions of Indian Ocean. Since the 1980s the US has largely recognised India's special role in South Asia, including the maritime South Asian states. In recent years it has encouraged India to increase its naval presence in the northeast Indian Ocean and increasingly also in the southwest. In contrast, the northwestern Indian Ocean region remains an area where the United States is perceived to be less forthcoming in encouraging an enhanced Indian naval presence—perhaps reflecting both US naval predominance in that region and a relatively high level of naval cooperation between the US and Pakistan.

Some have argued that, despite its rhetoric about encouraging India to take a greater role in the Indian Ocean, that the United States has resisted a greater role for India in the northwest. Some have claimed that the United States, which holds a predominant role in Gulf security, has not encouraged India to develop a security role in the region in the way that it has encouraged India to expand its role elsewhere in the Indian Ocean. Certainly, the US–Pakistan military relationship in the northwest has not been helpful to India. But some of the constraints are self-imposed: India refuses to participate in the US-sponsored Combined Military Forces in and around the Persian Gulf, at least in part because of its objections to working alongside Pakistan and concerns about maintaining strategic autonomy. This means that India needs to forge its own relationships in the region, with one or more Gulf Arab states or with Iran.

India's high degree of ambivalence about operational cooperation or even operation coordination with the United States is exemplified by its refusal to join the Proliferation Security Initiative (PSI). The PSI, first proposed by the United States in 2003, is an arrangement under which the US and its partners could aggressively search and seize 'suspicious' ships on the high seas. Although lacking UN endorsement, the PSI is now supported by 90 states. India continues to take a deliberately ambiguous approach to PSI and has neither declared an intention to join the initiative nor expressly rejected its principles. India remains leery of the PSI due to domestic political opposition and concerns about both its grounding in international law and its application to non-NPT countries. From one perspective, India has every reason to contribute to an international regime that would help mitigate WMD proliferation in South Asia and the Indian Ocean. India has itself been involved in the interdiction of North Korean vessels in its territorial waters suspected of transporting illicit cargo. However, the PSI faces significant Indian domestic opposition on several grounds. These include opposition to security cooperation with the United States where India might be perceived as a junior partner; fears of joining cooperative security arrangements not blessed by the United Nations; India's historical 'mistreatment' at the hands of international non-proliferation regimes; and residual fears that the regime could be used against India.[59] This has not prevented the Indian and US navies undertaking PSI-style exercises (e.g. maritime interdiction and visit, board, search and seizure operations) as part of bilateral exercise programmes. While practical cooperation between the US and Indian militaries under the political radar—including the sharing of intelligence on suspect ships—can go some way to addressing the problem, lack of Indian political endorsement of PSI inevitably limits India's activities in this area.

The future of the India–US relationship in the Indian Ocean

From the record of US–Indian naval cooperation it seems that India will be an unpredictable maritime security partner to the United States. Even if the interests of the two are broadly aligned, India will likely only publicly coordinate its operations with the United States on an occasional case-by-case basis.

India's nonaligned legacy of so-called 'merit-based' decisions means that it is little inclined to support coalition partners out of concern for the overall relationship and may be willing to take coordinated action only when it sees its interests are directly threatened. Despite its participation in Operation *Enduring Freedom* in 2002, India will, if at all possible, seek to avoid joining any international coalition under the operational leadership of the United States or its allies. A need to demonstrate that it is acting autonomously seems strongly rooted in the Indian national psyche and may sometimes lead to India avoiding cooperation with the United States even when it is plainly in its national interests to do so.

Some might argue that there may be good strategic reasons for India avoiding a perception of having too close a security relationship with the United States (whether in the maritime or other dimensions). While India derives significant leverage against China from having a good relationship with the United States, that leverage could actually be reduced if the US–India relationship is perceived as moving towards an anti-China alliance.

However, there are likely to be many cases where an ideological opposition to cooperation with the United States will make it more difficult for India to project power in the region or to effectively inherit the benefit of the United States' existing relationships. Paradoxically, in this respect, India's objective of strategic autonomy will likely constrain or delay the growth of Indian strategic influence in the Indian Ocean.

Notes

1 Department of the Navy (2007) *A Cooperative Strategy for 21st Century Seapower.* Online: www.navy.mil/maritime/Maritimestrategy.pdf (accessed 10 October 2013).
2 Robert Kaplan (2009) 'Center stage for the twenty-first century', *Foreign Affairs*, Vol. 88, No. 2, pp. 31–2.
3 Walter Russell Mead (2012) 'The Energy Revolution Part One: the biggest losers', 8 July. Online: http://blogs.the-american-interest.com/wrm/2012/07/08/the-energy-revolution-part-one-the-biggest-losers/ (accessed 10 October 2013).
4 Admiral Jonathan Greenert (2011) 'Value of maritime crossroads', 4 November. Online: http://cno.navylive.dodlive.mil/2011/11/04/%E2%80%9Cvalue-of-maritime-crossroads%E2%80%9D-3/ (accessed 10 October 2013).
5 Andrew Erickson, Walter C. Ladwig and Justin D. Mikolay (2010) 'Diego Garcia and the United States' emerging Indian Ocean strategy', *Asian Security*, Vol. 6, No. 3.
6 Juli A. Macdonald (2002) 'Indo–US military relationship: expectations and perceptions', report by Booz Allen Hamilton for the Director, Net Assessment, Office of the Secretary of Defense, October.
7 Kaplan, 'Center stage for the twenty-first century', p. 24.
8 Rahul Bedi (2005) 'US–India defense relations', *SPAN Magazine*, New Delhi, March–April.
9 Kaplan, 'Centre Stage for the twenty-first century'.
10 Mike Mullen (2010) speech in New Delhi, 23 July.
11 Manu Pubby (2009) 'China proposed division of Pacific, Indian Ocean regions, we declined: US admiral', *Indian Express*, 15 May.
12 Sandeep Dikshit (2011) 'Hillary's leadership call to India not aimed at Pakistan', *The Hindu*, 9 August.

13 James Holmes *et al.* (2009) *Indian Naval Strategy in the Twenty-first Century*, Abingdon: Routledge, Ch. 3.

14 Dean G. Acheson (1955) *A Democrat Looks at his Party*, New York: Harper, p. 64.

15 This analogy was first made by the US ambassador to India, Chester Bowles, in trying to persuade Nehru to adopt a Monroe Doctrine for Southern Asia. Chester Bowles (1954) 'A fresh look at Free Asia', *Foreign Affairs*, Vol. 33, No. 1, pp. 54–71.

16 US Navy, *Cooperative Strategy for 21st Century Seapower*.

17 Holmes *et al.*, *Indian Naval Strategy in the Twenty-first Century*, p. 122.

18 Rajat Pandit (2007) 'US eyes naval ties with India', *Times of India*, 19 April.

19 Stephen Cohen (1992) 'The Reagan Administration and India', in Harold A. Gould and Sumit Ganguly (eds), *The Hope and the Reality: US–Indian Relations from Roosevelt to Reagan*, Boulder, CO: Westview Press, pp. 139–53.

20 Ashok Kapur (1982) *The Indian Ocean: Regional and International Power Politics*, New York: Praeger, p. 210.

21 Jyotika Saskena and Suzette Grillot (1999) 'The emergence of Indo–US defense cooperation: from specific to diffuse reciprocity', in Gary K. Bertsch, Seema Gahlaut and Anupam Srivastava (eds), *Engaging India: US strategic relations with the world's largest democracy*, London: Routledge, pp. 144–68.

22 Continental Electronics also constructed the US Navy's VLF submarine communications station at Northwest Cape in Australia.

23 Desmond Ball (1993) *Signals Intelligence in the Post-Cold War Era*, Singapore: Institute of Southeast Asian Studies, p. 75.

24 'Marine Commandos: India's flexible elite' (1996) *Jane's Intelligence Review*, Vol. 008/005, 1 May.

25 K.P. Nayar (1998) 'Vajpayee describes India and US as natural allies', *The Telegraph*, 29 September.

26 Rajiv Chandrasekaran (2001) 'India offers bases to US for retaliatory attacks', *Washington Post*, 17 September.

27 Office of the Spokesperson, US Department of State (2005) 'Background briefing by Administration officials on US–South Asia relations', Washington, DC, 25 March.

28 Quoted in Daniel Twining (2007) 'America's grand design in Asia', *The Washington Quarterly,* Vol. 30, No. 3, pp. 79–94.

29 Ashley Tellis (2004) 'Assessing America's War on Terror: confronting insurgency, cementing primacy', *NBR Analysis*, Vol. 15, No. 4.

30 For a discussion of the 123 agreement, see Teresita C. Schaffer (2009) *India and the United States in the Twenty-first Century: Reinventing Partnership*, Washington, DC: The CSIS Press.

31 Condoleezza Rice (2005) speech at Sophia University, Tokyo, 19 March.

32 Merle David Kellerhals Jr. (2010) 'India an indispensable partner, US officials say', *IPP Digital*, 1 June. Online: www.america.gov/st/peacesec-english/2010/June/ 2010 601090431dmslahrellek0.7037622.html (accessed 10 October 2013).

33 T.P. Sreenivasan (2010) 'Obama has gone further than Bush on India', *Rediff.com*, 9 June. Online: http://news.rediff.com/column/2010/jun/09/tps-sreenivasan-on-the-obama-platter-for-india.htm (accessed 10 October 2013).

34 'A third country role cannot be envisaged nor is it necessary' (2009) *Outlook India*, 18 November.

35 While India and the United States both subscribe to the principle of freedom of the seas, there are also some important differences between them over international law. For example, India takes a position on military and hydrographic research activities in its EEZ that is very similar to China's objections to US activities in China's claimed EEZ in the South China and East China seas. This has led to Indian complaints over the activities of US naval survey ships in India's EEZ near the Andaman Islands and in the vicinity of India's submarine base near Visakhapatnam. These differences have not yet played out. See Jon M. Van Dyke (2004) 'Military ships and

planes operating in the exclusive economic zone of another country', *Marine Policy*, Vol. 28, pp. 29–39; and Ranjit Bhushan (2004) 'Port Hole', *Outlook India*, 7 June.

36 Bronson Percival (2010) 'Regional security environment in the Indian Ocean: threats on the margins; partnership with India', in C. Uday Bhaskar and Kamlesh K. Agnihotri (eds), *Security Challenges along the Indian Ocean Littoral: Indian and US Perspectives*, Delhi: National Maritime Foundation, pp. 21–32.

37 US Department of Defense (2011) 'Report to Congress on US-security cooperation', November.

38 Gupta (2011) 'US–India defence ties: the limits to interoperability', East Asia Forum, 31 July.

39 'Defence purchases worth over Rs 37,000 cr with US since 2004: Govt' (2011) *The Economic Times*, 10 August.

40 There were also reportedly serious discussions over the transfer of the USS *Kitty Hawk*, an 80,000-tonne aircraft carrier. M.D. Nalapat (2007) 'Will the USS *Kitty Hawk* cement US–India military ties?', *Intellibriefs*, 28 November. Online: http://intelli briefs.blogspot.com.au/2007/12/will-uss-kitty-hawk-cement-us-india.html (accessed 10 October 2013).

41 Brian Shoup and Sumit Ganguly (2006) 'Introduction', in Sumit Ganguly *et al.*, *US–Indian Strategic Cooperation into the Twenty-first Century: More than Words*, London: Routledge.

42 Schaffer, *India and the United States in the Twenty-first Century*, p. 79.

43 '216716: Scenesetter for Secretary of State Clinton's visit to India' (2011) *The Hindu*, 28 March.

44 Sandeep Unnithan (2011) 'Lone dissenter', *India Today*, 9 April.

45 Gupta, 'US–India defence ties'.

46 Macdonald, 'Indo–US Military Relationship', p. xxviii.

47 Indian Navy (2007) *Freedom to Use the Seas: India's Maritime Military Strategy*.

48 Bronson Percival (2010) 'Growing Chinese and Indian naval power: US recalibration and coalition building', in Sam Bateman and Joshua Ho (eds), *Southeast Asia and the Rise of Chinese and Indian Naval Power: Between Rising Naval Powers*, London: Routledge, pp. 36–47.

49 US Department of Defense (2011) 'Report to Congress on US-security cooperation', November.

50 Ibid., p. 51.

51 Vijay Sakhuja (2002) 'Indo–US naval cooperation', Institute of Peace and Conflict Studies, No. 898, 25 October.

52 Sandeep Unnithan (2008) 'The hijack dilemma', *India Today*, 17 October 2008; and 'Lack of consensus holding back anti-piracy policy', *Thaindian News*, 20 November.

53 Indian Navy, *India's Maritime Military Strategy*, p. 117.

54 See generally, Lawrence S. Prabhakar (2009) 'India's Maritime Surveillance and Reconnaissance Initiatives and the quest to secure its Maritime-Aerospace', *Strategic Affairs*, September.

55 'India will purchase the MQ-4C BAMS drone aircraft' (2012) *Avionews*, 2 April.

56 Lawrence S. Prabhakar (2010) 'India's options and role in the PSI: alliance of necessity', *Strategic Affairs*, February.

57 Medcalf, 'India Poll 2013', pp. 5, 9.

58 Gupta, 'US–India defence ties'.

59 James R. Holmes (2007) 'India and the Proliferation Security Initiative: a US perspective', *Strategic Analysis*, Vol. 31, No. 2, pp. 315–37.

10 China

China is now a major factor in India's strategic aspirations in the Indian Ocean. India's ambitions to dominate the Indian Ocean are coming into direct conflict with China's interests, particularly its concerns to ensure the unobstructed flow of energy across the ocean. Many see the potential for a security dilemma arising between them as 'defensive' moves taken by each are seen by the other as threatening its security. While the relationship in the Indian Ocean is only a subset of a broader strategic relationship, it is the area in which China is most vulnerable. Some believe that it is in India's interests to maintain China's strategic vulnerability in the Indian Ocean, as a potential bargaining chip for other areas of rivalry.

China's strategic imperatives in the Indian Ocean

China's overwhelming strategic imperative in the Indian Ocean is the protection of its sea lines of communication across the Indian Ocean, especially the transport of energy to China through the Malacca Strait.

China is keenly aware that its SLOCs are highly vulnerable to threats from state and non-state actors. Like India, China faces a 'Hormuz Dilemma' in the Persian Gulf, where some 40 per cent of China's oil imports transit the Strait of Hormuz. China is even more vulnerable in the Malacca Strait, through which around 82 per cent of China's oil imports pass (which includes imports from the Persian Gulf, Sudan and West Africa).[1] According to Chinese president Hu Jiantao, this last chokepoint represents China's 'Malacca Dilemma'. Chinese strategists are concerned that China's inability to protect its SLOCs or keep the Malacca Strait open could be used as a bargaining chip against it in the context of a wider dispute. China has so far implicitly accepted the role of the United States in maintaining stability in the Middle East and protecting the maritime SLOCs, but it takes quite a different view of India's aspirations in the region.

The overall strategic relationship between India and China is somewhat difficult and unstable. As Mohan Malik describes it, 'Just as the Indian sub-continental plate has a tendency to constantly rub and push against the Eurasian tectonic plate, causing friction and volatility in the entire Himalayan mountain range, India's bilateral relationship with China also remains volatile, friction- and tension-ridden'.[2] There are numerous unresolved strategic issues between them, including a major border dispute in the Himalayas, Tibetan autonomy, China's *de facto* alliance with Pakistan and its relationships elsewhere in South Asia. Probably most infuriating of all for New Delhi is China's refusal to recognise India's claims to great power status. Some observers believe that there has been a material deterioration in the Sino–Indian strategic relation- ship in recent years, propelling the countries towards a wider strategic rivalry. According to a 2013 opinion poll, some 82 per cent of Indians considered China to be a threat to the security of India in the next ten years.[3]

Rivalry in the Indian Ocean is just part of this mix, but it is also the theatre in which China is most strategically vulnerable to India. As a result, Beijing is firmly opposed to India's aspirations there. As General Zhao Nanqi, director of the Chinese Academy of Military Sciences, commented, 'this is something we cannot accept. … we are not prepared to let the Indian Ocean become India's Ocean'.[4] Many Chinese analysts believe that in coming years a 'Great Game' will be played out between China and India in the Indian Ocean, frequently (if inaccurately) quoting US sea power theorest Alfred Mahan: 'Whoever controls the Indian Ocean dominates Asia. This ocean is the key to the Seven Seas'.[5]

China has sought to address its perceived imperatives and vulnerabilities in the Indian Ocean in several ways. First, it is developing capabilities to project limited naval and air power into the Indian Ocean. Second, it is developing considerable economic influence with littoral states, but only a very limited security presence. Third, it is attempting to reduce its vulnerabilities through diversifying its energy transport options in the region. Many in New Delhi consider these actions as potentially threatening India's strategic advantages over China in the Indian Ocean.

The expansion of China's blue-water naval capabilities

China began implementing plans to develop a so-called 'blue-water' navy in the mid-1980s. Although these plans are overwhelmingly focused on the Taiwan Strait and China's other interests in the western Pacific Ocean, they also have long-term implications for India and the Indian Ocean. Over the last two decades or so, China has embarked on a major naval expansion programme, which includes programmes for the development and acquisition of anti-ship ballistic missiles, anti-ship cruise missiles, land-attack cruise missiles, surface-to-air missiles, submarines, aircraft carriers, destroyers and supporting ISR systems.[6] Of particular concern to the United States is China's develo- pment of anti-access area denial (A2AD) capabilities, which have the poten- tial to change the balance of power in the western Pacific. The most potent of these weapons are anti-ship ballistic missiles (ASBMs) equipped with manoeuvrable re-entry vehicles designed to hit moving ships at sea which, due to their ability to change course, are extremely difficult to intercept. Some observers regard this as a 'game-changing' weapon. While the A2AD threat is generally perceived to be in the western Pacific, the range of China's land-based ASBMs could in theory include parts of the Bay of Bengal/Andaman Sea and even the Arabian Sea.[7]

Overall, China's naval capabilities now exceed India's by a considerable margin in both quantitative and qualitative terms. But despite much alarm among some analysts, China's power projection capabilities in the Indian Ocean are very limited and are likely to remain so for the foreseeable future. The PLA Navy (PLAN) has extremely limited experience in projecting power beyond coastal waters. Despite its naval expansion programme, it has only a limited number of blue-water naval combatants and very limited long-range air strike capabilities. China's ability to project power into the Indian Ocean is also restricted by the long distance from Chinese ports (the closest major Chinese naval base to the Indian Ocean is on Hainan Island in the South China Sea), its lack of logistical support in the Indian Ocean, and the need to deploy to the Indian Ocean through chokepoints. A 2011 report by the US Department of Defense about China's naval capabilities concluded that by the latter half of the current decade, China will likely be able to project and sustain a modest-sized force, perhaps several battalions of ground forces or a naval flotilla of up to a dozen ships, in low-intensity operations far from China, but that China will not be able to project and sustain large forces in high-intensity combat operations far from China until well past 2020.[8] Another US review of PLAN's out-of-area capabilities concluded:

> The PLAN cannot currently conduct a full-scale joint forcible entry operation, maintain maritime superiority out of area, conduct multicarrier or carrier strike group operations, or provide comprehensive protection against threats to an out of area task force (antiaircraft warfare, ASW, and antisurface warfare). The PLAN appears to be expanding its out of area operations incrementally. This will allow the United States, its allies, and other countries time to work out (with each other and with the Chinese) how to respond to opportunities for greater cooperation and potential challenges posed by a more capable PLAN. China has an even longer way to go before it can be considered a global military power. In particular, it has no network of facilities and bases to maintain and repair its ships. The possession or absence of such a network may ultimately be the best indication of China's future intentions. If China lacks such a support network, it will have great difficulty engaging in major combat operations (MCOs) far from its shores.[9]

Even China's relatively small anti-piracy deployment to the Gulf of Aden has reportedly severely strained the PLAN's logistical capabilities. According to the International Institute for Strategic Studies, 'Any conflict involving supply lines stretching further than 200 miles or [which] did not involve a contiguous land corridor would prove challenging for the PLA and would severely restrict its ability to deploy and maintain its forces'.[10]

Since 1987 the PLAN has made several adjustments to its strategic doctrine that affect its role in the Indian Ocean, including adding the 'line' of SLOC security to its focus on the 'point' of Taiwan and expanding the traditional idea of territorial defence to cover 'all maritime areas that have a key bearing on China's national security'.[11] More recently the PLAN has given increased emphasis to naval operations against non-traditional security threats, including exploring the concept of Military Operations Other Than War. However, Australian analyst You Ji argues that Beijing has realised that the use of the military option to meet conventional threats to Indian Ocean SLOCs is not realistic and that military means for protecting SLOCs will be a last resort in Beijing's hierarchy of choices. The PLAN has thus given priority to seeking cooperation with the littoral states, while the acquisition of expeditionary capabilities is more of a hedging strategy. You concludes that while the PLAN's maritime strategy is blue-water in theory, its operational principles are still largely shaped by the doctrine of green-water defence based on a light force structure.

China's anti-piracy deployments

China's first steps in projecting naval power into the Indian Ocean region have been in response to the piracy crisis in the Gulf of Aden. In December 2008, following the hijacking of two Chinese-registered ships, China deployed three ships to waters off Somalia to conduct anti-piracy operations—only the third deployment of Chinese naval ships into the Indian Ocean in more than six centuries. The PLAN has since made successive deployments to waters of Somalia, operating in parallel (although barely in coordination) with the US-sponsored CTF 151. Like India, China has repeatedly declined proposals to cooperate in protecting the International Recommended Transit Corridor (IRTC) or operate within a multinational command structure. Instead, it conducts its escort operations approximately five nautical miles north and south of the IRTC. But the PLAN has taken some small steps to enhance coordination with other navies in the Indian Ocean, including: participating in the Contact Group on Piracy off the Coast of Somalia and the SHADE group; joining the *Mercury* web-based communication system, which is used by all naval forces in the area apart from Iran; and concluding a coordination agreement with Japan and India in January 2012. The PLAN's deployment seems to have been conducted in a manner intended to avoid arousing the 'China threat' theory. Before the PLAN was deployed in the Indian Ocean, China waited to gauge the international reaction to the counter-piracy mission and they ensured that the deployment had the authorisation of both the Somali government and the UN.[12]

The PLAN flotillas in the northwest Indian Ocean have received logistical support primarily out of Salalah and Aden. The United States officially welcomes China's anti-piracy deployment, commenting that it 'underscores an area where mutual interest can foster cooperation'.[13] Chinese commentators have made much of China's anti-piracy deployments in the Gulf of Aden as a demonstration or even 'breakthrough point' for China's image as a 'great responsible power'. The view that narrow self-interest no longer exclusively animates Chinese foreign policy reportedly enjoys substantial weight in Chinese policy and academic circles.[14] In contrast, many Indian analysts see China's anti-piracy deployment in the Gulf of Aden as part of a slippery slope towards a permanent Chinese naval presence in the Indian Ocean.

The expansion of China's influence in the Indian Ocean

Over the last decade or so there has been a major expansion of China's economic role in the Indian Ocean region, providing it with a level of influence that in many cases far exceeds that of India. But the full strategic impact of this is not yet clear.

Pakistan has long anchored China's strategic presence in the Indian Ocean region; China pursued the relationship following the 1962 war, establishing itself as a major supplier of arms to Pakistan and providing it with considerable diplomatic support against India. The so-called 'all-weather friendship' with Pakistan, alongside its relationship with North Korea, is the closest China has come to a long-term alliance. Since the 1960s, the China factor has played a major role in limiting India's strategic options with Pakistan and keeping India strategically preoccupied in South Asia. The perceived military threat from China and its *de facto* alliance with Pakistan was a primary motivation for India's security relationship with the Soviet Union and a key limitation on India's room for manoeuvre during the 1971 Bangladesh War. During the 1980s and 1990s the relationship gained a new dimension when China assisted in the proliferation of nuclear weapons and missiles to Pakistan. The economic relationship has also grown, and China is now Pakistan's second largest trading partner.

In recent years, China has also developed important economic and political relationships elsewhere in South Asia, for instance with Nepal, Bangladesh, Sri Lanka and the Maldives. Although South Asia is within India's core sphere of influence, India's dominance is not well reflected in the economic dimension and South Asia remains one of the least economically integrated regions in the world. China is making economic inroads in Nepal and is now Bangladesh's largest trading partner. It is also developing strong economic and political links with Sri Lanka. Although India remains Sri Lanka's biggest trading partner, China has become its major source of investment, particularly in the post-war years. Several projects have attracted controversy, including the Hambantota port project, discussed below.

The strength of China's economic relationships in the Indian Ocean region, compared with India's, is particularly evident in Southeast Asia. In 2010, bilateral trade between the ASEAN states and China (excluding Hong Kong) was worth US$232 billion, compared with US$55 billion for India. This disparity is paralleled in investment, which may be a better long-term gauge of economic influence and interdependence than trade: net foreign direct investment (FDI) from China to ASEAN aggregated US$8.9 billion between 2008 and 2010, compared with FDI from India to ASEAN of US$3.9 billion in the same period.[15] China has applied a concerted strategy of developing trading arrangements with ASEAN, including signing trade agreements on goods and services that gave ASEAN early access to the Chinese market in certain areas and concessional tariffs on agricultural items. This has helped promote China's image as a benevolent and responsible power. An ASEAN–China free trade area commenced in 2010 that provides for zero-tariffs on around 90 per cent of man-ufactured products. China hopes that the Yuan, which is currently largely only used in border trade, will grow to play a significant role as a regional currency, partially replacing the current role of the US dollar. In contrast, India has been relatively slow and non-strategic in developing formal economic linkages with ASEAN, signing a trade agreement with ASEAN—involving extensive exceptions—only in August 2009.

China's economic influence is growing even among India's closest security partners in the Indian Ocean. China is now the largest sources of tourism for Maldives, providing some 22 per cent of arrivals, and in September 2012 agreed to provide $500 million in soft loans for infrastructure and housing projects. Although the Maldives government went out of its way to downplay its stra-tegic significance, the size of the deal will inevitably increase China's political influence in that tiny country. China is also becoming a major investor in Mauritius, part of a strategy of using Mauritius as a platform to service South-ern Africa. In 2010 Mauritius announced a Chinese-financed $730 million expansion of Mauritius' airport and a special economic zone (although there has been little progress in construction). According to Mauritian deputy prime minister, Ramakrishna Sithanen, China's approach to Mauritius was 'extremely aggressive' and its approach of combining business and governmental interests contrasted with India's fragmented approach.[16]

China's economic influence in the region is bringing with it considerable poli-tical clout. But to date China has had only a very limited security presence in the region. As noted, China faces severe geographical constraints on its ability to project power into the Indian Ocean, including the long distance from Chinese ports and the lack of logistical support in the Indian Ocean. Many analysts have claimed that China is trying to mitigate these disadvantages through pursuing a 'String of Pearls' strategy involving the development of a string of dependent ports or potential naval bases in the Indian Ocean.[17] Over the last decade or so, Chinese companies have been involved in the funding and construc-tion of numerous commercial port facilities in the region, for instance in Pakistan (Gwadar), Sri Lanka (Hambantota), Bangladesh (Sonadia) and several ports in Myanmar. All these are located close to the key sea lanes used by China and could in theory be used by the PLAN if it developed a presence in the Indian Ocean. However, China has been careful to avoid any overt military presence or even, in most cases, any commercial role in the operation of these ports and has flatly denied that it has any intention to establish any military bases in the Indian Ocean.[18] Nevertheless, numerous Indian strategic commentators claim that these port developments are part of a Chinese strategy of 'encirclement' or 'containment' of India. They claim that China has negotiated secret access rights to allow it to use these ports as logistics hubs or even naval bases in the event of conflict.[19] This is used by a number of 'hawks' to justify a policy of 'counter-encirclement' of China through developing security relationships and military facilities around China's periphery. It is not clear to what extent the 'String of Pearls' theory is considered seriously by the upper echelons of Indian foreign policy makers, although it has certainly become a significant element in Indian public debate about China.

The port of Gwadar in western Pakistan (around 600 km from the Strait of Hormuz) is regarded as particularly significant by many analysts. There is little doubt that through the development of Gwadar, Pakistan is attempting to make China a factor in the naval balance in the Indian Ocean. Some Indian analysts argue that the development of a Chinese military presence at Gwadar would create a 'Hormuz Dilemma' for India analogous to the 'Malacca Dilemma' faced by China. Gwadar could potentially also provide a transit terminal for an oil pipeline through Pakistan to the western provinces of China. Although China has been the proponent of developing Gwadar as part of a transportation route, it is very hesitant about having any military connections with the port. But Pakistan has been less hesitant—in the wake of the deterioration of US–Pakistan relations after the killing of Osama bin Laden in May 2011, the Pakistan defence minister Ahmed Mukhtar, announced that China would build a naval base there in an attempt to play a 'China card' against the United States. Although this was denied by Beijing, a Chinese state-owned company took over from the original Singaporean commercial operator of the port in September 2012, but there are as yet no indications of any Chinese military presence.[20] According to one analyst, 'Beijing is treading carefully, and with good reason. A combination of compelling economic, security, and political factors ensure that a fully functioning commercial port—let alone an operational military base—remains a distant prospect'.[21] China has several reasons to be cautious. The development of a Chinese military presence in Gwadar would likely provoke a significant reaction from both the United States and India, which may damage its interests elsewhere. There are also real security concerns. Chinese engineers in Gwadar have been attacked several times by insurgents, and a Chinese military presence may draw China into combating the Baluchi separatist insurgency.[22]

Another controversial symbol of China's supposed military ambitions in the Indian Ocean is the new port at Hambantota on the southern tip of Sri Lanka. China funded the development of a new port and an associated international airport costing around US$1 billion, which are now operated by Sri Lankan entities. The Sri Lankan government hopes that Hambantota will become a major economic driver for southern Sri Lanka, but to date it has not been a commercial success. The location of Hambantota very close to the sea lanes that round the southern tips of India and Sri Lanka is taken as proof by many analysts that it is a 'pearl' in China's string, available for use by the PLAN. But these claims are not supported by the evidence. The Sri Lankan government first offered the project to India, which did not take up the opportunity.[23] Some Indian officials see this as a major mistake, demonstrating a lack of a vision and assertiveness in Indian foreign policy.[24] But New Delhi may have had good reason to turn down the proposal. According to one official, India did not feel the need to bid for the project since Trincomalee port had recently been upgraded by the Indian Oil Corporation and it did not see the Hambantota project as reducing India's influence in Sri Lanka.[25] There were also domestic considerations—among other things, the southern Indian states of Kerala and Tamil Nadu also have ambitions to develop the ports at Vizhinjam, Cochin and Tuticorin, which will compete directly with Sri Lanka for the region's lucrative transhipment trade. Hambantota probably has much less strategic significance than it appears. Beyond Chinese financing of its construction there is little else to support the contention that Hambantota will one day serve as a base for Chinese warships.[26]

Through the 1990s, Chinese interests were also involved in the development or upgrading of several ports in Myanmar on the Bay of Bengal, including Sittwe, Bassein, Hainggyi, Seikkyi, Monkey Point, Moulmein, Mergui and Kawthaung. China also supplied signals intelligence equipment to the Tatmadaw, including providing assistance in constructing a signals intelligence facility at Great Coco island. The purported 'Chinese' facility at Great Coco, which is located some 20 km from India's North Andaman Island, has been the subject of much controversy, variously described by analysts as being used to spy on India's naval base at Port Blair, monitor commercial traffic through the Malacca Strait and/or monitor Indian missile testing being carried out in the Bay of Bengal. In 2005 the Myanmar government, which had always emphatically denied the existence of electronic monitoring facilities or any other Chinese military presence in the Coco islands, invited the Indian Navy to carry out its own inspection of the islands, after which the Indian Navy conceded that there was no Chinese intelligence facility on Great Coco Island and neither were there any Chinese naval bases anywhere in Myanmar.[27] As Andrew Selth, an Australian specialist in Myanmar strategic affairs, commented, this 'was a remarkable about-face on two issues that had preoccupied Indian defence planners for more than a decade'.[28] Whether or not there was ever a Chinese presence at Great Coco, it is clear that no such facility exists today.

While some might see India as holding a strong security role in the southwest Indian Ocean, there are still fears in New Delhi that China might undermine or pre-empt Indian's relationships. According to the former Indian chief of naval staff, Admiral Prakash, India 'cannot afford to have any hostile or inimical power threatening the island states in this region'.[29] Political and economic relations between China and Mauritius and Seychelles respectively are closely watched by New Delhi and it has been claimed that a so-called Chinese 'thrust' towards these states presages Sino–naval rivalry in the western Indian Ocean.[30] While China may develop better economic and political interests in the area, it seems unlikely that it would be able to dislodge India as the dominant security provider to Mauritius and there are no indications at present that it would be able to seriously challenge India's maritime security role elsewhere in the southwest Indian Ocean.

Despite widespread claims about the 'String of Pearls' strategy, many analysts, particularly outside of India, are sceptical that China intends to develop any naval bases in the Indian Ocean.[31] According to Daniel Kostecka, a China analyst with the US Navy:

> Converting these facilities [Gwadar and Hambantota] into naval bases would require billions of dollars' worth of military equipment and infrastructure in order to ensure their viability in wartime. Even then, the exposed position of these facilities makes their wartime utility dubious against an enemy equipped with long-range precision strike capability.[32]

Holmes and Yoshihara, senior analysts with the US Naval War College, conclude that Gwadar is not readily defensible and would not prevent the interdiction of Chinese energy supplies inside the Persian Gulf.[33] As one Chinese analyst commented, given the distances separating any Chinese interests in the Indian Ocean, these ports look more like 'sitting ducks' than a string of pearls.[34]

Kostecka argues that the PLAN is instead pursuing a policy similar to the US military of 'places not bases', so that PLAN vessels can receive logistical support at ports where China has friendly and stable relationships. He sees this as a natural outgrowth of PLAN's expanding presence in the region, particularly its counter-piracy patrols off the Horn of Africa. According to Kostecka, PLAN's logistical support network in the northwestern Indian Ocean is likely to include Salalah, Aden, Djibouti (which already provides support for the US, French and Japanese navies, among others, and is therefore politically safe for China), and Karachi (which has the benefit of substantial repair facilities and possible parts-commonality with the Pakistan Navy's Chinese-built frigates). In the northeastern Indian Ocean, Kostecka believes that PLAN is likely to use Colombo and Singapore (although it would not be guaranteed access in the way that the US Navy is guaranteed access to Changi Naval Base). He argues that although China will continue to maintain positive relationships with Sri Lanka, Bangladesh and the Maldives, this does not mean China will seek to establish a military presence in those countries or that such a presence would even be permitted as it would undermine those countries' security and do very little to enhance China's.[35]

The popularity of the 'String of Pearls' narrative among the Indian security community may say more about Indian insecurities than actual Chinese strategic intentions. There is a danger that imagined threats from China in the Indian Ocean might cause India to take actions that are to its long-term detriment. As is demonstrated by the experience of many states (including Australia and countries in Southeast Asia), China's growing economic influence does not necessarily bring security cooperation with it. There seems little prospect that

China will establish a military base in the Indian Ocean in the current strategic environment. Borrowing from the terminology of nuclear deterrence, China's naval capabilities in the Indian Ocean might at the most be described as 'recessed'—i.e. an inchoate capability that can be activated if the circumstances require.

But the growth of Chinese economic influence in the region could well have a significant effect on India's ability to expand its military footprint in the Indian Ocean. Many of India's putative partners in the Indian Ocean region will seek to maintain good relations with China and avoid being seen as taking sides in any rivalry. The recent $500 million Chinese loan to the Maldives will no doubt be a relevant factor in its relationship with India. India's proposal to establish a signals intelligence facility in northern Madagascar was rumoured to have been stymied by Chinese lobbying. India's apparent attempt to corral South Africa into the IBSA grouping was also seemingly stymied by the strength of China's economic relationship with South Africa. Even close security partners, such as Maldives and Mauritius, may be very cautious about a public presence of Indian forces in their countries.

Attempts to diversify China's energy transport routes

China's growing economic and political influence in the region also provides an opportunity to mitigate its Malacca Dilemma through developing alternative energy transport connections through Pakistan, Myanmar and Thailand. China has also tried to reduce its reliance on oil transported across the Indian Ocean through constructing new oil and gas pipelines to Russia and Central Asia. These alternative connections have considerable strategic significance.

China plans to improve transport connectivity between its western Xinjian province and the Arabian Sea through Pakistan, including improved road/rail links to Karachi and a proposed oil pipeline and road/rail links from the Chinese border to Gwadar. The Chinese state-owned company that operates Gwadar port has announced investments of some $750 million on new infrastructure in Gwadar and Baluchistan province. But transport links to China would traverse regions of Pakistan where there are significant security issues. China has already had to deploy security forces in Pakistan-administered Kashmir near the Chinese border to protect Chinese construction workers from attacks by Islamic and tribal groups.[36] It seems that the adverse security environment in Pakistan's Baluchistan province and northeast territories makes it unlikely that a pipeline to Gwadar could be constructed in the foreseeable future.

China has made greater progress in developing transport connections to the Indian Ocean through Myanmar. This is part of what Beijing has called the national bridgehead strategy of turning Yunnan province into a bridgehead for strategic engagement with the Indian Ocean, as part of China's 'Two Ocean Strategy'. Although the strategy is currently focused on trade and transportation, Chinese officials acknowledge that it has a political and security component.[37] The Yunnan–Yangon Irrawaddy road/rail/river corridor has been operational for around a decade and has allowed significant improvements in freight transportation times to southern China. China is also constructing oil and gas pipelines between the Myanmar port of Sittwe and Yunnan province that will transport gas from Myanmar's offshore gas fields as well as oil shipped from the Middle East. There have also been proposals to build a canal (or land bridge) across Thailand's Kra Isthmus between the Andaman Sea and the Gulf of Thailand,which would allow shipping to avoid the Strait of Malacca and significantly shorten shipping transit times. But there are considerable doubts about the economic feasibility of this project.

All these projects are viewed with considerable suspicion by many in New Delhi. There is a visceral dislike of any Chinese presence anywhere in southern Asia, but some may also not wish to see any reduction of China's dependence on the Malacca Strait. But the creation of a security dilemma in the Indian Ocean is not necessarily to India's advantage. The father of Indian maritime strategy, K. M. Panikkar, recognised long ago the potential dangers of a Sino–Indian security dilemma in the Indian Ocean, and he suggested among other things that Rangoon should be turned by international treaty into a 'free port', which would provide China with a trading outlet on the Indian Ocean and alleviate its fears of blockade of its Pacific ports.[38] In any event, others question the extent to which these alternative connections to the Indian Ocean would mitigate China's Malacca Dilemma. One Chinese study concluded that the Kra Isthmus canal and the Sino–Myanmar and Sino–Pakistani oil pipelines would be rendered meaningless if Chinese tankers were intercepted in the Persian Gulf, the Arabian Sea or the Suez Canal.[39] Other analysts argue that it is a 'pipe dream' to believe that overland oil pipelines would mitigate China's Malacca Dilemma, due to their vulnerability to attack.[40]

Sino–Indian naval rivalry in the IOR

Competition with China has become a significant factor in India's strategic thinking about southern Asia and the Indian Ocean region. In many ways, fears in New Delhi of China's growing regional influence have only reinforced India's determination to become the dominant power in the Indian Ocean. Many in New Delhi firmly believe that the 'String of Pearls' is a coherent military strategy aimed at India. Although official declarations by the Indian government and the Indian Navy take great pains to emphasise that China currently has no military bases in the region, China's relationships in the region are generally not perceived in the Indian security community as being a legitimate reflection of Chinese interests in the Indian Ocean.[41] But few Indian analysts acknowledge China's strategic vulnerabilities in the Indian Ocean as being a legitimate cause for concern by Beijing. Rather, many perceive China's regional relationships as being directed against India: either as a plan of maritime 'encirclement' or to keep India strategically off balance in the region, just as China's relationship with Pakistan has long kept India off balance in South Asia. These reactions are consistent with an Indian sense of strategic vulnerability in the Indian Ocean that has existed since at least 1971.

While the Indian Navy's immediate strategic objectives in the Indian Ocean involve countering Pakistan and enforcing control over India's exclusive economic zone, the potential for China to project naval power into the Indian Ocean has become its principal long-term source of concern. Many in New Delhi see a significant risk that India and China will, as Arun Prakash, Indian chief of naval taff (2004–6), put it, 'compete and even clash in the same strategic space'.[42] Prakash's successor, Admiral Suresh Mehta, claimed on Indian television:

> [China] is shaping the maritime battlefield in the region. It is making friends in the right places. It you don't have the capability to operate in these waters, for a length of time, then you need friends who will support your cause, when the time comes, so definitely China is doing that, as there are Pakistan, Bangladesh, Myanmar, Sri Lanka and down below Africa. So it is a known fact that we are ringed by states which may have a favourable disposition towards China.[43]

Sino–Indian naval rivalry has the potential to spread across the Indian and Pacific oceans.

As has been discussed in previous chapters, India has responded to China's perceived presence in the Indian Ocean by trying to pre-empt China's relationships and by developing its own presence near the maritime chokepoints, particularly the Malacca Strait. India has also tried to exert pressure on China to keep off its 'patch' by increasing its presence and involvement in the South China Sea. Over the last several years India has become increasingly active in giving quiet support to ASEAN states in their territorial dispute with China. There has also been considerable speculation that India intends to establish a naval base at Cam Ranh Bay in Vietnam as a tit for tat for Chinese activities in the Indian Ocean. In June 2011, India reached an agreement with Vietnam under which it would be given regular access to (and, perhaps, a limited presence at) the port of Nha Trang, which, according to an Indian official, would allow the Indian Navy to create a 'sustainable presence' in the South China Sea.[44] This was possibly intended to signify something more than ship visits and something less than a military base.

In future years, there is a good chance that cross-ocean rivalry will extend into the nuclear dimension. As India's fleet of nuclear weapon-carrying ballistic missile submarines (SSBNs) grows, there is a high likelihood that they will be deployed to the western Pacific. Submarine deployments would be regarded as necessary for the Indian nuclear deterrent due to the inability of India's land-based ballistic missiles to reach China's eastern cities. China may also make counter-deployments to the Indian Ocean from its SSBN submarine base on Hainan Island in the South China Sea.[45] Indian and Chinese SSBNs would need to transit the deep-water Weitar Strait near East Timor—the other straits through the Indonesian archipelago being too shallow for operational deployments and the long voyage around the south of Australia being impractical. Such deployments would place both India and China in breach of their stated commitments to ASEAN's Southeast Asia Nuclear Weapons Free Zone Treaty, which prohibits the passage of nuclear weapons through Southeast Asian waters.[46]

Many argue that a security dilemma now exists between India and China in the Indian Ocean as 'defensive' moves taken by each are seen as reducing the other's security. If that is true, then that negative dynamic will be difficult to mitigate.[47] But despite talk of 'encirclement' among Indian commentators, few have credibly argued that a Chinese maritime presence in the Indian Ocean presents any realistic military threat to India. On the contrary, the Indian Ocean is the one area in which India holds a clear military advantage over China. As Admiral Mehta commented, 'The weak area for China today is the Indian Navy. We sit in the Indian Ocean and that is a concern for China and they are not happy as it is not so easy for them to come inside'.[48] Because India does not have the economic capacity to match PLAN's capabilities it will need to place greater reliance on geography. In strategic jargon, the Indian Ocean represents 'exterior lines' for China and 'interior lines' for India. That is, India has a natural advantage in the Indian Ocean, including short lines of communication to its own bases and resources, and China has corresponding disadvantages.[49] The maritime chokepoints between the Indian and Pacific Oceans offer another major advantage for India. As the Indian Navy's 2004 Maritime Doctrine argues, 'Control of the chokepoints could be useful as a bargaining chip in the international power game, where the currency of military power remains a stark reality'.[50] John Garver, an expert on Sino–Indian relations, comments:

> In the event of a PRC-ROI conflict, India might be tempted to escalate from the land dimension, where it might suffer reverses, to the maritime dimension, where it enjoys substantial advantages, and employ those advantages to restrict China's vital Indian Ocean trade.[51]

From this perspective, any mitigation of China's relative vulnerability in the Indian Ocean could have a significant effect on the balance of power between India and China. But the Indian reaction to any Chinese presence in the Indian Ocean is not just about maintaining a bargaining chip—it is much more visceral than that. There is also a sense that China is seeking to rob India of its legitimate sphere of influence in the Indian Ocean, the key building block for India's destined status as a great power. China's refusal to acknowledge an Indian sphere of influence in the Indian Ocean is seen as part of an incomprehensible refusal by Beijing to acknowledge India's destiny.

The future India–China relationship in the Indian Ocean

A basic strategic choice that India and others will face in the Indian Ocean in coming years is whether to try to limit any Chinese naval or maritime presence or facilitate the role of China as a responsible stakeholder in Indian Ocean security. India could work with the United States and its allies such as Australia to enhance their collective military capabilities in the Indian Ocean to sustain or even increase China's strategic vulnerability. Some may see this as potentially restraining China from taking an overly assertive stance in, say, the South China Sea or the Taiwan Strait. However, it could also easily lead to instability and strategic rivalry. Alternatively, India could work with the United States and China to find ways to accommodate the legitimate interests of all powers and facilitate the development of China's role as a legitimate and responsible stakeholder in Indian Ocean security. This may reduce the risk of strategic rivalry in the Indian Ocean.

There have been some tentative suggestions from both Indian and Chinese sources about the desirability of reaching an understanding of their respective roles in the Indian Ocean. In 2009, the Indian national security advisor, Shiv Shankar Menon, proposed a cooperative security arrangement among major Asian powers (including the United States) that would encompass the Indian Ocean and the western Pacific.[52] As Menon later commented:

> The larger issue is whether India and China can work together to help manage the complicated regional security environment in Asia. India's preference is for the open security architecture and the sort of multi-polarity that China too has advocated previously for global issues, and from which we have both benefited in the recent past. To do so, India, China and other rising Asian powers must be willing and capable of contributing to global public goods in terms of security, growth and stability that the region and world require. How will we help to preserve security in the global commons?[53]

There have also been reports of China signalling its openness to discussions about a cooperation mechanism on sea lanes in the Indian Ocean.[54] Some analysts argue that China recognises the need for cooperation with littoral states, especially India, for SLOC security. Australian analyst, You Ji, claims that while China would not be prepared to acknowledge the Indian Ocean as an 'Indian Lake', it would be prepared to acknowledge India's special interests in the Indian Ocean.[55] A January 2012 agreement between India, China and Japan to coordinate their naval anti-piracy efforts in the Gulf of Aden was an important, if largely symbolic, indication of a willingness to countenance limited maritime security cooperation.

Despite much talk from the commentariat, in reality both India and China have been cautious about developing any significant naval presence in each other's maritime sphere, although each would like the option to create such a presence if the need arose. Each has largely resisted attempts by partners such as Pakistan and Vietnam to draw them into disputes with their giant neighbours. While China is trying to develop alternative transport links between southern and western China and the Indian Ocean, it has been careful not to establish any significant military presence in the Indian Ocean beyond the anti-piracy deployment. Similarly, despite some talk, India has not established such a presence in the western Pacific. In July 2012, the retiring Indian naval chief of staff, Admiral Verma, commented that any active deployment of the Indian Navy to the Pacific and South China Sea 'is not on the cards'.[56] An understanding between China and India not to develop a permanent presence on each other's 'patch' may be helpful in reducing tensions. However, given the broader context of Sino–Indian strategic rivalry, it seems unlikely that China would be prepared to rely on India for its maritime security needs in the Indian Ocean region in the absence of a broader strategic understanding between the two.

Notes

1 Department of Defense, *Annual Report to Congress (2012)*, p. 42.
2 Mohan Malik (2011) *China and India: Great Power Rivals*, Boulder, CO: FirstForumPress, p. 9.
3 Rory Medcalf (2013) 'India Poll 2013: facing the future—Indian views of the world ahead', Lowy Institute for International Policy, p. 10.
4 'China's plan to build up its navy' (1993) *Hindustan Times*, 13 January, p. 14.
5 Toshi Yoshihara (2012) 'Chinese views of India in the Indian Ocean: a geopolitical perspective', *Strategic Analysis*, Vol. 36, No. 3, pp. 489–500.
6 For a detailed discussion of China's naval capabilities and doctrine, see US Congressional Research Service (2012) *China Naval Modernization: Implications for US Navy Capabilities—Background and Issues for Congress*, 31 July.
7 Department of Defense, *Annual Report to Congress*, p. 31.
8 Department of Defense, *Annual Report to Congress*, p. 27.
9 Christopher D. Yung *et al.* (2010) *China's Out of Area Naval Operations: Case Studies, Trajectories, Obstacles, and Potential Solutions*, Washington, DC: National Defense University Press, December.
10 International Institute of Strategic Studies (2011) *Strategic Survey 2011: the Annual Review of World Affairs*, London: Routledge, p. 134.
11 You Ji (2012) 'The Chinese navy, its regional power and global reach', *Strategic Analysis*, Vol. 36, No. 3, pp. 477–88.
12 Jack Moore (2012) 'China's Growing Role In Counter-Piracy Operations', *Therisky shift.com*, 5 September. Online: http://theriskyshift.com/2012/09/china-growing-role-counter-piracy-operations/ (accessed 10 October 2013).
13 United States, Department of Defense, *Annual Report to Congress: Military and Security Developments Involving the People's Republic of China 2011*.
14 Toshi Yoshihara, and James R. Holmes (2010) *Red Star over the Pacific: China's Rise and the Challenge to US Maritime Strategy*, Annapolis, MD: Naval Institute Press, pp. 170–1.
15 ASEAN Secretariat. Online: www.aseansec.org/ (accessed 10 October 2013).
16 James Lamont (2010) 'China makes foray into Mauritius', *Financial Times*, 25 January.
17 The term was first used in a 2005 report titled 'Energy futures in Asia', prepared for the US Secretary of Defence by the private consultants, Booz-Allen-Hamilton and quickly adopted by Indian analysts.
18 'China has no plan for Indian Ocean military bases' (2012) *The Hindu*, 4 September.
19 See, for example, Ramtanu Maitra (2005) 'India bids to rule the waves', *Asia Times*, 19 October; and Sudha Ramachandran (2007) 'China moves into India's back yard', *Asia Times*, 13 March.

20 Syed Fazl-e-Haider (2012) 'China set to run Gwadar port as Singapore quits', *Asia Times*, 5 September. There are unsubstantiated claims that China has established a signals intelligence facility at Gwadar. 'Pak offers China monitoring facilities on Makrana Coast' (2002) *The Times of India*, 29 June.

21 Urmila Venugopalan (2011) 'Pakistan's black pearl', *Foreign Policy*, 3 June.

22 Which, according to B. Raman, a former Indian intelligence chief, was one of the reasons why Pakistan's President Musharraf proposed the project to China. B. Raman (2011) 'Balochistan: greater realism in China and Iran', *India Defence Review*, 8 June.

23 R.S. Vasan (2009) 'It's advantage India in the Indian Ocean', *New Indian Express*, 15 September. Sri Lankan President Rajapaksa also reportedly approached the United States several times to fund the project. Nilanthi Samaranayake (2011) 'Are Sri Lanka's relations with China deepening? An analysis of economic, military and diplomatic data', *Asian Security*, Vol. 7, No. 2, pp. 119–46, at p. 27.

24 B. Raman (2007) 'China's Strategic Triangle', *Outlook India*, 6 March.

25 Sudha Ramachandran (2007) 'China moves into India's back yard', *Asia Times*, 13 March.

26 Daniel J. Kostecka (2010) 'Hambantota, Chittagong and the Maldives—unlikely pearls for the Chinese navy', *China Brief*, Vol. 10, No. 23, 19 November, p. 8.

27 'Interview with Admiral Arun Prakash, chief of naval staff, Indian Navy' (2005) *Asian Defence Journal*, October, p. 22.

28 Andrew Selth (2008) 'Burma's Coco Islands: rumours and realities in the Indian Ocean', Southeast Asia Research Centre Working Paper Series, No. 101, November, p. 11.

29 Arun Prakash (2007) *From the Crow's Nest: a compendium of speeches and writings on maritime and other issues*, New Delhi: Lancer, p. 7.

30 C. Raja Mohan (2009) 'Sino–Indian rivalry in the western Indian Ocean', *ISAS Insights*, No. 52, 24 February.

31 See for example, Andrew Selth (2007) 'Chinese military bases in Burma'; and You Ji, 'Dealing with the Malacca Dilemma: China's effort to protect its energy supply', *Strategic Analysis*, Vol. 31, No. 3, May, pp. 467–89.

32 Daniel J. Kostecka (2010) 'The Chinese navy's emerging support network in the Indian Ocean', *China Brief*, Vol. 10, No. 15, 22 July, pp. 3–5.

33 James R. Holmes and Toshi Yoshihara (2008) 'China's naval ambitions in the Indian Ocean', *Journal of Strategic Studies*, Vol. 31, No. 3, June, pp. 379–80.

34 Ye Hailin (2009) 'Securing SLOCs by cooperation—Chinese perspectives of maritime security in the Indian Ocean', paper presented at Karichi, Pakistan.

35 Kostecka, 'Hambantota, Chittagong, and the Maldives'.

36 Chinese troops likely numbered in the hundreds and not the thousands as reported in the *New York Times*. Selig Harrison (2010) 'China's discreet hold on Pakistan's northern borderlands', *New York Times*, 26 August.

37 Yun Sun (2012) 'China's strategic misjudgement in Myanmar', *Journal of Current Southeast Asian Affairs*, Vol. 31, No. 1, p. 83.

38 K.M. Panikkar (1943) *The Future of Southeast Asia: An Indian View*, New York: The Macmillan Company, p. 103.

39 James R. Holmes and Toshi Yoshihara (2008) 'China's Naval Ambitions in the Indian Ocean', *Journal of Strategic Studies*, Vol. 31, No. 3, June, pp. 367–94.

40 Andrew S. Erickson and Gabriel B. Collins (2010) 'China's Oil Security Pipe Dream', *Naval War College Review*, Vol. 63, No. 2, Spring, pp. 91–2.

41 See for example, 'No Chinese military bases in the Indian Ocean, says Menon' (2009) *The Indian Express*, 11 September.

42 Arun Prakash (2007) 'India's maritime strategy', *Indian Defence Review*, Vol. 137, No. 568, April–June, pp. 157–76.

43 'India not competing with China: Navy Chief' (2007) NDTV India, 26 December.

44 Sridhar Kumaraswami (2011) 'India eyes South China Sea pearl', *Asian Age*, 26 June.

45 Although such deployments may be primarily aimed at the United States, China might use these assets to open a seaward front against India in time of crisis. C. Raja Mohan (2012) *Samudra Manthan: Sino–Indian Rivalry in the Indo–Pacific*, Washington, DC: Carnegie Endowment for International Peace, p. 81.

46 Both India and China have announced that it would comply with the terms of the treaty. India is unable to formally accede to the treaty because it is a non-NPT state.

47 Mohan, *Samudra Manthan*, p. 190.

48 'China afraid of India's naval presence in the Ocean' (2009) *Zeenews.com*, 13 August.

49 James R. Holmes (2012) 'Inside, outside: India's 'exterior lines' in the South China Sea', *Strategic Analysis*, Vol. 36, No. 3, pp. 358–63.

50 Indian Navy, *Indian Maritime Doctrine*, p. 64.

51 John Garver (2001) *Protracted Contest: Sino–Indian Rivalry in the Twentieth Century*, Washington, DC: University of Washington Press, p. 277.

52 Shiv Shankar Menon (2009) 'Maritime imperatives of Indian foreign policy', speech to the National Maritime Foundation, New Delhi, 11 September.

53 Shiv Shankar Menon (2010) 'India and China: public diplomacy, building understanding', speech at the Indian Council of World Affairs, New Delhi, April.

54 Reshma Patil (2011) 'China signals desire for talks on Indian Ocean', *Hindustan Times*, 11 August.

55 You Ji (2008) 'The Indian Ocean and China's Naval Build-up', in Ravi Vohra and P.K. Ghosh, *China and the Indian Ocean*, Delhi: National Maritime Foundation, pp. 46–68.

56 'India against direct intervention in South China Sea disputes despite having stakes in the region' (2012) *India Today*, 8 August.

11 India as an Indian Ocean power

Will the Indian Ocean become India's Ocean? In many ways, India is the natural centre of strategic gravity in the Indian Ocean. But there are considerable uncertainties as to its future role. Might it, for example, seek to impose a muscular hegemony, exercise benign leadership or contribute to security using a cooperative model, or some combination of these? Will India seek to sponsor a new regional security order in the Indian Ocean that recognises its special role?

India as the natural centre of gravity in the Indian Ocean

After a gap of some 60 years, India is returning as the centre of gravity of the Indian Ocean. There are many good reasons for seeing India as having a 'naturally' dominant role in the region. The size and geographic centrality of the Indian peninsular makes it physically dominate the entire northern Indian Ocean. Its massive population provides the basis of a large military establishment, a huge market, and a labour force that can affect the whole region's demographics. In coming years it will likely become one of the world's largest economies and a natural trading and investment hub for the region. Importantly, India's elite more or less see an imperative to make the Indian Ocean 'India's Ocean' as part of India's destiny to become a great power.

During the colonial era, Britain exploited India's attributes to create a 'subordinate' empire over much of the Indian Ocean. India was a hub for administration of this British Indian Ocean empire and provided the soldiers, workers and merchants necessary for Britain's rule. With the growth of its national power, India now has the opportunity to again extend its influence over the Indian Ocean, if in a quite different way. Since independence, India has demonstrated its ability to take a leadership role in the international system and for some decades it has effectively exercised hegemony over much of South Asia. India's strategy towards the broader Indian Ocean is just taking shape.

The states in and around the Indian Ocean are highly diverse in almost every measure: social and economic development, geography and religion, and they range from among the world's smallest countries to the largest and from the richest and most stable nations to fragile or failed states. In the modern era, interaction among states across the Indian Ocean has been limited—the ocean has represented a highway used by others but not usually a unifying factor for its residents. But the rise of India as a central power in the Indian Ocean may change the entire political nature of the area and make it look more like a 'region'. Already India is the most important relationship for some of the smaller countries and represents an increasingly important relationship for the middle powers. As India rises, Indian Ocean states will also increasingly interact with each other through India.

Constraints on India's power in the Indian Ocean

In coming decades India will likely have the material capabilities to be the dominant power in the Indian Ocean, at least *vis a vis* other littoral states, and it certainly has aspirations to become so. But there are real doubts as to whether it is likely to achieve these ambitions. India's growing power in the Indian Ocean will be subject to some major constraints, both internal and external, and it is not yet clear to what extent India will be able to overcome them.

The most obvious constraint on the expansion of India's strategic role in the Indian Ocean is the military predominance of the United States. Although US military resources are currently under strain, the United States will likely have the *capability* to be the predominant Indian Ocean power for decades to come. But the more apt question is how long the United States will *choose* to commit the necessary resources to dominate the Indian Ocean. Washington appears willing to cede—and indeed encourage—a major security role for India in the Indian Ocean. But there will be limits to US support for India, particularly if it is perceived as acting inconsistently with US interests. The biggest potential area of contention (apart from the US relationship with Pakistan) is Iran, which India regards as a potential strategic partner but which the United States is seeking to contain and isolate. Although Washington has placed only very limited demands on India, there is an expectation that India will act in a reasonably cooperative manner in addressing security issues in the Indian Ocean.

A further constraint on India's role is its relatively weak relationships with the middle powers. New Delhi has been successful in developing security relationships with smaller countries such as Singapore, the Maldives, Mauritius, Mozambique and Oman, but has been slow to develop cooperative relations with larger or more powerful states such as Indonesia, Saudi Arabia, South Africa and Australia. This may be a function of India's lack of strategic direction or a bias against security cooperation except where it can dominate the relationship. Middle powers such as Australia, Indonesia and South Africa see considerable benefits in developing strategic partnerships with India, but while at least some of them may be willing to cede a leading security role to India under certain conditions, they will expect India to properly recognise their interests.

It seems unlikely that Pakistan will be prepared to accept claims by India to an extended area of influence in the Indian Ocean. While Pakistan no longer represents a conventional military challenge to India in the Indian Ocean, its security relationships in the northwest present a major obstacle to an enhanced strategic role for India, particularly in the Persian Gulf. Despite its historic role as a regional hegemon during the colonial era, Hindu India is now largely excluded from playing a major security role in the northwest region and there is little indication that this will change in coming years without some major changes to the strategic environment.

Nor does China accept that the Indian Ocean is India's Ocean. Indeed, China does present a threat to India's regional ambitions, but probably in a different manner than is sometimes assumed. India's sustained economic growth after the Cold War has allowed it to expand its economic and political influence in the region and has underpinned the development of its power projection capabilities. But India's economic power is much less than China's and India is less effective in using it for strategic advantage. For many countries in the Indian Ocean, China is a more important economic partner. While China has often been relatively cautious about converting its economic power into the security dimension, its growing influence will create important constraints on India's power and its ability to develop security relationships.

India also faces considerable cultural constraints on its ability to project power and influence in a consistent manner. Stephen Cohen describes India as having a culture of 'strategic restraint' that is deeply rooted in the Indian strategic psyche. Caution or restraint has been a major factor in Indian strategic behaviour since independence and will continue to be an important limiting factor even as India gains the material resources to play a more active strategic role beyond South Asia.[1] But while a cultural bias against military action could limit India's ability to act as a regional security provider, it has also helped India's relatively benign standing in the region.

Another important constraint on India's role in the Indian Ocean is its instincts against security cooperation with other states. During the Cold War this was manifested in the creed of non-alignment, which forbade India from entering into formal military alliances (although it did not prevent a *de facto* alignment with the Soviet Union). This instinct also lies behind the current devotion to strategic autonomy and fears that cooperation with the United States—and even with lesser powers—will in some way undermine India's destiny to become a great power. This constraint is more evident among India's political elite than in India's military: the Indian Navy, in particular, has strong cultural instincts towards cooperation, although it is often restrained from doing so by its political and bureaucratic masters. Although this taboo might be expected to lessen somewhat over time, for the foreseeable future there will be a strong preference towards cooperation only in politically non-controversial areas or in a manner that is not overly visible.

It should be remembered that before the United States became a global power it also tried to avoid entering into 'entangling alliances'. This helped the United States to stand apart from the rivalries and disputes among European powers while it grew its national power. But any analogy with India is flawed. While the United States had the ability to dominate its own hemisphere in the nineteenth and twentieth centuries without the need for local alliances, that option is unlikely to be available to India in the Indian Ocean. India may be the largest local power in the Indian Ocean, but there are other key regional powers that India will need to co-opt and rely upon if it is to take a leading role. Ironically, an ideological insistence on strategic autonomy, whether or not it helped India during the Cold War, now acts as a significant constraint on India's influence in the Indian Ocean. The provision of security on a unilateral basis is becoming increasingly untenable even for powers such as the United States, and India will be increasingly expected by others to demonstrate regional leadership in a cooperative manner.

Another factor having a negative impact on India's role in the Indian Ocean is the gap between India's rhetoric and its capabilities.[2] This is an oft-noted feature of Indian strategic behaviour and stands in considerable contrast with the approach taken by China, until recently, as it rises as a power in East Asia. Deng Xiaoping's famous '24 character strategy' of the early 1990s advised Beijing's leaders to: 'observe calmly; secure our position; cope with affairs calmly; hide our capacities and bide our time; be good at maintaining a low profile; and never claim leadership'. Until recent years this approach of reassurance facilitated the quiet expansion of China's strategic influence. Similarly, in India's case, there is a risk that unrealistic rhetoric may be counterproductive to India's image of a peaceful rise.

The shape of India's power in the Indian Ocean

There are also many questions as to how India might exercise a leading role in the Indian Ocean. Indian strategic thought about the Indian Ocean is comprised of a mish-mash of different influences and ideas, which include imperial perspectives, non-alignment and strategic autonomy, the Monroe Doctrine and a not insignificant slice of nominative determinism—it is called the 'Indian Ocean' after all. This leads to a lack of clarity among Indian decision-makers about India's desired role in the region. Nevertheless, it is possible to identify some consistent themes in Indian thinking. These include a widespread belief in India's 'manifest destiny' to become the dominant power in the Indian Ocean as part of India's larger destiny to become a world power, an instinct to exclude extra-regional powers from the region, and a desire to create a benign sphere of influence. How might these ideas guide India's strategic behaviour in the Indian Ocean?

A basic distinction is whether India will seek a dominant role in the Indian Ocean through demonstrating *leadership* or whether it will try to do so through the creation of a *hegemonic* regional order. Leadership is characterised by a commonality of goals between the leader and the followers, while a hegemon aims primarily to realise its own goals through presenting them to subordinate states as collective goals. A key feature of hegemony is the existence of a hierarchical relationship in which the subordinate states recognise the special status and prerogatives of the dominant state. But a hegemon does not just impose its will through the use or threat of military power—its relationship with subordinate states is usually more complicated. As one observer put it, the successful exercise of hegemony rests on a delicate balance between coercion and consensus, between the exercise of direct and indirect power of the hegemonic state and the provision of a degree of respect for the interests of the weaker state.[3]

India's political elite overwhelmingly see India as a moral and benign international leader without territorial ambitions or claims to hegemony. As Tanham described it, India's self-perceived regional role is that of a 'friendly policeman' seeking peace and stability for the entire Indian Ocean region.[4] During the Cold War, India's self-perceived international role was as a moral and disinterested leader of the Third World, trying to secure peace and stability for developing states against the inimical intrusions of neo-imperialists. Consistent with this approach, many in the Indian elite believe that India will achieve a dominant strategic role in the Indian Ocean through demonstrating benign and principled leadership as what New Delhi is now calling the region's 'main resident power.' The tasks of the main resident power include organising friendly states, providing public security goods and helping to resist the 'intrusion' of outside powers into the region. Over the last two decades, the Indian Navy has used a leadership model in developing security relationships throughout the Indian Ocean. In doing so, it is helped by India's noticeable lack of historical baggage—even in Islamic states where India's role is constrained by the Pakistan factor, India is rarely seen as a direct threat.

But India's dominant world view also places considerable emphasis on hierarchy and India's position in that hierarchy. India has also been described as a 'status-inconsistent' power—that is, there is a discrepancy between its perceptions of its own achievements and its ascribed status at an international level.[5] Although India currently possesses only some great power capabilities (e.g. nuclear weapons, a large population and military), and has the potential to possess others (e.g. economic strength and military power projection capabilities), many in New Delhi believe that India is unfairly denied recognition of its proper international status. In other words, many in India perceive an entitlement to status based on India's potential rather than actual capabilities. As Selig Harrison, a US expert on South Asia, put it, 'Many Indians have what might be called a 'post-dated self image'. They are confident that India is on the way to great power status and want others to treat them as if they had, in fact, already arrived'.[6]

To outsiders, India sometimes appears preoccupied with the recognition by others of its status as a great power and its accompanying prerogatives. At a material level, a preoccupation with status encourages the acquisition of major power status symbols such as aircraft carriers and nuclear submarines. Considerations of hierarchy may underlie India's relative openness to engaging with small states and its caution in engaging with middle powers such as Australia, Indonesia and South Africa which may be less willing to acknowledge India's special status. Such considerations, for example, were an important factor underlying India's irritation at Australia over its refusal to supply uranium even thought it had no pressing need for supplies of the commodity. China's refusal to recognise India's leading status in the Indian Ocean is particularly incomprehensible and infuriating and creates considerable hostility in New Delhi towards China's growing economic and political influence in the Indian Ocean.

Another major factor is India's instinct to try to *exclude* extra-regional powers from the Indian Ocean, previously the United States and now China, an instinct which is very imperfectly expressed in India's so-called Monroe Doctrine. India has made clear to its South Asian neighbours—at least the ones that it has a significant degree of power over—that any Chinese security presence would be unacceptable to it. Even further afield, strong economic relationships with China (as is the case with Australia or Southeast Asia), are viewed with some suspicion. It has been argued that fellow Indian Ocean powers may silently acquiesce in India's Monroe Doctrine, lending it a kind of quasi-legal standing, or at least an air of permanence, provided that New Delhi can develop the necessary capabilities and mindset to show regional leadership.[7] But while this might be the case with some small or weak states that may see India as a security provider, it seems unlikely with the middle powers of the Indian Ocean. Many of these states will encourage the United States to maintain its regional predominance for as long as possible. In playing a leadership role, India will need to come to terms with the fact that many other states do not see the presence of extra-regional powers such as the United States in negative terms. Pakistan sees a Chinese presence positively and it is possible that in future decades other Indian Ocean states might come to see China in a similar way.

Prospects for an Indian-led regional security order in the Indian Ocean

Will India be able to construct a regional security order in the Indian Ocean in which it plays a dominant role? If so, what might that order look like? Some believe that India will seek to create an old-fashioned sphere of influence in the Indian Ocean where it is the recognised hegemon, just as Britain did in the nineteenth century and as India attempted to do in South Asia in the 1970s and 1980s. But while India might have the potential to create such a sphere of influence in South Asia or among some of the island states of the southwest, it seems unlikely elsewhere in the Indian Ocean. Its role in Africa is constrained by several factors, including China's growing economic power. Its role in the northwest Indian Ocean is constrained by Pakistan and India's inability to find a regional partner. While India is generally seen in benign terms in the northeast, in Southeast Asia it is ultimately seen as just one of several extra-regional powers that provide a useful balance to each other. Australia sees India as a potentially important security partner in the Indian Ocean and the Pacific, but not as a security provider to it.

India could seek to sponsor multilateral security arrangements among Indian Ocean states that implicitly (if not formally) acknowledge India's leadership while recognising the 'legitimate' interests of extra-regional powers. But building such a mechanism among the Indian Ocean states would be a difficult task given that the area has few institutions and little or no tradition of collective action. Previous attempts by India to sponsor regional groupings have not been successful. The IOZOP proposal in the 1970s and 1980s foundered on unrealistic hopes that the United States and other extra-regional powers would voluntarily exclude themselves from the Indian Ocean and a failure to understand that many in the region saw considerable benefit in the presence of US forces. The failure of IOR-ARC to take off in the 1990s demonstrated a lack of perceived common interests among Indian Ocean states. Although India has sought to develop a regional dialogue through its sponsorship of the Indian Ocean Naval Symposium (IONS) for the naval chiefs of Indian Ocean states, the results there have also been disappointing to some. Another key problem in developing a multilateral security order will be New Delhi's expectations of recognition of India's special role—what Indian leaders are now referring to as the 'main resident power' in the Indian Ocean region.[8] It seems unlikely that Indian Ocean states could reach consensus on what India's leading role might be. Given the broader context of Sino–Indian strategic rivalry, it also seems unlikely that China would be prepared to rely on India for its maritime security needs in the Indian Ocean without an overarching security arrangement.

Alternatively, India could seek to sponsor a sort of concert of powers among major powers that have substantial interests in the Indian Ocean. In recent years there has been considerable academic discussion about a concert of powers in the Asian Pacific as a way of engaging with China as a responsible member of a new strategic order.[9] The idea harks back to the first half of the nineteenth century when a so-called 'concert' of four or five powers explicitly took collective managerial responsibility for the security of Europe. This was seen as a way of mitigating competition between them and reducing the risk of unintended conflicts. It required major powers to assume a leadership role in maintaining security and for the lesser powers to accept that role. In 2009, Shiv Shankar Menon, former Indian foreign secretary and now national security advisor, proposed such a concert as a way of addressing the Sino–Indian security dilemma in the Indian Ocean. Importantly, he recognised that any such concert of powers dealing with maritime security issues would need to span both the Indian and Pacific oceans, commenting that, 'none of Asia's seas or oceans can be considered in isolation'.[10] Menon's proposal assumes that the Sino–Indian security dilemma that is becoming evident in the Indian Ocean cannot be resolved by bilateral means, but also that India would be unlikely to agree to fetter its position in the Indian Ocean without being recognised as having a legitimate security role in the South China Sea and the western Pacific. The development of a working concert of major powers would also be consistent with India's overall objective of encouraging the development of a multipolar order. But while there are some attractions of a concert of power there is also a degree of scepticism about it. Some argue that the creation of such system is unlikely except following a major strategic upheaval, such as a major war. Others do not believe that the middle and smaller powers accept a system that does not give them a direct voice in major decisions. The experience with ASEAN in recent years suggests that even the smallest powers are unlikely to easily give up their voice in regional decision-making.

Such proposals also bring into relief debates about whether the Indian Ocean should be viewed as a discrete strategic entity or as part of what is now seen as a larger 'Indo–Pacific' strategic construct. As US secretary of state, Hillary Clinton, commented: 'How we translate the growing connection between the Indian and Pacific Oceans into an operational concept is a question that we need to answer if we are to adapt to the new challenges in the region'.[11] The term Indo–Pacific is popular among some in New Delhi because it apparently recognises India as occupying a more central position in Asia.[12] But its broader strategic implications are not yet clear: some see the concept of the 'Indo–Pacific' as a way of bringing both India and China into a security arrangement that spans both oceans, while others see it as supporting the development of India's security relationship with the United States and its allies to balance against China.[13]

Although India's role as an Indian Ocean power will almost inevitably grow in coming years, there is no obvious path as to how its power will develop. As with other areas of Indian policy, there is a good chance that India will continue along at its own civilisational pace without any overarching or coordinated strategic plan, seeking to expand its power and influence here and there on an *ad hoc* basis, as and when opportunities present themselves. This may represent a low-risk approach for New Delhi, particularly if it takes the view that time is on its side. But a failure to properly come to terms with China's interests or co-opt the middle powers of the region may restrict India from fully achieving its ambitions to become the leading power of the Indian Ocean. In coming decades, India's Ocean may look a bit more like a Hindu world than a European one, a society bound together by a common understanding of things, but also full of compromises, uncertainties and inconsistencies that allow its disparate parts to rub along.

Notes

1 Stephen Cohen and Sunil Dasgupta (2010) *Arming without Aiming: India's Military Modernisation*, Washington, DC: Brookings Institution Press.
2 See, for example, Harsh Pant (2009) 'India in the Indian Ocean: growing mismatch between ambitions and capabilities', *Pacific Affairs*, Vol. 82, No. 2, Summer, pp. 279–97.
3 Sandra Destradi (2012) *Indian Foreign and Security Policy in South Asia: Regional Power Strategies*, London: Routledge, pp. 19–20.
4 George Tanham (1992) *Indian Strategic Thought: an Interpretive Essay*, Santa Monica, CA: Rand, p. 69.
5 Baldev Raj Nayar and T.V. Paul (2003) *India in the World Order: Searching for Major Power Status*, New York: Cambridge University Press, pp. 1, 25.

6 Selig Harrison (1998) 'A nuclear bargain with India', paper presented at the conference 'India at the Crossroads', Southern Methodist University, Dallas, Texas, 27 March, quoted in Nayar and Paul, *India in the World Order*, p. 77.

7 James R. Holmes (2011) 'Looking south: Indian Ocean', in David Scott (ed.), *Handbook of India's International Relations*, London: Routledge, pp. 156–66.

8 See, for example, the speech by Indian foreign secretary, Nirupama Rao, to the National Maritime Foundation, 19 November 2010.

9 See, for example, Coral Bell (2007) *The end of the Vasco da Gama era: the next landscape of world politics*, Double Bay NSW: Longueville Media.

10 Shiv Shankar Menon (2009) 'Maritime Imperatives of Indian Foreign Policy', speech to the National Maritime Foundation, New Delhi, 11 September.

11 Hillary Clinton (2011) 'America's Pacific century', *Foreign Policy*, November.

12 See, for example, A. Prakash (2009) 'A moment for India: Shangri-La dialogue 2009', *Force*, July, pp. 5–7.

13 Dennis Rumley (2012) Timothy Doyle and Sanjay Chaturvedi, '"Securing" the Indian Ocean? Competing regional security constructions', *Journal of Indian Ocean Region*, Vol. 8, No. 1, pp. 1–20.

References

'216716: Scenesetter for Secretary of State Clinton's visit to India' (2011) *The Hindu*, 28 March.

'A third country role cannot be envisaged nor is it necessary' (2009) *Outlook India*, 18 November.

Abhyankar, Rajendra M. (2008) *West Asia and the Region: Defining India's Role*, New Delhi: Academic Foundation.

Acheson, Dean G. (1955) *A Democrat Looks at his Party*, New York: Harper.

Agencia de Informacao de Mocambique (2012) 'Mozambique: anti-piracy patrols should move further north', 10 July.

Aiyar, Mani Shankar (ed.) (1993) *Rajiv Ghandi's India: A Golden Jubilee Retrospective, Vol. 3*, New Delhi: UBSPD.

Albinski, Henry (1982) *Australian–American Security Relationship: A Regional and International Perspective*, Brisbane: Queensland University Press.

Allchin, Joseph (2011) 'India flexes diplomatic, military muscle in Myanmar', *Eurasia Review Newsletter*, 18 October.

Alves, Philip (2007) 'India and South Africa: shifting priorities', *South African Journal of International Affairs*, Vol. 14, No. 2, pp. 87–109.

Andersen, Walter K. (1979) 'India in Asia: walking on a tightrope', *Asian Survey*, Vol. 19, No. 12, pp. 1241–53.

Anonymous (1988) 'Maldives—the coup that failed', *Asiaweek*, 18 November, pp. 37–8.

'Anti-apartheid India found to have SA links' (1988) *The Star*, 23 September.

Appadorai, A. (1981) 'Non-alignment: some important issues', *International Studies*, Vol. 20, No. 1, pp. 3–11.

Australian Government (2009) *Defending Australia in the Asia Pacific Century: Force 2030*, Canberra: Commonwealth of Australia.

Avirgan, Tony and Martha Honey (1982) *War in Uganda: The Legacy of Idi Amin*, Westport, CT: Hill.

Ayoob, Mohammed (1990) *India and Southeast Asia: Indian Perceptions and Policies*, New York: Routledge.

Babbage, Ross (1988) *Should Australia Plan to Defend Christmas and Cocos Islands?* Canberra: Strategic and Defence Studies Centre.

Baker, Deane-Peter (2012) 'The South African Navy and African maritime security', *Naval War College Review*, Vol. 65, No. 2, pp. 145–65.

Balachandran, V. (2010) 'The day media turned a patriot into a traitor', *Sunday Guardian*, 19 September.

Ball, Desmond (1980) *A Suitable Piece of Real Estate: American Installations in Australia*, Marrickville, NSW: Southwood Press.

——(1993) *Signals Intelligence in the Post-Cold War Era*, Singapore: Institute of Southeast Asian Studies.

——(1996) *Signals Intelligence (SIGINT) in South Asia: India, Pakistan, Sri Lanka (Ceylon)*, Canberra: Australian National University.

Banerjee, Dipkar (ed.) (1995) *Towards an Era of Cooperation: An Indo–Australian Dialogue*, New Delhi: Institute for Defence Studies and Analyses.

Baruah, Amit (2003) 'India–Mauritius ties "umbilical and sacred"', *The Hindu*, 22 November.

——(2007) 'Not seeking exclusive sphere of influence', *The Hindu*, 11 February.

Bateman, Sam and Anthony Bergin (2010) *Our Western Front: Australia and the Indian Ocean*, Australian Strategic Policy Institute, March.

Bateman, Sam and Joshua Ho (eds) (2010) *Southeast Asia and the Rise of Chinese and Indian Naval Power: Between Rising Naval Powers*, London: Routledge.

Beazley, Kim C. and Ian Clark (1979) *The Politics of Intrusion: the Super Powers and the Indian Ocean*, Sydney: Alternative Publishing Cooperative.

Bedi, Rahul (2003) 'US closes in on South Asia's 'strategic jewel', *AsiaTimes Online*, 7 January.

——(2005) 'US–India defense relations', *SPAN Magazine, New Delhi*, March/April.

——(2007) 'Sri Lanka turns to Pakistan, China for military needs', *IANS*, 6 February.

——(2009) 'India strengthens military co-operation with the Maldives', *Jane's Defence Weekly*, 21 August.

Behera, Laxman K. (2012) 'India's defence budget 2012–13', *IDSA Comment*, 20 March.

Bell, Coral (2007) *The End of the Vasco da Gama Era: The Next Landscape of World Politics*, Double Bay, NSW: Longueville Media.

Beri, Ruchita (2000) 'Indo–South African defence cooperation: potential and prospects', *Strategic Analysis*, Vol. 23, No. 10, pp. 1681–705.

——(2003) 'India's Africa policy in the post-Cold War era: an assessment', *Strategic Analysis*, Vol. 27, No. 2, pp. 216–32.

Berlin, Donald L. (2004) *India–Iran Relations: A Deepening Entente*, Honolulu, HI: Asia Pacific Centre for Security Studies, October.

——(2006) 'India in the Indian Ocean', *Naval War College Review*, Vol. 59, No. 2, Spring, p. 60.

Bertsch, Gary K., Seema Gahlaut and Anupam Srivastava (eds) (1999) *Engaging India: US Strategic Relations with the World's Largest Democracy*, London: Routledge.

Bhaskar, C. Uday and Kamlesh K. Agnihotri (eds) (2010) *Security Challenges along the Indian Ocean Littoral: Indian and US Perspectives*, Delhi: National Maritime Foundation.

Bhaumik, Anirban (2011) 'China wooing NE insurgents in Myanmar', *Deccan Herald*, 2 October.

Bhaumik, Subir (2011) 'Arakanese rebels freed from Indian jail', *AsiaTimes*, 21 May.

Bhushan, Ranjit (2004) 'Port hole', *Outlook India*, 7 June.

Bhutani, S.K. (1995) 'India–Australia bilateral relations', in Dipankar Banerjee (ed.), *Towards an Era of Cooperation: an Indo–Australian Dialogue*, New Delhi: Institute for Defence Studies and Analyses.

Bilveer, S. 'Operation Cactus: India's "prompt action" in Maldives', *Asian Defence Journal*, Vol. 2, No. 89, pp. 30–3.

Blyth, Robert J. (2003) *The Empire of the Raj: India, Eastern Africa and the Middle East 1858–1947*, London: Palgrave Macmillan.

Bobb, Dilip (1980) 'Blunting the edge', *India Today*, 1 September, p. 85.

——(1987) 'High stakes gamble', *India Today*, 15 December, p. 81.

Boquérat, Gilles (2003) 'French interests in the Indian Ocean and the relevance of India', *Journal of Indian Ocean Studies*, Vol. 11, No. 2, August, pp. 234–46.

Bouchard, Christian and William Crumplin (2012) 'The *Marine nationale* in the southwest and southern Indian Ocean', paper presented at the Royal Australian Navy Sea Power Conference, Sydney, February.

Bowles, Chester (1954) 'A fresh look at free Asia', *Foreign Affairs*, Vol. 33, No. 1, pp. 54–71.

Bowman, Larry W. and Ian Clark (eds) (1981) *The Indian Ocean in Global Politics*, Boulder, CO: Westview, pp. 59–86.

Boyce, P.J. and J.R. Angel (eds) (1983) *Independence and Alliance: Australia in World Affairs 1976–80*, Sydney: George Allen and Unwin.

Brewster, David (2009) 'India's Security Partnership with Singapore', *The Pacific Review*, Vol. 22, No. 5, December, pp. 597–618.

——(2009) 'The strategic relationship between India and Vietnam: The search for a diamond on the South China Sea? *Asian Security*, Vol. 5, No. 1, January, pp. 24–44.

——(2010) 'The Australia—India Security Declaration: the Quadrilateral redux?', *Security Challenges*, Vol. 6, No. 1, Autumn, pp. 1–9.

——(2011) 'The evolving security relationship between India and Indonesia', *Asian Survey*, Vol. 51, No. 2, March/April, pp. 221–44.

——(2012) *India as an Asia Pacific Power*, London: Routledge.

Brewster, David and Ranjit Rai (2011) 'Flowers are blooming: the story of the India Navy's secret operation in the Seychelles', *The Naval Review*, Vol. 99, No. 1, pp. 58–62.

——(2013) 'Operation Lal Dora: India's aborted military intervention in Mauritius', *Asian Security*, Vol. 9, No. 1, pp. 62–74.

Brobst, Peter John (2005) *The Future of the Great Game: Sir Olaf Caroe, India's Independence and the Defence of Asia*, Akron, OH: University of Akron Press.

Bruce, Robert H. (1988) *Australia and the Indian Ocean: Strategic Dimensions of Increasing Naval Involvement*, Perth: Centre of Indian Ocean Studies.

——(ed.) (1989) *The Modern Indian Navy in the Indian Ocean: Developments and Implications*, Perth: Centre for Indian Ocean Regional Studies.

——(ed.) (1990) *Indian Ocean Navies*, Perth: Curtin University of Technology.

Burrell, R.M. and Alvin J. Cottrell (1974) *Iran, Afghanistan, Pakistan: Tensions and Dilemmas*, Beverly Hills, CA: Sage.

Buzan, Barry (1982) 'The Indian Ocean in global politics', *Survival*, Vol. 24, p. 44.

Buzan, Barry and Gowher Rizvi (1986) *South Asian Insecurity and the Great Powers*, New York: St Martin's Press.

Buzan, Barry Ole Waever and Jaap de Wilde (1998) *Security: A New Framework for Analysis*, Boulder, CO: Lynne Rienner Publishers.

Chand, Attar (1991) *Rajiv Gandhi: His Mind and Ideology*, New Delhi: Gian.

Chandramohan, Balaji (2011) 'Indo–Maldives relations continue to blossom', *Atlantic Sentinel*, 22 November.

Chandraprema, C.A. (2012) *Gōta's War: The Crushing of Tamil Tiger Terrorism in Sri Lanka*, Colombo: Ranjan Wijeratne Foundation.

Chandrasekaran, Rajiv (2001) 'India offers bases to US for retaliatory attacks', *Washington Post*, 17 September.

Cheeseman, Graeme (1992) *Selling Mirages: The Politics of Arms Trading*, Canberra: Strategic and Defence Studies Centre.

'China afraid of India's naval presence in the Ocean' (2009) *Zeenews.com*, 13 August.

'China has no plan for Indian Ocean military bases' (2012) *The Hindu*, 4 September.

'China's plan to build up its navy' (1993) *Hindustan Times*, 13 January.

'Chinese arms, radar for Sri Lanka military' (2007) *LankaNewspapers.com*, 5 June.

Choudhury, Ratnadip (2011) 'Bertil Linter: Myanmar will not cooperate with India in crossborder insurgencies', *Tehelka*, 28 September. Online: www.tehelka.com/story_main50.asp?filename=Ws280911Myanmar.asp (accessed 10 October 2013).

Clinton, Hillary (2011) 'America's Pacific century', *Foreign Policy*, November.

Cohen, Saul B. (1973) *Geography and Politics in a World Divided*, 2nd edn, New York: Oxford University Press.

Cohen, Stephen P. (2001) *India: Emerging Power*, Washington, DC: Brookings Institution.

Cohen, Stephen P. and Sunil Dasgupta (2010) *Arming without Aiming: India's Military Modernisation*, Washington, DC: Brookings Institution Press.

Cole, D.H. (1931) *Imperial Military Geography*, 6th edn, London: Sifton Praed.

Cole, Thomas R. (2007) *Imperial Connections: India in the Indian Ocean Arena 1860–1920*, Berkeley, CA: University of California Press.

Conley, Jerome M. (2001) *Indo–Russian Military and Nuclear Cooperation: Lessons and Options for US Policy in South Asia*, Lanham, MD: Lexington Books.

Cooper, Tom and Farzad Bishop (2000) *Iran–Iraq War in the Air, 1980–1988*, Atglen PA: Schiffer.

Copley, Gregory R. (2009) *Such a Full Sea: Australia's Options in a Changing Indian Ocean Region*, Melbourne: Sid Harta Publishers.

Coutau-Bégarie, Hervé (1983) *La Puissance Maritime Sovietique* [Soviet Sea Power], Paris: Economica.

da Cunha, Derek (1990) *Soviet Naval Power in the Pacific*, Boulder, CO: Lynne Rienner.

Datta-Ray, Sunanda K. (2009) *Looking East to Look West: Lee Kuan Yew's Mission India*, Singapore: Institute of Southeast Asian Studies.

de Borchgrave, Arnaud (2003) 'Pakistan, Saudi Arabia in secret nuke pact: Islamabad trades weapons technology for oil', *The Washington Times*, 22 October.

Deshmukh, B.G. (2004) *A Cabinet Secretary Looks Back*, New Delhi: HarperCollins, p. 197.

DeSilva-Ranasinghe, Sergei (2009) 'Sri Lanka—The New Great Game', *The Diplomat*, 28 October.

——(2011) 'China–India rivalry in the Maldives', *The Jakarta Post*, 17 June.

——(2012) 'India's Iranian sanctions predicament', FDI Strategic Weekly Analysis, Vol. 3, No. 4, 8 February.

——(2012) 'Post-war posture', *Jane's Defence Weekly*, 9 May, p. 27–32.

——(2012) 'Fact sheet: The Indian Ocean and Australia's national interests', Future Directions International Strategic Analysis Paper, 29 May.

Destradi, Sandra (2012) *Indian Foreign and Security Policy in South Asia: Regional Power Strategies*, London: Routledge.

Dikshit, Sandeep (2011) 'Hillary's leadership call to India not aimed at Pakistan', *The Hindu*, 9 August.

Dixit, J.N. (1989) 'IPKF in Sri Lanka', *USI Journal*, Vol. 119, No. 49, July, pp. 249–50.

——(1996) *My South Block Years: Memoirs of a Foreign Secretary*, New Delhi: UPS Publishers.

——(2004) *Makers of India's Foreign Policy: Raja Ram Mohun Roy to Yashwant Sinha*, New Delhi: HarperCollins.

Dodd, Mark (2012) 'Defence urged to shift presence to the north', *The Australian*, 31 January.

'Don't allow differences to stop South Asian integration: NSA' (2012) *The Economic Times*, 9 March.

Dorling, Philip, 'Chinese bid to set up East Timor spy base' (2011) *Sydney Morning Herald*, 10 May.

Dowdy, William L. and Russell B. Trood (eds) (1985) *The Indian Ocean: Perspectives on a Strategic Arena*, Durham, NC: Duke University Press.

Downer, Alexander (1998) 'Australian response to India's nuclear tests', Media Release, 14 May.

Dubey, Ajay Kumar (1990) *Indo–African Relations in the Post-Nehru Era (1965–1985)*, Delhi: Kalinga.

——(1997) *Government and Politics in Mauritius*, Delhi: Kalinga.

Dutta, Sujan (2009) 'Indian Navy eyes Maldives—counter to China's "String of Pearls" plan', *The Telegraph* (India), 20 August.

Egreteau, Renaud (2003) *Wooing the Generals: India's New Myanmar Policy*, Delhi: Authorspress.

Ellis, Stephen (1996) 'Africa and international corruption: the strange case of South Africa and Seychelles', *African Affairs*, pp. 165–96.

Embree, Ainslie T. (1989) *Imagining India: essays on Indian history*, New York: Oxford University Press.

Erickson, Andrew S. and Gabriel B. Collins (2010) 'China's oil security pipe dream', *Naval War College Review*, Vol. 63, No. 2, Spring, pp. 91–2.

Erickson, Andrew S., Walter C. Ladwig and Justin D. Mikolay (2010) 'Diego Garcia and the United States' emerging Indian Ocean strategy', *Asian Security*, Vol. 6, No. 3, pp. 214–37.

Express News Service (2008) 'Won't stop military cooperation with Lanka: Pranab', *Indian Express*, 24 October.

Fazl-e-Haider, Syed (2012) 'China set to run Gwadar port as Singapore quits', *Asia Times*, 5 September.

Foreign Affairs Reports (New Delhi), Vol. 36, July–Oct 1987, p. 208.

Forsberg, Steven J. (2007) 'India stretches its sea legs', *United States Naval Institute Proceedings*, Vol. 133, No. 3, March, p. 38–42.

Fraser, Lovat (1911) *India Under Curzon and After*, London: William Heinemann.

Ganguly, Sumit (2012) 'India's misguided autonomy', *The Diplomat*, 25 June.

Ganguly, Sumit, Brian Shoup and Andrew Scobell (eds) (2006) *US–Indian Strategic Cooperation into the Twenty-first Century: More than Words*, London: Routledge.

Garver, John W. (1992) 'China and South Asia', *Annals of the American Academy of Political and Social Science*, Vol. 519, January, p. 72.

——(2001) *Protracted Contest: Sino–Indian Rivalry in the Twentieth Century*, Washington, DC: University of Washington Press.

Gilboy, George J. and Eric Heginbotham (2012) *Chinese and Indian Strategic Behaviour: Growing Power and Alarm*, New York: Cambridge University Press.

Godage, K. (2005) 'Why won't India show her hand?', *Sunday Island*, 6 February.

Goh Chok Tong (2005) 'Constructing East Asia', speech to Asia Society, 15th Asian Corporate Conference, Bangkok, 9 June.

Gopal, D. (ed.) (2002) *Australia in the Emerging Global Order: Evolving Australia–India Relations*, New Delhi: Shipra.

Sandy Gordon (2010) 'Strategic interests of the major Indian Ocean powers: an Australian perspective', in H. Singh, *Pentagon's South Asia Defence and Strategic Yearbook, 2010*, New Delhi: Pentagon Press.

Gordon, Sandy with Desmond Ball, Paul Dibb and Amin Saikal (1996) *Security and Security Building in the Indian Ocean Region*, Canberra: Strategic and Defence Studies Centre.

Gould, Harold A. and Sumit Ganguly (eds) (1992) *The Hope and the Reality: US–Indian Relations from Roosevelt to Reagan*, Boulder, CO: Westview Press.

Grare, Frederick and Amitabh Mattoo (eds) (2001) *India and ASEAN: The Politics of India's Look East Policy*, New Delhi: Centre de Sciences Humaines.

Greenert, Jonathan (2011) 'Value of Maritime Crossroads', 4 November, http://cno.navy live.dodlive.mil/2011/11/04/%E2%80%9Cvalue-of-maritime-crossroads%E2%80%9D-3/ (accessed 10 October 2013).

Gulf Research Centre (2008) *India's Growing Role in the Gulf: Implications for the Region and the United States*, Dubai: Gulf Research Centre, November.

Gunaratna, Rohan (1993) *Indian Intervention in Sri Lanka: The Role of India's Intelligence Agencies?* Colombo: South Asian Network on Conflict Research.

Gupta, Amit (1990) 'The Indian arms industry: a lumbering giant', *Asian Survey*, Vol. 29, No. 9, pp. 846–61, p. 858.

Gupta, Anirudha (1974) 'Ugandan Asians, Britain, India and the Commonwealth', *African Affairs*, Vol. 73, No. 292, pp. 312–24.

Gupta, Bhabani Sen (1983) 'The Indian doctrine', *India Today*, 31 August.

Gupta, Sourabh (2011) 'US–India defence ties: the limits to interoperability', East Asia Forum, 31 July.

Gurry, Meg (1996) *India: Australia's Neglected Neighbour? 1947–1996*, Griffith: Centre for the Study of Australia–Asia Relations.

Haass, Richard N. (1987) 'Arms control at sea: The United States and the Soviet Union in the Indian Ocean 1977–78', *The Journal of Strategic Studies*, Vol. 10, No. 2, pp. 231–47.

Habib, Adam (2009) 'South Africa's foreign policy: hegemonic aspirations, neoliberal orientations and global transformation', *South African Journal of International Affairs*, Vol. 16, No. 2, August, pp. 143–59.

Hafiz, Brig (Retd) (1995) 'An insecure security', *The Morning Sun* (Dhaka), 17 June.

Harrison, Selig (1998) 'A nuclear bargain with India', paper presented at the India at the Crossroads Conference, Southern Methodist University, Dallas, Texas, 27 March.

——(2010) 'China's discreet hold on Pakistan's northern borderlands', *New York Times*, 26 August.

Harrison, Selig and K. Subrahmanyam (1989) *Superpower Rivalry in the Indian Ocean: Indian and American perspectives*, New York: Oxford University Press.

Hathaway, Robert (ed.) (2004) *The 'Strategic Partnership' between India and Iran*, Washington, DC: Woodrow Wilson Centre.

Hazarika, Prabeer Hazarika (2005) 'India faces secret Saudi–Pakistan defence alliance', *India Daily*, 23 March.

Heathcote, T.A. (1995) *The Military in British India: The Development of British Land Forces in South Asia, 1600–1947*, Manchester: Manchester University Press.

Hebditch, David and Ken Connor (2005) *How to Stage a Military Coup: From Planning to Execution*, London: Greenhill.

Hewitt, Vernon Marston (1992) *The International Politics of South Asia*, Manchester: Manchester University Press.

Hoagland, Jim (1975) 'Syrian–Iraqi dispute flares: Damascus accused of aiding Kurds Syria, Iraq split over aid to Kurds', *Washington Post*, 27 February, p. A16.

Hoare, Mike (1986) *The Seychelles Affair*, New York: Bantam.

Holmes, James R. (2007) 'India and the Proliferation Security Initiative: a US perspective', *Strategic Analysis*, Vol. 31, No. 2, pp. 315–37.

——(2012) 'Inside, outside: India's 'exterior lines' in the South China Sea', *Strategic Analysis*, Vol. 36, No. 3, pp. 358–63.

Holmes, James R., Andrew C. Winner and Toshi Yoshihara (2009) *Indian Naval Strategy in the Twenty-first Century*, Abingdon: Routledge.

Hurley, Matthew M. (1992) 'Saddam Hussein and Iraqi air power: just having an air force isn't enough', *Airpower Journal*, Vol. 6, No. 4, p. 4–16.

Huxley, Tim (1992) 'India's naval expansion and Australia', *Contemporary South Asia*, Vol. 1, No. 33, pp. 407–23.

'India, Mauritius to fast-track PTA' (2012) *The Hindu*, 6 July.

India, Ministry of Defence *Annual Report 2000–2001*.

'India, Qatar ink defence pact' (2008) *The Financial Times*, 11 November.

'India, Qatar to ramp defence, economic, energy ties (roundup, combining different series)' (2008) *Thaindian News*, 10 November.

India. High Level Committee on the Indian Diaspora (2001) *Report of High Level Committee on Indian Diaspora*, New Delhi: Ministry of External Affairs.

'India: Air Force' (2009) *Jane's World Air Forces*, 1 June.

'India: PM vows to defend tiny Qatar "if needed"' (2008) *ADN Kronos International*, 12 November.

'India's nuclear forces, 2007' (2007) *Bulletin of Atomic Scientists*, Vol. 63, No. 4, July/August, pp. 74–8.

'India–Mauritius ties more than diplomatic: Jugnauth' (2009) *The Hindu*, 3 December.

'India against direct intervention in South China Sea disputes despite having stakes in the region' (2012) *India Today*, 8 August.

'India and Iran: end of an alliance' (2005) *Jane's Intelligence Digest*, 5 October.

'India and Iran expand links' (2003) *Jane's Intelligence Digest*, 29 January.

'India and Mozambique to cooperate on maritime security, anti-piracy efforts' (2011) *Defenceweb*, 30 June.

'India begins supplies radars to Sri Lanka' (2007) *India Defence*, 8 June.

'India breaks silence on Myanmar, hedges its bets' (2007) *BDNew24.com*, 27 September. Online: http://ns.bdnews24.com/details.php?id=76312&cid=1 (accessed 10 October 2013).

'India jets poised to aid Mugabe' (1986) *The Observer* (London), 31 August, p. 13.

'India not competing with China: Navy Chief' (2007) NDTV India, 26 December.

'India offers $500m credit line to Mozambique' (2010) *The Hindu*, 1 October.

'India to supply coastal security equipment to Mauritius' (2009) *Indo–Asian News Service*, 6 November.

'India will purchase the MQ-4C BAMS drone aircraft' (2012) *Avionews*, 2 April.

'Indian Air Force chief to visit Malaysia; boost in military ties' (2008) *India Defence*, 17 August.

Indian Navy (2004) *Indian Maritime Doctrine*.

——(2007) *Freedom to Use the Seas: India's Maritime Military Strategy*.

'Indian Navy activates listening post, monitoring station in Madagascar, Indian Ocean' (2007) *India Defence*, 7 July.

'Indian Navy awaits regional nod for patrolling Malacca Straits' (2006) *India Defence*, 7 June.

'Indian ship to patrol Seychelles, Mauritius' (2009) *Deccan Chronicle*, 24 November.

Indo Asian News Service (2008) 'India says treat Iran with respect ahead of Ahmadinejad visit', 20 April. Online: www.thaindian.com/newsportal/uncategorized/india-says-treat-iran-with-respect-ahead-of-ahmadinejad-visit_10040097.html (accessed 10 October 2013).

——(2009) 'Want dialogue? Then contain terror, PM tells Gilani', *Thaindian News*, 16 July.

'Indonesia and Malaysia keen on buying BrahMos' (2007) *Frontier India Strategic and Defence*, 13 April.

'Indonesia asks India to help maintain Malacca Strait security' (2009) *Xinhua*, 5 March.

International Crisis Group (2008) 'Sri Lanka's return to war: limiting the damage', Asia Report No. 146, 20 February.

International Institute of Strategic Studies (2011) *Strategic Survey 2011: the Annual Review of World Affairs*, London: Routledge.

International Monetary Fund, World Economic Outlook Database, April 2012.

'Interview with Admiral Arun Prakash, chief of naval staff, Indian Navy' (2005) *Asian Defence Journal*, October, p. 22.

'Iran and India: big men locally' (1974) *The Economist*, 4 May, p. 52.

Iyer, Nandhini (1985) *India in the Indian Ocean: Groping for a Policy, 1947–70*, New Delhi: ABC Publishing.

Jackson, Ashley (2011) 'Britain in the Indian Ocean', *Journal of the Indian Ocean Region*, Vol. 7, No. 2, December, pp. 145–60.

Jain Commission Interim Report, *Growth of Sri Lankan Tamil Militancy in Tamil Nadu*.

Jonas, Maggie (1987) 'Tide turns against MNR', *New African*, May, p. 20.

Kadian, Rajesh (1990) *India's Sri Lankan Fiasco: Peace Keepers at War*, New Delhi: Vision Books.

Kanhye, Ashwin (2011) 'L'Inde offre $10 m pour la surveillance de notre ZEE', *Le Matinal*, 31 March.

Kaplan, Robert D. (2009) 'Center Stage for the Twenty-first Century', *Foreign Affairs*, Vol. 88, No. 2, pp. 16–29.

Kapur, Ashok (1982) *The Indian Ocean: Regional and International Power Politics*, New York: Praeger.

Karanjia, R.K. (1977) *The Mind of a Monarch*, London: Allen & Unwin.

Kassim, Yang Razali (1986) 'India angered by claim over Soviet subs', *Straits Times*, 13 October.

Keenan, Andrew (1988) 'Cut-price plan for islands coup', *Sydney Morning Herald*, 13 May.

Keesing's Contemporary Archives (1976) London: Keesings.

Kellerhals, Merle David, Jr. (2010) 'India an indispensable partner, US officials say', *IPP Digital*, 1 June. Online: www.america.gov/st/peacesec-english/2010/June/ 201006 01090431dmslahrellek0.7037622.html (accessed 10 October 2013).

Kemp, Geoffrey (2010) *The East Moves West: India, China and Asia's Growing Presence in the Middle East*, Washington, DC: Brookings Institution.

'Kenya violence: centre not to evacuate Indians' (2008) *Business Standard*, 4 January.

Kerin, John, (2011) 'Cocos Base under review' *Australian Financial Review*, 21 November.

Khanna, V.N. (1997) *Foreign Policy of India*, New Delhi: Vikas.

Khilnani, Sunil, Rajiv Kumar, Pratap Bhanu Mehta, Prakash Menon, Nandan Nilekani, Srinath Raghavan, Shyam Saran and Siddharth Varadarajan (2007) *Nonalignment 2.0: A Foreign and Strategic Policy for India in the Twenty-first Century*. 30 June. Online: www.cprindia.org/sites/default/files/NonAlignment%202.0_1.pdf (accessed 10 October 2013).

Khurana, Gurpreet S. (2009) 'China–India maritime rivalry', *Indian Defence Review*, Vol. 23, No. 4.

Kissinger, Henry (1979) *The White House Years*, Boston, MA: Little, Brown.

Kodikara, Shelton U. (ed.) (1990) *South Asian Strategic Issues: Sri Lankan Perspectives*, New Delhi: Sage Publications.

Kostecka, Daniel J. (2010) 'The Chinese navy's emerging support network in the Indian Ocean', *China Brief*, Vol. 10, No. 15, 22 July, pp. 3–5.

——(2010) 'Hambantota, Chittagong and the Maldives—unlikely pearls for the Chinese navy', *China Brief*, Vol. 10, No. 23, 19 November, p. 8.

Krishna (2000) *Postcolonial Insecurities: India, Sri Lanka, and the Question of Nationhood*, New York: Oxford University Press.

Kronstadt, K. Alan and Kenneth Katzman (2006) 'India–Iran relations and US interests', Congressional Research Service Reports and Issue Briefs, 2 August.

Kumaraswami, Sridhar (2011) 'India eyes South China Sea pearl', *Asian Age*, 26 June.

Kumaraswamy, P.R. (ed.) (2004) *Security beyond Survival: Essays for K. Subrahmanyam*, New Delhi: Sage.

'Lack of consensus holding back anti-piracy policy' (2008) *Thaindian News*, 20 November.

Lamont, James (2010) 'China makes foray into Mauritius', *Financial Times*, 25 January.

Legum, C. (ed.) (1985) *Africa Contemporary Record: Annual Survey and Documents*, London: Collings.

Lenczowski, George (ed.) (1978) *Iran under the Pahlavis*, Stanford, CA: Hoover Institution Press.

'Libya backed Maldives coup' (1988) *Intelligence Digest*, 7 December, p. 8.

Lintner, Bertil (1994) 'Enter the Dragon', *Far Eastern Economic Review*, 22 December, p. 24.

——(2010) 'Australia's strategic little dots', *Asia Times*, 25 June.

Lutz, Catherine (ed.) (2009) *The Bases of Empire: the Global Struggle against US Military Posts*, New York: New York University Press.

Macdonald, Juli A. (2002) 'Indo–US military relationship: expectations and perceptions', report by Booz Allen Hamilton for the Director, Net Assessment, Office of the Secretary of Defense, October.

'Maldives not in favour of Chinese naval expansion in Indian Ocean' (2011) *Times of India*, 26 February.

'Maldives says China to grant Maldives $500 million loan' (2012) *South Asia Monitor*, 5 September.

Malhotra, Jyoti (2000) 'Lanka offers free access to Trincomalee, India mulls over it', *Indian Express*, 12 May.

——(2009) 'There's a Maldivian link to 26/11', *Business Standard*, 25 October.

Malik, J. Mohan (1994) 'Sino–Indian rivalry in Myanmar: implications for regional security', *Contemporary Southeast Asia*, Vol. 16, No. 2, September, pp. 137–56.

——(2011) *China and India: Great Power Rivals*, Boulder, CO: FirstForumPress.

Mamdani, Mahmood (1983) *Imperialism and Fascism in Uganda*, Nairobi: Heinemann.

Manor, J. and G. Segal (1985) 'Causes of conflict: Sri Lanka and Indian Ocean strategy', *Asian Survey*, Vol. 25, No. 12, December, pp. 1165–85.

'Marine Commandos: India's flexible elite' (1996) *Jane's Intelligence Review*, Vol. 008/005, 1 May.

'Mauritius: a change in direction?' (1983) *The South African Institute of International Affairs*, Brief Report No. 53, December.

McDonald, Hamish (1999) 'Nuclear posturing—out on a street-cred limb', *Sydney Morning Herald*, 8 February.

McDonald, John W. and Noa Zanolli (2008) *The Shifting Grounds of Conflict and Peacebuilding: Stories and Lessons*, Lanham, MD: Lexington Books.

Medcalf, Rory (2013) 'India Poll 2013: Facing the future—Indian views of the world ahead', report for the Lowy Institute for International Policy.

Medcalf, Rory and Amandeep Gill (2009) 'Unconventional partners: Australia–India cooperation in reducing nuclear dangers', policy brief for the Lowy Institute for International Policy, October.

Menon, Shiv Shankar (2009) 'Maritime imperatives of Indian foreign policy', speech to the National Maritime Foundation, New Delhi, 11 September.

——(2010) 'India and China: public diplomacy, building understanding', speech at the Indian Council of World Affairs, New Delhi, April.

Mills, Greg (1998) *South Africa and Security Building in the Indian Ocean Rim*, Canberra Papers on Strategy and Defence No. 127, Canberra: Australian National University.

Ming Zhang (2006) 'The Malacca Dilemma and the Chinese navy's strategic choices', *Modern Ships*, No. 274, October, p. 23.

'Minister clarifies Mauritius island offer' (2012) *The Times of India*, 7 July.

Misra, Raj Narain (1986) *Indian Ocean and India's Security*, Delhi: Mittal.

Mohan, C. Raja (2003) *Crossing the Rubicon: the Shaping of India's New Foreign Policy*, London: Palgrave Macmillan.

——(2003) 'Beyond India's Monroe Doctrine', *The Hindu*, 2 January.

——(2004/5) 'What if Pakistan fails? India isn't worried. ... yet', *Washington Quarterly*, Vol. 28, No. 1, p. 127.

——(2008) 'India's geopolitics and Southeast Asian security', *Southeast Asian Affairs*, pp. 43–60.

——(2009) 'Sino–Indian rivalry in the Western Indian Ocean', *ISAS Insights*, No. 52, 24 February.

——(2010) 'India and the changing geopolitics of the Indian Ocean', speech at the National Maritime Foundation, New Delhi, 19 July.

——(2012) *Samudra Manthan: Sino–Indian Rivalry in the Indo–Pacific*, Washington, DC: Carnegie Endowment for International Peace.

——(2012) 'An uncertain trumpet? India's role in Southeast Asian security', paper presented at RSIS South Asia Programme Workshop, Singapore, 30 November.

——(2013) 'India's regional security cooperation: the Nehru Raj legacy', ISAS Working Paper No. 168, 7 March.

Monsonis, Guillem (2010) 'India's strategic autonomy and rapprochement with the US', *Strategic Analysis*, Vol. 34, No. 4, July, pp. 611–24.

Moonien, Vel (2010) 'Arrivée de Shantam Mukherjee, le nouveau conseiller du PM en matière de sécuritié', *L'Express*, 9 December.

Moore, Jack (2012) 'China's growing role in counter-piracy operations', *Theriskyshift.com*, 5 September. http://theriskyshift.com/2012/09/china-growing-role-counter-piracy-operations/.

'Mossad comes to Sri Lanka' (1984) *Tamil Times*, June.

Mughisuddin, Mohammed (ed.) (1977) *Conflict and Cooperation in the Gulf*, New York: Praeger.

Mukherjee, Pranab (2006) address to the 5th IISS Asian Security Summit, 3 June.

——(2007) 'International relations and maritime affairs: strategic imperatives', speech for the Admiral A.K. Chatterjee Memorial Lecture, Kolkata, 30 June.

Mullen, Mike (2010) speech in New Delhi, 23 July.

Muni, S.D. (1993) *Pangs of Proximity: India and Sri Lanka's Ethnic Crisis*, New Delhi: Sage Publications,

Murphy, Damien (2009) 'Reds out from under the beds', *Sydney Morning Herald*, 31 December.

Murthy, Padmaja (1999) 'The Gujral Doctrine and beyond', *Strategic Analysis*, Vol. 23, No. 4, pp. 639–52.

Naidu, G.V.C. (1991) 'The Indian navy and Southeast Asia', *Contemporary Southeast Asia*, Vol. 13, No. 1, June, p. 81.

Naidu, Sanusha (2011) 'South Africa joins BRIC with China's support', *East Asia Forum*, 1 April. Online: www.eastasiaforum.org/2011/04/01/south-africa-joins-bric-with-china-s-support/ (accessed 10 October 2013).

Nalapat, M.D. (2007) 'Will the USS Kitty Hawk cement US–India military ties?', *Intellibriefs*, 28 November.

Namboodiri, P.K.S., J.P. Anand and Sreedhar (1982) *Intervention in the Indian Ocean*, Delhi: ABC Publishing, p. 260.

Natsukawa, Kazuya (2006) opening address, Indo–Japan Dialogue on Ocean Security, Tokyo, 12 October.

Nayar, Baldev Raj and T.V. Paul (2003) *India in the World Order: Searching for Major Power Status*, New York: Cambridge University Press.

Nayar, K.P. (1998) 'Vajpayee describes India and US as natural allies', *The Telegraph*, 29 September.

Nehru, Jawaharlal (1961) *India's Foreign Policy: Selected Speeches, September 1946–April 1961*, Delhi: Government of India.

——(1985) *Selected Works of Jawaharlal Nehru*, Vol. 3, Series 2, New Delhi: Jawaharlal Nehru Memorial Fund.

Nicolle, David and Tom Cooper (2004) *Arab MiG-19 and MiG-21 Units in Combat*, Oxford: Osprey.

'No Chinese military bases in the Indian Ocean, says Menon' (2009) *The Indian Express*, 11 September.

Office of Spokesman, US Department of State (2005) 'Background briefing by administration US–South Asia relations', Washington, DC: 25 March.

O'Malley, Nick (2012) 'Perth naval base 'plan' would cost too much: study author', *National Times*, 2 August.

Ong, Yong (2004) 'Advancing the ASEAN–India partnership in the New Millenium', address in New Delhi, 18 October.

Onley, James (2009) 'The Raj reconsidered: British India's informal empire and spheres of influence in Asia and Africa', *Asian Affairs*, Vol. 40, No. 1, pp. 44–62.

Oodiah, Malenn D. (1989) *Mouvement Militant Mauricien: 20 ans d'histoire, 1969–1989*, Port-Louis: s.n.

Padfield, Peter (1974) *The Great Naval Race: Anglo-German Naval Rivalry 1900–1914*, London: Hart-Davis, MacGibbon.

'Pak offers China monitoring facilities on Makrana Coast' (2002) *The Times of India*, 29 June.

'Pakistan Navy frogmen trained Kasab, other terrorists: Headley' (2010) *The Times of India*, 19 July.

Pandit, Rajat (2007) 'US eyes naval ties with India', *Times of India*, 19 April.

——(2010) 'Strategically important A& n Command to get a boost', *Times of India*, 6 February.

Panikkar, K.M. (1945) *India and the Indian Ocean: An Essay on the Influence of Sea Power on Indian History*, London: George Allen & Unwin.

Pant, Harsh V. (2009) 'India in the Indian Ocean: growing mismatch between ambitions and capabilities', *Pacific Affairs*, Vol. 82, No. 2, Summer, pp. 279–97.

——(ed.) (2012) *The Rise of the Indian Navy: Internal Vulnerabilities, External Challenges*, Farnham: Ashgate.

Pasha, A.K. (ed.) (1999) *India and Oman: History, State, Economy and Foreign Policy*, New Delhi: Gyan Sagar.

Pathak, Vidhan (2006) 'France and Francophone Western Indian Ocean Region: implications for Indian interests', *Journal of Indian Ocean Studies*, Vol. 14, No. 2, August, pp. 186–203.

Patil, Reshma (2011) 'China signals desire for talks on Indian Ocean', *Hindustan Times*, 11 August.

Paul, T.V. (ed.) (2010) *South Asia's Weak States: Understanding the Regional Security Predicament*, Stanford, CA: Stanford Security Studies.

Pearson, Michael Naylor (2003) *The Indian Ocean*, London: Routledge.

Peerthum, S. (1998) 'L'ingérence néocolonialiste', in *L'Express, Portrait d'une nation*, 12 March, p. 56.

Pettman, Jan (1974) *Zambia: Security and Conflict*, New York: St Martin's Press.

Phillips, Andrew (2012) 'Australia and the challenges of regional order building in the Indo–Pacific Age', submission to Australian Senate Enquiry, April.

Prabhakar, Lawrence S. (2009) 'India's maritime surveillance and reconnaissance initiatives and the quest to secure its maritime-aerospace', *Strategic Affairs*, September.

——(2010) 'India's options and role in the PSI: alliance of necessity', *Strategic Affairs*, February.

Prakash, Arun (2006) 'China and the Indian Ocean region', *Indian Defence Review*, Vol. 21, No. 4, p. 11.

——(2007) *From the Crow's Nest: a compendium of speeches and writings on maritime and other issues*, New Delhi: Lancer.

——(2009) 'A moment for India: Shangri-La dialogue 2009', *Force*, July, pp. 5–7.

Pretorius, Joelien (2011) 'Africa–India nuclear cooperation: pragmatism, principle, post-colonialism and the Pelindaba Treaty', *South African Journal of International Affairs*, Vol. 18, No. 3, December, pp. 319–39.

Pubby, Manu (2009) 'China proposed division of Pacific, Indian Ocean regions, we declined: US Admiral', *Indian Express*, 15 May.

——(2009) 'India bringing Maldives into its security net', *Indian Express*, 13 August.

——(2012) 'India to train, support Indonesian Sukhoi fleet', *The Indian Express*, 17 October.

Rabinovich, Itamar and Haim Shaked (eds) (1978) *From June to October: the Middle East between 1967 and 1973*, New Brunswick, NJ: Transaction Books.

Rai, Rangit (2010) 'Why the Indian Navy did 'sweet Fanny Adams' in the 1965 War', *The Naval Review*, Vol. 98, No. 4, November, p. 379–84.

Rajapaksa, Gotabaya (2011) 'Key factor in defeating terrorism was political leadership', speech in Colombo, 6 January.

Rajghatta, Chidanand (2001) 'Singhing Bush's praise', *Times of India*, 13 April.

——(2005) 'India shows its sphere of influence to the world', *Times of India*, 5 January.

Rajkumar, Philip, 'The Indian Air Force in Iraq'. Online: www.bharat-rakshak.com/IAF/History/1990s/Rajkumar-Iraq.html (accessed 10 October 2013).

Ramachandran, Sudha (2006) 'India navy drops another anchor', *Asia Times*, 17 October.

——(2007) 'China moves into India's back yard', *Asia Times*, 13 March.

——(2007) 'India's quiet sea power', *Asia Times*, 2 August.

Raman, B. (2002) *Intelligence: Past, Present and Future*, New Delhi: Lancer.

——(2007) *The Kaoboys of R&AW: Down Memory Lane*, New Delhi: Lancer.

——(2007) 'China's strategic triangle', *Outlook India*, 6 March.

——(2008) 'India's strategic thrust in S. E. Asia: before and after 9/11', *South Asia Analysis Group*, Paper No. 2643, 26 March.

——(2011) 'Balochistan: greater realism in China and Iran', *India Defence Review*, 8 June.

Ramchandani, R.R. (ed) (1980) *India and Africa*, New Delhi: Radiant.

Ramtanu Maitra (2005) 'India bids to rule the waves', *Asia Times*, 19 October.

Rana, Kishan S. (2003) 'Island diplomacy', *Indian Express*, 7 June.

——(2006) *The 21st Century Ambassador: Plenipotentiary to Chief Executive*, New Delhi: Oxford University Press.

Ranjan, Amitav (2004) 'India says not yet to Indonesian plea', *India Express*, 21 April.

Rao, Nirupama (2010) 'India as a consensual stakeholder in the Indian Ocean: policy contours', speech to the National Maritime Foundation, 19 November.

Rasgotra, Maharajakrishna (ed.) (1998) *Rajiv Gandhi's India: A Golden Jubilee Retrospective Vol. 3: Ending the Quest for Dominance*, New Delhi: UPSPD.

Rasler, Karen A., William R. Thompson (1994) *The Great Powers and Global Struggle, 1490–1990*, Lexington, KY: University Press of Kentucky.

Reddy, C. Narendra (1987) 'Expectations of Indian government', *Indian Express*, 1 August.

Rehman, Iskander (2011) 'An ocean at the intersection of two emerging maritime narratives', *ISDA Issue Brief*, 11 July.

Renouf, Alan (1986) *Malcolm Fraser and Australian Foreign Policy*, Sydney: Australian Professional.

Rice, Condoleezza (2005) speech at Sophia University, Tokyo, 19 March.

Richardson, Michael (1989) 'East Asia and Western Pacific brace for Indian ascendency', *The International Herald Tribune*, 4 October.

Ricks, Thomas E. (2012) 'Why India is so half-hearted about the US rebalance towards Asia', *Foreign Policy*, 14 August.

Ridge, Brian (1988) 'India—a threat to Australia?', *Defender*, Winter, pp. 37–42.

Riedel, Bruce (2008) 'Saudi Arabia: nervously watching Pakistan', Brookings Institute, 28 January.

Robins, Brian (2011) 'Qatar gas challenge', *Sydney Morning Herald*, 30 November.

Robinson, David (2006) 'Curse on the land: a history of the Mozambiquan Civil War', doctoral thesis, University of Western Australia.

Rubinstein, Alvin Z. (ed) (1983) *The Great Game: Rivalry in the Persian Gulf and South Asia*, New York: Praeger.

Rudd, Kevin (2009) 'From fitful engagement to strategic partnership', address to the Indian Council of World Affairs in New Delhi, 12 November.

Rumley, Dennis, Timothy Doyle and Sanjay Chaturvedi (2012) '"Securing" the Indian Ocean? Competing regional security constructions', *Journal of Indian Ocean Region*, Vol. 8, No. 1, pp. 1–20.

Sahni, Varun (2002) 'Indo–US naval cooperation', *Institute of Peace and Conflict Studies*, No. 898, 25 October.

——(2005) 'India's security challenges out to 2000', paper presented at the Australia–India Security Roundtable, Canberra, 11–12 April.

——(2006) 'India and the Asian security architecture', *Current History*, Vol. 105, No. 690, April, pp. 163–7.

Sakhuja, Vijay (ed.) (2012) *Reinvigorating IOR-ARC*, New Delhi: Indian Council of World Affairs.

Sally, Razeen (2010) 'Regional economic integration in Asia: The track record and prospects', ECIPE Occasional Paper No. 2.

Samaranayake, Nilanthi (2011) 'Are Sri Lanka's Relations with China Deepening? An Analysis of Economic, Military and Diplomatic Data', *Asian Security*, Vol. 7, No. 2, pp. 119–46.

Sawhneym Rajeev (2006) 'Redefining the limits of the Straits: A Composite Malacca Straits Security System', *RSIS Commentaries* No. 37, 18 May.

Schaffer, Howard B. (1993) *Chester Bowles: New Dealer in the Cold War*, Cambridge, MA: Harvard University Press.

Schaffer, Teresita C. (2009) *India and the United States in the Twenty-first Century: Reinventing Partnership*, Washington, DC: The CSIS Press.

Scott, David (2006) 'India's "Grand Strategy" for the Indian Ocean: Mahanian visions', *Asia Pacific Review*, Vol. 13, No. 2, pp. 97–129.

Scott, David (ed.) (2011) *Handbook of India's International Relations*, London: Routledge.

Sebolao, Pearl (2010) 'South Africa: India's developmental model an inspiration to country', *Business Day*, 31 August.

'Securing footprints' (2012) *Strategic Affairs*, May, p. 68.

Selth, Andrew (1996) 'Myanmar and the strategic competition between China and India', *Journal of Strategic Studies*, Vol. 19, No. 2, pp. 213–30.

——(2007) 'Chinese military bases in Burma: The explosion of a myth', *Regional Outlook Paper* No. 10, Brisbane: Griffith University.

——(2008) 'Burma's Coco Islands: rumours and realities in the Indian Ocean', *Southeast Asia Research Centre Working Paper Series*, No. 101, November.

'Seychelles: General Ward, US Africa Command visit 19 August helps cement new, closer relationship', 8 September 2009. Online: www.cablegatesearch.net/cable.php?id=09PORTLOUIS271&q=india%20security%20seychelles (accessed 10 October 2013).

'Seychelles: The Game of Nations' (1987) *Africa Confidential*, Vol. 28, No. 22, 4 November.

Shaheed, Dr Ahmed (2009) 'Building a framework for India–Maldives security co-operation: an oceanic agenda for the future', Open Society Association, 22 August.

Shahi, Agha (1988) *Pakistan's Security and Foreign Policy*, Lahore: Progressive Publishers.

Shahzad, Syed Saleem (2011) 'Pakistan ready for Middle East role', *Asia Times*, 2 April.

'Shake-up for Indian spies' (2000) *Jane's Foreign Report*, 28 June.

Sharma, Pranay (2011) 'Sailing up the Tigris: for India's new envoy to Iraq, a quiet renewal', *Outlook India*, 4 July.

Sharma, Rajeev (2011) 'BRIC vs IBSA = China vs India?', *The Diplomat*, 2 March.

Sidhartha (2006) 'India acquiring global footprint', *Times of India*, 25 November.

——(2006) 'India eyes island in the sun', *Times of India*, 25 November.

——(2012) 'Mauritius offers India two islands in effort to preserve tax treaty', *The Economic Times*, 6 July.

Sidiropoulous, Elizabeth (2011) 'India and South Africa as partners for development in Africa?', *Chatham House Briefing Paper*, March.

Sikri, Rajiv (2009) *Challenge and Strategy: Rethinking India's Foreign Policy*, New Delhi: Sage.

Singh (2009) 'PM inaugurates naval academy at Ezhimala', 8 January.

Singh, Dalit (1990) 'Military intelligence not up to the mark', *Illustrated Weekly of India*, 14 October, pp. 30–2.

Singh, H. (2010) *Pentagon's South Asia Defence and Strategic Yearbook, 2010*, New Delhi: Pentagon Press.

Singh, Jasjit (ed.) (1999) *Kargil, 1999: Pakistan's Fourth War for Kashmir*, New Delhi: Knowledge World.

Singh, Manmohan (2012) speech at Tenth India–ASEAN Summit, Phnom Penh, November.

Sinha, Rakesh (2005) 'Jakarta says no to Indian patrol in Malacca Straits', *Indian Express*, 13 July.

Sinha, Yashwant (2004) 'Geopolitics: what it takes to be a world power', speech in New Delhi, 12 March.

Sisodia, N.S. (ed.) (2008) *Changing Security Dynamics in Southeast Asia*, New Delhi: Institute for Defence Studies and Analyses.

Smith, James (1991) 'Developments in the Indian Air Force', *Jane's Intelligence Review*, November, p. 523.

Sokolski, Henry (ed.) (2007) *Gauging U.S.–Indian Strategic Cooperation*, Carlisle, PA Strategic Studies Institute.

Solomon, Hussein (2012) 'Critical reflections of Indian foreign policy: between Kautilya and Ashoka', *South African Journal of International Affairs*, Vol. 19 No. 1, pp. 65–78.

Solomon, Hussein and Sonja Theron (2011) 'Behind the veil: India's relations with apartheid South Africa', *Strategic Review for South Africa*, Vol. 33, No. 1, pp. 102–19.

Sreenivasan, T.P. (2010) 'Obama has gone further than Bush on India', *Rediff.com*, 9 June. http://news.rediff.com/column/2010/jun/09/tps-sreenivasan-on-the-obama-platter-for-india.htm.

Sridharan, Kripa (1996) *The ASEAN Region in India's Foreign Policy*, Aldershot: Dartmouth Publishing.

Srivathsan, A. (2011) 'US saw Indian "hidden agenda" in Mauritius', *The Hindu*, 2 April.

Standard Life (2012) *The Weekly Focus: a market and economic update*, 8 October.

Straits Times, 7 November 1988.

'Strategic shift in South Asia' (2003) *Jane's Intelligence Weekly*, 28 January.

Subramanian, Nirupama (2011) 'How India kept pressure off Sri Lanka', *The Hindu*, 17 March.

Sun Cheng (2008) 'A comparative analysis of Abe's and Fukada's Asia diplomacy', *China International Studies*, No. 10, Spring, pp. 58–72.

Sun, Yun (2012) 'China's strategic misjudgement in Myanmar', *Journal of Current Southeast Asian Affairs*, Vol. 31, No. 1, pp. 73–96 at p. 87.

Suryanarayan, Dr V. (2008) 'India–Singapore relations: an overview', *Chennai Centre for China Studies*, C3S Paper No. 140, 2 April.

——(2008) 'Malaysian Indian society in ferment', *South Asia Analysis Group*, Paper No. 2880, 14 October.

Suryanarayana, P.S. (2010) 'Indonesia to "learn" from India's defence sector', *The Hindu*, 18 June.

Suter, Keith (1989) 'Kerguelen: a French mystery', *Newsletter of the Antarctic Society of Australia*, No. 16, March, pp. 5–10.

Swamy, M.R. Narayan (1995) *Tigers of Lanka: From Boys to Guerrillas*, Delhi: Konark.

Tanham, George (1992) *Indian Strategic Thought: An Interpretive Essay*, Santa Monica, CA: Rand.

Tanham, George Kanti P. Bajpai and Amitabh Mattoo (eds) (1996) *Securing India: Strategic Thought and Practice in an Emerging Power*, New Delhi: Manhora.

Taylor, Donald (2005) *Launching out into the deep: the Anglican Church in the history of the Seychelles to 2000 AD*, Victoria: Board of Church Commissioners.

Taylor, Rob (2011) 'Australia backs security pact with US, India', *The Australian*, 30 November.

'Tel Aviv worried about New Delhi's ties with Iran' (2003) *The Times of India*, 11 September.

Tellis, Ashley (2004) 'Assessing America's War on Terror: confronting insurgency, cementing primacy', *NBR Analysis*, Vol. 15, No. 4.

The Economist (1986) 13 September, p. 30.

The Economist (1979) *Foreign Report, No. 1569*, 31 January.

Tomlinson, Hugh (2012) 'Saudi Arabia to acquire nuclear weapons to counter Iran', *The Times*, 11 February.

Tow, William T. (1978) 'ANZUS: a strategic role in the Indian Ocean?', *The World Today*, Vol. 34, No. 10, pp. 401–8.

Towle, Phillip (1979) *Naval Power in the Indian Ocean*, Canberra: Australian National University.

Twining, Daniel (2007) 'America's grand design in Asia', *The Washington Quarterly*, Vol. 30, No. 3, pp. 79–94.

United States, Department of Defense (2011) *National Defense Budge Estimates for FY 2012*, March.

——(2011) 'Report to Congress on US-security cooperation', November.

——*Annual Report to Congress: Military and Security Developments Involving the People's Republic of China 2011*.

——*Annual Report to Congress: Military and Security Developments Involving the People's Republic of China 2012*.

United States, Department of State (2005) *Foreign Relations of the United States, 1969–1976: Vol. XI, South Asia Crisis, 1971*, Washington, DC: US GPO

United States, Department of the Navy (2007) *A Cooperative Strategy for 21st Century Seapower*.

Unnithan, Sandeep (2011) 'Lone dissenter', *India Today*, 9 April.

Upadhyaya, Shishir (2009) 'India and Australia relations: scope for naval cooperation', *National Maritime Foundation*, 4 December.

US Congressional Research Service (2012) *China Naval Modernization: Implications for US Navy Capabilities: Background and Issues for Congress*, 31 July.

US Embassy Colombo cable to US State Department (2007) 'Sri Lanka requests US military team to assess air defense following LTTE air attack', 1 April. Online: www.cablegatesearch.net/cable.php?id=07COLOMBO516 (accessed 10 October 2013).

——(2007) 'Indian Navy reportedly lifts objections to US-provided maritime radar', 13 June. Online: www.cablegatesearch.net/cable.php?id=07COLOMBO838 (accessed 10 October 2013).

——(2010) 'Maldives assistance overview: US and other donors', 13 January. Online: www.cablegatesearch.net/cable.php?id=10COLOMBO26 (accessed 10 October 2013).

US Embassy Doha cable to US State Department (2008) 'First-ever Indian PM visit to Qatar aims to spark better ties', 18 November. Online: www.cablegatesearch.net/cable.php?id=08DOHA810 (accessed 10 October 2013).

US Embassy Muscat cable to US State Department (2010) 'Oman—government's Number Two gives his views of the region', 22 February. Online: www.cablegate search.net/cable.php?id=10MUSCAT99. (accessed 10 October 2013).

US Embassy New Delhi cable to US State Department (2009) 'Indian officials to visit Maldives to raise concerns about stability there', 26 June. Online: www.cablegatesearch. net/cable.php?id=09NEWDELHI1334 (accessed 10 October 2013).

US Energy Information Administration (2011) *International Energy Outlook 2011*, 19 September.

——(2012) *World Oil Transit Chokepoints*, 22 August.

US Secretary of State cable to US Embassy Colombo (2010) 'Maldives Ambassador's Washington Consultations', 26 February. Online: www.cablegatesearch.net/cable. php?id=10STATE18437 (accessed 10 October 2013).

Van Dyke, Jon M. (2004) 'Military ships and planes operating in the exclusive economic zone of another country', *Marine Policy*, Vol. 28, pp. 29–39.

Vasan, R.S. (2009) 'It's advantage India in the Indian Ocean', *New Indian Express*, 15 September.

Velloor, Ravi (2010) 'A man who loves his country', *Straits Times*, 17 March.

Venugopalan, Urmila (2011) 'Pakistan's black pearl', *Foreign Policy*, 3 June.

Vohra, Ravi and P.K. Ghosh (2008) *China and the Indian Ocean*, Delhi: National Maritime Foundation, pp. 46–68.

Werake, Mahina and P.V.J. Jayasekera (1995) *Security Dilemma of a Small State, Part 2: International Crisis and External Intervention in Sri Lanka*, Kandy: Institute for International Studies.

Wilson, Dominic and Anna Stupnytska (2007) 'The N11: more than an acronym', *Goldman Sachs Global Economics Paper* No. 153, 28 March.

Ye Hailin (2009) 'Securing SLOCs by cooperation: Chinese perspectives of maritime security in the Indian Ocean', paper presented at Karichi, Pakistan.

Yoshihara, Toshi (2012) 'Chinese views of India in the Indian Ocean: a geopolitical perspective', *Strategic Analysis*, Vol. 36, No. 3, pp. 489–500.

You Ji (2007) 'Dealing with the Malacca Dilemma: China's effort to protect its energy supply', *Strategic Analysis*, Vol. 31, No. 3, May, pp. 467–89.

——(2012) 'The Chinese navy, its regional power and global reach', *Strategic Analysis*, Vol. 36, No. 3, pp. 477–88.

Young, Bronwyn (1990) 'Government cops plenty of flak over Indian Mirage sale', *Australian Financial Review*, 27 April.

Yung, Christopher D. and Ross Rustici with Isaac Kardon and Joshua Wiseman (2010) *China's Out of Area Naval Operations: Case Studies, Trajectories, Obstacles, and Potential Solutions*, Washington, DC: National Defense University Press, December.

Zumwalt, Elmo R. (1976) *On Watch: A Memoir*, New York: Quadrangle.

Index

Abe, Shinzo 155
Aden 6–8, 20, 104, 185, 190
Afghanistan 7, 19, 27, 29, 43, 114–15, 137, 148, 152, 170, 174, 175; Soviet intervention in 10,48, 71, 149, 168; US intervention in 3, 9, 11, 164, 169, 174, 176
African National Congress (ANC) 89–90, 93, 95
Agalega islands 74–76
Albuquerque, Afonso de 5–6
Amin, Idi 87–88
Andaman Islands 124–26, 129, 134, 139
Andaman Sea 123–25, 129, 136, 141, 151, 184, 192
Antarctica 36, 79, 152
Antony, A.K. 61, 78, 173, 177
ANZUS Treaty 9, 148–50
APEC 150
ASEAN 8–9, 30–32, 34, 36, 110, 127–32, 134, 136, 141–42, 153, 157, 186–87, 193–94, 206
Asia Pacific 4, 44, 152
Australia 4, 6–7, 9, 13–14, 20, 37, 54, 58, 80, 93, 114, 125–27, 130–32, 134, 147–65, 171–73, 175–76, 180, 185, 189–90, 194–95, 200, 203–4; and India 152–59

Bahrain 7, 9, 104, 107, 110, 152
Bangladesh 25, 27–30, 43–45, 49–50, 63, 72, 90, 106, 124–25, 141, 143, 186–87, 190, 193
Bangladesh War 45, 49, 90, 106, 110, 116, 112, 143, 167, 186
Bay of Bengal 14, 20, 31, 39, 45, 123–25, 133, 136, 141, 143, 151, 154, 167,172, 175, 184, 189
Berenger, Paul 70–74, 81–82

Bhutan 19, 28–29, 43, 50–51
BIMSTEC 131, 136, 141
Boodhoo, Harish 71, 73, 81
Botswana 88, 90–91, 96, 100
Bowles, Chester 27, 180
BRICS 95
Britain 40, 48, 57, 76, 90–91, 93,111, 133, 152, 166; in colonial era 1, 4–8, 12, 5, 19–21, 25–26, 32, 86–88, 103–4, 137, 147, 176, 199, 204
British Indian Army 6–8, 14, 16, 19, 104
Burma see Myanmar
Bush, George W 36, 116, 169–70
Buzan, Barry 4, 43, 137

Caroe, Olaf 19–20
Central Intelligence Agency (CIA) 64, 71, 81, 170
Central Treaty Organization (CENTO) 9, 106
Ceylon see Sri Lanka
Chahbahar 114–15
Chatterji, A.K. 30–31
China 1–3, 7, 11–13, 15, 19, 21, 27, 29–30, 32–34, 36–37, 40, 60, 83, 86–92, 109, 114, 123–27, 130–36, 163–66, 170–72, 177, 179, 182–98, 201, 202, 204–6; and Australia 155–58, 162; and Bangladesh 45, 186; and Maldives 58, 60, 186–87, 191; and Myanmar 53, 124, 137, 140–42, 187–89, 191–92; and Pakistan 105, 109, 186–91; and Seychelles 76, 78–79; Sri Lanka 48, 54–56, 62, 187–90
Christmas Island 151, 160
Clinton, Bill 169–70
Clinton, Hillary 166, 206
Cocos Islands 54, 149, 151

Combined Task Force (CTF) 150 118, 175
Combined Task Force (CTF) 151 112, 118, 175, 185
Curzon, George 19, 50

Dawson, O.S. 72, 153
Desai, Morarji 88, 90, 99, 129
Diego Garcia; and the Cold War 9, 28, 31, 48, 51, 57–59, 71, 74, 149–50, 153, 167–68; post Cold War 9–10, 29, 31, 75, 176
Dixit, J.N. 47–48, 50

Egypt 7, 104, 108, 117
Exercise *Malabar* 154–55, 171–72, 175

France 19, 21, 27, 40, 97, 109, 173; and the Southwest Indian Ocean 69, 76, 79–80, 83
Fraser, Malcolm 149, 153

Gan Atoll 28, 59, 114
Gandhi, Indira 20, 25, 29, 30, 47, 49–50, 70–74, 77, 81, 87, 108, 114, 133, 177
Gandhi, Rajiv 12, 20, 28–29, 47, 49, 51–52, 74, 77–78, 91, 109
Gayoom, Maumoon Abdul 57–58, 65
Great Coco island 140, 189
Gujral Doctrine 28–29, 45, 53
Gwadar 106, 109, 115, 187–88, 190–91

Hambantota 56, 186–90

IBSAMAR 95–96
IBSA 94–95, 191
Indian Air Force 13–14, 50–53, 57, 71–72, 90–91, 96, 108–9, 112, 115, 125, 127, 133, 137, 171–72,
Indian Army 13–14, 28, 33, 49, 65, 72–73, 81, 90, 96, 108, 112, 125, 133, 139, 171
Indian Navy 6, 12–15, 18, 20, 30–36, 39, 52–53, 58–59, 64, 69, 72–74, 77–78, 83, 92–93, 98, 105–6, 108, 112, 115, 124–25, 129, 133, 137, 140, 158, 168–9, 174–75, 189, 192–94, 196, 201, 203
Indian Ocean Naval Symposium (IONS) 34, 205
Indian Ocean Rim Association for Regional Cooperation (IOR-ARC) 80,97, 150, 156, 205
Indian Ocean Zone of Peace (IOZOP) 21–22, 38, 168, 205

Indira Doctrine *see* Monroe Doctrine
Indonesia 2–3, 13, 36, 37, 106, 123–24, 126–37, 142, 148, 150–51, 157, 159, 165, 193, 200, 203
Iran 2–3, 7, 9, 27, 59, 79, 96, 103, 106–7, 109, 112–18, 120, 168, 170, 176, 178, 185, 200
Iraq 7, 9, 103–4, 106, 108–9, 114, 117, 148, 152; US intervention in 3, 9–11, 116, 164

Japan 2, 32, 33, 114, 125, 127, 130–32, 154–67, 164–67, 170, 172–73, 175–76, 185, 190, 195; and World War II 23, 33, 124, 147
Jayawardene, J.R. 48, 51
Jinnah, Muhammad 105, 118
Jugnauth, Anerood 70–74

Kao, R.N. 49–50, 72–73
Kenya 7, 76, 87–88, 92, 98
KGB 71
Kissinger, Henry 30
Kuwait 7,9, 104, 109–10, 148

Lee, Kwan Yew 58, 111, 133
Liberation Tigers of Tamil Eelam (LTTE) 50, 52–55, 64, 176
Libya 59, 64, 65, 70, 73, 81

Madagascar 70, 76, 79, 83, 191
Mahan, Alfred Thayer 20, 26, 34, 183
Malacca Strait 2,5–7, 14, 30, 32, 36, 109, 111, 123, 125–27, 129, 133, 135–37, 141, 169, 174, 182, 188–89, 191–93
Malaysia 2, 7, 57, 106, 123, 126–27, 129–37, 142, 149–51, 157, 160
Maldives 12, 24–25, 28–29, 35, 43–44, 46, 56–62, 114, 129, 168, 176, 186–87, 190–91, 200
Mauritius 6, 7,9, 20, 24, 34, 65, 69–70, 75–76, 79–81, 90,97, 114, 187, 189–91, 200; Indian intervention in 12, 71–74
Mehta, Suresh 36, 193–94
Mekong Ganga Cooperation (MGC) 11, 131, 136, 141
Menon, Shivshankar 55, 195, 205
Michel, James 78
MILAN 107, 125
Monroe Doctrine 18, 24–30, 32–33, 39, 46, 49, 105, 137, 166, 168, 202, 204
Mozambique 5, 79, 88, 91–93, 98, 200

Mozambique Channel 2, 5, 69, 75, 79, 91–93, 98
Mugabe, Robert 90–91
Mukherjee, Pranab 29, 33, 36, 54, 133
Myanmar 6, 7, 25, 27, 53, 72, 123–25, 131, 136–41, 176, 187, 189, 191–93

Namibia 89–90, 96, 100
Narayanan, M.K. 54–55, 116
Nasheed, Mohamed 59–61
Naval Arms Limitation Treaty (NALT) 148, 159
Nehru, Jawaharlal 8,11,20, 24–27, 30, 36, 86, 128, 180
Nepal 19, 28–29, 43, 186
Nixon, Richard 30–31
Non-Aligned Movement 21, 58, 77, 86–87, 108
Nuclear Non-Proliferation Treaty (NPT) 96, 131, 178, 198
Nuclear submarines 10, 15, 105; Chinese 193; Indian 15, 105, 124, 169, 193, 203; US 10, 148, 159
Nuclear weapons 3, 9, 13, 15–16, 21–22, 29–31, 34, 45, 83, 95–96, 107, 113, 116–17, 131, 153–56, 161, 163, 168–70, 186, 191, 193, 194, 203

Obama, Barack 60, 141, 170–71, 177
Oman 2, 7, 9, 24, 34, 91, 104, 107, 110–12, 114, 119, 200
Operation *Cactus* 57–58
Operation *Enduring Freedom* 126, 174, 179
Operation *Lal Dora* 72–73, 81

Pakistan 9, 10, 12–13, 25, 27–34, 43–45, 47–48, 50, 53–54, 56–59, 61, 72, 86–87, 89–91, 99, 103, 105–7, 110–12, 114–20, 124, 129, 135–36, 140, 150, 153, 164–65, 167, 169–70, 174–75, 177–78, 183, 186–88, 190–93, 195, 200, 203–4
Pakistan Navy 39, 105, 107, 175, 190
Panikkar, K.M. 20, 28, 93, 125, 192
Persian Gulf 2, 3, 5–6, 8–9, 11, 13, 36, 76, 103–4, 107, 109, 112–15, 118, 126, 150, 178, 182, 190, 192, 201
PLAN (Chinese Navy) 78, 184–85, 187, 189–90, 194
Portugal 4–6, 27, 88
Prakash, Arun 14, 32, 127, 189, 193
Proliferation Security Initiative (PSI) 178

Qatar 9, 104, 110–11

Rajapaksa, Gotabhaya 56
Rajapaksa, Mahinda 55–56, 197
Ramgoolam, Navin 74–75
Ramgoolam, Seewoosagur 70, 74–75, 81
Rebalancing strategy 11, 163–64
René, Albert 76–78, 82
Research and Analysis Wing (RAW) 113; and Africa 87–88, 90; and Mauritius 71–74, 79 and Myanmar 138–39; and Sri Lanka 48–51, 64
Reunion 79–80
Rhodesia *see* Zimbabwe
Rice, Condoleezza 170
Royal Australian Navy 150, 152, 158
Royal Navy: in colonial era 5, 15, 19, 33–34, 129, 148; post-1947 8, 12, 21, 28, 39, 70, 133
Rudd, Kevin 155
Russia 6, 9–10, 15, 19, 21–22, 30–31, 33, 35, 40, 48, 59, 62, 64–65, 70–71, 73, 76, 81, 86, 88–90, 93–96, 104, 106–8, 110, 113–16, 119, 129, 131, 135, 137, 139, 142, 148–49, 153, 167–69, 172–73, 186, 201

Saddam Hussein 108–10
Saudia Arabia 9, 13, 91, 110, 117, 150, 200; and Pakistan 106–7
Sen Gupta, Bhabani 25, 38, 39, 49
Seychelles 9, 12, 34, 69–71, 76–80, 82–83, 97, 189
Shah of Iran 113–14, 120, 168
Shaheed, Ahmed 59–60, 62
Sikkim 19, 28
Singapore 6, 7, 9, 53, 80, 90, 111, 149, 151, 154, 157, 164, 172, 176, 188, 190, 200; and India 20,24, 34, 36, 75, 123, 126–34, 142
Singh, Jaswant 36
Singh, Manmohan 36, 93, 131
Singh, V.P. 52
Sinha, S.K. 72–73, 81
South Africa 6–7, 13, 20; and Apartheid era 37, 70–71, 74, 76–77, 80, 86–87, 89–93; and post-Apartheid era 85, 93–98, 150, 191, 200, 203
South African Navy 93, 96–97
South Asian Association for Regional Cooperation (SAARC) 44, 58, 60
South China Sea 36, 125, 132–33, 135, 142, 151, 158, 165, 184, 193, 195–96, 205

South East Asian Treaty Organization (SEATO) 9, 47
Southern African Development Community (SADC) 96–98
Southwest Africa *see* Namibia
Soviet Navy 71, 77, 113, 129, 143, 148, 149
Soviet Union *see* Russia
Sri Lanka 5–7, 43–44, 55–64, 186–90, 193, 197; civil war and Indian intervention 12, 25, 28–29, 38, 46–55, 71, 91, 129, 139, 168–69, 176
Sri Lankan Navy 53–55
Strait of Hormuz 2–3, 5, 109–11, 115, 174, 182, 188
Strategic autonomy 18, 20, 23–24, 114, 152, 158, 167–68, 177–79, 201–2
String of Pearls strategy 187–90, 192
Suntook, N.F. 73

Tajikistan 115
Tanzania 76, 87–88, 92–93, 98
Thailand 9, 27, 123, 126, 131–32, 134, 136–37, 142, 191–92
Trincomalee 6, 28, 39, 48–49, 51, 53–54, 63–64, 189

Uganda 7, 71, 87–88, 92
United Arab Emirates (UAE) 7, 9, 78, 104, 107, 110–11

United Nations 14, 27, 57–58, 85, 111, 158, 178; and Security Council 15, 85, 117, 171, 175
United States Africa Command (USAFRICOM) 78, 174
United States Central Command (USCENTCOM) 9, 107, 111, 118, 149, 174
United States Pacific Command (USPACOM) 107, 166, 172–74
Uranium 96, 155–56, 203
US Navy 9, 30–31, 34, 39, 48, 60, 124, 148, 151, 160, 162–64, 167, 171–76, 180, 190
USS *Enterprise* 30–31, 34, 39, 124, 167, 172

Vajpayee, A.B. 90, 169
Verma, Nirmal 37, 196
Vietnam 129, 132, 142, 144, 157, 193, 195
Voice of America 48

Waheed, Mohamed 61

Yemen 108, 119

Zambia 88, 90, 96, 99, 100
Zimbabwe 88–92, 99